DARK TERRITORY IN THE INFORMATION AGE

For Antje
A most unaccountable German

and in memory of
Peter R. Gould (1932-2000)
Glen S. Elder (1967-2009)

Dark Territory in the Information Age

Learning from the West German Census Controversies of the 1980s

MATTHEW G. HANNAH
Aberystwyth University, UK

Routledge
Taylor & Francis Group
LONDON AND NEW YORK

First published 2010 by Ashgate Publishing

2 Park Square, Milton Park, Abingdon, Oxon OX14 4RN
711 Third Avenue, New York, NY 10017, USA

Routledge is an imprint of the Taylor & Francis Group, an informa business

First issued in paperback 2016

British Library Cataloguing in Publication Data
Hannah, Matthew G.
Dark territory in the information age : learning from the
West German census controversies of the 1980s.
1. Germany (West)--Politics and government--1982-1990.
2. Germany (West)--Census, 1983--Public opinion.
3. Germany (West)--Census, 1987--Public opinion.
4. Public opinion--Germany (West)--History--20th
century. 5. Protest movements--Germany (West)--History--
20th century. 6. Privacy, Right of.
I. Title
323.4'48'0943'09048-dc22

Library of Congress Cataloging-in-Publication Data
Hannah, Matthew G.
Dark territory in the information age : learning from the West German census controversies of the 1980s / by Matthew G. Hannah.
p. cm.
Includes bibliographical references and index.
ISBN 978-1-4094-0813-0 (hardback) 1. Germany (West)--Census, 1987. 2. Boycotts--Germany (West)--History
--20th century. I. Title.

HA1234 1987d
304.6072'3--dc22

2010014640

ISBN 978-1-4094-0813-0 (hbk)
ISBN 978-1-138-27363-4 (pbk)

Contents

List of Figures

List of Abbreviations

The German abbreviations below appear in the text with the first appearance of the terms they abbreviate, and with the English translation. Subsequently the English translations and the German abbreviations are used interchangeably.

afas	*archiv für alternatives schrifttum*	Archive for alternative written materials
AL	*Alternative Liste*	Alternative List [West Berlin]
APIS	*Arbeitsdatei "PIOS-Innere Sicherheit"*	Working database "PIOS – Internal Security"
APO	*Ausserparlamentarische Opposition*	Extraparliamentary opposition
B2J	*Bewegung 2. Juni*	Movement of the Second of June
BBU	*Bundesverband Bürgerinitiativen Umweltschutz*	Federal Association of Citizens' Initiatives for Environmental Protection
BDSB [or BfD]	*Bundesdatenschutzbeauftragter* [long form: *Bundesbeauftragter für Datenschutz*]	Federal Data Protection Commissioner
BDSG	*Bundesdatenschutzgesetz*	Federal Data Protection Law
BKA	*Bundeskriminalamt*	Federal Criminal Bureau
BND	*Bundesnachrichtendienst*	Federal Intelligence Agency
BRD	*Bundesrepublik Deutschland*	Federal Republic of Germany [West Germany]
BStatG	*Bundesstatistikgesetz*	Federal Statistical Law
BStU	*Bundesbeauftragter für die Unterlagen des Staatssicherheitsdienstes der ehemaligen Deutschen Demokratischen Republik*	Federal Commissioner for the Records of the State Security Service of the former German Democratic Republic [Stasi archive]
BVerfG	*Bundesverfassungsgericht*	Federal Constitutional Court
BVerfSch	*Bundesverfassungsschutz* or simply *Verfassungsschutz*	Federal Constitutional Protection Agency
CDU	*Christlich Demokratische Union*	Christian Democratic Union
CSU	*Christlich Soziale Union*	Christian Social Union
DDR	*Deutsche Demokratische Republik*	German Democratic Republic [East Germany]
DKP	*Deutsche Kommunistische Partei*	German Communist Party
DSB	*Datenschutzbeauftragter*	Data Protection Commissioner
FAZ	*Frankfurter Allgemeine Zeitung*	[national newspaper]

FDGO	*Freiheitliche demokratische Grundordnung*	Free, democratic basic order
FDP	*Freie Demokratische Partei*	Free Democratic Party
FoeBuD, e.V.	*Verein zur Förderung des öffentlichen bewegten und unbewegten Datenverkehrs*	Society for the support of public mobile and immobile data traffic [a privacy/open source advocacy organization]
FR	*Frankfurter Rundschau*	[national newspaper]
GAL	*Grün-Alternative Liste*	Green-Alternative List [Hamburg]
GG	*Grundgesetz*	Basic Law [Constitution]
GSG9	*Grenzschutzgruppe 9*	Border Protection Group 9 [special anti-terrorist unit of Federal Police]
HISF	*Hamburg Institut für Sozialforschung*	Hamburg Institute for Social Research
IM	*Inoffizielle Mitarbeiter*	"Unofficial" informant working for the East German *Stasi*
INPOL	*Informationssystem der Polizei*	Police Information System [database]
KPD	*Kommunistische Partei Deutschlands*	Communist Party of Germany
LDSB [or LfD]	*Landesdatenschutzbeauftragter* [long form: *Landesbeauftragter für Datenschutz*]	State Data Protection Commissioner
NSG	*Notstandsgesetze*	Emergency Laws
NSMs		New social movements
PIOS	*Personen, Institutionen, Objekten, Sachen*	Persons, Institutions, Objects, Things [BKA database]
RAF	*Rote Armee Fraktion*	Red Army Faction
RAV	*Republikanische Anwaltsverein*	Republican Attorneys' Guild
RISB	*Recht auf Informationelle Selbstbestimmung*	Right of Informational Self-Determination
RZ	*Revolutionäre Zellen*	Revolutionary Cells
SDS	*Sozialistischer Deutscher Studentenbund*	Socialist German Student Federation
SED	*Sozialistische Einheitspartei Deutschlands*	Social Unity Party of Germany
SEW	*Sozialistische Einheitspartei Westberlin*	Socialist Unity Party of West Berlin
SFB	*Sender Freies Berlin*	[radio and television broadcaster – West Berlin]
SPD	*Sozialistische Partei Deutschlands*	Socialist Party of Germany
SPK	*Sozialistisches Patientenkollektiv*	Socialist Patients' Collective
StaLA	*Statistisches Landesamt*	State Statistical Bureau
Stasi	*Staatssicherheitsdienst*	State Security Service
taz	*tageszeitung*	[national alternative newspaper]
VoBo Ini	*Volkszählungsboykott Initiative*	Census boycott initiative

VZ	*Volkszählung*	Census
VZG	*Volkszählungsgesetz*	Census law
WG	*Wohngemeinschaft*	Residential Collective
ZDF	*Zweites Deutsches Fernsehen*	[national television broadcaster]

Preface and Acknowledgments

This book is an historical geography with explicit political intent. Ten years ago or so, an energizing involvement in the People's Geography Project established by Don Mitchell, and long conversations with my good friend radical historian Jay Moore as well as with the late radical philosopher Will Miller, deepened my interest in exploring regimes of power/knowledge not so much as systems to be analyzed abstractly but rather through the lenses of struggle. From what little I knew about the West German boycotts, they seemed to represent a fascinating field in which to explore what organized oppositional politics might look like if it were aimed explicitly at the techniques and rationalities of power so subtly analyzed by Foucault and other scholars. Often aggregated under terms such as "surveillance society", "the security state", or "risk society", such techniques constitute one of the most difficult forms of power to address critically in a sustained and coordinated way, to make the target of a coherent oppositional politics. The root political motivation of this book is the belief that such a politics grows ever more necessary and urgent in the 21st century.

The boycotts developed forms of activism that, in addition, were inherently geographical. They highlight the contestability of what can be termed "epistemic sovereignty", a dimension of territorial sovereignty expressing a state's presumptive claim to knowledge of what goes on in the territory it governs. Epistemic sovereignty, though always to some degree aspirational, is arguably an indispensable precondition for the sorts of biopolitical and governmental projects, whether state-driven or not, that geographers and other scholars have been exploring for some time now. A study of activism challenging the scope of epistemic sovereignty promises, among other things, to link notions of citizenship with recent theorizations of "counter-governmentality". It also has the advantage of highlighting the complex relations between "publicity" and "privacy" at the intersection between physical and virtual spaces. These were the initial ideas that fueled my fascination with the boycotts, and they clearly touch a whole range of important issues in critical political theory, as well as the theorization of social movements.

As the research progressed, however, it became increasingly clear that the details of what happened constituted a goldmine of insights on their own terms, and that the best way to showcase the relevance of the boycotts was not to overwrite them with a great deal of explicit theory but first of all to recount them in empirical detail. The point is not to try to "escape" theory in any way; I am well aware that the resulting historical geography (or spatial history) is no less theory-laden for leaving the theory implicit. I did eventually return to the issue of framing the census boycotts in explicitly theoretical terms, and have published a few pieces outlining some of the implications they might have.[1] Traces of my original, broadly Foucauldian concerns have survived in the manuscript wherever they seemed to add something useful to the narrative, and academic readers will notice a couple of references to Agamben, as well as the occasional influence of Actor-Network Theory. However, the explicit theory that turns up in the narrative emerges, mostly in the Interlude and Conclusions, from the attempt to discern and develop the indigenous political logics running through the controversies in 1983 and 1987. Thus, while the book was originally conceived in the context of critical debates in political geography and social theory, working out exactly where and how it intersects with those debates is a task that remains to be done.

Even simply to take the census boycott movements seriously as political episodes, I have learned in numerous conversations with German colleagues and acquaintances, is to take a position on them. While I ultimately do not pass judgment on whether the boycotts were successful in achieving their goals at the time, I do intend this study, at one level, as a tribute to the thousands of West Germans who carried them off with such dedication and imagination. One form of tribute would be to offer a rich and comprehensive ethnographic history of the boycotts as such, a task I have not undertaken here. Instead I focus in this book on certain specific aspects of the boycotts that seem particularly useful for creative and proactive critical informational politics across many different geographical and political contexts in the 21st century. While I take due care to report on the arguments and activities of those who opposed the boycotts, the primary object of the book is to attend to the boycott movements, and to read them as crucibles of new, potentially transferable political logics.

To piece together the course of events, I have relied mainly on archived press coverage of the census controversies by national newspapers and newsweeklies, supplementing this material with holdings in a range of social movement archives, as well as with key government documents. First-hand recollections of a number of individuals have also provided me with valuable perspective, though a systematic program of interviewing was called for neither by the nature of my interests nor by the larger purpose of the book. In geographical terms, chiefly due to the reporting of the national alternative daily newspaper the *tageszeitung* (taz), the focus on press coverage has resulted in a disproportionate emphasis on events in West Berlin, most obviously at the expense of the boycott movements in Hamburg, which was the other main center of the boycotts. I have tried to keep this bias to a minimum,

---

1 Hannah, M. 2008a. Die umstrittene Konstruktion von Vertrauen und Misstrauen in der westedeutschen Volkszählungsboykottbewegung 1983. *Social Geography* [Online journal], 3, 11-21. Available at http://www.soc-geogr.net/3/11/2008/sg-3-11-2008.pdf. Hannah, M. 2008b. Mapping the under-scrutinized: the West German census boycott movement of 1987 and the dangers of information-based security, in *Geospatial Technologies and Homeland Security*, edited by D. Sui. New York: Springer, 301-314. Hannah, M. 2009. Calculable territory and the West German census boycott movements of the 1980s. *Political Geography* 28, 66-75.

but admittedly with only limited success. More generally, the course of boycott controversies in larger cities received the bulk of press attention, so there is an urban bias as well in what follows. Qualitatively, coverage in the press was clearly structured by spin, and the various spun versions in turn played a major structuring role in how the controversies played out at the time. Furthermore, regardless of the particular political line, all press sources, from the left as well as from the center and right, tended toward the eye-catching or sensational rather than the mundane. None of this interferes fundamentally with the sort of "history of the present" I am attempting here, but it still deserves brief acknowledgment.

This book has occupied me for nearly a decade, and the experience of working on it has been personally as well as professionally transformative. Thus I want to thank all the people who have helped along the way in a fashion that goes beyond a mere alphabetical listing of names. I am not by training a scholar of German social politics, so this research project first of all required an intensive immersion in a whole new political-cultural world. Above all, I needed to acquire a new language fairly quickly and in considerable depth. I am grateful to Wolfgang Mieder, David Scrase, Helga Schreckenberger, and Theresia Hoeck of the Department of German and Russian at the University of Vermont for ushering me skillfully through the earliest phases of this process. The extremely generous material and institutional support of the Alexander von Humboldt Foundation (especially Cäcilia Nauderer) made possible not only the research itself but also intensive preparatory language training at the Goethe-Institut in Berlin. The Humboldt Foundation is in my view a model of how the support of research and researchers should be organized. (The findings and judgments expressed in this book do not reflect the position or opinion of the Humboldt Foundation or of any one of its representatives, but are solely mine.) Once the initial intensive language training was completed, Benno Werlen at the Friedrich-Schiller-Universität-Jena, my academic host during the fellowship, then took the crucial step of committing both of us, and all of his co-workers, to the maintenance of an English-free environment during my initial six months centered at the Friedrich-Schiller-Universität Jena in 2001. For this I can hardly exaggerate my gratitude. It got me over the hump in linguistic terms, allowing my acquisition of German to become a self-reinforcing process thereafter. Many thanks to Antje Schlottmann, Roland Lippuner, Holger Gertel, and Tilo Felgenhauer for good-natured tolerance of my sometimes bizarre fledgling German and for help with many practical aspects of the initial research. Nadine Wassner has been wonderful about continuing to mail me requested materials in the intervening years. I am grateful to Gunther Philler of the Jenaer Bücherstube, for additional assistance in acquiring research materials. Peter Meusburger of Ruprecht-Karls-Universität Heidelberg offered generous support in the form of multiple invitations to present work at conferences in Heidelberg and Obergürgl, Austria, and to get to know more German scholars, as well as by urging me to seek materials at the Stasi archive which ultimately provide some of the most fascinating insights into the significance of the boycotts (see Chapter 3). Heike Jöns, Tim Freytag, Annika Matissek and Caroline Kramer have been very welcoming and supportive. I have profited as well from many conversations with Julia Lossau at the Humboldt University in Berlin, and from a brief but fruitful exchange with Berndt Belina, then at Potsdam, now at Frankfurt. In Vermont again, Dennis Mahoney, also of UVM's Department of German and Russian, provided invaluable support for subsequent forays into the more difficult terrain of writing in German, and Antje Schlottmann has continued to be extremely generous with assistance on this score. The translations from the German throughout the book are my own unless otherwise indicated. They attempt to strike a balance between literality and readability in English, undoubtedly with uneven success.

As the research has led me to a range of archives, I have benefited repeatedly from the assistance of excellent archivists, often working under very difficult financial conditions to maintain under-funded collections of material relating to social movements. Jürgen Bacia and Dorotheé Leidig at the archiv für alternatives schrifttum (afas), Duisburg, have been especially welcoming and inventive in locating materials relating to the census boycotts, and have become friends in the process. I would also like to thank Erdmute Horn, Head Archivist at the Pressearchiv at Otto Suhr Institut of the Freie Universität Berlin; "mister kaufman" and associates at the archive of the *tageszeitung* in Berlin; Christoph Becker-Schaum and staff at Archiv Grünes Gedächtnis in Berlin; Reinhard Schwarz and Dieter Schröder at the Hamburg Institut für Sozialforschung; and Ulrike Kochniß at the Stasi Archive (Der Bundesbeauftragte für die Unterlagen des Staatssicherheitsdienstes der ehemaligen Deutschen Demokratischen Republik or "Birthler-Behörde"). In addition, a number of individuals responded to an advert placed in the taz in 2001 by sending me materials from their attics and desk drawers relating to the boycott movements. In some other cases individuals who sent materials asked not to be identified, but I have misplaced my notes regarding exactly which individuals they were. In the interest of data protection, then, I am unfortunately bound to thank all of these generous people anonymously. Andreas Paust sent me his unpublished thesis on the 1987 boycotts, which was very helpful. I am grateful to Harald Juch, the caricaturist who drew the cover illustration (also Figure 1.4) as well as other political caricatures influential during the boycotts, to the photographer Gerhard Vormwald (Figure 1.2), and to "mister Kaufman" and Corinna Urbach at the taz archive, as well as Peter Stroh and Sybille Bauer at dpa-Picture-Alliance GmbH for their generous help with copyright permissions for the figures. Excerpts from *Seeing* © José Saramago and Editorial Caminho SA, Lisbon, 2004, English translation copyright © 2006 by Margaret Jull Costa. Published by Harvill Secker and reprinted by permission of The Random House Group Ltd (excluding USA/Canada). Published and reprinted by permission of Houghton Mifflin Harcourt Publishing Company (USA/Canada).

A number of former West Germans related their experiences in connection with the boycott movements, or in some cases simply made passing comments that got me thinking in useful ways. I would like to thank Tim Freytag, Caroline Kramer, Ingrid Lottenburger, Dieter Schröder, Reinhard Schwarz, Hans Gephardt, Christiane Schönfeld, and Ulf Strohmayer for their thoughts. For additional reflections, comments, criticisms or for alerting me to information on the research project itself I am grateful to Peter Meusburger (again); Ruth Leuze; Gerry Kearns; Karen Till; Christoph Waack; Larry Frohmann; Mike Heffernan; David Matless; Stephen Legg; audiences at the University of Vermont, the University of Wales, Aberystwyth (as it was then known); Cambridge University; the University of Bristol; Nottingham-Trent University; Black Sheep Books and the Langdon Street Cafe in Montpelier, Vermont; and at various ICCG, AAG and IBG conferences. At Nottingham-Trent University, Steve Legg very generously organized a discussion after my visit aimed at providing me with in-depth feedback on questions I had posed regarding how to frame the overall argument.

My colleagues in the Department of Geography at the University of Vermont, and, since 2007, in the Institute of Geography and Earth Sciences at Aberystwyth University, have been wonderfully supportive over many years. I would especially like to thank Pádraig Carmody for first alerting me to the possibility of funding for this project through the Humboldt Foundation, and Joni Seager for being a great friend and keeping my horizons broad for many years. The sudden tragic death of friend and long-time colleague Glen Elder cast a shadow over the final stages of writing this book. As with every one of my research projects, Glen contributed to this one, too, with general support as well as a few carefully placed gems of his razor-sharp intelligence, tossed off with an arch of the eyebrow and a twinkle of the eye. I wish he were still around to see the results. My new colleagues in Aberystwyth have also been very supportive. I would especially like to thank Deborah Dixon and Mark Whitehead for their valuable comments on parts of earlier drafts. In the later stages of writing the manuscript, Peter Wissoker lent his professional editorial eye to a draft and provided invaluable feedback on all aspects of the project. Jessica Pykett, Don Mitchell and Ulf Strohmayer all likewise read the manuscript from start to finish and offered excellent comments and criticisms. Thanks to Jessica especially for suggestions on the concluding chapter, to Don for a variety of points throughout and for a great alternative title suggestion ("Rock, paper, scissors"), and to Ulf for detailed interpretations of some of the finer points of the political context, for scrutiny of my translations of German terms, and for correcting one very basic geographical mistake. I have not followed all the suggestions made by these readers, but the book has been immensely improved by their thoughtful engagement. Katy Low and Emily Pace at Ashgate have been extremely helpful at all stages of manuscript submission and editing.

Just as I was finishing this manuscript in 2009, a short monograph was published in German on the census boycott movements by Nicole Bergmann, an historian.[2] Up to that point I had been in the enviable position of working on a book about events in (West) Germany which had never been the subject of a book-length treatment either in English or in German. I admit to having opened Bergmann's thin volume with some trepidation. But in retrospect it came at the perfect time.

2 Bergmann, N. 2009. *Volkszählung und Datenschutz: Proteste zur Volkszählung 1983 und 1987 in der Bundesrepublik Deutschland*. Hamburg: Diplomica Verlag.

In fewer than 100 pages, she does a remarkably efficient job of describing what happened in 1983, and offers a brief but insightful contrast to the 1987 boycott. Her work has proven a very useful mirror in which to reflect, suddenly with much more clarity, on what I have done (and not done) with much of the same material.

The embodied process of writing up this research has been a long one, revolving around the basic challenge of finding a conducive and congenial place to sit. Much of the sitting has taken place during summers or on sabbaticals somewhere away from whatever counted as "home" at the time. I am deeply indebted to friends and family for their generous hospitality: Kelvin Chu and Jennifer Appleyard; Claudia Hannah; Mike Powell and Jerri Smith; Brad, Irene, Rachel and Eric Wolf, Dennis Wallace, Kathleen McGranaghan and Hugh Wallace; Reese, Lucy and Ogden Hersey; Jay Moore and Jude Sargent; Joni Seager and Cynthia Enloe; and Emily Johansen and John Johnson. Coffee shops have served as important places of work, as well. My most productive regular ersatz offices have been Mayorga (Silver Spring, MD); Capitol Grounds and Langdon Street Cafe (Montpelier, VT); Muddy Waters (Burlington, VT); and Diesel Cafe (Somerville, MA). No less important have been the providers of fine coffee beans for home-brewed coffee: Capitol Grounds in Montpelier, Vermont and The Mecca in Aberystwyth, Wales.

Around the time this research project began, I had the good fortune to be introduced by my former Vermont neighbor Bob Light to a group of people who have nothing to do with census politics, but who have anchored me to a particular place more firmly than they could know throughout the entire life of this research project: Bill Howe; Dennis Wallace; Kathleen McGranaghan; Greg Titus; Greg Hooker; Paul Nichols; Dave Bookchin; Bob Minsenberger; Jimmy Kennedy; and more recently, Tom Treese and Noah Hahn, and the recrudescent Rick White, as well as Daisy and Prelvis. It has been a true privilege to re-create with such fine people and noble animals. Thanks are due also to Mark Whitehead and Gareth Hoskins for their enthusiastic adoption of the same peculiar outdoor hobby in the wetter and windier conditions of Wales.

Finally, I am deeply grateful to my partner Antje Ricken, for unflagging and unselfish general support, for some very concrete help with sorting out the endnotes, corrections and index and for more things besides than it is possible to enumerate. This book is dedicated to her.

Introduction

> The presiding officer got up, took a few uncertain steps around the table, went into the voting chamber, looked inside and came back. The representative of the party in the middle spoke up to remind the others of his prediction that the abstention rate would go sky-high, the representative of the party on the right once more played the role of pacifier, the voters had all day to vote, they were probably just waiting for the rain to let up.
>
> (José Saramago, *Seeing*, p. 5)

In the Spring of 1983, a boycott movement developed in West Germany against the federal government's plans to take a national census [*Volkszählung* or VZ]. In the space of three months, the movement, which first took hold in West Berlin and Hamburg, quickly developed into a loose nationwide network of hundreds of citizens' initiatives, most densely concentrated in the larger cities and university towns, but also present in rural areas. Roughly a quarter of West German adults surveyed in March of 1983 said it was possible they would participate in the boycott. The accuracy of this figure was never put to the test, however. In April, shortly before the enumeration date, the West German Federal Constitutional Court [*Bundesverfassungsgericht* or BVerfG] halted the census in response to a pair of suits brought against the government, arguing that the justices needed time to consider the constitutional implications of new electronic information technologies. In December of 1983, the Court ruled that some parts of the census law were void, and sent the Helmut Kohl administration, the new conservative government only in power for six months, back to the drawing board. After much wrangling between political parties and legislative houses, a new law was passed in 1985, with the enumeration date set for May of 1987. This time, the enumeration did go forward, but was anticipated and dogged throughout by a boycott movement more widespread and well organized than the first. The months before, during and after the count saw the census become a lightning rod and touchstone for a broad array of domestic political issues. Most of the former West Germans I have talked with who were old enough at the time still vividly recall the 1987 boycott, though opinions differ markedly as to what it meant or how important it was.

The present study reads the boycotts as crucial moments in the emergence of new forms of active citizenship that respond to new meanings of "the political" in the information age. As challenges to the epistemic sovereignty of the West German nation-state, the boycotts were aimed not only at preserving some "dark territory" against the searching gaze of state agencies, but also, I will argue, experimented with new ways of taking part in decisions about what sorts of knowledge can or should "come to light" in the processes of governance. The *magnum opus* of Alberto Melucci, one of the major theorists of New Social Movements since the 1960s, is entitled *Challenging Codes: Collective Action in the Information Age.*[1] The "codes" Melucci has in mind are primarily qualitative, shaping meaning, thought, "culture". Informational citizenship, as I would like to develop the concept here, is concerned in addition with the ways in which the virtual identities constructed out of electronic data files shape the relations of individuals and groups to the social orders of which we are a part. Michel Foucault, commenting on the new social movements of the 1970s and 1980s, ties both forms of identity politics to the question "Who are we?": at their core lies "a refusal of these abstractions, of economic and ideological state violence which ignore who we are individually, and also a refusal of a scientific or administrative inquisition which determines who one is."[2] In a similar vein, Melucci and Leonardo Avritzer argue that "the definition of democracy in complex societies should include two further freedoms: the freedom not to belong as the right to withdraw from one's constituted identity in order to form a new one, and the freedom not to be represented."[3] These formulations are fine as far as they go, but "refusal" is too limited a term for the kind of informational citizenship taking shape during these decades. It fails to capture the pro-active, *creative* political possibilities inherent in epistemic relations between individuals or groups and large organizations such as states or corporations. A core presupposition of this study is the conviction that, at least in liberal capitalist societies of the Global North, statistical representation, especially in electronic form, is in the process of eclipsing our electoral representation as the locus of our chief political relevance as both subjects and objects of government. How and in what ways modern citizens (and non-citizens such as immigrants and refugees) literally "count" for questions of policy and politics is ever more closely tied to our presence or absence in data files, the categorical frameworks into which those files sort us, the mechanics of survey and sampling techniques, in short, to a whole range of issues not customarily understood as "politics". If this is so, it raises the following linked questions: To what extent and in what ways can the realm of digital representations be transformed into an arena for *active* political participation, and how does this transformation in turn potentially alter the meaning of politics in the 21st century? How can we imagine "a more interactive way of building one's informational world"?[4] How can we become more self-determining

1 Melucci, A. 1996. *Challenging Codes: Collective Action in the Information Age*. Cambridge: Cambridge University Press.

2 Foucault, M. 1982. The Subject and Power, in *Michel Foucault: Beyond Structuralism and Hermeneutics*, edited by H. Dreyfus and P. Rabinow. Chicago: University of Chicago Press, 208-228, pp. 211-212.

3 Melucci, A. and Avritzer, L. 2000. Complexity, cultural pluralism and democracy: collective action in the public space. *Social Science Information* 39, 507-527, p. 522.

4 Melucci, *Challenging Codes*, 195.

subjects as well as docile objects of the "geo-coded world"?[5] The West German census boycott movements of the 1980s provide a rich and suggestive context in which to identify some provisional answers to these questions.

The West German census boycott movements were among the earliest major social movements aimed directly at core features of the "information age."[6] They drew heavily on the experience and resources of the New Left movements of the 1960s and 1970s, and displayed many of the organizational, ideological and sociological features common to post-1960s movements in general. But at the same time their emergence *between* the legitimation and "governability" crises of the 1970s[7] and the era of "globalization" heralded in the 1990s was crucial. This period can be seen in retrospect as a brief window of time in which the basic trajectory of the information age as a technological transformation was broadly visible while its larger political and economic implications remained more shrouded in speculation (not least because Cold War geopolitics still dominated the international stage). Further, the 1980s preceded the spread of a newly heightened perception that the nation-state might be headed for obsolescence. Thus it was still possible, indeed it seemed necessary to many, to oppose features of the information age by opposing state power.

The term "the information age", like any big historical abstraction, is assailable from a variety of directions, first and foremost in its apparent privileging of technological change over other possible criteria of historical periodization, and in its character as a broad-brush simplification. However, Manuel Castells' basic understanding of the term can be useful as a description of one part of the context for the West German boycott movements. The information age emerged in the specific matrix of the 1970s United States as a cumulative effect of technological innovations in electronic computing and communications since the mid-20th century (the silicon chip, the personal computer, fiber optics, the internet, etc.), and over subsequent years quickly gained footholds and independent centers of innovation in East Asia and Europe. Without too much simplification, the key technological innovations can be said to have advanced electronic technology in four interrelated directions: (1) ever faster, more miniaturized and less expensive *information processing* capacity; (2) ever-expanding, more miniaturized and less expensive *data storage* capacities; (3) ever-expanding, ever faster *transmission and switching* capacities; and (4) ever more efficient *translation* between various types and applications of electronic data, as technologies increasingly take advantage of "the common digital language in which information is generated,

5 Pickles, J. 2006. *A History of Spaces: Cartographic Reason, Mapping and the Geo-Coded World*. London: Routledge.

6 Castells, M. 2000. *The Rise of the Network Society (2nd Ed.)*. Oxford: Blackwell.

7 Habermas, J. 1975. *Legitimation Crisis* (trans. T. McCarthy). Boston: Beacon Press; Offe, C. 1984. Ungovernability: On the Renaissance of Conservative Theories of Crisis (trans. A. Buchwalter), in *Observations on the Spiritual Situation of the Age*, edited by J. Habermas, Cambridge, MA: MIT Press, 67-88.

stored, retrieved, processed, and transmitted."[8] Castells rightly stresses that a key source of the longer-term significance of these technological trends lies in their uptake into the globalized capitalist political economy.[9] The specific issues of privacy and surveillance so central to the West German census boycott movements are portrayed by Castells as having less to do with dangers posed by the state than with the threat of private (corporate) control of information. "The Big Brother imagery must be empirically dismissed", he declares; information technologies "actually undermin[ed] the centralizing logic of one-way instructions and vertical, bureaucratic surveillance."[10]

Yet this was certainly *not* the perception of many West Germans in the 1980s. The boycotts there were clearly directed against a particular national state, and they emerged from a particularly vital and coherent, if extremely polarized, national civil society.[11] Because of its emergence out of the profoundly shocking crimes and extreme politics of the Nazi era, West German political culture was arguably unique at the time in the intensity of investment, both on the part of what might be termed "the establishment" and on the part of its critics, in struggles over the meaning of legitimate political contestation. At the same time, the boycotts were aimed at broader conjunctural aspects of the fledgling information age central to Castells' account. The boycotts were a symptom of the confluence of the particularities of postwar West German political dynamics, still basically understood within a nation-state model of politics, though also strongly inflected by the Cold War, and a particular historical moment in the unfolding of the tendentially trans-national information age. That moment can be described in terms of the rapidly changing institutional context of the four broad dimensions of

---

8 Castells, *Network Society*, 29.

9 Castells, *Network Society*, 13.

10 M. Castells (2004), *The Power of Identity (2nd Ed.)*. Oxford: Blackwell, pp. 340-341.

11 Sabine von Dirke argues that "a coherent and functioning public sphere no longer existed" at this time. (von Dirke, S. 1997. *"All Power to the Imagination": The West German Counterculture from the Student Movement to the Greens*. Lincoln: University of Nebraska Press, 101.) This is certainly true if the yardstick is something like Habermas's "ideal communication community." (Habermas, J. 1992. *The Theory of Communicative Action* (2 Vol.) (trans. T. McCarthy) Boston: Beacon Press.) However far apart the mainstream and alternative positions were, though, they were far apart *on a common set of issues*, most notably the (il)legitimacy of various forms of violence. In addition, not only was the left intimately familiar with the arguments of mainstream politicians and press, some prominent defenders of the status quo were actually quite conversant with, and attempted seriously to address, radical analyses. Most notable in this regard was Kurt Sontheimer, the foremost mainstream liberal interpreter of the West German political system from the 1970s until after unification. (Sontheimer, K. 1976. *Das Elend unserer Intellektuellen*. Hamburg: Hoffmann und Campe; Sontheimer, K. 1979. *Die verunsicherte Republik: Die Bunderepublik nach 30 Jahren*. Munich: Piper; Sontheimer, K. 1980. *Der unbehagliche Bürger: vom deutschen Umgang mit der Demokratie*. Zürich: Edition Interfrom).

technological development noted above (computing speed, data storage capacity, switching and transmission capacity, and translatability between applications). The early stages of the informational revolution were marked by significant state involvement and centralized control of information, both because information technologies (especially powerful computers) were still extremely expensive, cumbersome, and only profitable in certain economic sectors, and because (as in the case of the internet) governments often took the initial steps in developing them. A major turning point came in the mid-1980s:

> [S]ince the mid-1980s, microcomputers cannot be conceived in isolation: they perform in networks, with increasing mobility, on the basis of portable computers. This extraordinary versatility, and the capacity to add memory and processing capacity by sharing computer power in an electronic network, decisively shifted the computer age in the 1990s from centralized data storage and processing to networked, interactive computer power-sharing.[12]

The census boycott movements emerged on the cusp of this change, during a fairly short span of years in which the rapid development of computing speed and data storage were widely known but the decentralizing possibilities of networking were still a few years away from being mainstreamed. Thus "Big Brother" imagery centered on the surveillance state was still very much a plausible lens through which to interpret issues of surveillance and privacy. As I will emphasize in the concluding chapter, an updated version of "the surveillance state" remains a surprisingly relevant specter in the 21st century.

Surveillance, information, and oppositional geographies in West Germany

As David Murakami Wood argues, the specific trajectories followed by both the technological trappings and the political discourses of "surveillance society" have differed across national and cultural contexts.[13] While the burden of this book is to argue for the general relevance of events in West Germany, appreciating this relevance requires an extended immersion in the specifics of the West German context. The contours of the political landscape in the aftermath of the West German student movements of the 1960s have been thoroughly mapped out by authors from a range of perspectives.[14] Two particular aspects of Left thought in this period are

12 Castells, *Network Society*, 43.

13 Murakami Wood, D. 2009. The "surveillance society": questions of history, place and culture. *European Journal of Criminology* 6(2): 179-194.

14 See for example Koenen, G. 2001. *Das rote Jahrzehnt: Unsere kleine deutsche Kulturrevolution*. Köln: Kiepenheuer und Witsch; Markovitz, A. and Gorski, P. 1993. *The German Left: Red, Green and Beyond*. Oxford: Oxford University Press; Sontheimer, *Verunsicherte Republik*; Aust, S. 1998. *Der Baader Meinhof Komplex* (expanded and

certainly relevant as general, if indirect motivational frames for the census boycott movements. First, though the student movement had eventually parted ways with representatives of the Frankfurt School over issues of violent resistance, the multifaceted "critique of instrumental reason" formulated in different ways by Frankfurt School thinkers such as Horkheimer and Adorno, Reich, Marcuse or Habermas had become a part of the *Weltanschauung* of many West Germans.[15] Secondly, the West German feminist movement, especially since the high-profile controversy over the anti-abortion law that exploded in 1971, had succeeded in establishing a new awareness of the contentious politics of private life.[16] As Edith Hoshino Altbach notes, long-standing distrust on the part of feminists of the broader German left to some extent blocked a more thorough exploration of the many commonalities of these two strands of thought and activism.[17] Nevertheless, it can hardly be doubted that a heightened sensitivity to the fact that "the personal is political" made it far easier for West Germans to perceive advances in electronic technology and its adoption by state agencies as an alarming political development. The wide resonance of concern for "data protection" (*Datenschutz*) in the mid-1970s is difficult to imagine apart from these new sensitivities.

Indeed, an articulated and contentious politics of surveillance, privacy and electronic technologies can be seen to link together many key issues that were perhaps much less strongly related in substantive terms. Rather than explore the by now quite well-researched constellation of left political positions and projects in thematic terms, this introduction will weave a context for the census boycotts at this common, underlying level of "policing" and "security". In the mid-1970s, the federal state's strenuous attempts to vanquish the Red Army Fraction (RAF) and other violent domestic extremist groups led politicians, police and security agencies into quite controversial projects aimed at identifying, rooting out and isolating "dangerous" individuals and small groups. This investigative zeal, especially the various ways in which it placed large numbers of average citizens under scrutiny, was the most glaring provocation for the data protection movement that led to the passage of privacy legislation.[18] Also beginning in the 1970s and continuing into the 1980s, public demonstrations and occupations organized by all sorts of

---

updated edition). Munich: Goldmann Verlag; Aly, G. 2008. *Unser Kampf: 1968*, Frankfurt: Fischer Verlag.

15 Kraushaar, W. 1998. *Frankfurter Schule und Studentenbewegung: von der Flaschenpost zum Molotowcocktail 1946 bis 1995* (3 Vols.). Hamburg: Rogner & Bernhard bei Zweitausendeins.

16 Markovitz and Gorski, *The German Left*, pp. 87-94; Hoshino Altbach, E. 1984. The New German Women's Movement. *Signs* 9(3), 454-469; Bergmann, *Volkszählung und Datenschutz*, p. 15.

17 Hoshino Altbach, "The New German Women's Movement", p. 462.

18 Flaherty, D. 1989. *Protecting Privacy in Surveillance Societies: the Federal Republic of Germany, Sweden, France, Canada and the United States*. Chapel Hill: University of North Carolina Press; see also Busch, H., Funk, A., Kauß, U., Narr, W.-D. and Werkentin, F. 1985. *Die Polizei in der Bundesrepublik*. Frankfurt: Campus Verlag, pp. 391-399.

oppositional groups, and given a new mass dimension especially by the peace, anti-nuclear and environmental movements, posed new challenges. Techniques of "mass" surveillance of large demonstrations, marches and occupations of land, as well as new forms of resistance to police measures, became the core issues. Through all of these struggles, electronic technologies of identification and data processing were an increasingly important theme, as were questions of the state's monopoly on legitimate violence, the definition of "violent" protest or "legitimate" civil disobedience, in short, the politics of coercion and resistance. Finally, both of these themes were inextricably focused upon, if not restricted to, the evolving "oppositional geographies" of the West German left. The state's policing and surveillance strategies were aimed at rendering these geographies visible. I will pause in the middle of the account of illustrative struggles that follows here to say more about these oppositional geographies and their political significance.

Domestic terrorism: Surveillance and the search for dangerous individuals

The constitutional order established in 1949 by the passage of the Basic Law [*Grundgesetz*] that established the Federal Republic of Germany ("West Germany") out of the former British, French and American occupied zones, was fundamentally shaped by a determination, on the part of the Allies as well as of the fledgling postwar German leadership, not to allow any future recurrence of the National Socialist ascendancy to power in the late 1920s and early 1930s. The Basic Law was explicitly forged in contrast to the democratic constitution of the Weimar Republic, which was perceived by the new founders as having been too weak and pliable to prevent Hitler's rise to, and legal seizure of, power.[19] The new political order would be a "fortified" or "militant" democracy, a system that could not be undermined from within, through the use of its own elements.[20] Thus the new constitution was kept free of any plebiscitary features that might allow demagogues to mobilize forms of direct democracy as a way of challenging or circumventing representative politics and legislative process: the Basic Law firmly prioritizes official representation over political expression outside the institutions of the state. Further, because of this strong ideological investment in process over substance, the postwar West German order taps into the longer German *Rechtsstaat* tradition. The core principle of the *Rechtstaat* (or "rule of law") approach requires all state action to be quite closely specified in enabling legislation, leaving much less room for executive interpretation than in the Anglo-American political

19 Sontheimer, K. and Bleek, W. 1999. *Grundzüge des politischen Systems der Bundesrepublik Deutschland*. Munich: Piper; Niclauß, K. 1998. *Der Weg zum Grundgesetz: Demokratiegründung in Westdeutschland, 1945-1949*. Paderborn: Ferdinand Schöningh.

20 Jesse, E. 1981. *Streitbare Demokratie*. Berlin: Colloquium Verlag; Schönbohm, W. 1979. *Verfassungsfeinde als Beamte? Die Kontroverse über die Streitbare Demokratie*. Munich: Günter Olzog Verlag.

tradition.[21] Similarly, in full awareness of the fact that Hitler had been able to take power within, and then perpetuate, a constitutionally permissible suspension of the normal institutions of democracy, the framers of the Basic Law made sure that a ruling government could only be removed on the condition that a new governing coalition of elected representatives already be in place to take over within an uninterrupted continuation of the institutions of democracy (the "constructive vote of no confidence").[22] The symbolic re-location of the capital from a Berlin laden with too many dark associations to the unprepossessing Rhenish town of Bonn (the "capital of self-effacement", according to Michael Z. Wise[23]), and the dispersal of various federal agencies to different cities throughout the newly formed country, were to symbolize a deliberate limitation of centralized national government, a new beginning for a pointedly modest and unambitious nation-state.[24] Finally, an important administrative complement to these federal-level precautions was the placement of police matters firmly in control of the individual states [*Länder*] that made up the federation [*Bund*, hence *Bundesrepublik*].

Even with all these initial safeguards in place, however, West Germany's acquisition of the normal powers of a nation-state in the decades after 1949 was met with substantial protest at each step: the re-establishment of a military and compulsory military service in the course of the 1950s provoked major protests.[25] One of the key flashpoints of controversy in the 1960s was the set of Emergency Laws through which the West German government would finally re-claim from the Allied Powers the ultimate authority to maintain domestic order in times of acute disruption or unrest. These *Notstandsgesetze* were among the first issues taken up by the young radicals of the SDS in the early 1960s, and the more politically advanced sections of the student movement of 1967-68 nurtured high hopes that common opposition to the emergency laws would overcome the considerable cultural barriers to alliance between militant students and the industrial working class.[26] This problem of building

---

21 Busch, *et al.* argue that, while close legal regulation of state activity might seem reassuring, it in fact stems from a construction of state power as fundamentally external and historically previous to democratic-parliamentary control. (Busch, *et al.*, *Polizei*, pp. 53-54; see also Sontheimer and Bleek, *Grundzüge*, pp. 184-185). This interpretation is confirmed by Albrecht Funk (Funk, A. 2000. Die Entstehung der Exekutivepolizei im Kaiserreich, in *Staat, Demokratie und innere Sicherheit in Deutschland*, edited by H.-J. Lange. Opladen: Leske und Budrich, 11-28, pp. 16-19).

22 Sontheimer and Bleek, *Grundzüge*, 30.

23 Wise, M. 1998. *Capital Dilemma: Germany's Search for a New Architecture of Democracy.* Princeton: Princeton Architectural Press.

24 Sontheimer and Bleek, *Grundzüge*.

25 Large, D. 1996. *West Germans to the Front: West German Rearmament in the Adenauer Era*. Chapel Hill: University of North Carolina Press.

26 Markovitz and Gorski, *The German Left*, 54-56; Thomas, N. 2003. *Protest Movements in 1960s West Germany: A Social History of Dissent and Democracy*. Oxford: Berg, pp. 87-93; Seifert, J. 1965. *Gefahr im Verzuge: Zur Problematik der Notstandsgesetzgebung.*

alliances with workers was the most politically important basic challenge facing militant student movements of the 1960s in many different countries, though it was approached in different ways in each. The upheavals of the 1960s in West Germany acquired a special intensity also from the Nazi past of many older Germans in positions of authority, whether parents, professors, judges or government officials. Youthful rebellion against the establishment, another common strand in many struggles at the time, was fuelled in West Germany by very specific and potentially damning suspicions about authority figures and their biographies.[27] These suspicions, in turn, were lent additional plausibility by the authoritarian response of establishment figures to even relatively mild forms of civil disobedience. The arbitrary and very lightly punished fatal shooting of the student Benno Ohnesorg in June of 1967 by a policeman in the aftermath of a protest in Berlin was the most spectacular and galvanizing example of state brutality, but it was part of a much more general pattern.[28]

The suspicion that a commitment to order rather than democracy animated state actions and the mainstream political culture was nurtured as well by the situation in Bonn. Federal power had been shared since 1966 in a Grand Coalition of the two mass parties, the conservative Christian Democratic Union/Christian Social Union (CDU/CSU) on the one hand, and the Social Democratic Party of Germany (SPD) on the other. Many in the student-led extra-parliamentary opposition [*ausserparlamentarische Opposition*, henceforth APO] as well as on the left of the working class saw the gradual rightward migration of the SPD as a particularly bitter betrayal. The SPD is the oldest surviving political party with parliamentary representation in Germany, and arguably the most important socialist party of the European 20th century, having served as the electoral home of the German and then West German industrial working class, and as the main steward of social justice ideals, since the late 19th century.[29] Viewed from the radical left, the SPD had made two historic blunders in the 20th century: the decision to take national power rather than join the Bolsheviks in pushing for international revolution in the aftermath of WWI, and the explicit renunciation of basic opposition to the capitalist system in the 1959 Godesberger Program. Its support for the Emergency

Frankfurt: Europäische Verlagsanstalt; Anon. (ed.) 1967. *Vorbereitung auf den Notstand? 10 Antworten auf eine aktuelle Frage*. Frankfurt: Fischer Bücherei.

27 Jaspers, K. 1966. *Wohin treibt die Bundesrepublik?* Munich: Piper; Frei, N. 2001. *Karrieren im Zwielicht: Hitlers Eliten nach 1945*. Frankfurt: Campus Verlag; Reichel, P. 2001. *Vergangenheitsbewältigung in Deutschland: Die Auseinandersetzunn mit der NS-Diktatur von 1945 bis heute*. Munich: C.H. Beck; Markovitz and Gorski, *The German Left*, p. 52.

28 The recent revelation that the police officer who shot Ohnesorg was in the pay of the East German Stasi does not alter the fact that the shooting was, if not welcomed, also not strongly condemned by many mainstream West Germans and Berlin residents. The clear reluctance of police officials and politicians to punish the shooting was likewise not a result of Stasi manipulation.

29 Sassoon, D. 1996. *One Hundred Years of Socialism: The West European Left in the Twentieth Century*. New York: New Press.

Laws only confirmed its arrival in the establishment. Nevertheless, the SPD remained the only parliamentary option and hope for many on the left. That the SPD was now arrayed with the forces of order on the other side of the barricades signaled a profound shift in the terms of political struggle in West Germany.[30] SPD ascendancy in 1969 to a dominant position in a ruling coalition with the smaller Free Democratic Party (FDP) would last through the 1970s to the Kohl "turn" in 1982, and would bring in train a thoroughgoing reorientation of ideologies across the entire political spectrum. Of crucial importance was the fact that the SPD, and not the conservatives, oversaw the development of repressive programs through which the state responded to domestic extremist violence.[31] The census boycotts were among the many developments that would have been impossible to imagine before this long-term shift in the landscape of party politics.

At the level of oppositional political practice, the protest wave of 1968 failed to stop the Emergency Laws, and failed as well to shake the government's support for the US adventure in Vietnam. The APO then gradually disintegrated over the next couple of years into a kaleidoscope of smaller organizations and affinity groups focused on a wide range of political issues (anti-fascism, feminism, peace, environmentalism, anti-racism, local participatory urban planning, as well as Marxist-inspired revolution), but oriented as well, in many cases, more toward alternative lifestyles than "issue politics".[32] Most of these groups eschewed violence (if not civil disobedience), but it was the very few who were willing to pursue their goals over dead bodies that drove struggles over the authority and provoked the coercive powers of the state in the 1970s. The Red Army Faction (RAF) remains the most notorious of these groups in retrospectives on the period, but a number of others were equally deadly at the time.[33] The challenge they posed was illustrated in the early 1970s when celebrated journalist Ulrike Meinhof and co-conspirators freed Andreas Baader, who had been in custody for his role in attempting to torch a department store, at the eventual cost of the life of a guard who had been shot in the action. Together with Baader, his girlfriend and accomplice Gudrun Ensslin, and a small group of others, Meinhof went underground to form the RAF or Baader-Meinhof gang. Until the capture of most of the major figures in 1972, this "first generation" RAF staged a series of bombings and other violent actions. Alongside scattered extremist acts by the Movement of the Second of June (*Bewegung 2. Juni* or B2J), the Socialist Patients' Collective (SPK), the Revolutionary Cells and

30 Cobler, S. 1978. *Law, Order and Politics in West Germany* (trans. F. McDonagh). Harmondsworth: Penguin Books, 53.

31 Sassoon, *One Hundred Years of Socialism*, 521.

32 Kraushaar, W. (ed.) 1978a. *Autonomie oder Getto? Kontroversen über die Alternativbewegung*. Frankfurt: Verlag Neue Kritik; Markovitz and Gorski, *The German Left*; von Dirke, *"All Power to the Imagination!"*; Thomas, *Protest Movements*.

33 Aust, *Baader Meinhof Komplex*; Koenen *Das rote Jahrzehnt*; Schiller, M. 2001. *Es war ein harter Kampf um meine Erinnerung: ein Lebensbericht aus der RAF*. Munich: Piper.

other groups, the doings of the RAF, especially of the "second generation" that would carry on through the mid-1970s, provoked the West German state into an active program to update and re-define "militant" democracy.

The most controversial measures taken by state officials were, first, the so-called "Order on Radicals" [*Radikalenerlaß*] passed by the conference of provincial interior ministers in 1972, and second, the addition of the soon-to-be infamous Paragraph 129a to the criminal code. The Order on Radicals, popularly known as the Employment Ban (*Berufsverbot*), decreed that applicants for state employment had to undergo background checks to make sure they had no connection with organizations "hostile to the constitution". This involved requesting information from the Constitutional Protection Agency (*Bundesverfassungsschutz* or BVerfSch), the most feared domestic spying agency. As a result of such background checks, the number of prospective teachers, welfare workers, university professors and others who were denied state jobs over the course of the 1970s and 1980s was relatively modest, running into the hundreds nationwide.[34] But its symbolic importance as an expression of what many took to be a basic government distrust of its citizens was enormous.[35] A high-profile international Russell Tribunal meeting in March and April of 1978 in Frankfurt made headlines by investigating this practice and concluding that it violated basic human rights.[36] Paragraph 129a defined "terrorist organizations" as legally relevant entities for the first time, and provided for the punishment of any individual involved in either forming or belonging to any organization so designated.[37]

34 Jesse, *Streitbare Demokratie*, 65-72; Bethge, H., Bünemann, R., Enderlein, H., Kurz, I., Roßmann, E., Schiller, T., Stein, H., and Stuby, G. (eds.) 1976. *Die Zerstörung der Demokratie in der BRD durch Berufsverbot.* Köln: Pahl-Rugenstein Verlag; Braunthal, G. 1990. *Political Loyalty and Public Service in West Germany: The 1972 Decree against Radicals and its Consequences.* Amherst: University of Massachusetts Press.

35 Hannover, H. and Wallraff, G. 1982. *Die Unheimliche Republik: Politische Verfolgung in der Bundesrepublik.* Hamburg: Rowohlt.

36 The text of the Tribunal's report concludes that "the extent of human rights violations by the practice of *Berufsverbote* and the consequences which have resulted must be regarded as extremely serious ... The distinction between loyalty to constitutional principles, loyalty to the state and loyalty to those who administer the state is fast disappearing." (Third Russell Tribunal 1978. *Berufsverbote Condemned.* Nottingham: the Bertrand Russell Peace Foundation Ltd., p. 9.) The first tribunal, organized by Bertrand Russell and Jean-Paul Sartre in Stockholm in 1967, was modeled on the Nuremberg trials, and brought evidence against top US politicians for crimes against humanity in Vietnam. Russell died in 1970, but the tradition of calling tribunals of high-profile public figures continued. The second tribunal took place in Rome in 1973-76 and concerned human rights violations by the *Apartheid* regime in South Africa. The fourth and last, staged in Rotterdam, focused on human rights violations against the native peoples of the Americas. Mailänder, U. and Zander, U. 2003. *Das kleine Westberlin-Lexikon: von "Autonome" bis "Zapf" – die alternative Szene der siebziger und achtziger Jahre.* Berlin: Schwarzkopf und Schwarzkopf, p. 233.

37 Cobler, *Law, Order and Politics*, pp. 109-118.

Thus members of the RAF or other such groupings could be tried and jailed even without being connected to any particular crime against persons or property. The federal government built a special high-security prison at Stuttgart-Stammheim in which to incarcerate members of the RAF and other such groups. The plight of the first-generation RAF leaders held there until their deaths in 1976 and 1977 became a lasting point of controversy. While most on the West German left rejected the RAF's violent approach, and the imprisoned leadership practiced systematic provocation of the authorities at every opportunity, the exceptional measures taken at Stammheim and in other high security tracts to isolate and control Baader, Meinhof, Ensslin, Jan-Carl Raspe, Irmgard Möller, and their allies were widely denounced as inhumane. The organization *Rote Hilfe* mobilized financial assistance for the legal defense of the inmates and arranged visits to prisoners where that was allowed. Suspicions that RAF-hired attorneys were smuggling correspondence between second-generation cells still at large and the high-security tracts led the government to suspend client-attorney confidentiality, and the attorneys had to undergo searches at entry and exit. In addition, attorneys were denied the otherwise routine right to a "double mandate", that is, to represent more than one client in trials relating to terrorist organizations. The offices of one of the defense attorneys, Klaus Croissant, were suspected of doubling as an RAF communication center, and some of Croissant's associates were arrested by police. Croissant fled to France, claiming political asylum, but was extradited back to West Germany.[38] For Sebastian Cobler, writing in 1976 (more than 20 years before Giorgio Agamben would make a similar connection), all of these measures together conjured up Carl Schmitt's notion of the "state of exception", and in effect confirmed the fears raised in the 1960s regarding the authoritarian dangers posed by the Emergency Laws. Reflecting on the new militant West German democracy, he concluded succinctly, "People may now legally be put outside the law."[39]

The updated version of West German "militant democracy" made use not only of legal instruments but also of ideological strategies. Government officials sought to cast oppositional politics in a criminal light, in part by attempting to taint those "sympathizers" who objected to the treatment of imprisoned RAF leaders as guilty of indirect complicity in terrorist crimes. The most spectacular instance of this tactic followed the assassination of Federal Prosecutor Siegfried Buback in April of 1977. Buback was one of a series of establishment figures targeted by the second generation RAF, and after his killing, an anonymous student at Göttingen University published a commentary under the name of "Mescalero". Mescalero confessed to a certain amount of "secret joy" (*klammheimliche Freude*) at the assassination, but then went on to criticize the killing as wrong. Journalists and state officials ignored the latter part of the note, seizing instead upon the phrase "secret joy" to accuse wide swathes of the left of being terrorist sympathizers. When Peter Brückner, a well-known leftist professor of psychology, organized a public letter from prominent intellectuals urging open discussion of the growing

38 Aust, *Baader Meinhof Komplex*, pp. 427, 440, 573-575.

39 Cobler, *Law, Order and Politics*, pp. 40, 143.

mutual distrust between state and West German youth that could lead to such "secret joy", he was suspended from teaching by his university.[40] The climax of killing came in late 1977, when, along with Buback, Dresdner Bank CEO Jürgen Ponto was killed by the second generation RAF in late July. The abduction on September 5th of West German Industrial Council chief Hans-Martin Schleyer, and the hijacking of a Lufhansa jet were intended to force the release of Baader and company from incarceration, but the West German state refused any such deal. The hijackers were killed by the elite commando unit GSG9 in Mogadishu on October 18th, 1977. The next day, Baader, Ensslin and Raspe were found dead in their cells and Möller wounded (Meinhof had already died in her cell the previous year). Most accounts conclude that these were suicides, but some on the left argue that the RAF leaders may in fact have been murdered. Hans-Martin Schleyer, held for six weeks in a high-rise apartment block near Köln, was shot the next day near the Belgian-French border, and his body abandoned in the trunk of a car.[41]

As this increasingly bitter contest unfolded through the mid-1970s, the West German State searched tirelessly for ways to move beyond a purely reactive posture with respect to terrorist acts. The figure who came to symbolize the push for anticipatory and preventive policing was Horst Herold, head of the Federal Criminal Agency [*Bundeskriminalamt*, BKA].[42] When Herold took over the post in 1972, he was already recognized in police circles as an innovator. Unusually for a police director, he was a lifelong Social Democrat. He was an avid reader of left-leaning social thought, including Marx, and had become convinced that the best way to fight criminality was to address the underlying social problems through cybernetic social engineering based on statistical analysis. As he put it in a 1976 speech accepting the Beccaria Medal for achievement in crime-fighting,

> Toward the end of the 20th century the pressing task arises of subordinating the institutions of police and justice to the procedures and processes, similar to feedback-loops, of self-steering and self-optimization, in order thus to develop a capacity for learning which at a higher qualitative level replaces repression with prevention, stubborn persistence [in traditional methods ... *Beharrung*] with dynamism, hypotheses with prognoses, [personal] leadership with steering and purported experience with logical expertise.[43]

Herold was fascinated much earlier than his police colleagues and political superiors with the possibilities computer technology seemed to hold out for realization of

---

40 See von Dirke, *"All Power to the Imagination!"*, pp. 96-103 for an interesting analysis of the wider cultural significance of "Mescalero's" "Buback obituary".

41 Aust, *Baader-Meinhof Komplex*, pp. 632-637; 643-647.

42 Schenk, D. 1998. *Der Chef: Horst Herold und Das BKA*. Hamburg: Spiegel Buchverlag; Busch, *et al.*, *Die Polizei*; Hauser, D. 1997. *Baader und Herold: Beschriebung eines Kampfes*. Frankfurt: Fischer Verlag.

43 Herold 1976, quoted in Schenk, *Der Chef*, 230.

this vision. When he took over the BKA, Herold expected to bring computer-based cybernetics to bear primarily upon "endemic", everyday criminality. His ultimate goal, as he would later recount it to Sebastian Cobler in an interview, was the complete automation of the criminal justice process: "I am striving to achieve a criminal process that – if you allow me to formulate it in extreme terms – is free of witnesses and experts. [A process] that is based exclusively on scientifically verifiable, measurable evidence. According to my theory, as terrible as it sounds, the judge would also be dispensable."[44] But soon after he started, he found that the struggle with domestic terrorism, and especially the RAF, consumed much of his time and energy, and indeed would come to define his public image. While in one sense, the chief domestic political issue of the 1970s would thus divert him from his initial goal of cybernetically engineering "normal" society, it would also justify a massive accumulation of resources and official competencies at the BKA, transforming a small agency into a major center of information, criminological expertise and federal coordination of efforts to fight serious crime.

Herold's strategic approach to combating domestic extremism revolved around the attempt to recognize patterns in the planning and execution of attacks as well as in the underground infrastructures developed by the RAF and other groups to support their activities. Herold's method called for the collection and electronic processing of huge amounts of data, and the refinement of surveillance and identification techniques of all sorts. Along with a growing number of allies in provincial and federal government, he was at the forefront of attempts to establish national electronic police databases.[45] The most successful of these was INPOL, which allowed the sharing of information between different provincial police organizations through a central clearinghouse at BKA headquarters in Wiesbaden.[46] The more specialized PIOS-Terrorism system, brought into operation in 1975, involved the digital entry of personal information on known or suspected extremists along with supplementary narrative information and references to police file numbers as an aid to investigators.[47] PIOS would play a role in the 1987 census boycott controversy.

Through the use of an ever-growing supply of data, Herold hoped to complete a comprehensive map of the oppositional geographies of West Germany. Where politicians had attempted to stigmatize the "sympathizer scene" around the RAF and other extremist groups, Herold and his police colleagues intended to register it as fully as possible. In the mid-1970s, the first steps in this direction were taken with the build-out of databases containing the handwriting of everyone known to be associated with imprisoned extremists, lists of all visitors they received,

---

44 H. Herold quoted in Cobler, S. 1981. Herold gegen Alle: Gespräche mit dem Präsidenten des Bundeskriminalamtes. *Transatlantik* [n.v.n.], photocopy in Hamburg Institut für Sozialforschung, Bestand SBe 444, Box 2.

45 Busch, *et al.*, *Die Polizei*, Chapter 4.

46 Busch, *et al.*, *Die Polizei*, pp. 118-119.

47 Busch, *et al.*, *Die Polizei*, pp. 136-137.

and even parents, spouses, more distant relatives, owners of the vehicles used to visit the high-security prisons, etc.[48] By 1979, according to a report of the Federal Ministry of the Interior [*Bundesministerium des Innern*, BMI], the BKA held information on 6,632 such "contacts", and 60,000 pieces of handwriting. More broadly, the digital representation of the oppositional "scene" had mushroomed well beyond those with direct contacts to imprisoned extremists. The 1979 BMI report found that the databases at BKA headquarters encompassed 4.7 million names and some 3,100 organizations in the *Bundesrepublik*. Among these were a fingerprint file (2.1 million persons), a photographic collection (1.9 million), a "Person Identification Central" file with 3,500 individuals, a "Commune file" with data on residential collectives (approximately 4,000 persons and 1,000 "objects"), and an "Organization file" containing data from various security services on citizens' initiatives, human rights organizations, etc. PIOS by this time contained information on 135,000 people, 5,500 institutions, 115,000 "objects" of surveillance and 74,000 things.[49] According to Herold's biographer, by the late 1970s "there would hardly have been a citizens' initiative with democratic goals that hadn't been infiltrated" by undercover agents.[50]

As a series of media stories steadily raised public awareness of the growing mass of data stored in BKA and other police computers, concern about exactly what Herold and his criminologists were doing with this data also grew.[51] From the perspective of the 21st century, the kinds of data-sifting routines developed at the BKA might seem rather obvious and rudimentary. But at the time, the much-discussed *Rasterfahndung* [roughly "grid-search" or "data dragnet"] fed growing fears of the imminent surveillance state and the "glass person". As a technique, *Rasterfahndung* can be applied "positively" or "negatively". In a positive *Rasterfahndung*, two or more data files (in the simplest case, say, one file containing names of wanted persons and the other containing names of electricity customers) are compared for matches. The term "positive" indicates that the individuals being sought are already positively identified, the task being merely to find them with the aid of additional data. In a negative *Rasterfahndung*, by contrast, the individuals being sought are not yet known. All that is known beforehand is a set of characteristics which, in combination, raise the likelihood that any person who possesses all of them is an extremist or criminal. Through rounds of sifting of different kinds of information on a large number of people, more and more individuals can be filtered out as uninteresting, until only those remain who show the sought-for combination of specific characteristics.[52] In a much-publicized case of successful negative *Rasterfahndung* in 1979, an RAF hideout in Frankfurt was discovered and Rolf

48 Schenk, *Der Chef*, pp. 206-207.

49 Aust, *Baader Meinhof Komplex*, pp. 216-217.

50 Schenk, *Der Chef*, p. 240.

51 The first major series dealing with the "surveillance state" appeared in the magazine *Stern* in May and June of 1978 (Schenk, *Der Chef*, pp. 371-374).

52 Busch, *et al.*, *Die Polizei*, pp. 139-141; Schenk, *Der Chef*, pp. 398-399.

Heißler, a member of the second generation RAF, arrested. The BKA started with the records of the electric utility in order to locate those electrical customers who paid in cash. Of the 16,000 cash customers in the city, those who had properly registered their addresses with the local residency offices were eliminated. Then the resulting reduced pool was successively compared with databases on automobile registration, driver's licenses, receipt of child subsidies and other common forms of registration. After all these rounds of reduction, only two addresses remained, one the home of a drug dealer and the other the sought-for RAF hideout. The same technique was to be used again in 1979 in Hamburg, but media picked up on the plan and the resulting negative publicity spelled the end of its use.[53] Indeed, 1979 marked Herold's definitive fall from grace, as his informational ambitions became a political liability to the SPD and a thorn in the side of Interior Minister Gerhard Baum. But while Herold would soon take early retirement, many of the data acquisition projects he had championed, and much of his approach to social order, would become part of accepted police and security practice.

The underlying logic of the negative *Rasterfahndung* is important for understanding the story told in the chapters to follow. It provoked such outrage as a police technique because, unlike in a positive search, a negative *Rasterfahndung* implicitly treats *everyone* registered in the relevant databases as initially suspect. Only if individuals show a combination of attributes that render them uninteresting do they cease to be suspicious. In short, the presumption of innocence at the heart of liberal justice systems is reversed: the population, represented in large databases, is not "innocent until proven guilty", but rather "suspicious until proven innocent".[54] By the late 1970s, West Germans had had ample experience of the state's zeal in pursuing extremists. The Employment Ban, the Order on Radicals and other features of "militant democracy" suggested to many, especially younger adults, that the logic of the negative *Rasterfahndung* had permeated the entire government approach to society. From citizens to be respected and dealt with as the basis and source of legitimacy for the liberal democratic social order, many felt they had been transformed into "security risks", now external and potentially threatening to the maintenance of a state power that had become its own justification.[55] In this scenario, it became a matter of great concern that electronic data could be stored indefinitely and copied so easily. This, too, would be a major issue in the census boycotts.

Oppositional geographies from the 1960s to the 1980s

The oppositional geographies this welter of data sought to capture were multilayered and complex. From the perspective of state officials and many mainstream West Germans, they represented an alien growth on the socio-political body, a dark territory harboring deadly terrorists, and thus a threat against which

53 Schenk, *Der Chef*, p. 399.

54 Busch *et al.*, *Die Polizei*, p. 141; Schenk, *Der Chef*, p. 376.

55 Busch, *et al.*, *Die Polizei*, p. 360.

"Modell Deutschland", the economically successful liberal democratic system that arose from the ruins of defeat in WWII, had to be defended.[56] But for many, especially younger West Germans, these geographies constituted a vibrant "scene" for alternative, oppositional life. Many of the people, organizations and "objects" stored in Horst Herold's databases were located concretely in the main nodes of a very loose national network, such as West Berlin's Kreuzberg and Schöneberg neighborhoods, Frankfurt's Bockenheim and Nordend, and the fabled St. Pauli neighborhood in Hamburg. West Berlin's Kreuzberg neighborhood in particular was iconic as a hot-house of alternative living experiments and radical political activity, the "claustrophobia" of being hemmed in by the Berlin Wall after 1961 adding a peculiar intensity to conflicts.[57] West Berlin was technically under Allied rule. Although BRD citizens could travel to and from the city, it was not part of West German territory. Thus the 24 month military service obligation for young West German men did not apply to those whose primary residence was West Berlin. For this reason and others, the walled city became a magnet for many youth not at home in the mainstream. The national alternative scene also included parts of other large cities (Bremen or Munich) and university towns such as Göttingen, Bielefeld or Heidelberg. Within any one of these nodes a heterogeneous array of residential and social spaces became increasingly established and important through the 1970s, comprised of alternative bookshops, cafes, collective childcare centers established by feminists, neighborhood centers, and left or alternative bars, clubs, galleries and movie theaters. Such places constituted an infrastructure for the circulation of oppositional populations, for the organization and staging of public extra-parliamentary political activities, and for the reproduction of alternative forms of life. Especially the development and proliferation of "residential collectives" [*Wohngemeinschaften*, WGs], households formed voluntarily by like-minded people, and small alternative businesses and agencies, lent oppositional geographies more durability than the ephemeral actions, sit-ins and protests of the 1960s.[58]

56 Foucault, M. 2003. *Society Must Be Defended: Lectures at the Collège de France 1975-1976* (trans. D. Macey). New York: Picador.

57 Till, K. 2005. *The New Berlin: Memory, Politics, Place*. Minneapolis: University of Minnesota Press, p. 69, 77. Ingrid Lottenburger reports that this claustrophobic atmosphere was very important to the 1987 boycotts in West Berlin (Personal conversation 2002).

58 Markovitz and Gorski, *The German Left*, p. 84. This variegated network nicely illustrates Walter Nicholl's argument regarding the nature of the infrastructure for the New Social Movements, of which the census boycotts were just one example. Nicholls contends that it is too simple to think of these networks as composed of local spaces providing community cohesion and larger-scale connections allowing distant coordination. He argues, in effect, that local juxtapositions and chance meetings also play a role in supporting large-scale movement coordination, and conversely, that movement activists traveling to distant nodes can help generate the "quasi-local" personal relations and trust that support commitment of resources to a cause (Nicholls, W. 2009. Place, networks, space: theorizing the geographies of social movements. *Transactions of the Institute of British Geographers* NS 34, 78-93).

Local city magazines often served as an additional source of community glue, and would prove important in the census boycotts.[59] The establishment of the alternative *tageszeitung* (taz) in West Berlin in 1979 strengthened the national coherence of the scene. The catalyst for the foundation of an independent, national alternative daily was the mainstream press's spineless obedience to the government's news blackout request during the climax of the German Autumn of 1977, as security services feverishly sought to control what the public and the RAF captors knew of events around the attempt to find and free Hans-Martin Schleyer.[60] The taz initially concentrated its reporting on government security measures, environmental issues and women's issues, and covered the squatter's movement (see below) from an angle critical of the West Berlin government. In every aspect of its organization and decision-making structure, its approach to layout and its involvement of lay citizens in grassroots journalism, even the practice of encouraging editorial annotations by the typesetters, the taz sought to model a democratic approach to journalism.[61] Mindful of the aggressive investigative energy of state security services, and at the same time wishing to de-emphasize the notion of "authoritative authorship", taz journalists often signed articles merely with given names, or in some cases just initials.[62] The taz regularly published calls to action from various citizens' initiatives, which by the 1980s had become the organizational backbone of most major social movements.

The emergence and evolution of oppositional geographies in West Germany during the 1960s, 1970s and 1980s was inextricably bound up with what was perhaps the central strategic question for Left politics over that period: whether radical social change could be most effectively pursued by attempting to take over and transform existing structures of political, economic and social power, or whether instead a more promising approach was to establish relatively independent beach-heads, islands or laboratories for alternative social existence that would attract growing interest from and exert growing influence over ever wider swathes of mainstream society. These two strategies were already discernable in the late 1960s in the political cauldron of West Berlin. The iconic residential experiment that provided the first rough blueprint for building an alternative social order was the *Kommune I*, inspired by the "Yippies" in the US. The more traditional approach of working toward revolutionary takeover of institutional power and the eventual overthrow of capitalism was represented by the Marxist leadership of the SDS, especially Rudi Dutschke. Yet any strict division between the strategies represented by these two

59 Markovitz and Gorski, *The German Left*, pp. 83-84.

60 von Dirke, *"All Power to the Imagination!"*, p. 120.

61 von Dirke, *"All Power to the Imagination!"*, pp. 122-142. Inevitably, as von Dirke notes, the taz has been controversial on the left, with some critics arguing that it sacrificed its ideals in order to survive.

62 von Dirke, *"All Power to the Imagination!"*, pp. 133-134. This practice largely explains why so many of the citations in the footnotes of Chapters 1-4 below are anonymous.

groups is too simplistic. The *Kommune I*, whose most famous members included Dieter Kunzelmann, Fritz Teufel, and Rainer Langhans, was founded in 1967. It was born in part out of the insight that the familiar, inherited repertoire of public protest could be widened, that satire and various other theatrical devices could be used to stage both provocations and the predictable responses to them much more effectively.[63] But *Kommune I* was not simply about public actions. As Ulrich Enzensberger, a long-term *Kommune I* member, put it in retrospect, "We took the line that a fulfilled individual life of freedom and the freeing of desires is directly linked to meaningful political work."[64] The communards attempted to put into practice some of the insights of Wilhelm Reich and Herbert Marcuse, who drew on Marx and Freud to analyze the ways in which capitalism failed to meet human needs, distorting and diverting natural drives by forcing individuals into the roles of obedient producer and mass consumer.[65] Only by rejecting the nuclear family, "repressive tolerance" and other forms of cooptation and complacency in their own lives could activists truly begin to undermine mainstream society and begin to form what Marcuse had called "islands of the future".[66]

The *Kommune I* itself was highly controversial within the Left at the time. It was criticized, for example, for not offering any particular program of larger-scale social change that could address such phenomena as imperialism. However, it was indisputably important as an early model for alternative living arrangements, and for raising the issue of the link between new public politics and new subjectivities. Feminists were prominent in establishing women-only organizations and WGs during the 1970s as political and lifestyle alternatives to the patriarchal life politics not only of mainstream society but also of many male-dominated "left" projects.[67] In the late 1970s, the impulse of the early Kommunes would be revived by a wide range of urban groups and rural agricultural communes under the loose banner of the "alternative movement".[68] The highest-profile event associated with the movement was the *"Tunix Treffen"* ("Do-nothing gathering") organized by the Frankfurt spontaneists or "Spontis" in 1978 and drawing several thousand participants to West Berlin.[69] The three main aims of this meeting, according to Sabine von Dirke, were to "remedy the identity crisis that the counterculture had suffered in the context of terrorist violence and the government's sweeping countermeasures"; to

63 Enzensberger, U. 2006. *Die Jahre der Kommune I: Berlin 1967-1969*, Munich: Goldmann; Thomas, *Protest Movements*, pp. 98-104.

64 Quoted in Thomas, *Protest Movements*, p. 104.

65 Negt, O. 2001. *Achtundsechzig: politische Intellektuelle und die Macht*. Göttingen: Steidl Verlag; von Dirke, *"All Power to the Imagination!"*.

66 Quoted in Kraushaar, W. 1978b. Thesen zum Verhältnis von Alternativ- und Fluchtbewegung, in *Autonomie oder Getto? Kontroversen über die Alternativbewegung*, edited by W. Kraushaar. Frankfurt: Verlag Neue Kritik, 8-67, p. 8.

67 Hoshino Altbach, The New German Women's Movement, pp. 455-456; Markovitz and Gorski, *The German Left*, p. 90.

68 von Dirke, *"All Power to the Imagination!"*, Chapters 4 and 5.

69 von Dirke, *"All Power to the Imagination!"*, pp. 111-120.

express "dissatisfaction with the sociopolitical situation in the Federal Republic and with the left's traditional strategies of opposition", and finally, "to provide a forum for self-assertion and mutual encouragement on the part of the alternative culture."[70] The flyer advertising the gathering included a manifesto that covered many familiar left themes (including surveillance), but with a special emphasis on non-conformity: "We no longer want to do the same job, make the same faces over and over again. They have bossed us around enough, have censored our thoughts and ideas, checked our apartments and passports, and bashed us in the face. We will no longer let ourselves be bottled up, made small and made the same."[71]

The alternative movement, like the early communes, was controversial on the left, and for similar reasons. As Wolfgang Kraushaar summarized the general skepticism,

> The unfolding of a separate countercultural social scaffolding, the "scene", must be seen from the beginning as ambivalent. It can prevent the disintegration of structures emerging from political struggle and to a certain degree make possible spaces for testing out alternative forms of life; but these latter will remain without revolutionary or society-transforming effect so long as they don't place their own social realities in specific relation to the social context and its contradictions … The ideological misrecognition of left radicalism driven into the corner of social isolation as the autonomous position of an independent, historically novel force approaches the status of an alternative praxis of self-betrayal. Instead of becoming a danger to the system, the communal movement increasingly takes the form of a social agency whose task is to secure the survival of drop-outs.[72]

Horst Herold and other government officials pushing a security agenda did not accept the notion that there was a strict distinction between "turning away" from society and endangering the system. The oppositional geographies sketched above were tendentially dangerous to the state if for no other reason than that they represented "dark territory"; they obscured the government's view of who was where doing what at any given time. The cover illustration of this book, by caricaturist Harald Juch, nicely evokes the limits to the official gaze represented by WGs. The memberships of WGs were notoriously fluid, and it was a normal part of alternative culture, especially in the cities, to offer temporary housing to relative strangers. The most transgressive form of WG (excluding underground extremist hideouts) was the urban squat, the illegal occupation of abandoned housing. There was great scope for squatting in the larger cities of West Germany, as extensive tracts of urban housing compromised by Allied bombing in WWII had still not been cleared or renovated decades later. Squatting had enjoyed phases of local popularity throughout the 1970s, notably in Frankfurt and some university

70 von Dirke, *"All Power to the Imagination!"*, pp. 111-112.

71 Quoted in von Dirke, *"All Power to the Imagination!"*, p. 115.

72 Kraushaar, "Thesen", p. 21.

towns, but gained the most publicity in West Berlin in late 1980 and early 1981, when the police and squatters engaged in running street battles provoked by police attempts to clear some of the houses that had been occupied in the neighborhoods of Kreuzberg and Schöneberg.[73] Some of the more militant and politically sophisticated squatters seemed to confirm the fears of conservative politicians that taking over empty houses meant creating subversive "law-free spaces" in which and from which to undermine the West German political status quo.[74] Members of the West Berlin squat "Kukuk" linked the squat clearances by police to larger dynamics of capitalist urban politics:

> The attacks on us are actually completely understandable. Our actions are an attack on their system. That is very clear in this housing battle [*Häuserkampf*]. We have stirred up a wasp's nest. It becomes clear in this whole building, demolition and renovation business how inhumanely this system functions. Our lifestyles as well, and the fact that we remove ourselves from their labor processes are by themselves already an endangerment of the system. Because what we are doing inspires imitation. Others see this and say to themselves, Hey, they have a great life, great also because they're willing to live with the consequences of transgressing the law.[75]

In West Berlin, despite a housing shortage, many absentee property owners, especially in the Kreuzberg area, were widely perceived to be allowing their empty houses to deteriorate far enough that they would be granted permission from the city to tear the buildings down. They would then be able to erect new, more profitable buildings on the cleared lots.[76] The economic injustice suggested by this scenario was a major pillar of squatters' justification for their actions:

> Consciousness of the magnitude of socially produced wealth – whose just distribution to all is only hindered by this system – leads to the conclusion: We take for ourselves what we need, we take what is owed us, we take it if it is not given to us voluntarily. Community shoplifting by residential collectives on the weekend at Kardstadt or Hertie [two department store chains] is a result of this attitude as much as is routine free-riding on the subway and the bus, and the

---

73 Wirsching, A. 2006. *Abschied vom Provisorium: Geschichte der Bundesrepublik Deutschland 1982-1990*. Munich: Deutsche Verlags-Anstalt, pp. 399-402.

74 Anon. 1981. Rechtsfreie Räume, in *Hausbesetzer: Wofür sie kämpfen, wie sie leben und wie sie leben wollen*, edited by S. Aust and S. Rosenbladt. Hamburg: Hoffman und Campe, 127-169, p. 145.

75 Anon. 1981. Bullenparanoia und das Gefühl vom Paradies: Michael Wieczorek sprach mit Vertretern des "Kukuk", in *Hausbesetzer: Wofür sie kämpfen, wie sie leben und wie sie leben wollen*, edited by S. Aust and S. Rosenbladt. Hamburg: Hoffman und Campe, 97-126, p. 109.

76 Mailänder and Zander, *Westberlin-Lexikon*, p. 127.

> occupation of empty houses. Nobody has the feeling of doing anything unjust. Something forbidden, yes.[77]

But not all the squats were so politically tuned. As a member of the Kukuk explained, "there are houses devoted mainly to working on prisoner issues [a number of squatters had been given stiff jail sentences in the aftermath of West Berlin riots in December of 1980], or others concerned only with the house itself and simply trying to keep the life of the house running. Others are busy just with fixing the house up [*Instandsbesetzung*, "squatting into shape"], etc. It's a very broad spectrum."[78]

Squatting, whether motivated by a desire to disconnect as thoroughly as possible from mainstream society, to establish a base for fighting it, or merely to fix up a living space in an urban environment plagued by a housing shortage, usually meant facing forcible eviction by the police sooner or later. Depending on the brutality of the police and the personal background and politics of squatters, this experience could have a radicalizing effect. Stefan Wisniewski and some other members of the RAF had connections to squats.[79] Partly due to suspected links to terrorism and partly due to pressure from property owners, squatters had to reckon with constant surveillance.[80] Filmed, photographed and fingerprinted repeatedly, their houses sometimes infiltrated by undercover security agents, squatters felt the surveillance state more intensely than most West Germans. A group of medically trained emergency responders [*Sanitäter*], organized within the squatting scene in West Berlin to treat injuries suffered in street battles with police, were able to generalize from experience at many clashes: "In general the tactics of the police at the moment seem to be that they want to register the entire scene. They have definitely already registered [*erkennungsdienstlich behandelt*, a classic example of bureaucratic German that would translate literally as "treated by recognition services"] hundreds of people."[81] Squatters were among the first to be given

---

77 Anon., Rechtsfreie Räume, p. 151.

78 Anon., Bullenparanoia, pp. 114-115.

79 Wisniewski, S. 1997. *Wir waren so unheimlich konsequent: ein Gespräch zur Geschichte der RAF mit Stefan Wisniewski*. Berlin: ID Verlag, p. 17; Tolmein, O. 1999. *"RAF: Das war für uns Befreiung": Ein Gespräch mit Irmgard Möller über bewaffneten Kampf, Knast und die Linke*. Hamburg: Konkret Literatur Verlag.

80 Rosenbladt, S. 1981. Nürnberg: "Die großen Lumpen schwer aufs Hirn hauen", in *Hausbesetzer: Wofür sie kämpfen, wie sie leben und wie sie leben wollen*, edited by S. Aust and S. Rosenbladt. Hamburg: Hoffman und Campe, 60-96, p. 75; Busch, *et al.*, *Die Polizei*, 343, 345-346. Suspicion of links between the *Hausbesetzer* scene and underground extremists was fuelled as well by the fact that some squats were named in honor of members of captured or killed militants. Mailänder and Zander, *Westberlin-Lexikon*, pp. 46-47, 101-102.

81 "Heide", quoted in Sanitäter-Gruppe 1981. Im Fadenkreuz: Drei Mitglieder der Sanitäter-Gruppe über sich selbst, in *Hausbesetzer: Wofür sie kämpfen, wie sie leben und wie sie leben wollen*, edited by S. Aust and S. Rosenbladt. Hamburg: Hoffman und Campe, 170-192, p.186.

intimate insights into the increasingly preventive character of surveillance, nicely diagnosed by a member of a West Berlin squat:

> For me all the house searches going on now are not actually house searches but rather prophylactic measures. This is how it goes: gathering of personal information, registration of the people, so that in the worst-case scenario, when things really get much more strongly out of hand here, the people can be more easily identified and silenced for a long time on the basis of a record of previous offences.[82]

Public protest and mass surveillance

As the struggles around violent extremism, alternative spaces and squats all illustrate, a major focus of the state's interest in knowledge was the residential element of oppositional geographies. Pinning an identified individual to a known address remained at the core of the logic of surveillance. But oppositional or alternative life and its "dark territories" were of course also about public spaces. Public protests, marches and demonstrations had been an integral part of post-1960s West German oppositional politics, and a long-standing flashpoint for clashes with the police and security services from the famous 1968 attacks on Springer Press buildings in the aftermath of the shooting of Rudi Dutschke onward. (Dutschke, the most important leader of the West German student movement, had been shot on the heels of a naked campaign of demonization in the influential, low-brow *Bild* newspaper and other papers owned by the conservative magnate Axel Springer.) As with squatting, police tactics in dealing with street protests during these years was also heavily focused on surveillance. Police forces in a number of large cities had, by the 1980s, taken to encircling entire demonstrations, and forcing everyone to remain standing (sometimes in summer heat) for hours, without access to toilets. Wilhelm Kewenig, Interior Senator for West Berlin in the early 1980s was a well known advocate of this so-called "cauldron" or "kettle" tactic. The West Berlin police sometimes offered protestors the option of leaving a kettle, but only if they allowed their personal details to be recorded. Kewenig dryly termed this practice "collective aggregation for individual registration" [*kollektive Zusammenfassung zu individuellen Kontrollen*].[83] The kettle was the analogue, in public space, to the database so beloved of Horst Herold. Everyone caught inside had lost the presumption of innocence, and was unlikely to leave the category of the suspect without leaving behind a record of identity and presence.

Alongside the more familiar street protests, the issues raised by mass demonstrations, and state attempts to register and identify large crowds, took on a new urgency beginning with the protests against the planned building of

82 Anon., "Bullenparanoia", p. 107.

83 Quoted in Anon. 1987. Ordentlich schleppern. *Der Spiegel* June 22, p. 23.

a nuclear power plant at Wyhl in Baden-Württemberg in the early 1970s.[84] By the mid-1980s, the list of iconic mass protests and mass occupations organized by the anti-nuclear, environmental and peace movements would also include the nuclear facilities Brokdorf, Kalkar, and Gorleben, as well as the planned new Frankfurt airport runway Startbahn West and many others. The messages sent by large protests were varied. In general most public demonstrations sought at least to communicate the fact that large numbers of people opposed or supported the particular policies at issue. Numbers apart, though, in some cases even just the possibility that *anyone* would publicly proclaim particular messages or reject unwanted policies was already important. The West German peace movement and environmental movement also sought, especially in the 1980s, to send more symbolic messages through their demonstrations, for example forming rings around areas or objects to symbolize protection or perhaps threats to be contained, or, as in the human chain, to symbolize connection.[85] Occupations of forbidden spaces or installations such as nuclear plants symbolized claims for democratic control over energy policy or democratic challenge to police control.

A key issue for the anti-nuclear, peace and environmental movements was how to reach the large numbers of mainstream citizens who were indeed not happy with government policy but who were also uneasy about openly opposing it. In addition to the types of message noted above, organizers also strove to cultivate a strong sense of "personal impact" [*Betroffenheit*]. Steve Breyman argues that the peace movement was particularly well placed in this respect: "The very essence of the targeted evil – the indiscriminate nature of nuclear explosives and the all-encompassing (if hypothetical) character of nuclear winter – sets anti-nuclear weapons movements apart from most other movements, old and new. Peace movements have few, if any, competitors for the breadth and expansiveness of their self-proclaimed constituency,"[86] It was in this sense that "Gorleben is everywhere", as the popular slogan put it in referring to a controversial nuclear waste storage facility that became the target of long-running protests.[87] But in addition to making the sense of *Betroffenheit* as wide as possible, protest movements also needed to render it intense and immediate enough to motivate potential recruits. The famous "die-ins" that have since entered the standard repertoire of peace protestors worldwide were an innovative attempt to do just that.[88] The census boycott movements were interesting in this respect because while the threat posed by the census was not understood by most West Germans to be a matter of life and death, it was certainly universal within the national

84 Busch, *et al.*, *Die Polizei*, pp. 328-329.

85 Balistier, T. 1996. *Straßenprotest: Formen oppositioneller Politik in der Bundesrepublik Deutschland.* Münster: Westfälisches Dampfboot, Chapters 2, 3 and 4.

86 Breyman, S. 1998. *Movement Genesis: Social Movement Theory and the 1980s West German Peace Movement*. Boulder: Westview Press, p. 185.

87 Balistier, *Straßenprotest*, p. 139.

88 Balistier, *Straßenprotest*, pp. 228-232.

boundaries, as well as direct and immediate, in the sense that an enumerator would visit every household and ask for information.

The anti-nuclear, peace and environmental movements had remarkable success in these years in attracting mainstream citizens. The conservative Kohl government came to power in 1982, through a successful constructive vote of no-confidence in the previous Schmidt government. Its alliance with the primitive anti-communism of Reagan and Thatcher as they sharpened the superpower standoff helped elevate the threat of (nuclear) war to a major motivator of widespread opposition. But the environmental movement and strong opposition to nuclear power were equally prominent flashpoints, and both had been developing since the mid-1970s. By 1983 West Germany was internationally recognized as the home of the most advanced sections of the international peace and environmental movements. The formation and evolution of the Green Party became a beacon and a closely watched process for environmental activists around the world, while opposition to NATO's planned stationing of mid-range Pershing nuclear-tipped missiles on West German soil generated giant demonstrations involving hundreds of thousands of citizens. Neidhardt and Rucht document a peak of protest events in the late 1960s and another in the early 1980s.[89] The latter peak coincided with the height of the peace movement, which was marked by some huge protests, such as a human chain of some 250,000 stretching between Ulm and Strasbourg, and a protest estimated to have attracted 500,000 people to Bonn, the largest protest in the history of the BRD.[90]

These new, massive mobilizations posed two related challenges to police and politicians who sought to stigmatize and defuse opposition. The first was the new difficulty in sifting out "bad apples", individuals and groups seeking to subvert or overthrow state authority, from the mass of "normal", generally law-abiding citizens who showed up in ever-increasing numbers at these events.[91] The familiar equation of protestor with "radical", "extremist" or "chaotist" was ever-more patently mendacious. Captive to the long-standing logic of surveillance, police still sought to link individuals to known addresses. But since most people at the large demonstrations were clearly mainstream citizens who were otherwise law-abiding, the justification for gathering and holding their personal information was ever-more obviously paper-thin. Tied to this problem was the difficulty of identifying real threats to the system simply in terms of their "violence". The problem of violence and state authority in connection with public demonstrations emerged in the 1960s and continued to reappear on the front pages throughout the 1970s and

---

89 Neidhardt, F. and Rucht, D. 2001. Protestgeschichte der Bundesrepublik Deutschland 1950-1994: Ereignisse, Themen, Akteure, in *Protest in der Bundesrepublik Deutschland: Strukturen und Entwicklungen*, edited by D. Rucht. Frankfurt: Campus Verlag, 27-70, pp. 36-37; Balistier, *Straßenprotest*, pp. 14-15.

90 Balistier, *Straßenprotest*, pp. 120, 129, 136-137; Koopmans, R. 1993. The dynamics of protest waves: West Germany, 1965 to 1989. *American Sociological Review* 58, 637-658, p. 639; Markovitz and Gorski, *The German Left*, pp. 106-112.

91 Busch, *et al.*, *Die Polizei*, p. 353.

1980s, forming a major theme for domestic governmental discourse.[92] Intellectuals and activists connected to the peace, Green and anti-nuclear movements sought to carve out defensible justifications not just for street protests but for civil disobedience, and to define it in ways that could appeal to mainstream citizens.[93]

Not surprisingly, state officials sought to define "violence" at demonstrations and protests as broadly as possible, so as to stigmatize opposition, much in the way that "sympathizers" were being tarred in connection with incarcerated members of the RAF. Nobel Prize-winning author Heinrich Böll's ironic definition of "sympathizers" would also have applied to leftists debating civil disobedience at large protests: "People who have committed the criminal sin of making distinctions.'[94] Conservative politicians were strident in their rejection of the sorts of distinctions left activists were making, between non-violent and violent protestors in the context of a single event, between bodily harm and destruction of property, between active attacks on police and defensive resistance to arrest.[95] The perspective expressed by Minister of the Interior Friedrich Zimmermann in a July 1983 *Spiegel* interview was common among state officials throughout this entire period: "If the local police officer says, "Please clear the area," and [the person addressed] does not leave, then he is no normal citizen … He is in any case not a peaceful one."[96] Zimmerman, who would remain in this post and thus play a major role in both the 1983 and the 1987 census controversies, held to his strict views on violence throughout the decade, going as far in a 1988 speech as to state that "non-violent resistance is violence".[97]

---

92 Wirsching, *Abschied*, pp. 399-404; Negt, *Achtundsechzig*, Part II. See also Hill, W. (ed.) 1984. *Widerstand und Staatsgewalt: Recht im Streit mit dem Gesetz*. Gütersloh: Gütersloher Verlagshaus Mohn; Kutscha, M. (ed.) 1986. *Demonstrationsfreiheit: Kampf um ein Bürgerrecht*. Köln: Presseverlag Theurer.

93 See, for example, the contributions to Glotz, P. (ed.) 1983. *Ziviler Ungehorsam im Rechtsstaat*. Frankfurt: Suhrkamp. The ongoing relevance and potentially limitless scope of this debate is suggested by the range of readings compiled for participants in a June 1987 discussion of the Green Party *Bundestag* delegates on the 20th anniversary of the watershed killing of the student Benno Ohnesorg by police in West Berlin. Along with statements by political contemporaries, the readings included pieces by Gandhi, Rosa Luxembourg, Marx, Engels, Henry David Thoreau, the Catholic Bishops of the US, and theologians of all stripes, past and present. Küntzel, M. Kolodzeiej, G. and Ebermann, T. 1987. "Gewalt": Debatte der Bundestagsfraktion Die Grünen am 2.6.87, unpublished typescript, Archiv Grünes Gedächtnis, Bestand B.II.1, File 3381.

94 Cited in Cobler, *Law, Order and Politics*, p. 41.

95 In a much discussed speech in Berlin in 1967, Herbert Marcuse had insisted that there was no overarching definition of violence, but instead that violence was always tied to specific situations, so that "there is a violence of liberation, and there is a violence of repression. There is a violence of the defense of life, and there is a violence of aggression." (quoted in Negt, *Achtundsechzig*, p. 90).

96 Quoted in Balistier, *Straßenprotest*, p. 65.

97 Quoted in Balistier, *Straßenprotest*, p. 254.

As was also clear in the "kettle" technique discussed above, police strategy and tactics at mass protests gave material expression in public space to this rejection of a hard-and-fast distinction between disruptive and peaceful participants in public demonstrations.[98] Most spectacularly in the 1970s, state officials responded to planned mass demonstrations against nuclear installations by banning demonstration throughout entire districts, or by erecting control points along roads and in rail stations and registering or searching everyone traveling toward the city or town in which the demonstration was to take place, whether or not they were actually planning to attend it. In 1978, the *Bundestag* passed a law authorizing police to ask anyone for identifying documents, even if they were not suspected of a crime.[99] These practices were taken to an extreme in preparation for a demonstration at Kalkar in North-Rhine-Westphalia in 1977, where some 3,500 police officers, manning 96 control points registered or searched 122,000 people and 68,000 vehicles.[100] This, coupled with ceaseless intonations of the dangers of "chaotists" and "terrorists", sent a clear signal to the West German public that opposition to government policy entailed being treated like a suspected criminal. The focus of police forces upon information-gathering continued in the 1980s, though the temporary massive mobilizations and webs of control points like that at Kalkar would not be repeated. Instead what seemed to be emerging was a tendentially permanent "zonation" [*Verlandung*] of the *Bundesrepublik* "through zones of special security and correspondingly more limited citizens' rights." Not only nuclear reactors and waste storage facilities but also scientific laboratories or research installations (such as for genetic technology) and regions surrounding the sites of atomic, biological or chemical weapons would be nested in protective buffers.[101] Among the rights sacrificed in these zones was the right to anonymity and freedom from automatic suspicion on the part of the authorities.

Questions of the legitimacy of participation in protests, and of the disputed distinction between "peaceful" and "violent" protestors, led the Federal Constitutional Court to hand down a number of rulings relating to public space and political expression. A key principle, set out in its 1985 "Brokdorf" decision (named for the planned atomic power plant in Schleswig-Holstein that became the target of a major demonstration in 1981), denied the state's broad definition of a "violent protest": "If there is no reason to fear that a demonstration as a whole will take a disruptive course, or that the organizer[s] and associates are striving for, or at least are willing to condone such a course, then the protection of the freedom of assembly guaranteed to every citizen remains in force even if disruptions by individuals or a minority [of demonstrators] are to be expected."[102] Nevertheless,

98 Busch, *et al.*, *Polizei*, pp. 200-201.

99 Markovitz and Gorski, *The German Left*, p. 75.

100 Busch, *et al.*, *Polizei*, p. 338.

101 Busch, *et al.*, *Polizei*, pp. 426-427.

102 Bundesverfassungsgericht 1985. 1 BvR 233, 341/81, May 14. *Entscheidungen des Bundesverfassungsgerichts*, v. 69. Tübingen: JCB Mohr (Paul Siebeck).

police practice at demonstrations continued to tend towards stigmatizing all protestors as potential criminals.

The issue that perhaps best represents the common logic linking surveillance of public space and the sort of informational surveillance that raised concerns about privacy and data protection is that of "masking" [*Vermummung*], that is, wearing handkerchiefs or other cloth coverings over the face at public demonstrations. Along with what the police termed "passive armament", wearing motorcycle helmets and/or other padding to protect against police batons, masking was a logical response to some of the new ways the police were dealing with demonstrators, both in smaller-scale urban protests and at mass mobilizations.[103] Many commentators at the time, citing the increasingly fearsome appearance of riot police, with helmets, gas masks, knee pads and other protective clothing, jackboots and transparent plexiglass shields, spoke of the "militarization of the police". Certainly one of the intended effects of this impressive get-up was to intimidate protestors. But as Busch *et al.* pointed out, such gear was actually part of a larger effort by police agencies to fill the so-called "gap" between the old-fashioned baton and the potentially deadly firearm as means to coerce obedience. Conspicuously absent from the new suite of gear were more deadly or powerful guns. The idea was that a more elaborately equipped police force could deal more easily with physical attacks such as the time-honored throwing of paving stones, could hold their ground or continue to drag away protestors even when being kicked, punched or scratched, and could continue to operate if gas were released among, or water cannons trained upon, protestors.[104] These new physical capabilities, coupled with the routine photographing and information-gathering police now engaged in at public demonstrations, were supposed to maximize the flexibility and precision of their actions. Masking and helmeting made sense, from the perspective of protestors, as protection precisely against the non-deadly means by which police sought improved control over crowds.[105] Masking served the dual purpose of covering the face to thwart photographic identification and helping to protect against gas. It can also be construed as embodying a more "classical" message about citizenship, even where this was not the explicit intention. In this view the important thing about citizens expressing political opinions in public is

103 For a darkly humorous take on the Orwellian formulation "passive armament", see Schwenger, H. 1983. *Im Jahr des grossen Bruders: Orwells deutsche Wirklichkeit.* Munich: Piper, pp. 49-51. Schwenger suggests that the state could save a good deal of money by denying social aid to those guilty of "passive exploitation", and could finally satisfy male supremacist urges to share the guilt for violent sexual crime between men and women by giving legal standing to the notion of "passive rape". Seen in retrospect after 30 years of neoliberal "workfare" programs, the first neologism is no longer so amusingly outlandish. The latter never was.

104 Busch, *et al.*, *Polizei*, pp. 185-187.

105 Meyn, J.-H. 1988. *Die sogenannte Vermummung und passive Bewaffnung: Verfassungs- und verwaltungsrechtiliche Probleme unter besonderer Berücksichtigung der Änderung des Versammlungsgesetzes von 1985.* Frankfurt: Verlag Peter Lang, p. 6.

not the specifics of their individual identities, through which it might be tempting to read "underlying" or "real" motives that could "explain away" the message, but rather the merits of the message or the act of opposition itself, and the fact that significant numbers of (anonymous and interchangeable) citizens share it. Read in this manner, masking at demonstrations was strongly analogous to some of the ways in which census boycotters sought to insist on complete anonymity in exchange for consenting to be counted. It should come as no surprise that Kohl's Interior Minister Friedrich Zimmermann, while struggling in 1983 to cope with the first census boycott movement, was simultaneously pushing hard to have the *Bundestag* pass a law banning both masking and "passive armament". These measures would become law in 1985. The text of the legislation forbade the carrying, "at outdoor public demonstrations or marches, [of] protective weapons, or objects suited to be used as protective weapons and intended to defend against enforcement measures of state officials [*Träger von Hoheitsbefugnissen*]." It also banned participation in a demonstration "in a get-up [*Aufmachung*] that is suited and in the circumstances intended to hinder the establishment of identity."[106]

Contemporary critical analysis of the West German "surveillance state'

Taken together, the transformations and political flashpoints outlined in the foregoing sections make clear that the term "dark territory" in the title of this book refers not simply to the kinds of apparently "private" space suggested by the cover illustration but also, and in profoundly intertwined ways, with public spaces both physical and virtual. Rather than begin to develop this notion further here, though, perhaps a more useful initial way to summarize the changes in the coordinates of West German surveillance and privacy issues from the mid-1970s to the mid-1980s is to see what kind of sense Left theorists through this period made of them. Conservatives, as well as some prominent social democrats, tended in general to naturalize police and security measures as simply necessary for the maintenance of the FDGO, the "free democratic basic order", to dismiss critics as immature, idealistic or dangerous, and thus effectively to abstain from detailed analysis of these matters. Even those social democrats, such as political scientist Kurt Sontheimer, who made more sustained efforts to engage left critiques of the heavy security emphasis of 1970s fortified democracy, ultimately considered the problem to inhere not in any aspect of the political-institutional system but rather in the psychological or ideological distortions of the Left.[107]

Much of the left critical discussion of the security state that went on in West Germany at this time was broadly Marxist in orientation, but also incorporated ideas from Foucault and other theorists of power. In a classic 1977 paper, Oskar

106 Quoted in Meyn, *Sogenannte Vermummung*, pp. 23-24.

107 Sontheimer, *Das Elend unserer Intellektuellen;* Sontheimer, *Die verunsicherte Republik*; Sontheimer, *Der unbehagliche Bürger*.

Negt located the weakness of West German democracy in the fact that the German bourgeoisie, unlike its counterparts in England or France, had historically "failed to liberate itself from feudal coercive domination and the absolutistic state through self-conscious revolutionary action and to assert itself as an autonomous political class. Yet, only in doing so could it have acquired the objective potential for regarding liberal freedoms as its own affair to be strongly defended."[108] For Negt, the absence of a bourgeois revolution had also put the German working class on a path of state-centered historical development. This "negative" German exceptionalist argument was made famous initially by Marx himself, who had quipped that, in Jack Zipes' paraphrase, "Germans have always been backwards; they've never shared in the revolutions of other countries, only their restorations."[109] In an influential 1976 book, Sebastian Cobler eschewed a class analysis in favor of a more exclusive focus on political ideology.[110] Cobler saw the sometimes latent, sometimes open repressive law-and-order program of the West German state, its propagation of a continuous "state of emergency", as rooted above all in militant anti-communism.[111] In language that resonated with that in which Foucault was lecturing at the Collège de France in the year his book appeared, Cobler described West German state repression of the left as follows: "Political opponents, their criticisms of existing conditions and their demands, are presented as criminal, to avoid the need for a political confrontation with them. They are presented as biological phenomena or evil forces and so denied the right to be treated as human beings.'[112] In this way "the politically isolated and disastrous activities of a few desperadoes – in the literal sense of the word – [the RAF and other violent extremists] serve as a welcome pretext for sealing off a whole society against any possibility of the growth of political extra-parliamentary opposition."[113] Anti-communism has indisputably formed the one constant ideological strand stringing together the entire sequence of hegemonic political cultures holding sway in western Germany from Weimar democracy through Nazi fascism and the "Bonn" *Bundesrepublik* on to its present, reunited "Berlin" successor. Cobler thus had little trouble finding documentary evidence to highlight continuities in the authoritarian and anticommunist mentality of security officials from the 1950s to the 1970s. Even in 1987, during the second census boycott movement, state officials and conservative publicists would dust off the hallowed, if increasingly outdated, tactic of ascribing widespread opposition to the manipulations of small communist cadres.

---

108 Negt, O. 1977. The misery of bourgeois democracy in Germany. *Telos* 34 (Winter 1977-78), 123-136, pp. 128-129.

109 Zipes, J. 1977. From *Berufsverbot* to Terrorism. *Telos* 34 (Winter 1977-78), 136-147, p. 137.

110 Cobler, *Law, Order and Politics*.

111 Cobler, *Law, Order and Politics*, p. 23.

112 Cobler, *Law, Order and Politics*, p. 41.

113 Cobler, *Law, Order and Politics*, p. 12.

In a paper presented in New York City in 1979, critical publicist Hans-Magnus Enzensberger offered a somewhat different account of contemporary West German security policy, shifting attention more toward the new. He argued that the "peculiarly German flavor" of state control measures in those years were not merely to be understood in the long shadow of the missing bourgeois revolution, but should be attributed to a mix of traditional authoritarian conservatism and technocratic systems built on electronic surveillance.[114] For Enzensberger, Horst Herold represented the new approach to combating social disorder, but Herold and his ilk still had to share the halls of power with the likes of Franz-Josef Strauß, the arch-conservative long-time ruler of the Bavarian Christian Social Union (CSU). The two logics they represented were "not reconcilable, all they have in common is the mad idea of perfect internal security."[115] The curious thing was that, however accurate Enzensberger's account of the longer-term generational change, the political transition of the early 1980s actually ran in the opposite direction, with older-style authoritarians taking over from technocrats. This circumstance would add yet another twist especially to the publicity battle around the 1983 boycott movement.

In a widely cited 1983 work, state theorist Joachim Hirsch, drawing on contemporary innovations in Marxist political theory from Gramsci, Althusser and Poulantzas, sought to explain the intensifying drive for security by way of the shifting position of the West German economy in the global division of labor, and the increasingly central role of the state in securing the conditions for capital accumulation.[116]

> [T]he extreme integration into the world market on the part of the West German economy, which has been the basis, on the one hand, for relative economic stability and prosperity up to the present, on the other hand causes a growing economic-social pressure to adapt to changed conditions of competition in the world market. This adaptation, however, presupposes continued success in carrying out economic-social restructuring with its increasingly deep consequences for the working and living conditions of the population.[117]

The maintenance of social order despite the stresses placed upon the population by the demands of the global market became increasingly problematic, according to Hirsch, due to

114 Enzensberger, H.-M. 1979. An address on German democracy to the citizens of New York. *New Left Review* 118 (Nov./Dec.), 3-14, p. 12.

115 Enzensberger, Address, p. 9.

116 Hirsch, J. 1983. *Der Sicherheitsstaat: Das "Modell Deutschland", seine Krise und die neuen sozialen Bewegungen.* Frankfurt: Europäische Verlagsanstalt.

117 Hirsch, *Sicherheitsstaat*, p. 18.

> the dissolution of class-based social milieux, driven forward by the capital restructuring process and so far almost unbridled (destruction of residential and communication arrangements, de-differentiation and re-mixing of social positions, forced mobility), the growth of the "middle class" and a "negative socialization" marked by the exclusion of large social groups from economic conditions of reproduction and [by] social marginalization. In this way stable social contexts, living spaces and the political-organizational structures built upon them are undermined, [and] socially disintegrated subjects immediately [transformed into] objects of administrative "provision" and control.[118]

This basic diagnosis of social disorientation from the late 1960s onward, whether given an economic inflection as in Hirsch or a more socio-political one, as in much of the literature on New Social Movements, was one important point of consensus among many left commentators. There was also a degree of consensus attaching to the idea that the "security state", however defined in detail, was a symptom of the increasing difficulty of maintaining political-economic order in the face of this disorientation.

The most empirically rich and grounded attempt to capture these links was a heavy collaborative tome published in 1985 by Heiner Busch, Albrecht Funk, Udo Kauß, Wolf-Dieter Narr and Falco Werkentin, entitled *The Police in the Federal Republic*.[119] Rather than focus upon the rather abstract category of "the state", Busch and his colleagues argued forcefully that the core issue in understanding recent shifts in strategies of social control was the web of specific state institutions making up the police and security services. Taken together, so they argued, these institutions were the concrete embodiment and collective guardian of the state's aspirational monopoly on violence, the effective core of its sovereignty. Thus the best way to grasp the evolving contours of the security state was to study the various empirical dimensions of the reform of police policy, institutions and practices since the early 1970s. This would allow more differentiated judgments on the extent to which fears of an omniscient and omnipresent "security state" were justified. They undertook an extended analysis of the changing organizational structures, recruiting practices, weaponry and information technology of the various domestic police and security services from the early 1970s to the mid-1980s, as well as a survey of police practice on the ground in various situations. On the basis of this research they agreed in general with other left commentators that the higher profile of police and security in West German society was a symptom of an overarching political failure to come to terms with rapid social change. They portrayed the trappings of the emergent security state as a "substitute for politics" [*Politikersatz*] characterized by a number of related trends: (1) a "thickening" of the web of security institutions, rules, etc.; (2) an increasing reach of these institutions down into the lives of individual citizens; (3) a simultaneous distancing

118 Hirsch, *Sicherheitsstaat*, pp. 24-25.

119 Busch, *et al.*, *Polizei.*

of the state from society through "depoliticization" of social policy and yet an increasingly intimate proximity between the two as state regulation suffuses ever more social fields; (4) an increasing tendency, therefore, for state institutions to be pulled into all conflicts; (5) a corresponding extension of the effective field of the state monopoly on violence into every area where state institutions are present ("every state measure becomes a part of security policy"); (6) an increase in the *political* relevance and centrality of the state monopoly on violence in the form of police institutions, which encourages a new prophylactic approach to disorder ("prepression"); and (7) a growing state role in "social synthesis", that is, in providing key structures on and through which society attains elements of coherence (here, according to Busch *et al.*, the state had "sucked dry heteronomous forms of social organization", and, ironically, precisely through their increasing presence, police institutions had acquired the political function of ensuring that certain problem areas remain unpolitical).[120]

In this context, Busch and his colleagues argued that the move to electronic information gathering and data processing during the 1970s was important but did not necessarily signal the advent of a total surveillance state. Computers and data files supported the larger trend of centralization, standardization and coordination among police forces dictated in part by the increasing mobility of the population (and thus also of crime). But they also facilitated the entry of security institutions into ever more areas of social life, even in the absence of larger cybernetic visions of the sort that had initially motivated Horst Herold. At the same time, however, Busch *et al.* noted that through the use of the *Rasterfahndung* and related methods, more police work had become abstract in nature, and tended to take place in the interior office spaces of the police apparatus rather than on the street or through direct contact with citizens.[121] Thus the adoption of new information technology was a driving force in the seemingly paradoxical third trend in the list above, the simultaneous suffusion of society with police and distancing of police from society. Crucially, they pointed out that new concerns over data protection raised by electronic data processing amounted to a recognition that *information gathering is in itself a form of intervention in society*. Information gathering had always been part of police work, but fears of the "glass person" now helped make plain the fact that registration and identification, the gathering of social knowledge more generally, are never merely neutral functional steps in the project of fighting crime or addressing social ills.[122] This insight would play a major role in the census boycott movements. I will argue in the concluding chapter that despite (or perhaps precisely because of) the familiarity and banality it has acquired in the last three decades, the potential political significance of this particular point for struggles of the 21st century has yet to be fully appreciated.

---

120 Busch, *et al.*, *Polizei*, pp. 461-464.

121 Busch, *et al.*, *Polizei*, pp. 145-146.

122 Busch, *et al.*, *Polizei*, p. 116.

Although they strove throughout to avoid over-dramatizing the changes of the 1970s, Busch and his co-authors did warn, in no uncertain terms, against the tendential outcomes of all these changes:

> Citizens now fully become STATE-citizens [*STAATS-Bürger*, a play on the usual German term for citizen, *Staatsbürger*]. They receive an identification card. They are categorized in many different ways, they are not permitted, once filed, to pull out of this order "anarchistically". The disposition, ordering, identification is the work of the bureaucracy. It produces a second image of the citizen, the one that now actually counts publicly. The secondary, bureaucratic reality becomes primary.[123]

The Police in the Federal Republic ends with a brief look at strategies of resistance to the ongoing expansion and abstraction of West German security apparatuses. Along with a call to expand autonomous, democratic, non-state-mediated ways to address social problems (such as women's shelters and other self-help and community groups), the authors pointed to an Achilles-heel of massive identification and data schemes such as the proposed national, machine readable identity card. A national identity card, so they argued, can only work for the state if every adult actually carries it with them at all times. Even a relatively small percentage of people refusing or failing to do so spoils the purpose of sorting individuals accurately in the basis of a complete mass of data.[124] They closed with a thinly disguised endorsement of actions like the census boycott, the first round of which had already taken place when their book appeared, the second round still to come two years later: "For these reasons it is worth keeping in mind the possibilities for resistance that would allow the 'right of informational self-determination' highlighted by the Federal Constitutional Court to be exercised, if necessary through withdrawal from technically perfected attempts at mass monitoring."[125]

Like many others in Europe, Michel Foucault was following events in West Germany in the mid- to late 1970s with great interest and alarm, and, like his West German colleagues, attempting to develop forms of analysis adequate to evolving security regimes. In a December 1977 public letter to "certain leaders of the left" in France, Foucault condemned the French state's refusal to grant political asylum to Klaus Croissant, one of the attorneys representing imprisoned RAF leaders, as well as its prosecution of the two French women who had given Croissant

123 Busch, *et al.*, *Polizei*, pp. 468-469.

124 Such a strict understanding of what would be necessary for ID cards to work would not prevent them from being made mandatory for West Germans in the years following those chronicled in this book.

125 Busch, *et al.*, *Polizei*, p. 476.

shelter.[126] As noted above, Croissant was accused by the West German government of having abetted terrorists by passing communications between the imprisoned RAF leaders and accomplices still at large. Anticipating the socialist ascendancy to power in his own country, Foucault attempted to warn socialist leaders against too strong an investment in "security":

> You know that in the future you may have to deal with an important problem: governing one of these modern states that prides itself on offering populations not so much territorial integrity, victory over the enemy, or even general enrichment as "security": a staving-off and repair of risks, accidents, dangers, contingencies, diseases, and so on. This security pact entails dangerous extensions of power and distortions in the area of recognized rights. And it leads to reactions aimed at contesting this "securitizing" function of the state. In short, we risk entering a regime in which security and fear will challenge and reinforce one another.[127]

In his authoritative study of Foucault's entire "critique of political reason", Thomas Lemke highlights this "security pact" proposed by Foucault as an important if unremarked feature of the "dispositive of security", and links it to other suggestions Foucault made to the effect that an "anxiety state" is the flipside of the *Rechtsstaat*: "The abuses, legal transgressions and irregularities of the state are not unavoidable deviations or the divergence between ideal and reality, but rather constitute the basis and guarantee for the durable and regular existence of the *Rechtsstaat*."[128] This brings us very close to the analysis of Giorgio Agamben and, again, echoes one of Sebastion Cobler's concluding comment in his 1976 book ("People may now be legally put outside the law").[129] A sense of resonance between the early 1980s and the early 21st century is not accidental. I would like to suggest that the situation in West Germany at that time anticipated many features of the political conjuncture in the first decade of this century, and that the census boycott movements became so widespread then for reasons that are still very much in play today. Such periods of heightened fears for public security only serve to highlight the importance of cultivating dark territory.

* * * * *

The chapters to follow tell the story of the census boycott movements. Chapter 1 explains how the idea for a nationwide boycott first emerged in late 1982 and early

---

126 Foucault, M. 1994. Letter to certain leaders of the left, in *Power*, edited by J. Faubion. New York: New Press, 426-428.

127 Foucault, Letter, p. 427 (see Lemke, T. 1997. *Eine Kritik der Politischen Vernunft: Foucaults Analyse der modernen Gouvernmentalität*. Hamburg: Argument Verlag, pp. 191-192 [Note 51]).

128 Lemke, *Kritik*, p. 192 [Note 51].

129 Agamben, G. 1998. *Homo Sacer: Sovereign Power and Bare Life*. Palo Alto: Stanford University Press; Cobler, *Law, Order and Politics*, p. 143.

1983 from within established eco- and peace movements, and lays out the range of critical and historical analyses of the proposed census developed by movement organizers. The rich palette of boycott strategies debated by the citizens' initiatives is likewise explored and placed in a longer historical context of 20th century German politics. The 1983 boycott movement never had a chance to test these strategies, however, as the Constitutional Court first delayed and then cancelled the census in that year. Chapter 2 places this momentous decision in the context of the range of state responses to the nascent boycott movement in the Spring of 1983. A comparison of the stances taken toward the census by conservative statists, Data Protection Commissioners and the Constitutional Court highlights the challenge posed by the controversy to received understandings of the relation between state and citizenry. Overall, the 1983 boycott controversy was significant primarily as an occasion for development and discussion of new analyses of the problems of surveillance and security and of new strategies for combating their intensification. The imaginative plans of the boycott movement, together with the ruminations of the Constitutional Court, begin to trace some of the contours of the "informational citizenship" I seek to develop. However, the practical dimensions of informational citizenship, the adaptation of strategies and tactics to the shifting circumstances of a real political struggle, were not elaborated much further until 1987, when an overhauled version of the census was finally taken in the face of a stronger and better organized boycott movement. Issues of surveillance, privacy and data protection never left the public stage between 1983 and 1987. But the field of political forces in which the second boycott movement took up the struggle changed fundamentally over these four years. The most important change was the institutional anchoring of the Green Party in the *Bundestag* and in a number of state parliaments. As a federally recognized party the Greens now had access to financial and organizational resources that enabled them to play a key, though never entirely dominant role in shaping the 1987 boycott movement into a more formidable force than its predecessor. The Kohl administration, too, had learned from 1983, and now invested much more effort in the project of justifying the census and pushing it through. Before tracing the course of events in 1987, the narrative pauses for an Interlude, which briefly chronicles the decisively important rise of the Greens as a significant new point of both linkage and confrontation between social movements and state power, and previews the more practical political aspects of informational citizenship that would come to the fore in the 1987 boycott controversy.

The second half of the book tells the story of the 1987 controversy, and completes the picture of informational citizenship sketched in part one. Chapter 3 highlights the strategizing and the publicity campaigns of both camps in the lead-up to the May 1987 enumeration, showing how the boycott issue led propagandists on both sides to tap into and in some cases re-formulate the entire range of domestic political issues that had bubbled up repeatedly in one form or another throughout the post-war decades. Along the way, material from the files of the East German Stasi on the census controversy provides a fascinating external window on the whole issue. Chapter 4 narrates the playing out of all these issues during and after the enumeration, on the streets, in local courtrooms throughout West Germany and West Berlin, and in the virtual world of police and security databases. The "hard boycott" strategy adopted by most of the citizens' initiatives, the varied responses of state officials at all levels, and the slow denouement of the census struggle over subsequent months and years together highlight the profound questions raised for inherited notions of citizenship and citizen-state relations. A clearer sense begins to emerge in 1987 of what it might mean to approach the prospect of "being counted" or "being registered" as an opportunity for active political (self-)representation for individuals and groups. In addition, relations between acts of knowledge gathering and seemingly far more "intrusive" forms of authoritative intervention such as physical coercion, as well as between registration and resistance, emerge as far more complex questions than courts and political theorists have tended to assume they are. The concluding chapter briefly surveys the continued relevance of the West German census boycott movements in the re-united Germany of the last two decades, ties together the concept of informational citizenship as a set of perspectives and strategic considerations applicable to a wide range of settings, and discusses a few of the scattered controversies in a range of liberal democracies that seem to indicate the growing, if not yet systematically understood relevance of such struggles for the politics of the 21st century.

Chapter 1
The 1983 Boycott Movement: Development, Themes and Tactics

> When he replaced the receiver, he looked over at his colleagues, but without, in fact, seeing them, it was as if he had before him a landscape composed entirely of empty voting chambers, immaculate electoral rolls, with presiding officers and secretaries waiting, party representatives exchanging distrustful glances as they tried to work out who might gain and who might lose from this situation, and, in the distance, the occasional rain-soaked poll-clerk returning from the door to announce that no one was coming.
>
> (José Saramago, *Seeing*, p. 7)

It was out of the political hothouse of West Berlin and onto the pages of taz that the first national public call for a census boycott came in December of 1982. With the slogan "Politicians ask – citizens don't answer" ["*Politiker fragen – Bürger antworten nicht*"], members of a West Berlin anti-nuclear group announced the formation of a "VoBo Ini" ["***Vo****lkszählungs* (census) ***Bo****ykott* ***Ini****tiative*"]. The slogan would eventually catch on and be adopted throughout West Germany, although the group's specific program for a boycott would find little resonance elsewhere. The West Berlin group had formed in September of 1982 out of a pre-existing West Berlin chapter of an international anti-military-service organization [*Internationale der Kriegsdienstgegner*].[1] The ad in the taz proposed a trade: citizens would give the federal government their personal information only if Bonn would divulge the locations at which it planned to station mid-range nuclear missiles. According to Michael Schroeren, "[w]e make exactly the same claim to information regarding rocket locations that the government makes on citizens with the census."[2] According to taz, the local Greens had already signed on with their support of the boycott. In a letter to peace and eco-activists from November of 1982, before placing the ad, Schroeren had laid out the strategic logic behind the bargain, arguing that despite all the massive protests it had organized, the peace movement would not be able to hinder the Reagan-Kohl arms build-up with its current repertoire of actions. The census seemed an opportunity not to be missed: "Because each individual, each household, each family and each business is

1 Initiative Volkszählungsboykott 1982. Flyer, in Archiv Grünes Gedächtnis, Bestand BII1, File 2896.

2 Anon. 1982. Politiker fragen – Bürger antworten nicht. *die tageszeitung*, December 16, p. 4.

impacted [*betroffen*] by the census, it offers a point of connection for a mass act of civil disobedience."[3] *Der Spiegel*'s later account of the movement's local origins in Hamburg also places the decisive moment in late 1982, when an unnamed woman who had been notified that she was to be a census enumerator stood up to voice her concerns at a public presentation and started the discussion that led to the formation of the first VoBo Ini in West Germany proper.[4]

There was an important historical precedent for the 1983 West German boycott. Many Dutch citizens had objected to the census taken in the Netherlands in 1971, and had sabotaged it in sufficient numbers to cast real doubt on the usefulness of its results.[5] Unlike in West Germany, however, the Dutch state gave credence to citizens' fears and decided not to take a census in 1981, thereby defusing the issue for some time. Some state officials in the *Bundesrepublik*, as we shall see, inhabited a quite different world of thinking on obedience to government measures. The clash between this authoritarian tradition and an equally insistent activist culture is ultimately what makes the West German story so fascinating, as will become especially clear in part two of this study. The duration, breadth and energy of the census controversy generated a rich penumbra of arguments, strategies, and tactics that, I argue, can be of great use to democratic politics in the future. But more on that later.

The speed with which VoBo Inis sprouted up all over the *Bundesrepublik* between December of 1982 and March of 1983 can only be explained against the background of the web of surveillance and security measures detailed in the introduction. The 1983 boycott, then, was the beginning of something new in terms of the political scope the issue would eventually take on. The role of the critical press was crucial. If taz can be credited with first explicitly raising the census issue for a national audience from its West Berlin stronghold, the alternative *Hamburger Rundschau* played that role in the other major headquarters of the movement, with an article on January 27th, 1983.[6] But it was *Der Spiegel* more than any other periodical that ensured the census controversy would be born into a context marked by a high level of public awareness of the larger issue of the surveillance state and the prospect of comprehensive, technologically mediated social control, or, as activists in Hamburg termed it, "cybernocracy" [*Kybernokratie*].[7] *Der Spiegel* had run a long piece in its first number of January 1983 detailing all the ways in which George Orwell's dystopian world of

3 Schroeren, M. 1982. Letter to activists, November 19. Archiv Grünes Gedächtnis, Bestand BII1, File 2896.

4 Anon. 1983. "Ohne Drohgebärde, ohne Angst". *Der Spiegel*, April 18, p. 20. See Bergmann, *Volkszählung und Datenschutz*, pp. 40-41 for a more detailed account of the movement's origins.

5 Vieten, G. 1983. Holland – ein Land lässt sich nicht zählen, in *Die Volkszählung*, edited by J. Taeger. Reinbek bei Hamburg: Rowohlt, 270-282.

6 Mathes, R. and Pfetsch, B. 1991. The role of the alternative press in the agenda-building process: spill over effects and media opinion leadership. *European Journal of Communication* 6: 33-62, pp. 41-42.

7 I am grateful to Dieter Schröder at the Hamburg Institut für Sozialforschung for alerting me to the importance of the term *Kybernokratie*.

1984 could be considered to have arrived right on time, or even a little early. Horst Herold's visions of the transparent society, and his methods of surveillance, anchor a story that, while it made no mention of the planned census, focused centrally on the problem of data protection in a world of ever-more-formidable computer and communications technology.[8] The next week, a follow-up article detailed the methods used by the West German security services in 1981 to wire an entire neighborhood in Heidelberg in an attempt to detect and head off an expected RAF attack on NATO generals.[9] The focus of this second article was the rapidly advancing technology of video surveillance, and the ways in which it had already eroded constitutional and legal rights. Berndt Schmidt, a development engineer at the BKA, had been in charge of organizing the cutting-edge surveillance system in Heidelberg. But he had come to oppose the methods of surveillance used by the BKA when he saw how surveillance cameras, bugs and stake-outs came to be used more and more to register and follow not only suspected terrorists but law-abiding members of their "environment". He quit his job and resolved to do what he could to warn his fellow citizens about what he had come to see as a runaway security apparatus. This *Spiegel* article raised most of the key ethical, legal and constitutional issues that would, within just a few weeks, come to shape the controversy over the census. In January of 1983, taz built on this theme, publishing articles on attempts by local and state governments to circumvent data protection regulations, and, a day after *Der Spiegel*'s second article, its own three-part interview with Berndt Schmidt. To his taz interviewers, Schmidt recounted his discomfort upon learning, for example, that every resident of 145 separate households was observed and researched by the BKA simply because they were located on the same street as a suspected "conspiratorial apartment" [*konspirative Wohnnung*].[10] The video footage and statistical information the BKA was able to collect on the people in those 145 households was assembled on the basis of perfectly legal activities by residents (walking down the street, telephone use, ownership of an automobile, loan payments). But transferred into the context of a security investigation, it became something different: inherently suspicious raw material for the discovery of criminal activities. Represented in BKA files by the informational traces they had left, these few hundred people unknowingly became suspicious until proven innocent. Fears that this basic relation of distrust would become the norm underlay much of the critique aimed at the census in 1983 and again in 1987.

---

8 Anon. 1983. Die neue Welt von 1984. *Der Spiegel*, January 3, pp. 19-30.

9 Sternsdorff, H.-W. 1983. Auf dem Weg zum Überwachungsstaat. *Der Spiegel*, January 10, pp. 46-64.

10 Dickerlitz [no first name given] 1983. "Wunschpost TE" Interview mit dem Bundeskriminalamts-Aussteiger Berndt Schmidt. *die tageszeitung*, January 12, p. 3. Surveillance cameras had first been introduced in West Germany in the 1950s, chiefly to manage the rapidly growing volume of automobile traffic (see Kammerer, D. 2009. Police use of public video surveillance in Germany from 1956: management of traffic, repression of flows, persuasion of offenders. *Surveillance and Society* 6(1): 43-47 [Online]. Available at: http://www.surveillance-and-society.org [accessed: February 22, 2010]).

The 1982 census law

In March of 1982, with the unanimous support of all parties, the West German *Bundestag* had passed the law providing for the 1983 census (the *Volkszählungsgesetz*, or VZG).[11] The two and a half page law included 13 paragraphs encompassing: (1) announcement of the census (reference date for the enumeration: April 27th) and preparatory surveys; (2) types of data to be gathered (but not the exact questions to be asked) on the population and employment part of the census (the part all residents were required to answer); (3) types of data to be gathered in the census of residential buildings and spaces; (4) types of data to be collected on workplaces (the third main part); (5) specification of the obligation to respond to the different parts of the census; (6) specification of the obligation to act as an enumerator (all adults between 18 and 65, with some exceptions, could be required to act as enumerators) and some of the basic outlines of enumerator duties; (7) the duty of governments at all levels to make officials available to act as enumerators; (8) the obligation of local tax authorities to provide census offices with names and addresses of owners of the buildings to be surveyed in the second part of the census; (9) description of the conditions under which, and the form in which, census data could be transferred to statistical and administrative government agencies or non-government researchers; (10) specification of the number, scope and permissible types of questions to be included in test-surveys taken previous to the census itself; (11) the financial contribution of the Federal Government to lower levels of government to offset the cost of the census; (12) application of the VZG to West Berlin; and (13) indication that the law came into force the day after its signing.

Nine months later, by January 26th, 1983, taz journalists had gotten hold of the census form [*Fragebogen*] and had a chance to comb through the law. The headline for that day, "Big brother orders a count" ["*Großer Bruder läßt zählen*"], appeared below a cartoon by Harald Juch showing the Virgin Mary ripping a census form in half while Joseph and the donkey shrink away startled. Mary's exasperated comment: "What, go to Bethlehem so pregnant for a census? This Herod with his surveillance state can [kiss my rear end]!" ["*kann mich mal*"][12] An extended analysis of the law and the census form appeared on page three, along with an article originating with the Hamburg VoBo Ini that surveyed the darker sides of the state's justifications for the census. The focus in both pieces was on what happens to personal data after it is surrendered to an enumerator. Citing the census law's list of the various different public and private organizations for which the census would serve as an "indispensable basis" for planning, the articles detailed many of the ways in which the state and federal statistical agencies could

11 *Gesetz über eine Volks-, Berufs-, Wohnungs- und Arbeitsstättenzählung (Volkszählungsgesetz) 1982* [henceforth VZG 1982]. *Bundesgesetzblatt* 1982, Teil I, nr. 13, March 25, Z5702A, 369-372. Bonn: Bundestag.

12 Anon. 1983. Großer Bruder lässt zählen. *die tageszeitung*, January 26, p. 1.

become a data "supermarket", to the disadvantage of individuals and vulnerable groups. Data on housing and rent levels could be used by landlords to raise rents among populations expected to put up minimal resistance; as mentioned earlier, the BKA and other security agencies could incorporate census data, especially on WGs, both into their pursuit of terrorists and into the ever-finer evaluation of the "protest- and resistance-potential" of urban neighborhoods and larger regions; large business firms could use census data on income and unemployment to locate plants in places where wages could likely be kept at the lowest possible level, or where resistance to associated infrastructure upgrades could be expected not to flare up; and information on primary residence and automobile registration could be used to ferret out young men seeking to avoid military service by claiming falsely to live in West Berlin.

The most controversial provision of the census law was clearly going to be § 9, which detailed the ways in which personal information gleaned from the census form could be shared. Paragraph 9, part (1) was immediately singled out as particularly problematic, because it provided that personal data *including name, address, telephone number, sex, birthdate, family status, membership (or not) of a religious confession and citizenship* could be used by local authorities to correct residency registers.[13] The residency register, or *Melderegister*, a peculiarly German institution, was (and remains) a registry maintained by special offices of local municipal governments, at which all individuals are required to register upon moving to a new home, and are required to register their departures when they move away. The establishment of many day-to-day institutional connections, such as opening a bank account or registering one's automobile, require residents to show that they have visited the registry office [*Einwohnermeldeamt*] and been recorded in the local register. However, since registering does not happen automatically but requires actively presenting oneself at a government office, and since it is possible to arrange daily life without relying entirely on local institutions, a significant minority of West Germans (especially students) had always neglected to fulfill this obligation. Even among the majority of citizens who did register upon arriving at a new address, a significant group had always forgotten to register their departures upon leaving for a new home. As a result, the *Melderegister* were rightly assumed in 1983 to be inaccurate, and in particular it was thought that in the aggregate, they over-estimated the West German population by up to a million people.[14] Paragraph 9 section (1) specified that personal census data could be used to address this problem, but the explicit limitations it placed on what the local registry offices could do with the data were vague. In section (1) itself, the law states that "information gleaned from these data may not be used as the basis for

13 VZG 1982, 371.

14 Eickeler, R. 1983. Orwells Vision vom "gläsernen Menschen" ist noch eine Legende statt Realität. *Handelsblatt* February 24, n.p.n.; Anon. 1983. "Überfällig und unerlässlich" neue Daten für Wirtschaft und Politik/Kritik an der Volkszählung, *Frankfurter Allgemeine Zeitung*, February 25, n.p.n.

measures taken against individual respondents [*Auskunftspflichtige*]"; section (5) dictates that in the *other* instances of data transfer foreseen in § 9, "individual data may only be used by recipients for the purposes for which they are transferred".[15] There were no specifics about how compliance with these safeguards would be monitored. The taz analysis also devotes considerable space to the other kinds of data sharing envisaged in § 9. The law required that data shared with other government agencies (besides the *Einwohnermeldeämter*), with non-government entities such as businesses or political parties, and with researchers, be anonymized before transfer. But, as taz pointed out, re-identifying individuals whose data had had the name removed would be child's play. The census form asked for the telephone number of the respondent, which would allow re-identification by means of a basic search program. Giving one's telephone number was actually not required, but enumerators were not instructed to notify residents of this fact. The critical analysis begun in the January 26th issue of taz would soon be fleshed out, as we shall see, and many more problems large and small discovered. But again, the core target of objections remained the correction of the residency registers.

"Resistance, humor and imagination": Boycott analysis and publicity

As it developed, the critical discourse about the census came to revolve around an interlocking set of basic questions: (1) In what senses or circumstances are official statistics dangerous to human dignity and human rights? (2) Does the danger lie in the misuse, or already in the everyday use, of statistics? (3) To what extent, and at what scale, is it legitimate to mistrust the government, and to design legislation and other regulations on the basis of mistrust? Especially this last question touches on one of the core points of contention shaping West German political debates throughout the decade immediately preceding the boycotts. Where the critical analyses differed was on whether the reductive representation of human life in statistical form is *inherently* or only *contingently* dangerous. Radical critics writing in the taz tended to argue that the engineering of social life follows numbers *as a rule*, that the connection between statistics and damaging social manipulation is an internal, necessary one.

Nowhere was this connection more disturbingly illustrated than during the Nazi period in Germany. On March 18th, a two-full-page article appeared in taz outlining the history of the Nazis' unprecedented elaboration of a vast statistical infrastructure during the 1930s and 1940s.[16] The article, entitled "Statistics in its essence is already closely connected to the National Socialist movement", carries the attribution *Projektgruppe "Autonomie"*. The authors of the unsigned article were

15 VZG 1982, 371.

16 Projektgruppe Autonomie 1983. "Schon nach ihrem Wesen steht die Statistik der Nazionalsozialistischen Bewegung nahe" – Statistiker als "wissenschaftliche Soldaten", *die tageszeitung*, March 18, pp. 12-13.

probably Götz Aly and Karl-Heinz Roth, whose research into the history of Nazi statistics appeared in book form in 1984 as *Die restlose Erfassung* [*The Complete Registration*, translated into English in 2004 as *The Nazi Census*][17] Roth, a physician and historian, had been wounded in a shootout between police and members of B2J in 1975, and jailed.[18] Aly, a militant West Berlin activist, would go on to become a preeminent, though controversial, historian of the connections between social scientific knowledge, planning, the welfare state, and administration of the "Final Solution" in Nazi Germany.[19] The original article showed how much importance the Nazis attributed to censuses (the first Nazi census was taken immediately after Hitler's seizure of power in 1933, the second in 1939). Nazi planners and statisticians viewed the census as the basis for a range of more specialized registries making possible the mobilization of German and conquered populations for production and/or military service, the monitoring and management of demographic ("racial") health, and the organization of the dispossession, resettlement and finally extermination of Jews and other "undesirables". The taz article quotes a German statistician surveying the prospects for his discipline in 1934:

> It is a fact ... that our statistical work has proliferated immensely in quantitative terms. To verify this in more detail appears superfluous; it is only necessary to mention a few key terms such as Work Creation Program, ... Birth Policy, Ancestry Courts, Race Policy, etc., all tasks that can only be successfully taken up by the administrative agencies through the comprehensive use of statistical information.[20]

The aspects of Nazi statistics covered in the taz article were clearly chosen with the 1983 census in mind. They focus, *inter alia*, on the indispensable role played by the residency registers [*Melderegister*] in allowing the Nazis to locate individuals; on the vacuity of confidentiality provisions; on innovations in automated data processing using IBM Hollerith machines;[21] and on attempts to connect and coordinate all the

---

17 Aly, G. and Roth, K.-H. 2000 [1984]. *Die restlose Erfassung: Volkszählen, Identifizieren, Aussondern im Nationalsozialismus*. Frankfurt: Fischer. Translated as Aly, G. and Roth, K.-H. 2004. *The Nazi Census: Identification and Control in the Third Reich* (trans. E. Black). Philadelphia: Temple University Press.

18 Mailänder and Zander, *Westberlin-Lexikon*, 47-48.

19 Aly, G. 1995. *"Endlösung": Völkerverschiebung und der Mord an den europäischen Juden*. Frankfurt: Fischer Verlag; Aly, G. and Heim, S. 2002. *Architects of Annihilation: Auschwitz and the Logic of Destruction* (trans. A. Blunden). Princeton: Princeton University Press; Aly, G. 1997. *Macht Geist Wahn: Kontinuitäten deutschen Denkens*. Frankfurt: Fischer Verlag; Aly, G. 2005. *Hitlers Volksstaat: Raub, Rassenkrieg und nationaler Sozialismus*. Frankfurt: Fischer Verlag.

20 Quoted in Projektgruppe Autonomie, "Schon nach ihrem Wesen ..." p. 12.

21 Edwin Black has since expanded upon their research into the IBM connection in Black, E. 2001. *IBM and the Holocaust: The Strategic Alliance between Nazi Germany and America's Most Powerful Corporation*. New York: Crown Publishers.

different databases, both via organizational changes and by assigning every person under Nazi control a unique and universal identification number. The title of the taz article ("Statistics in its essence is already closely connected to the National Socialist movement") clearly indicates the strong position the authors took on the dangerousness of statistics. This went hand in hand with an equally radical position on whether it was only the *misuse* of statistics that was to be feared, or whether on the contrary even their "normal", everyday *use* was a problem. As Götz Aly would put it in a scathing critique of ex-BKA worker Berndt Schmidt's defense of "the census in itself" as against the dangers of its abuse,

> Is it not perhaps less the misuse than the use of the census that constitutes an attack upon us? These numbers ... are they not the eternally meager mnemonic [*die ewig dürftige Eselsbrücke*] [linking] the administrators to the administrated? The count furthers the power of the objective, the rationality of arbitrariness. Entirely without misuse ... For two decades the statistical designation "outside toilet" served uncontroversially [as sufficient justification] for the leveling of [whole neighorhoods of] the city [West Berlin] ... Census, that is [another word for] frontal attack on the imagination and on the intelligent posing of questions for the future ... That we don't allow ourselves to be fully registered in indicator-profiles [*Merkmalsprofile*], is part of the value of the person. And it is a philosophical question to what extent we abandon the field to dumb empirics and simple quantities. It's about [human] needs and not about [consumer] demand figures.[22]

Relying only on numbers, Aly implied, even those administrators with the best intentions, implementing laws passed for the noblest purposes, would inevitably do damage. It was not a matter of the sinister designs of the occasional twisted bureaucrat; even the most benign city planning exercises were destined to have destructive effects. The scary thing about the Nazis was not that they had *misused* data, but that they had *used* it.

The Nazi use of statistics began to concretize the spectre of "total registration", a phrase that circulated freely through the 1983 VoBo debates. To highlight the continuities between that dark time and early-1980s West Germany, taz published a brilliant analysis, by a writer identified only as "Sabine", aimed at clarifying the role of the census in changing state strategies for the control of social deviance. Under the thematic heading "The Dangerousness of Statistics" and with the title "Making the Underground Transparent", Sabine and "Imma" (author of the thematic blurb introducing the article) linked the radical critique of the census to an analysis of recent socio-political trends that shared much with Foucault's ideas on biopower and security. To set the stage, Imma chided more liberal census critics for their distracting focus on the misuse of data and on the defense of individual anonymity:

---

22 Aly, G. 1983. "Volkszählung an sich". *die tageszeitung*, April 11, p. 16.

> As though a modern state cannot carry out its policies except through the surveillance and disciplining of the individual. That is only the last, most costly and worst method. What purpose is served by social policy, urban planning, educational policy, policy toward foreigners? By means of these instruments entire segments of the population can be far more effectively disciplined: unruly youth, work-shy academics, the workers forever calling in sick [*die ewig krankfeiernden Malocher*], and the fast-reproducing foreigners.[23]

In the main article, draped around a reproduction of a crime-frequency map of the industrial city Bochum, Sabine argued that censuses and many other social statistics are indeed directed precisely at the "deviant geographies" that could serve as the invisible basis for the oppositional political activities outlined in the Introduction. Her sophisticated framing of the changing geographical nature of social marginality and its official construction is worth quoting at length:

> The decisive question is that of the cybernetic control and steering of a population whose social composition, as contrasted with the 1970s, has changed in essential ways, and whose behavior [thus] calls for other steering mechanisms. With the dissolution of the traditional working class at the level of the factory, of the labor market and as social subject, the need increases among state institutions for a new form of control with respect to the dispersed atoms and segments of society, for the production of controlled social relations in data form. In the BRD a process of differentiating selection [*Aussonderung*] has begun, the creation of a new poor population and asociality (e.g. in the form of the "bad third" in health insurance), whose control no longer takes the form of traditional ghettoization (where the ghetto was simultaneously a social place in which counter-identities could develop from below), but of digitization [*Verdatung*] and individualization. So for example in Hamburg, asylum seekers, who are housed in homes spatially not far apart, are assigned to the agencies of different city wards based on nationality: a potential ghetto is hindered in this way … but only on the side of cohesion from below. The social bureaucracy nevertheless produces [its own cohesion] – in its files and with the help of its computers. Sociality is on the one hand shattered or hindered where possible; one the other hand it is produced by means of the pseudo-reality of data, as substitute, as shadow-world …
>
> The dissolution of social places and the rearticulation [*Neugliederung*] of social structures in the illusory world of data gives the census its special significance as the instrument of isolation [*Einkreisung*] and digital registration of all those who in the course of crisis fall out of the traditional schema of production and reproduction, and who thus can no longer be registered in those terms. The previously existing system of data registration and the inherited data inventory

23 Autonomie (Sabine). 1983. Volkszählung als Planungsinstrument: den Untergrund transparent machen. *die tageszeitung*, April 12, p. 3.

> [*Datenbestand*] is in wide areas bound precisely to the functioning of regular work and nuclear family reproduction …
>
> What is isolated with the help of data gained from the census, and what becomes available for social-political processing is the un-adapted part [of the population]. This means the half-legal and illegal border-zones of the labor market and immigrant labor; black-market workers, who maybe also pocket unemployment money; people who have no regular income and live off of occasional or systematic shoplifting; punks …[24]

The full-page spread featuring this analysis was completed by a short piece presenting criminal geography as itself a "criminal" undertaking, and detailing the criminal geographic research at the University of Bochum that led to the publication of the *Atlas of Criminality in Bochum* that was the source for the map. Returning to the Nazi connection, the authors asserted that "fighting 'crime' with the aid of criminal geography had its origins in the Nazi period. Then, for the first time, maps were produced that were supposed to pinpoint both criminality and political opponents (such as KPD [*Kommunistische Partei Deutschlands*] voters) in relation to place of residence."[25]

The historical precedent of the Nazi use of statistics, and Sabine's sophisticated analysis of the virtual rearrangement of worlds made possible by administrative databases served also to highlight the precarious position of foreigners living in West Germany in the 1980s. Whether legal or illegal, immigrants, "guest workers" or asylum seekers, non-Germans were on the one hand much more thoroughly registered than their German counterparts, and on the other hand much more directly exposed to real consequences of the fact that state agencies possessed their personal information.[26] But the plight of foreigners was not merely relevant to them alone. In a sense, as activists would again point out in 1987, foreigners could be seen already to be living the future awaiting all Germans in the coming surveillance state or "Kybernokratie": unlike Germans, almost all official data about them was already contained in a single massive database. Further, they had much more to lose if the barrier between "statistical" and "administrative" data proved too porous: deportation awaited registered foreigners who broke even minor laws, and in extreme cases, deportation could even mean death for some.

---

24 Autonomie (Sabine), Volkszählung als Planungsinstrument, p. 3.

25 Autonomie (Sabine), Volkszählung als Planungsinstrument, p. 3. See Busch, *et al.*, *Die Polizei*, pp. 170-180 for a description of the wider criminal research program of which this was a part.

26 Bergmann, *Volkszählung und Datenschutz*, p. 31.

Boycott strategies and tactics

These early radical analyses did not appeal to everyone, of course, but the number of West Germans concerned about the upcoming 1983 census was beginning to grow, and would soon increase dramatically. As two taz readers testified in a letter published on February 9th, "[c]olleagues who have never before laid a finger on taz" were asking to make photocopies of articles. These readers (rightly) expected that feelings of being personally impacted by the census, and of growing anger, would quickly spread "(and not only in the oh-so-radical scene)".[27] But the question of how to respond politically was not at all settled. The boycott form of protest made a great deal of sense as a general framework. After all, the success of a census depends upon the participation of every individual, in a way that an election does not. Even the more typical consumer boycott may or may not succeed in damaging the target business, depending on whether the boycott participants constitute a significant portion of the normal market share for the target product or service. Here was a situation in which the state literally needed everyone to cooperate. Thus every individual decision not to be counted would have an impact. The evolving debate over how to oppose the census revolved around two potential problems with the boycott form. First and most practically, refusal to answer the census fully and truthfully could bring a fine of between 5 and 10,000 DM. Although this way of enforcing participation had been pursued only very rarely in previous censuses, many West Germans were understandably nervous about exposing themselves to it. Secondly, from the perspective of activists who saw the census as part of the larger problem-complex of the "security state", the boycott form made it all too easy for mainstream West Germans to participate individually on entirely selfish grounds, without considering the connections between threats to their own interests and what progressive activists saw as the wider systematic inhumanities of Cold-War West German capitalist society.

The real prospect of aggressive state action against the boycott was illustrated in a letter from Berlin Senator Heinrich Lummer to the station director of *Sender Freies Berlin* (SFB), obtained by taz and published on February 23rd. In it, Senator Lummer took strong issue with the station's decision to allow Michael Schroeren to broadcast a call to boycott the census on its morning program of February 7th. Citing the specific paragraph of the Law on Misdemeanors that forbids public encouragement of a finable action, Senator Lummer declared his intent to pursue a fine against Mr. Schroeren, and ended with a clear statement on his expectations for media coverage:

> I am extremely disturbed that your institution provides space for the agitation of declared opponents of legally ordered state actions [agitation which] among other things deliberately minimizes the legal consequences that could follow for

27 Karin und Rüdiger 1983. Volkszählung – Leserbrief zum Artikel vom 2.2. *die tageszeitung*, February 9, p. 12.

> a citizen upon refusal to respond [and which] as a result could call into question the success of the census. Many enumerators, too, who make available their evenings and free weekends, will get the impression that SFB through its actions is stabbing them in the back. I would be extremely grateful [*verbunden*], *Herr Intendant*, if it could be firmly established that no further opportunities will be given the opponents of the census in the radio or television programs of your organization, to make propaganda.
>
> With friendly greetings,
> Lummer[28]

Senator Lummer made good on his promise of fining Michael Schroeren: in late March, Schroeren was in fact fined 3,150 DM (4 times 750 DM for four separate boycott calls, plus 150 DM).[29] To counter fears of paying such sums, taz cited a group of attorneys, who argued that there would be safety in numbers, that the state could not even attempt to bring legal action against thousands or tens of thousands of boycotters.[30] Since the level of individual risk would diminish as the number of boycotters swelled, one letter to taz recommended that the movement itself set up a sort of running estimate of the number of West Germans planning to boycott, as a means of reassuring those still too worried to commit.[31]

As Senator Lummer noted, the perceptions and attitudes of enumerators constituted another potential field of operation for opponents of the census. Michael Schroeren's original call for a boycott had already suggested that those required to be enumerators could help subvert the census by returning blank census forms to central offices.[32] Enumerators were recruited in part via open public information sessions, and in short order these sessions would be the scene of heated challenges from opponents of the census. Increasing numbers of enumerators would drop out over the next few weeks under various pretenses, and some VoBo Inis would encourage willing citizens to complete the enumerator trainings with the intent of dropping out *en masse* just before the day of the count (April 27th, 1983). For most considering a boycott, however, the issue was what exactly to do as an individual respondent. Michael Schroeren's recommendations were playfully worded ("One could send the [blank] census form back to the Interior Minister, light a little fire, make paper airplanes, or use it in the toilet").[33] But they raised more serious questions both about vulnerability to penalties and

28 Lummer, H. 1983. Boykott Bestrebungen aus "berufenem" Mund [reprinted letter from Berlin Interior Senator Lummer to SFB Intendant], *die tageszeitung*, February 23, p. 16.

29 Anon. 1983. Knast für Boykotteure angedroht. *die tageszeitung*, March 30, p. 16.

30 Anon. 1983. Bereits über 50 Inititiativen zum Volkszählungsboykott. *die tageszeitung*, February 14, p. 3.

31 Karin und Rüdiger, Volkszählung, p. 12.

32 Anon., Politiker fragen – Bürger antworten nicht, p. 4.

33 Quoted in Anon., Politiker fragen – Bürger antworten nicht, p. 4.

about the statistical effectiveness of different methods of subverting the census. Was it better to leave the whole form blank or fill it out? If the latter, would it be more effective to mix truthful and misleading answers, or to fabricate everything? And what about immigrants, guest workers and asylum seekers? What additional factors should be weighed in their decisions?[34] Letters to taz from all over West Germany urgently requested more precise information.[35] But because the VoBo Inis constituted in the early stages a true grass-roots movement, with a central information source (taz) but no unified organization, more time would pass before there would be anything approaching a "consensus" recommendation. And the larger question of what else to do beyond individual sabotage hung in the background unresolved. Schroeren's initial call to use the boycott to try to force Bonn to reveal rocket locations, to counter what he termed the "permanent refusal of information from above", was criticized for tying the VoBo to the specific issue of nuclear weapons and thereby unnecessarily limiting its potential appeal.[36] Ongoing discussion of the merits of "offensive" vs. "defensive" boycott strategies, petitions, and the like showed that the larger framework for the growing movement remained in flux and subject to widely varying interpretations. Nicole Bergmann follows discussions at the time in grouping the proposed boycott methods into "open" and "quiet" categories, the former intended to announce participation in the boycott, the latter to sabotage the census while escaping detection.[37] In 1987, when the census and the boycott both went ahead, this distinction became crucially important. Here, though, I am more interested in thinking through the implications of different tactics the light they shed upon the limits and possibilities of responses to statistical surveys as a potential vehicle for political representation.

One seemingly tongue-in-cheek contribution to the tactical debates is worth dwelling upon at length because, behind the humor, it raised quite profound questions. On March 21st the Berlin cabaret group *Die 3 Tornados* published a short guest column in taz:

34 Anon. 1983. Ausländerrechtliche Hinweise für die Volkszählung. Hamburg Institut für Sozialforschung, Bestand SBe 444, Box 2: VoBo Büro Hamburg.

35 [Various] 1983. Betr. Artikel über Volkszählung v. 26.1.83 [Letters to the editor]. *die tageszeitung*, February 1, p. 12; [Various] 1983 [Letters to the editor]. *die tageszeitung*, February 22, p. 12.

36 A criticism he readily granted, once it became apparent how much wider the boycott movement had become: Schroeren, M. 1983. Gemeinsam und offensiv [letter to editor]. *die tageszeitung*, February 21, p. 16.

37 Bergmann, *Volkszählung und Datenschutz*, pp. 49-51.

We are uncountable

Yesterday we were visiting with Wolfgang Neuss[38] and together we took a look at the form for the census. "Man," said Neuss, "is that all they want to know? I have more to say!" That's right, we said, everyday there is something in the newspaper about Prince Charles and Lady Di, where they go skiing, what they fight about and the color of their bathing suits. Now, for once, we are finally also interviewed and they pose such stupid questions: how many square meters is the apartment, and whether there is a telephone. That is really so uninteresting. We have more to say!!!

Are they really not at all interested in the fact that Werner represents a serious problem in our collective and Jörg wants to move out in two months, because he no longer gets along with Barbara? Manne is totally into BAP [a rock band] and keeps the stereo turned up all day listening to "*Verdamp lang her*", which annoys Petra, who in turn keeps her 140-watt stereo running all day with "*Geschichte wird gemacht, es geht voran*".

How are they supposed to govern us if they don't know that Holger is gay and Sigrid does aerobics? They really need to know that we don't feel like working anymore, that we need more time to dream. We're telling them now what we always wanted to say. What excites us and what stinks. We call on you to do the same: we didn't learn to read and write only to make X's and pencil marks. And include a couple of photos from vacation or from the meal at the Greek's place in 1980! Their computers won't be enough to hold what we have to report. We have a lot to say: let's lay it all out!

Die 3 Tornados[39]

It is not an accident that this suggestion had an exact parallel in activist responses to the campaign by state officials to ban masking [*Vermummung*] at demonstrations. Two years previously, in August of 1981, some 400 men and women, "liberated from all clothing ('total de-masking' [*Totalendmummung*])", had streaked along

38 Wolfgang Neuss was a legendary West Berlin cabarettist most famous throughout West Germany for his masterful hijacking of a television interview with Federal President Richard von Weizäcker in 1983, during which he refered to the statesman repeatedly as "Ritchie" (Mailänder and Zander, *Das Kleine Westberlin-Lexikon*, pp. 195-196.

39 *Die 3 Tornados*. 1983. Wir sind unzählbar. *die tageszeitung*, March 21, p. 2. Die drei Tornados were formed in West Berlin in 1976 by Arnulf Rating, Günter Thews and Hans-Jochen Krank. They directed their stage program "against reactionaries, *Spießer* [small-minded, self-satisfied *petit-bourgeois*], racists, the Church, militarists, atomic power, police and protectors of the state, and didn't spare the left public as well from biting satire." (Mailänder and Zander, *Westberlin-Lexikon*, p. 69.)

the Kurfürstendamm, West Berlin's main shopping street, and "impressed the public with their 'naked violence'."[40]

One set of issues potentially highlighted by "profligate" responses to state requests for information concerned gender and the relative invisibility of women in the domestic sphere. In March of 1983, Christel Dormagen published a piece on the census in the feminist magazine *Courage*. The article set the stage for specific analyses by giving a gender twist to critiques of the surveillance state: "Governing would be easiest if there were no people. A step toward the tendential marginalization of citizens would be their total registration, which finds expression in the administrative-logical rosy vision of a population of hens laying eggs in batteries, that hops in synch every morning onto the rack and then, in the evening, after group TV, the big Father turns the light out with a 'good night'."[41] Boycotting was to be recommended, but Dormagen foresaw an additional hurdle in convincing women to join in, namely, the temptation to take advantage of one of the few instances in which the state seemed to be interested in women's lives and dependent upon their participation.

> How well this supposed personal participation still appeals to women was explained to me by one of them: suddenly we women feel important and addressed. Now the powers that be [*die da oben*] are really interested in me. I have a place in the grid of tick-boxes they've worked out for the questionnaire. And they rely on my help. Not least with the enumeration.[42]

This logic throws the "bare-all" tactics suggested by the *3 Tornados* into a different light. In April of 1983, the magazine *Emma* ran an article on the under-explored issues of gender raised by the planned census, quoting Horst Herold on the uses of computers to discover "deviant behavior", and asking how lesbian couples or all-female WGs might appear to state authorities. *Emma* urged support for the boycott, and suggested an elegantly simple and plausible tactic for women, one which would counter the temptation to respond positively to the state's newfound curiosity about the private sphere: "It may happen that women don't come to the door. Who knows who it might be?"[43] An article by Ingrid Strobl in *Courage* in the lead-up to the 1987 boycott would bring the issue of women's relative invisibility to the state down to the specific, concrete issue of the "double career". Referring to the state's new publicity in 1987 targeting left-wing taz readers, Strobl would confess surprise at the new questions given prominence in government propaganda: "Where do women stand today in our society? What have they

---

40 Balistier, *Straßenprotest*, p. 47.

41 Dormagen, C. 1983. Die Häupter ihrer Lieben – Volks-ver-zählung. *Courage* (March 1983), p. 8. *archiv für alternatives schrifttum* [afas], 5.II [1983] n.s.

42 Dormagen, Die Häupter, p. 11.

43 Anon. 1983. Meine Daten gehören mir! *Emma* (April 1983), p. 6. afas, 5.II [1983].

achieved in their jobs? What remains to be done? The census will provide answers to these questions." Arguing that of course many of these kinds of information were already available in official statistics, she pointed out that "what the state nevertheless does not know is whether Ms. X is involved in non-job-related work that doesn't appear on her tax forms. Just for example."[44] Whereas the *3 Tornados* had suggested the tactic of swamping state statistical agencies with indigestible masses of narrative information, photographs, etc., Strobl highlighted the fact that for some social groups, the problem with social knowledge could be that the state had too little rather than too much. Nevertheless, Strobl, too, implicitly concurred with the point made by the *3 Tornados* that it was not just a matter of how much information the state had on specific social phenomena but also of the nature of the information. Thus, while outlining the specific positionality of women with regard to state knowledge, the coverage of the census in the feminist press did generally support the boycott.

There was another, very different, historical point of resonance for the tactic of responding to requests for information with an unmanageable avalanche of narrative. This episode is worth dwelling upon as well, because although it took place in a very different era, it also had to do with a census, in fact, with the census that helped establish the political basis of postwar West German life. In 1951, Ernst von Salomon, a nationalist German author and filmmaker who had fought with the nationalist militias [*Freikorps*] after WWI but kept his distance from the Nazis, published an autobiographical work in the form of a 600+ page response to the Allied questionnaire that formed the basis for the de-nazification program immediately after WWII.[45] The book, entitled *Der Fragebogen* [*The Questionnaire*], used the 131 questions of the de-nazification form to explore the entire sweep of German political and cultural life of the first half of the 20th century through the lenses of von Salomon's varied and controversial biography. *Der Fragebogen* angered the Americans particularly for its detailed condemnation of the arbitrariness with which the postwar detention camps for suspect Germans were run, for the unapologetic sassiness of von Salomon's style, and for the overall political message of the book.[46]

---

44 Strobl, I. 1987. Volkszählung. *Courage* (April 1987), p. 38. [afas], 5.II [1987] n.s.

45 von Salomon, E. 2007 [1951]. *Der Fragebogen*. Hamburg: Rowohlt. Published in English in 1955 as von Salomon, E. 1955. *The Questionnaire*. New York: Doubleday.

46 Anon. 1955. It just happened, review of *Der Fragebogen*. *Time* January 10 [Online]. Available at http://www.time.com/time/magazine/printout/0,8816,861117,00.html [Accessed: October 26, 2007]. See Klein, M. 2002. *Ernst von Salomon: Revolutionär ohne Utopie*. Aschau i. Ch.: San Casciano Verlag. pp. 246-249. This biography is itself controversial, as the doctoral thesis on which it is based was rejected by the University of Heidelberg for reasons that the conservative-nationalist Armin Mohler claims in a Foreword were merely ideological. The text, while scholarly in format and indeed thoroughly researched, does on the other hand certainly contain passages revealing an underlying nationalist orientation (for example the characterization of the de-nazification program on p. 237).

What von Salomon perceived as the stupidity of the de-nazification questionnaire, its structural inability to capture the rich and complex German situation, was most tellingly highlighted in an account of his oral interrogation by a young American soldier in 1945: "He didn't smile anymore, he had a furrow in his brow and asked slowly, 'How have you been able to reconcile living and working in Germany with your conscience?' I was completely taken aback. I observed this young man thoughtfully, this lanky, blond youth, obviously robbed of sleep by the most subtle questions. I said slowly, 'I haven't yet thought about it. I can happily promise you, though, that in the future I will think over very carefully where I wish to live and for whom I wish to work.'"[47] As was clear throughout the book, even had he meant this answer seriously, he probably would have remained in Germany in any case: in keeping with his general iconoclasm, von Salomon refused to accept that the horrors of Nazism had rendered all German nationalism dishonorable, even directly after the war had ended. Most germane to the census boycotts 40 years later, von Salomon linked the futility of the de-nazification program to a more general critique of statistical surveys. In his introductory comments, von Salomon assured his readers that "during that time-span between the 30th of January 1933 and the 6th of May, 1945, ... many questionnaires have lain before me, and I can testify that I have read through them all very carefully."[48] But he refused to harbor any illusions about what he saw as the extreme danger in official questionnaires: "The bureaucracies have always known the magic of a power that 'arrests' [*bannt*] the individual most securely in registering him. Registration is the most sublime form of terror, that out of which all of the consequences of the regime of terror follow ... No form has ever left an office that attached any importance to it, without taking on the character of a wanted poster."[49] Accordingly, von Salomon admitted that when he tried to put his finger on how he felt when confronted with the questionnaire, "I came to compare it most closely with that of a young student caught out, ... who stands right at the beginning of his experiences with those great and threatening powers that present themselves as law, custom, order and morality."[50] *Der Fragebogen* was a best-seller in West Germany, selling some 250,000 copies, and was translated into French, Italian and Spanish as well. In November of 1951, on the basis of this success, von Salomon was invited to take part in a broadcast of the "Köln Wednesday discussions", and used the opportunity to push his revived nationalist program.[51] While most of the press discussion of the 1980s census boycotts revolved around the activities and arguments of activist organizations chiefly peopled by the relatively young, it is plausible to imagine that many older West Germans still vividly remembered the very different links between censuses and arbitrary power dramatized by von Salomon. Anecdotally,

47 von Salomon, *Der Fragebogen*, p. 551.

48 von Salomon, *Der Fragebogen*, p. 6.

49 von Salomon, *Der Fragebogen*, pp. 40-41.

50 von Salomon, *De Fragebogen*, p. 6.

51 Klein, *Ernst von Salomon*, p. 248.

a number of former West Germans with whom I have discussed this episode recall seeing *Die Fragebogen* on their parents' bookshelves.

Some of the more mundane boycott tactics discussed in the Spring of 1983 can be seen as milder forms of this approach, for example "accidentally" crumpling census forms, spilling coffee on them or writing illegibly. These, too, signal the excess of real life over the severely constrained tick-boxes of the questionnaire. Their exquisite cleverness lies in the fact that, unlike the potentially time-consuming responses of von Salomon or the *3 Tornados*, these more mundane acts not only dramatize the inadequacy of questionnaires but do so in a way that simultaneously renders them unusable as material objects. In the 1987 boycotts, the materiality of the paper forms would become the focus of heated debates. In 1983, the discussion of tactics was not yet so advanced. To address the lack of coordination in the early stages of the 1983 campaign, meetings of initiatives began in Berlin in early February.[52] The *Initiative Volkszählungsboykott* of West Berlin then organized a working group entitled "Everyday resistance: census boycott" for the February 26th/27th national conference of independent peace groups in Frankfurt.[53] According to the report in Monday's taz following the weekend meeting, roughly 1,000 interested participants "stormed" the VoBo session.[54] A large national conference of VoBo Inis took place in Bochum in late March, and resulted in the announcement of a national "action day" on April 16th, as well as plans for coordinated nationwide burnings of census forms on the 27th, the reference day for the count. The Bochum conference also drew on legal expertise to establish principles for consistent advice to be given to any who asked. West German citizens were to be advised to do the following: (1) take the census form from the enumerator; (2) cut off the identification number and turn it in empty of any information to alternative collection points set up by the local initiatives; and (3) if the enumerator returned to inquire about the form, claim to have mailed it to the statistical agency. Because of the special risks involved, foreign residents should not be urged to join the boycott but instead should be invited to discuss the census and their specific situations on a case-by-case basis with qualified advisors. Finally, the Bochum conferees recommended embedding the whole census issue explicitly within the wider context of the surveillance state, and suggested a follow-up conference in May on that theme.[55] To provide more detail on legal issues, the *Humanistische Union*, a Hamburg organization dedicated to progressive causes, published a 60+ page pamphlet including critical and historical analyses, as well as legal advice for citizens and immigrants.[56] In April, the first

---

52 Bergmann, *Volkszählung und Datenschutz*, p. 42.

53 Schroeren, Gemeinsam und offensiv, p. 16.

54 Anon. 1983. Von Aktivitäten überrollt, *die tageszeitung*, February 28, p. 3.

55 Anon. 1983. Volkszählungsboykott: Aktionswoche ab 16. April. *die tageszeitung*, March 29, p. 4.

56 Humanistische Union (Landesverband Berlin), Jungdemokraten Berlin, and Liberale Demokraten Berlin, 1983. *Volkszählung 1983 – Bürgerbefragung oder Zwangserfassung?* West Berlin: Elefanten Press.

full-length book appeared, with 25 critical chapters (including a reprinted interview with the famous author Günter Grass) on various aspects of the census.[57] To further facilitate communication, taz announced the dedication of a census hotline number to make it easier for interested individuals to inform themselves and to report on their experiences, pass on information on "imaginative actions", etc.[58]

The organization of the VoBo movement received an additional boost when taz began in late February to collect and publish weekly compilations of contact information for all the VoBo Inis in West Germany and West Berlin. On the first listing there were already more than 150 Inis, and the contact addresses show, in addition to individual citizens, a mixture of alternative bookstores, health- and organic-food stores, peace groups, local offices of the Greens, local city papers, cafes, and neighborhood social service agencies. Many local city papers covered the census early and often, sometimes reprinting analyses and interviews from taz.[59] By the end of March the Inis listed in taz numbered approximately 400.[60] From early March to mid-April, activists brought into play the full instrumentarium of social movement publicity. Left political caricaturists and comic strip artists picked up the issue, and it was soon possible to order decals, postcards and buttons from the advertising pages of taz. The *Kasseler Kunstverein*, an artists' organization in the central German city of Kassel, hosted an exhibition of art relating to the boycotts, and published an accompanying collection of essays, placards and flyers for the use of the initiatives.[61] VoBo Inis sponsored film showings on the perils of the "surveillance state", and the station SFB (ignoring threats from Senator

57 Taeger, J. (ed.) 1983. *Die Volkszählung*. Reinbek bei Hamburg, Rowohlt.

58 Anon. 1983. taz-Volkszählungs-Telefon. Wer schweigt hat viel zu erzählen! *die tageszeitung*, April 11, p. 5.

59 See for example, Anon. 1983. Volksquälung. *De Schnüss* [Bonn], no. 3 (March), pp. 4-6. afas [no archival signature]; Anon. 1983. Volks(v)erfassung. *De Schnüss*, no. 4 (April), pp. 6-12. afas [no archival signature]; W./ Knast- u. Anti-Nato-Gruppe. 1983. Raster für Alle: Volkszählung und Widerstand. *Stadtzeitung* [Freiburg im Breisgau] April, pp. 20-21. afas 80.III.4; Anon. 1983. Alles was Du jetzt sagst, kann später gegen Dich verwendet werden! *der Tip* [Siegen], April, pp. 8-12. afas [no archival signature]; Anon. 1983. Ausgezählt! *Stadt Revue* [Köln] no. 4 (March 27-April 3), pp. 38-44. afas [no archival signature]; Anon. 1983. Volkszählung und Datenverarbeitung: Ein Gespräch mit Wilhelm Steinmüller. *Stadt Revue* [Köln], no. 5 (April 4-April 11), pp. 6-7. I am grateful to Jürgen Bacia and Dorothee Ledig of the *archiv für alternatives schrifttum* (afas) in Duisburg for locating this local coverage.

60 Anon. 1983. Politiker fragen – Bürger antworten nicht! *die tageszeitung*, February 25, p.15; [Same title]. *die tageszeitung*, March 3, p. 15; [Same title]. *die tageszeitung*, March 11, p. 15; [Same title]. *die tageszeitung*, March 18, p. 15; [Same title]. *die tageszeitung*, March 25, pp. 14-15. It is difficult to obtain an exact total number of initiatives for any week because in some larger cities a central address was designated as the contact point for multiple local groups.

61 Anon. 1983. Volkszählungsboykott – Bilder, Plakate, Flugschriften, Tips zur Volkszählung. afas 83.I.2.

Lummer) covered a knitting action in which the work of the knitters was intended to symbolize an alternative to the "data net" being woven by the security state.[62] In early April, SFB's programming would be interrupted by a pirate signal playing "99 Luftballons" to accompany a pro-boycott message.[63] The *Humanistische Union* announced a journalism competition to reward incisive coverage of the *Volkszählung*, generously reassuring potential entrants that they were eligible even if they had entered a pro-census journalism competition recently announced by the *Statistische Bundesamt*.[64]

Despite the gradual emergence of something like a consensus on boycott tactics, many individuals and groups made their own decisions about how to respond, and this of course always carried risks for boycott publicity. The only event that had the potential seriously to mar the image of "civility" enjoyed by the 1983 VoBo movement was a bomb attack on April 11th against an *Einwohnermeldeamt* [residency registration office] in Braunschweig. The *Frankfurter Allgemeine Zeitung*, staunch supporter of the census throughout 1983, noted that the Braunschweig police and District Attorney's office "did not rule out" the possibility that the attack was carried out by "militant opponents of the census".[65] Although there was no letter claiming responsibility, the editors clearly saw the attack as part of the VoBo movement, and urged authorities to act decisively: "The propagandists of a boycott of the census should be called to account". As it happened, nothing conclusive emerged from the subsequent investigation, and the incident was not followed by other violent attacks in 1983. Its imputed connection to the boycott movement remained speculative, and the whole matter was eclipsed only two days later by the Constitutional Court's temporary restraining order stopping the census. Apart from this one violent episode, which may or may not have been the work of anti-census activists, all of this activity showed a movement rich in what *Der Spiegel* called "resistance, humor and imagination".[66]

A key visual image deployed time and again in the 1983 boycott, and again in 1987, was the bar code. Bar codes were depicted in posters, photographs and caricatures on bare heads, bare bottoms, the Berlin Wall, and much else besides (see Figure 1.1). The new ubiquity of bar codes in the early 1980s was another aspect of the very particular stage reached by the intertwined technological developments of the "information age" traced in the Introduction. The search for a machine-readable code to help streamline the tracking and inventory management of physical products of all kinds goes back almost 80 years. Through the middle decades of the last century, a bewildering array of different symbologies were

62 Anon. 1983. Volkszählungsnews. *die tageszeitung*, March 30, p. 15.

63 Anon. 1983. Volkszählungsnews. *die tageszeitung*, April 8, p. 20.

64 Anon. 1983. Rumpelstielz-Preis. *die tageszeitung*, April 11, p. 16.

65 Anon. 1983. Schutz von Meldeämtern wird verstärkt. *Frankfurter Allgemeine Zeitung*, April 12, n.p.n.

66 Anon. 1983. Volkszählung: "Lasst tausend Fragebogen glühen". *Der Spiegel*, March 28, p. 32.

Figure 1.1 "Don't let yourself be registered!"

Note: The numbers at the bottom of the poster are the date of the enumeration day, April 27th, 1983.

Source: Permission to reproduce courtesy of dpa Picture-Alliance GmbH.

proposed for carrying identification and other information on packages. In the early 1970s the US grocery industry sponsored a systematic testing program that compared many of the different symbologies in terms of tolerance for printing errors, speed and cost of printing, and success of pilot systems in stores. As a result of these tests, a version of the IBM Universal Product Code (UPC) was officially adopted as the industry standard in 1973. European companies developed a compatible symbology, which was accepted as the standard of the newly formed European Article Numbering Association (EAN) in 1976. The EAN symbology incorporated an extra digit at the beginning as part of a country identifier lacking in the America UPC. Technically, although developed earlier, the UPC symbology was a subset of the more capacious EAN. European machines could read US products but many US readers could not handle the European code. By the early 1980s, however, US manufacturers had made the necessary changes, and the two symbologies had become fully compatible. The codes, too, the character sets corresponding to the unit symbols in bar codes, had by then been standardized.[67] By the time the anti-census protests flared up in West Germany, then, the image of the bar code represented a system whose material reach was intercontinental in scale.

The bar code, like any successful political symbol, struck many West Germans in the 1980s as immediately and intuitively understandable. But it is worth parsing this seeming obviousness to gain a fuller appreciation for the way the bar code image tied together a number of boycott themes. First and most obviously, it dramatized the elimination of privacy. Folded into this seemingly straightforward symbol of visibility, however, were a number of additional nuances or specific layers of meaning. The bar code is designed to be read by machines, and thus encodes in an opaque symbology an *impersonal* form of surveillance in the service of projects that may be utterly indifferent to individual purposes, goals and desires. The numbers along the bottom or top of a standard-format UPC do nothing to mitigate this indifference and lack of personal access, as most people (still today) do not know what these digits represent. Further, although bar codes all basically look the same to humans, we also know that each one encodes information that is totally unique. Something like a modern supermarket is in this sense on overwhelming illustration of our ignorance of the code. Miles of aisles full of colorfully juxtaposed, totally unique packages nevertheless all share this one seemingly identical visual element constituting an *open secret* to which we are not privy. Transcribed onto heads and other parts of human bodies as in the images of the anti-census movement, the bar code could embody yet another layer of symbolic suggestion: the evidence ("in black and white") of people's non-participation in, and exclusion from the medium of, their own surveillance is represented as itself publicly visible, on display. Total visibility to and objectification by the technical control apparatus of the surveillance state is made visible to one's fellow citizens, adding to the humiliation of the bar coded while reminding others of shared powerlessness. In many of these images, the bar code (like a tattoo) is inscribed on the naked body, and thus cannot be removed (see Figure 1.2). This nakedness suggests, further, that even where public display is not constant, the subjected lack control over the terms of their exposure to surveillance. In this respect the bar code images echo the tattoos inscribed onto the wrists of Holocaust victims: the literal hiddenness of the wrist tattoos under sleeves of shirts or pajamas was utterly contingent, as the Nazis had the power to undress and expose at will. This was also part of the message to the West German public reading the cartoons in the 1980s: to allow the state to inscribe a bar code onto one's identity, or worse,

67 Palmer, R. 2001. *The Bar Code Book: A Comprehensive Guide to Reading, Printing, Specifying, and Applying Bar Code and Other Machine-Readable Symbols* (*4th Ed.*). Peterborough, NH: Helmers Publishing, 11-14, 75-81; Brown, S. 1997), *Revolution at the Checkout Counter: The Explosion of the Bar Code*. Cambridge, MA: Harvard University Press, pp. 194-200.

Figure 1.2 Bar codes on bodies

Source: Copyright permission courtesy of Gerhard Vormwald.

to facilitate this inscription in an active way, is to sacrifice control over one's subsequent exposure. Again, a major strand of anti-census argument had to do precisely with the possibility of reconstructing unique personal identification out of anonymized census data. Thus the "connect-the-dots" image (Figure 1.3) was also apt: in filling out the census form, residents were actively "filling in" their identities by drawing together previously isolated data.

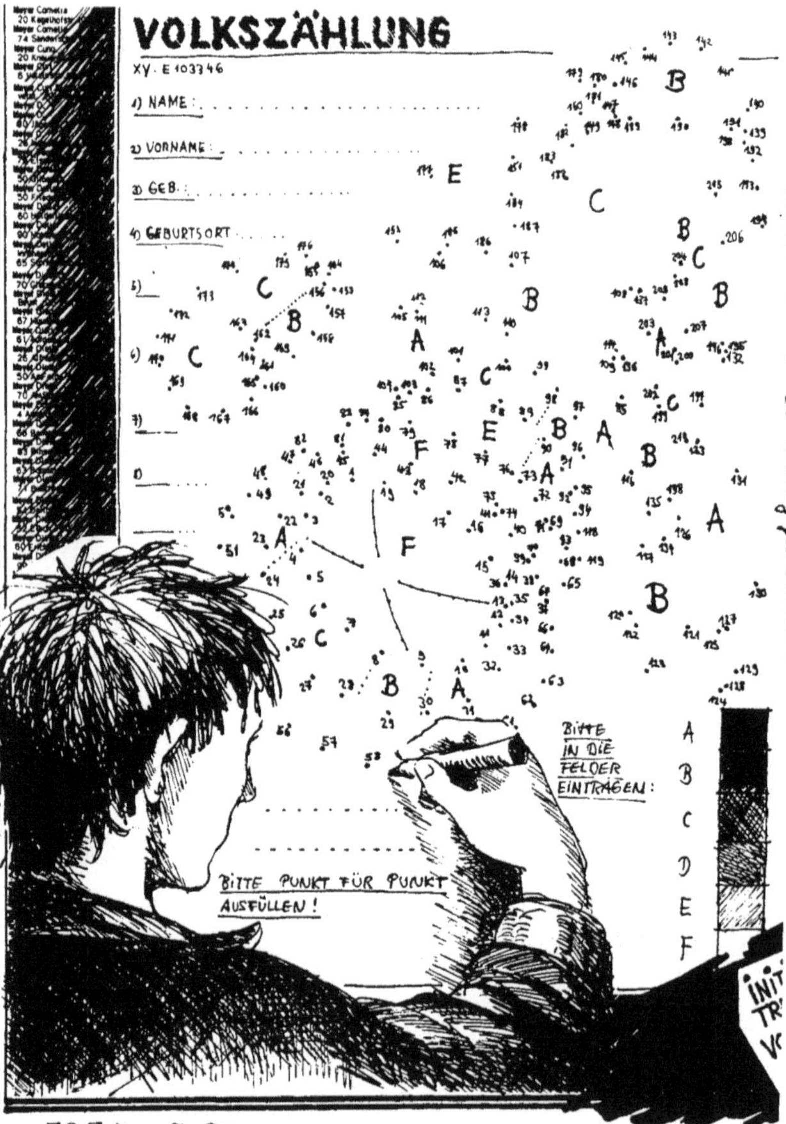

aus ZO-Zeitung für Ottensen

Figure 1.3 The census as a connect-the-dots exercise

Source: Permission to reproduce courtesy of *die tageszeitung* (taz) [aritist unknown].

Mainstream press coverage

Senator Lummer's letter to the SFB clearly illustrated the state's interest in keeping a lid on the discussion surrounding the boycott movement. The Federal Statistical Agency [*Statistisches Bundesamt*: StaBA] would doubtless have shared Senator Lummer's conviction that a responsible public discourse did not include the sort of arguments found in the pages of taz. In an evaluation of the previous (1970) West German census obtained by taz, the StaBA acknowledged the key role played by cooperative ("open-minded") media: "In very general terms it can be said that the press and television took up the theme of the census in a very open-minded way. The largely frictionless course of the count is certainly not least to be traced to the engagement of these mass media."[68] As we have seen, taz was working hard to ensure that the media's handling of the 1983 census would be more truly open-minded than in 1970. But even with the help of the sustained and imaginative engagement of the VoBo Inis, many census opponents realized, taz could never give the issue the prominence they felt it deserved in the minds of mainstream West Germans. For that, the mainstream media itself had to begin covering the VoBo.[69] Only then could the public discourse acquire the depth and breadth that would transform the census boycott movement into a true barometer of West German political culture.

For more liberal census critics, the Nazis and the Kohl government were connected much more distantly and tenuously than by the sort of steep slippery slope suggested by radical critics. The question of what was objectionable about the 1983 census *was*, for liberal critics, a question of degree, and the focus was more strongly on the erosion of individual privacy. As mentioned above, *Der Spiegel* set the stage for its coverage of the census boycott movement with two long feature articles in its first two issues of January 1983, entitled "The new world of 1984" and "On the way to the surveillance state".[70] The census itself is not mentioned in either article, but practically every other element of the increasingly comprehensive system of registration and surveillance is interpreted in Orwellian terms. This association was sustained over the next two months, and is best summarized in a passage from *Der Spiegel's* March 28th number:

> Video-surveillance of pedestrian zones, railway stations and intersections belong to everyday life in West Germany; dragnet data searches, bugging affairs and *Radikalenerlaß* [the infamous Executive Order on Radicals] have incited citizens against state snooping; now added to all this, just in time for the Orwell-year comes the not entirely counterfeit-proof but machine-readable personal ID

---

68 Quoted in Anon. 1983. Vor 13 Jahren war alles noch so gut. *die tageszeitung*, February 17, p. 7.

69 Olaf [no surname]. 1983. [Letter to the editor] *die tageszeitung*, February 22, p. 12.

70 Anon., Die neue Welt von 1984; Sternsdorff, Auf dem Weg zum Überwachungsstaat.

card for all, which makes it possible for the criminal police and secret services to throw a fine-meshed electronic dragnet over the country.

The term "*Volkszählung*" could come out of the lexicon of Orwell's "new-speak", in which war ministries are called peace ministries: the people are supposed not only to be counted but to talk about themselves. And the politicans' promise that the anonymity of respondents is guaranteed reveals itself upon closer inspection to be mere chatter [*bloßes Wortgeklingel*].[71]

A number of specific issues were woven into this skeptical vision, and would be ever more clearly separated out as the public debate zeroed in on concrete legal questions. The issue of how "total" the registration of the individual had become was not simply a matter of how much of one's life had been registered, but also of the anonymity of data, the storage of data, and the transfer of data gathered for one purpose into different databases or files serving other purposes. Even if the scope of the information collected were fairly comprehensive, other conditions would have to be in place for the registered data to lead to comprehensive social control. If the information could not be compiled from different databases into a unified profile of an individual, could not be stored beyond the time it took to add it to aggregate statistical totals, could not be accessed by any executive authorities able to use it against individual respondents, and, finally, if citizens were certain that all of these limits were in place, even a "total" registration would be fairly harmless. Much of the liberal critique of the census would thus focus on all the different ways in which the text of the census law and the strong government focus on security allowed or encouraged departures from the safeguards involved in this scenario.

The scope of the information to be collected in the census was far from "total", though census critics did not hesitate to portray it in maximalist terms. For many, though, the key dangers had more to do with the fact that what was collected could be *stored* for a considerable period of time, and that it could be *shared*, under certain conditions, with administrative agencies normally empowered to impose penalties. As noted above, the most glaring example of these dangers was the provision for the correction of the residency registers. There were nominal safeguards built into the law, for example, a requirement that personal data be destroyed after a set period of time, and a reassurance that personal information surrendered to census takers could not be used against respondents. But given the widespread climate of distrust of state motives, a climate fleshed out with ample details from taz, *Der Spiegel* and other publications, many West Germans were increasingly unwilling to be satisfied by the assurances of state officials. And these assurances were often rendered hollow by other actions taken by governments at all levels. For example, *Der Spiegel* would discover that the city of Munich had officially approved a premium to be paid to enumerators of DM 2.50 for every

71 Anon., Volkszählung: "Lasst tausend Fragebogen glühen", p. 30.

registration of a person previously not entered in the *Melderegister*.[72] This was not as gratuitously draconian as it may have sounded: cities could receive substantially expanded subventions from state coffers if their populations exceeded certain threshold levels.[73] Nevertheless, it did fit the larger picture of an aggressively intrusive census effort.

In an article for taz on March 10th, Wilhelm Steinmüller, Professor of Legal and Administrative Information Science at the University of Bremen, approached the issue of trust not in terms of the personal trustworthiness of bureaucrats but of the physical possibility of abuse implied by the co-location of databases.[74] In the midst of a wide-ranging critique of the census law, he noted that in many federal states, the offices responsible for carrying out the census also house many other important databases, often on the very same computers. Thus although the databases were nominally separate, they could function in an integrated way. Steinmüller made the further point that for databases to be linked up into a unified network, some means of unique identification would have to be found that allowed information in the various databases to be tied to the same person. He noted that because so many state databases were linked to the residency registers, the correction of these registers via census data would make it possible them to function as the equivalent of a national personal identification number (*Personenkennzeichen* or PKZ). In1976, the West German *Bundestag* had already explicitly rejected proposals for a national PKZ as, in its view, unconstitutional.

On March 24th, the *Frankfurter Rundschau* published an abbreviated version of a meticulous 61-page analysis of the census law presented to the Federal Constitutional Court by legal scholar Ulrich Mückenberger.[75] In it, Mückenberger brought concerns about the effects of data storage and data sharing into sharp focus, and assembled detailed legal evidence to support a highly skeptical view of the 1982 census law. "The problem of data protection", he wrote, "is increasingly a matter not only of the scope and intensity of registered data but also of the concentration of access to these data. Centralized data gathering and storage – even holding scope and intensity constant – in and of itself already heightens the danger of misuse."[76] The Constitutional Court had in an earlier decision drawn a strict line between "statistical" and "administrative" surveys, defining the former as entirely "receptive", "passive" collections and the latter as responsive or "furthering" [*fördernden*] surveys whose results could be used directly to influence the phenomena on which data are gathered. The correction of the residency registers foreseen in the 1982 census law was, according to Mückenberger, a clear violation of the court's ban on mixing the two. The census law offered inadequate protection

72 Anon. 1983. Heiße Ohren. *Der Spiegel*, April 11, p. 29.

73 I am grateful to Ulf Strohmayer for pointing this out to me.

74 Steinmüller, W. 1983. Der große Datenverbund. *die tageszeitung*, March 10, p. 3.

75 Mückenberger, U. 1983. "Anonymität bedroht, Menschenwürde beeinträchtigt". *Frankfurter Rundschau*, March 24, pp. 14-15.

76 Mückenberger, "Anonymität bedroht …", p. 14.

against such dangers also in the laxity of the conditions it stipulated for data sharing with other government agencies beyond the local residency offices. Mückenberger noted that its definition of potential recipients of shared data was functional rather than person-specific. Thus citizens responding to the census could have no clear picture of exactly who might gain access to their information, and the circle of potential recipients was largely self-defining: those agencies which could claim a need for census data were eligible to receive it. This was a problem in part because federal statistical and data protection law affirms the right of individuals to seek legal recourse against misuse of data. But if it is not possible to know which officials in which agencies have had access to one's personal information, this right of recourse cannot be exercised.

According to Mückenberger, the mixing of statistical and administrative goals and the possibility of data sharing raised two related and quite serious problems. On the one hand they further endangered the already thinly protected anonymity of respondents, and on the other, they undermined the *Nachteilsverbot*, the prohibition on disadvantage arising from response to a statistical survey. The so-called "micro-census decision" issued by the Constitutional Court in 1969 had established the principle that statistical surveys such as censuses involve an obligation to preserve anonymity, and not merely in the direct sense of keeping any identifying data confidential but also at the stage of processing and evaluating data: "the principle of anonymity thus requires that no connection between collected data and individually identifiable persons or groups of persons be established or be capable of being established."[77] The 1977 *Datenschutzgesetz* [data protection law] took up this principle and developed a citizen-friendly definition of anonymity summarized by Wilhelm Steinmüller in an interview with *Der Spiegel*: "each piece of data is and remains personal as long as one is able, with additional knowledge and/or additional procedures [but] without disproportionately great expense, to link it to [specific] persons."[78] If the correction of the residency registers and the census were entirely separate surveys, Mückenberger argued, anonymity in the latter could be protected. In pure form, a census would not even require any identifying information. But because of the mixed use foreseen by the census law, two key pieces of identifying information were necessary: a "household identification number" on the form itself, and the enumerator list of addresses. These would allow enumerators and the statisticians who processed the forms to identify individuals. Beyond these markers, however, Mückenberger raised a point highlighted also by Steinmüller and others, namely that even if data were shared in strictly anonymized form, the correlation of enough different pieces of information on a single person or household could easily allow "re-identification". The TV program *Panorama*

77 Mückenberger, "Anonymität bedroht …", p. 14.

78 Pötzl, N. 1983. "Beten, dass die Sicherungen halten", Interview with W. Steinmüller. *Der Spiegel*, March 21, p. 109; see also Bull, H.-P. 1983a. "Der Öffentlichkeit wurde zu wenig erklärt …" [reprinted information sheet]. *Frankfurter Rundschau*, March 25, p. 12.

ran a demonstration of re-identification in mid-March, catching the attention of a wide audience (and annoying federal officials). The simulation involved a search for an approximately 30-year-old office worker living in an apartment building at 11 Reeperbahn in Hamburg. The 214 people identified as living at this address were narrowed down to 23 by filtering them through a four-year window for birth year, and then the additional criterion of "office worker" narrowed the pool to two. With the final step of specifying an approximate workplace location, the search was complete and the individual identified.[79]

The second major implication of the correction of residency registers and other forms of possible data-sharing was the hollowing-out of the prohibition on disadvantage. Although the census law stated that no penalties could be imposed on individuals as a result of their responses to the census, critics had no trouble identifying a host of gray areas. Spiros Simitis, Data Protection Commisioner for the federal state of Hessen, expected that residency offices would not simply ignore evidence that West Germans were lying about their primary and secondary residences: "whoever, for example, reports a second residence in the countryside as a primary residence in order to save the auto insurance premium, or has rented a room in Berlin in order to avoid military service" would likely be called to account.[80] Mückenberger suggested that this would be possible because even if the residency offices or other agencies did not react directly to census responses showing irregularities, the law did not prevent them from initiating investigations on the basis of census data that could then "independently" verify transgressions and thus open the way for penalties.

Another set of problems with the prohibition on disadvantage could be grouped under the heading of conflicting duties. Mückenberger framed the issue in terms of the wider legal protection of individuals against self-incrimination, and argued that their duty to answer the census could violate this principle if the information they gave involved evidence of legal transgressions.[81] In such a situation, it could not be assumed that the protections established by the census law would hold, because it was not just citizens who faced conflicts of obligation. Potential problems arose also for government agencies and individual government officials obligated to fulfill other duties. In its first major piece on the VoBo, the highbrow weekly *Die Zeit* characterized the residency registers as an "open data market", and noted ominously that the *Melderechtsrahmengesetz*, the separate statute governing the residency registers, included a paragraph explicitly obliging registry offices to honor any requests for residency information submitted by any of the espionage, criminal or security agencies.[82] What the residency offices would do in weighing

79 Anon., Volkszählung: "Lasst tausend Fragebogen glühen", p. 31; Siemens, J. 1983. Fast alles falsch gemacht. *Frankfurter Rundschau*, March 17, n.p.n.

80 Quoted in Anon., Volkszählung: "Lasst tausend Fragebogen glühen", p. 31.

81 Mückenberger, "Anonymität bedroht …", p. 15.

82 Brunner, E., Pokatzky, K. and Schwelien, M. 1983. Erfasst, registriert, entmündigt. *Die Zeit*, March 18, p. 11.

the census law against the duty to pass on information to security agencies was not a question anyone could answer with confidence. And just as bureaucracies might be faced with contradictory duties, individual officials might be placed in untenable positions. *Der Spiegel* quoted the complaint of a police union official who objected to officers being required to serve as enumerators, since they would be confronted with the "dilemma between [respecting] the statistical principle of confidentiality and their duty to pursue punishable activity".[83]

There was no shortage of claims that the 1982 census law licensed unacceptable invasions of privacy. Mückenberger referred in his legal analysis to a gradation established by the Constitutional Court in an earlier decision, whereby the innermost "intimate sphere" was sacrosanct and off limits to state invasion, while the "remaining private sphere" could be queried within limits that were more stringent for matters of private life than, say, for information relating to employment.[84] Personal privacy issues would play a prominent role also in the decisions of the Constitutional Court. But given the endemic mistrust of the motives of the federal state, critical commentators, both liberal and radical, were at least as preoccupied with the implications of the census law for WGs, the residential collectives so central to the alternative and oppositional scene. A cartoon by Harald Juch appearing on the front page of taz on April 12th nicely evoked the confrontation between the inquisitive state in the person of a straight-laced census enumerator and the teeming democratic-oppositional geography of the stereotypical WG described in the introduction (see cover and Figure 1.4).[85] As the alarmed and confused enumerator has his briefcase torn from his hand by a dog running through his legs, and a census form folded into a paper airplane sails overhead, a tangle of WG residents struggles in the half-opened door over how to react. An arm stretches toward the enumerator offering a hot cup of coffee, another, sleeping tablets; a man dressed as a clown prepares to throw a cake at him while a woman tries to block the throw, shouting "Stop, only non-violent resistance!" Another man says he'll only talk to enumerators through his lawyer while yet another strains to pull the door closed, crying "Shut the door! Old WG decision: don't open it in the first place!" The punch-line is delivered by a friendly young woman near the bottom of the pile of bodies: "Sorry man, our WG couldn't agree on a form of boycott." The cartoon pokes fun at the difficulty of democratic decision-making in collectives, but also suggests the general futility of attempting to capture the richness of collective human life, especially in such a democratic form, by means of statistics. A key to the whole message is the darkness of the territory behind the door: WGs were fundamentally opaque to authorities. But this dark territory can be taken to symbolize issues that are central to the argument presented in this book, and thus relevant far beyond the particular circumstances

83 Anon., Volkszählung: "Lasst tausend Fragebogen glühen", p. 31.

84 Mückenberger, "Anonymität bedroht …", p. 15.

85 Imma [no surname]. 1983b. Man kann auf jeden zählen. *die tageszeitung*, April 12, p. 1.

Figure 1.4 The census and the "dark territory" of the *Wohngemeinschaft*

Source: Copyright permission courtesy of Harald Juch. Permission to reproduce courtesy of *die tageszeitung* (taz).

of West German living collectives. First, the space inside the doorway is not simply "dark": a set of distinct characters emerges from it, each with a different bodily or discursive relation to the prospect of becoming visible. In particular, the figure in the clown makeup suggests that what is really at stake here need not be simply a rejection of visibility but visibility *on terms not dictated from above by the state*. Second, the dark territory depicted is not simply "private space'… as the sheer variety of characters in the picture suggests, and as their eminently political spontaneous debate makes clearer still, the boundaries between public and private are blurred. The importance of both of these points will become clearer as the story moves along.

The early January *Spiegel* article on the hunt for terrorists and the video surveillance of whole neighborhoods in Heidelberg, as well as the early taz interview with former BKA employee Berndt Schmidt, had highlighted the fact that WGs were viewed by federal security services as inherently suspect. The search for RAF cells and other dangerous groups was often in large part the search for "conspiratorial apartments", the living spaces, usually rented by unsuspicious third parties, in which extremists spent the daylight hours, gathered equipment and planned their attacks. The opacity of WGs was, in the eyes of police services, inherently dangerous. Critics picked up fairly quickly on the potential threat posed to this opacity by the fact that the census form printed by the government was a *household* form, not an individual form. As Wilhelm Steinmüller noted in his March 21st *Spiegel* interview, the census form included the following definition: "To a household belong all persons who live together in a residential- and economic collective."[86] But, he insisted, there was no legal basis for taking census information in such a way that the internal social structure of a *Wohngemeinschaft* would be revealed: "Social explosives as big as anything one could imagine lie in the [possibility] that the social structure of all *Wohngemeinschaften* including names, would be registered. These data could be linked with some 500 further pieces of information per person. One can only pray that the confidentiality measures of the statistical officials hold against the data requests of other agencies."[87] Another critical analysis in the *Frankfurter Rundschau* pointed out that if all members of a WG were forced to use the same form, each would have the opportunity to see the information provided by other WG members, which would already amount to a violation of the legal requirement of confidentiality. Further, because the 1982 census law concerned itself only with "individual responses", but the general statute governing the collection of statistics explicitly stated that "the bringing together of responses of multiple respondents is not an individual response in the sense of the law," the form is in conflict with the law it is supposed to execute.[88] In a piece appearing March 28th, *Spiegel* editor Jochen Bölsche connected these fears back to the boycott movement itself, suggesting that the gravest danger came not from answering the census but from protesting it. Noting that some local authorities had instructed enumerators to report any individuals or households refusing to answer the census, Bölsche anticipated the completion of a nationwide "dissident file": "Already in 1984, the *Bundesrepublik* will be the only state in the history of humankind to have registered practically the entire protest potential in the population with names and information about the degree of individual willingness to resist – not in spite of but precisely because of the growth of the boycott movement."[89]

Parties and organizations

These critiques, despite the variety of their angles of attack and general orientations, evinced an underlying attitude toward the state of some degree of distrust, and, as we shall see in the next chapter, ran directly contrary to many features of the conservative political culture animating many state bureaucracies as well as

86 Pötzl, "Beten, dass die Sicherungen halten", p. 106.

87 Pötzl, "Beten, dass die Sicherungen halten", p. 107.

88 Bull, "Der Öffentlichkeit wurde zu wenig erklärt …", p. 12.

89 Bölsche, J. 1983. Der Geßlerhut des Orwell-Jahrzehnts. *Der Spiegel*, March 28, p. 47.

the conservative press. The focus on the hypothetical possibility of misuse; the critique of the flimsiness of data protection; in general, the unhappiness with the fact that the census law relied so heavily on the assumed *trustworthiness* of state agencies and officials, showed that the boycott movement had already burrowed to the core of the post-1945 political culture wars that had periodically convulsed West Germany. In addition to extraparliamentary activism and the press, to speak of "political culture" is also to speak of roles played in public decision-making by political parties, unions, and other organizations at all scales from the local to the national. From mid-February to mid-April 1983, an ever-longer list of organizations went public with serious reservations about the imminent count. In combination with the patterns of press coverage and the weakness of the official response to the VoBo movement (outlined in the next chapter), this trend helped move public opinion to a degree of skepticism that ultimately raised serious doubts about the expected accuracy of the census.

As already noted above, the 1983 boycott movement was truly a grassroots political phenomenon. Not surprisingly, the local citizens' initiatives that made it up were often interwoven with local party organizations, which took public positions at odds with the national parties' official support for the count. And where the renegade party locals had a share in power, local and state governments began to challenge federal policy. Thus cracks began to appear within the nested regional structures both of parties and of elected governments. As in the very earliest phase of the VoBo movement, the peculiar political dynamics of West Berlin made the half-city a unique case, and the earliest place in which support for the boycott was taken up by a party local. West Berlin was a center of budding Green Party influence, and the West Berlin Greens signed on to the first public call for a boycott ("Politicians ask, citizens do not answer") reported by taz in mid-December of 1982.[90] This call was also supported by the Federal Association of Citizens' Initiatives for Environmental Protection [*Bundesverband BürgerInitiativen Umweltschutz* or BBU]. The BBU was a key component of the Greens' national organization, and would facilitate the emergence of the Greens as the only generally pro-boycott party.[91] Outside Berlin, too, Green opposition to the census began early and continued through mid-April.[92] The announcement in taz on April 8th of an information session put on by the Munich Greens gives a sense for the practical orientation of much of this activity. In addition to the meeting, the Greens announce plans to print and distribute flyers, in Turkish and Greek as well as German, addressed primarily to foreign residents concerned about the "12-square-meter ordnance", the West German version of the time-honored use of

90 Anon., Politiker fragen – Bürger antworten nicht, p. 4.

91 The BBU, founded in 1972, was a major player in the development of the West German environmental movement (Markovitz and Gorski, *The German Left*, pp. 102, 105, 108).

92 Miehe, R. 1983. Eine Republik macht Inventur. *Frankfurter Rundschau*, February 19, n.p.n.

residential density ordnances to control the lives of urban immigrant communities.[93] For guest workers, asylum seekers and other immigrants, the general alarm at the sharing of census information with other agencies resolved itself into specific fears of the effects of having their data turned over to the Immigration Authority [*Ausländerbehörde*]. And, as the announcement from the Munich Greens indicates, a key concern was the rule governing maximum residential density: "Each foreigner must be able to show that 12 m^2 of living space [are available] per family member if he wants to avoid the danger of being deported."

In early March, the centrist-conservative *Frankfurter Allgemeine Zeitung* noted with alarm that the Greens of the federal state Hessen had plans to establish a boycott fund aimed especially at offering financial assistance to those boycotters "who are singled out as exemplary and sentenced to pay heavy penalties ..."[94] The members of the Green Party lined up to enter the national *Bundestag* when the Greens won seats there for the first time in March had already decided to come out in favor of the boycott on February 12th and 13th, but, according to an open letter published in taz on March 10th, the feverish activity surrounding the national elections in early March had prevented an organized public announcement and discussion.[95] The open letter declared the intention of the signatories not to cooperate with the census enumerators and urged West Germans to follow suit in the interest of resisting the slide toward a "1984" scenario. It was signed by Green and alternative delegates from a range of communal, local, state and national fractions. In early April, as soon as the Greens were sitting in the *Bundestag*, they called for a debate in that body over the census, and all Green delegates spoke against it.[96] Another expression of West Berlin's status as a hotbed of alternative politics was the presence of a group of delegates representing the *Alternative Liste* (AL), an umbrella organization bringing together Greens and other issue-specific oppositional clusters, in the city's House of Delegates. In mid-February of 1983, the AL fraction in the House of Delegates sponsored a large advertisement in taz urging citizens to boycott, urging those assigned as enumerators to refuse, and explaining that although the AL was "not against planning in and of itself", the upcoming census did not "conform to the standards [appropriate to] a survey of individuals in the service of citizen-friendly planning."[97] The AL would remain heavily involved in the West Berlin VoBo through April.

---

93 Anon. 1983. VoBo Termine. *die tageszeitung*, April 8, p. 11.

94 Quoted in Behr, A. 1983. Die Angst, ein "gläserner Mensch" zu werden. *Frankfurter Allgemeine Zeitung*, March 2, p. 10.

95 Schmidt, R., Baum, P., *et al*., 1983. Die Regierung fragt – Abgeordnete antworten nicht. *die tageszeitung*, March 10, p. 3.

96 Fraktion Die GRÜNEN. 1983. Keine Totalerfassung des Bürgers. *Das Parlament*, No. 14, April 9, p. 3.

97 Alternative Liste. 1983. Volkszählung? So nicht! [advertisement]. *die tageszeitung*, February 18, p. 18.

The Social Democrats (SPD), who had been the party in power when the VZG was passed in March 1982, saw regional and other internal splits develop around the boycott. Hamburg, like Berlin a key node in the web of boycott activities and publicity, was the scene of an important defection. Its SPD party fraction came out in early March in favor of a postponement of the census. According to the Executive Council, close reconsideration of the questions asked and the composition of the form itself would allow the federal government to "enhance the citizen-friendliness, to improve the results and to ensure the restriction of the list of questions to the indispensably necessary, as well as to strengthen the trust of the citizenry and the acceptance of the *Volkszählung*."[98] Ten days later, Björn Engholm, a top SPD candidate in the federal state of Schleswig-Holstein, declared his intention to support a postponement if his party won the state elections.[99] The developing skepticism regarding the census was not confined to the left parties. In mid-March taz reported grumblings against the census from the highest ranks of the Free Democratic Party (FDP), the pro-business party in coalition with the CDU/CSU. Party leader Otto Graf von Lambsdorff complained of inadequate public relations work to persuade citizens of the need for a census, and the FDP Interior Minister of North Rhine-Westphalia registered his opposition to the controversial plan to correct the residency registers.[100] To the delight of VoBo activists, the paleo-conservative Franz-Josef Strauß, long-time head of the Bavarian CSU, former Defense Minister and the moving force behind the infamous *Spiegel* Affair, distanced himself from the *Volkszählung* in an interview with *Stern*:

> I am no particular fan of the census. If citizens are anxious about it I am of the opinion that we can do without a census for another couple of years. In any case I consider the perfectionism typical of such actions superfluous. Completely senseless questions are often asked.[101]

Strauß's comments nicely highlight the split among West German conservatives between old-style defenders of deference and order and new-style technocrats identified by the liberal publicist Hans-Magnus Enzensberger in the speech he gave in New York City in 1979 (see Introduction).[102] Another interesting episode involving conservatives was centered on the CDU *Ministerpräsident* of the federal state Lower Saxony, Hans Albrecht. Two days before the national parliamentary elections, the German Press Agency reported that Albrecht had gone public with a statement in favor of postponing the census. Two days after the elections, Albrecht

---

98 Quoted in Anon. 1983. Anweisung an Volkszähler "… uns bei schwierigen Verweigerungen unterrichten". *die tageszeitung*, March 4, p. 4.

99 Imma [no surname]. 1983a. Volkszählung. Widerstand weitet sich aus. *die tageszeitung*, March 14, p. 7.

100 Imma, Volkszählung. Widerstand weitet sich aus.

101 Quoted in Anon., Anweisung an Volkszähler …, p. 4.

102 Enzensberger, "An address".

denied the report, blaming irresponsible journalists. The interpretation suggested by taz was that Albrecht recognized and sought to make use of growing uneasiness about the census in the context of the political campaign, but then returned to the pro-census party line once the election was over.[103]

All such news only confirmed the judgment reached by Gerhard Ziegler in an editorial for the *Frankfurter Rundschau* on March 10th that "the differences of opinion run across the parties".[104] In the lead article on the front page of *Die Zeit* for March 25th ("Freedom, free space and census forms"), Theo Sommer remarked at greater length on the seeming irrelevance of the usual party lines:

> It is peculiar how diagonally the fronts run in the census discussion. The opposition, otherwise data hungry and eager for planning, warns of the "glass person". The Union [CDU] ([whose slogan is] "Freedom instead of socialism") wants – with a few exceptions like Strauß and Barschel – not to postpone it, although it is precisely the conservatives who constantly preach limitation of the state. The FDP is once again open to all sides. The *Frankfurter Allgemeine* [*Zeitung*], sinking ever further from grand-bourgeois liberality into petty-bourgeois state-piety, makes a test of strength out of the carrying through [of the census], and [an implicitly trivializing] Spring theater out of the doubts.[105]

In addition to local parties, a hodgepodge of different organizations went public in March and April with various criticisms of the census or calls to join the boycott. A group of 100 Munich public defenders registered strong reservations about the conformity of the census legislation with basic principles of the rule of law [*Rechtsstaatsprinzip*].[106] They singled out for particular criticism the monetary bonuses set by the city of Munich to be paid to enumerators for each person counted in the census but not previously in the residency registers. They also reminded the public that respondents were legally required neither to enter their telephone numbers on the census forms nor to allow enumerators into their living spaces. A few days later, a conference of white collar workers belonging to the powerful national industrial union IG Metall declared their opposition to the census, to electronically readable personal ID cards, and to the comprehensive computerization and wiring of workplaces.[107] The union cited fears of the "surveillance state" and of a progressive loss of office jobs to technology and home-based work. The following

---

103 Anon. 1983. Nach der Wahl. Albrecht dementiert. *die tageszeitung*, March 10, p. 3.

104 Ziegler, G. 1983. Die Super-Befragung. *Frankfurter Rundschau*, March 10, n.p.n.

105 Sommer, T. 1983. Freiheit, Freiraum und Fragebögen – Warum die Volkszählung verschoben werden sollte. *Die Zeit*, March 25, n.p.n.

106 Anon. 1983. Integration des VZ-Boykotts? *die tageszeitung*, March 10, p. 3.

107 Anon. 1983. 11. Angestelltenkonferenz der IG-Metall – Metaller gegen Volkszählung. *die tageszeitung*, March 14, p. 4.

week, the national police union issued a statement recommending that officers refuse to act as enumerators on the grounds that their obligation to pursue illegal activity could place them in a position where they faced conflicts of legal duties.[108] In early April, 13 teachers in a small town near Hamburg asked a local court for a stay preventing the town from forcing them to take on enumerator duties.[109] Shortly afterward, a group of 250 mathematicians and information scientists working at universities throughout West Germany published an open letter to the Interior Ministry opposing the census in its current form. A similar statement was issued by the national association of sociologists.[110]

The connection to the Nazi era was raised again in alarming terms by Romani Rose, the Chair of West Germany's Central Council of Sinti and Roma, who called in a letter to taz for all Sinti and Roma to refuse to answer the census.

> The growing public critique of the census is supported by the Central Council. Among Sinti and Roma there are now additional fears, after it has become known that the term "Gypsy camps" [*Zigeuner-Lager*] appears in the "Introduction for enumerators" ... The registration of our ethnic group has played a fateful role in the recent German past. During the fascist period in Germany Sinti and Roma were registered on racist grounds by the *Reichssicherheitshauptamt* [the infamous umbrella security organization run by Heinrich Himmler], in preparation for genocide ... The Central Council emphasizes once more that on the basis of old racist ideologies the Sinti and Roma continue to be registered, surveilled, and electronically filed in the databanks of police and centrally in federal and state criminal bureaus as "traveling suspects", throughout the *Bundesrepublik* up to the present day, by means of "Traveler- Observation and Control Forms". This is supplemented [in the service of] the total registration of Sinti and Roma by the legal obligation of city agencies to share information on members of our ethnic group with criminal police authorities ... Orwell's "1984" has been in existence for Sinti and Roma since 1933.[111]

It is impossible to isolate the precise effect of each of these defections from the official government line on public opinion, but that public opinion had been swayed was undeniable. A poll by the "*Politbarometer*" of the television station ZDF in late March revealed that 52% of West Germans surveyed had misgivings about the census, and that roughly a quarter planned not to participate.[112] Around

108 Anon. 1983. Trotz neuer Proteste und Verfassungsbeschwerden – Bundesrat besteht auf Volkszählung. *die tageszeitung*, March 21, p. 2.

109 Anon. 1983. Lehrer klagen gegen Zwangsverpflichtung. *die tageszeitung*, April 11, p. 5.

110 Anon. 1983. Zählerei – Verweigerung aller Orten. *die tageszeitung*, April 11, p. 5.

111 Rose, R. 1983. Aufruf zur Volkszählung [letter to the editor]. *die tageszeitung*, April 7, p. 12.

112 Anon., Volkszählung: "Lasst tausend Fragebogen glühen", p. 30.

the same time, the Allensbach Institute found that 21% of respondents planned to boycott.[113] A mere two weeks before the planned enumeration date of April 27th, *Der Spiegel* reported mass attrition among enumerators throughout the country: 700 of the necessary 3,000 enumerators in the industrial city of Duisburg had abandoned their clipboards; 500 of the 2,850 needed in Hannover had refused, with more following every day; the number in Hamburg had shrunk from 13,800 to 11,600. The federal *Statistisches Bundesamt* in Wiesbaden insisted that rumors of such a trend were "exaggerated" but had no further specifics with which to counter *Der Spiegel*'s numbers, and acknowledged that it was aware of attrition.[114] Even just taken as very approximate indicators, these numbers strongly suggest that resistance among enumerators and citizens in general had reached a point at which both the mechanics of the count and the anticipated accuracy of its results were seriously threatened. What *Der Spiegel* termed an "unexampled" protest movement[115] had evidently crossed not only party lines but another line many West Germans perceived. This line ran between, on the one hand, habitual activists, members of the alternative scenes in the major cities and denizens of the oppositional geographies described in the Introduction, and on the other hand, "normal citizens", people whose political involvement in the affairs of the *Bundesrepublik* was otherwise limited to the formal electoral system and perhaps institutionally-circumscribed activism within the established parties. Taking stock in mid-April, *Der Spiegel* quoted the *Washington Post*, which had commented that with the planned census, the West German state had obviously reached the "limits of trust" on the part of its citizens.

> What critics of atomic energy, squatters and runway-demonstrators[116] had not succeeded in doing, the VoBo movement had achieved: it brought into existence a unique nationwide coalition of established and counter-culture. Citizens from all social strata and political corners got involved: medical professionals and data protections officials, union members, church people and professional politicians.[117]

113 Bergmann, *Volkszählung und Datenschutz*, pp. 44-45.

114 Anon., Heiße Ohren, p. 28.

115 Anon., Volkszählung: "Lasst tausend Fragebogen glühen", p. 30.

116 A major controversy had simmered through the 1970s and then erupted in the early 1980s over the potential ecological consequences of plans to build a new runway ("*Startbahn 18-West*") at the Frankfurt airport. The issue was an important focus for the development of Green politics (Orth, G. and Podlech, A. 1982. *Testfall Startbahn West: Erfahrungen und Perspektiven im Widerstand.* Wuppertal: Jugenddienst Verlag).

117 Anon., "Ohne Drohgebärde, ohne Angst", p. 20.

Chapter 2
"The Sensitivity of a Steamroller"? The State at Cross-Purposes

> You know better than anyone that no interior minister, in any age or in any country in the world, has ever opened his mouth to speak of the mean, dishonourable, treacherous, criminal deeds committed in the course of his work, so you can rest easy on that score because I will prove no exception.
>
> [T]he blank vote is as destructive a form of blindness as the first one, Either that or a form of clear-sightedness, said the minister of justice, What, asked the interior minister, who thought he must have misheard, I said that the blank vote could be seen as a sign of clear-sightedness on the part of those who used it, How dare you, in the middle of a cabinet meeting, utter such antidemocratic garbage, you ought to be ashamed of yourself, no one would think you were the minister of justice, cried the minister of defense, Actually, I wonder if I've ever been more of a minister of justice or for justice than I am at this moment.

(José Saramago, *Seeing*, pp. 119, 159)

As I have recounted the story thus far, it might seem almost as though the 1983 census boycott movement was unopposed, or blossomed into a political vacuum. Census critics developed their arguments and imagery, the mainstream press picked them up and fleshed them out, a growing tide of party locals and other organizations in civil society backed away from supporting the enumeration, and public opinion followed obediently. In fact there was both institutional and public support for the census, but it would be too simplistic by far to describe official support with the term "the state". Though the left tended to use the singular "the state", especially in connection with security policy and surveillance, the 1983 boycott would make plain just how far the complex institutional ensemble of state institutions and agencies was from programmatic unity on this issue. This chapter traces some of the main fissures and conflicts within and between state responses to the boycott. As the discussion in Chapter 1 of the breakaway party locals already suggested, this fragmentation itself tended to lend credibility to the boycott.

Champions of the census

The chief underlying source of support for the census was the great mass of the relatively quiescent mainstream population, content to take its cues from national media and high-profile political officials, or simply not inclined to believe, despite all the boycott propaganda, that the threat posed by the census was so dire as to make it worth disrupting normal life or defying the law, especially where this might mean making common cause with the activists of which many were still suspicious or actively disapproved. If a quarter of the population were considering participation in the boycott, that meant three quarters were not, even if they did not entirely trust the government. This diffuse political inertia was the main asset relied upon by the officials who were determined to carry out the census. Many state agencies, officials and leaders at all levels based their responses to the VoBo on the long-standing German statist tradition that saw state action as legitimate by definition, because the state (or a state agency) is an inherently legitimate actor.[1] If, by the statist logic, there was no need for additional legitimation of the census, the appropriate response to VoBo activities would not be any form of dialogue or persuasion but simply suppression. Other proponents of the census made some attempt at discursive engagement, but their arguments often placed more emphasis on the duty to obey the law than on detailed justifications of its content. Thus, especially in the early stages of the pro-census response, it often fell to the conservative media to outline a basic case for answering the census. But even this "case" remained fairly rudimentary, and never approached the level of empirical detail or theoretical sophistication to be found in the critiques surveyed in the previous chapter. The judgment of Erwin Brunner, Klaus Pokatzky and Michael Schwelien in an article in *Die Zeit* in mid-March regarding the limited angle of vision of two prominent government officials was applicable to a broader swathe of officialdom and of the conservative press: "The arguments against the *Volkszählung* are more comprehensive, more fundamental and above all more serious than [Federal Data Protection Commissioner Hans Peter] Bull and [Interior Minister Friedrich] Zimmermann want to believe."[2]

The letter West Berlin's Senator Lummer had sent to SFB demanding that it cease to air the opinions of Michael Schroeren and other census critics, and the fine Lummer was able to impose on Schroeren (see previous chapter), are paradigmatic of early reactions by many officials. In April, *Der Spiegel* would claim that suppression of the VoBo movement was sharpest in West Berlin.[3] In addition to Lummer's personal campaign, there were reports of West Berlin police tearing down boycott banners hung from the windows of a squatted house at

1 The Weimar Republic of 1918-1933 was the only period following the unification of Germany under Bismarck in 1871 in which the government in power was denied the benefits of this statism by most conservatives (see Mommsen, H. 2003. *Aufstieg und Untergang der Republik von Weimar 1918-1933*. Munich: Ullstein for the authoritative account of the politics of this period).

2 Brunner, E., Pokatzky, K., and Schwelien, M. 1983. Erfaßt, registriert, entmündigt. *Die Zeit*, March 18, p. 10.

3 Anon., "Ohne Drohgebärde, ohne Angst", p. 21.

Wilsnackerstrasse 15.[4] In late March, Lummer's colleague Senate Councilor Magen announced that anyone intending to turn in their census forms for destruction to the so-called "alternative collection points" organized by the boycott could reckon with a penalty for injury to state property (West Berlin VoBo Inis and the local bars that would serve as collection points responded with the assurance that they only intended to carry out a massive recycling action: "instead of stuffing masses of garbage cans full with the property of the state, the papers would be collected and then returned to their owner, the *Statistische Landesamt* [the provincial State Bureau of Statistics]"). Magen also warned taz explicitly against "incitement" to illegal activities.[5]

But similar repressive measures were also to be noted elsewhere in West Germany. Throughout the *Ruhrgebiet,* the industrial core of North Rhine-Westphalia, cities and towns refused to approve applications by VoBo Inis to set up information kiosks in public spaces. One Gelsenkirchen judge explained the ban on information stands in classic German bureaucratese: the information booths might move citizens to "realize the elements of a misdemeanor" [*Ordnungswidrigkeitstatbestände zu verwirklichen*].[6] To evade a similar ban in Hamburg, one of the local Inis put its table on wheels.[7] In Heddesheim, near Heidelberg, the mayor denied the local Green party both the use of town meeting space to hold an information session and permission to publish an anti-census article in the local paper.[8] Beyond denying VoBo supporters the use of public spaces and public media, conservatives sometimes explicitly urged or ordered the collection of information on census opponents. None seemed more clearly to confirm the darkest suspicions of census critics than Constantin Freiherr Heeremann, a local CDU politician from Emsdetten and long-serving president of the German Peasants' Union. Heeremann advocated the use of the boycott movement to "establish where the enemies of our free democratic order are hiding."[9] An internal memo obtained by taz and directed to all local district officials in the state of Schleswig-Holstein included the following passage: "We ask you to inform us of hard cases of refusal. These refusers are to be gathered together in an overview, out of which the current status of each individual case can be obtained".[10] Berlin police were instructed to take

---

4 Anon. 1983. Auch Polizisten wollen keine Zähler sein. *die tageszeitung*, March 11, p. 20.

5 Anon., Knast für Boykotteure angedroht.

6 Ludger [no surname given] 1983. Verfassungsgericht soll entscheiden. *die tageszeitung*, April 8, p. 9.

7 Anon., Lehrer klagen gegen Zwangsverpflichtung.

8 Anon. 1983. Bei diesem Thema nicht. *die tageszeitung*, April 8, p. 9.

9 Quoted in Anon. 1983. [No title, passage reprinted from *Emsdettener Zeitung* of February 2, 1983]. *die tageszeitung*, March 4, p. 4. See also Schwenger, *Im Jahr des grossen Bruders*, p. 63.

10 Anon. 1983. "... uns bei schwierigen Verweigerungen unterrichten". *die tageszeitung*, March 4, p. 4.

down personal information on all individuals caught distributing boycott flyers.[11] There were certainly some officials, in other words, who urged precisely the sort of comprehensive "dissident mapping" feared by Jürgen Bölsche (see Chapter 1).

Local authorities bent on suppressing opposition enjoyed explicit support for such measures from Interior Minister Friedrich Zimmermann, who quickly became the lightning rod of opposition to the census, urging citizens "not to allow themselves to be stirred up by people for whom the issue is not actually the census but rather the struggle against our democratic state system."[12] His fellow federal Minister (of Justice) Hans Engelhard agreed, stating that "boycotting the census is illegal and not [based on] a legitimate right of resistance."[13] In a story on March 2nd, the *Frankfurter Allgemeine Zeitung* noted the concerns of census critics that the correction of the residency registers could lead to the discovery of falsifications of primary residence to avoid tax burdens or military service. The article quoted the brief response of a statistician at the *Statistisches Bundesamt* in Wiesbaden: "Na, und?" ("And?") Among the many other interwoven assumptions lurking behind these sentiments was an implicitly unified view of state knowledge and state action: if the state gathers information for one purpose and discovers that it would be useful in the fulfillment of other commitments, why should it not pass on what it knows? In an interview with *Der Spiegel* in late March (discussed in more detail below), Interior Minister Zimmermann anticipated an attitude among citizens on this point as trusting as his own: "Concerning the few personal data required, I don't believe that the greater part of the citizenry has any reservations. In the end, [the citizen] knows that all of these data are required for opening an account at the bank or savings-and-loan."[14] Yet, again, the issue for many West Germans was not only or even primarily whether the census would require them to surrender any "new" data they hadn't had to give before. The problem was what was done with their data once it was in the hands (or databanks) of the authorities. Zimmermann's apparent ignorance of or indifference to this point did little to allay such concerns.

An article in the FAZ on March 2nd pulled together the basic elements of the pro-census position: (1) the 1982 census law was passed with the solid support of all three parties represented in the *Bundestag* at the time (here the author(s) conveniently neglected to mention that the Greens did not gain their first *Bundestag* seats until March of 1983), and was therefore the legitimate product of a democratic process; (2) the state needed updated demographic information for such things as planning for new schools and hospitals; (3) estimates of the size of the West German population based on the *Melderegister* were probably too high by roughly one

11 Anon. 1983. Staatsfeindlicher Akt? *die tageszeitung*, March 23, p. 16.

12 Pötzl, "Beten, dass die Sicherungen halten", p. 108.

13 Anon. 1983. Das Bundesverfassungsgericht prüft Beschwerden gegen umstrittene Volkszählung. *Süddeutsche Zeitung*, March 12/13, p. 1.

14 Pötzl, N. and Mettke, J. 1983. "Wo ist denn die Intimität?" Interview mit Innenminister Friedrich Zimmermann. *Der Spiegel*, March 28, p. 43.

million residents, because of the phenomenon noted above of people neglecting to register their departures when moving away from their old residences; (4) the census would cost something on the order of DM 370 million, of which a good portion had already been spent, so canceling it would waste a lot of money; and (5) some of the specific claims made by boycott supporters (for example, that enumerators would ask about personal income and savings) were false.[15] Under the hubristic headline "Why the census is necessary and will take place", a late March article in *Die Welt* opened by revisiting the fact that the 1982 law passed with broad support. Quoting Franz Kroppenstedt, President of the Federal Statistical Bureau [*Statistisches Bundesamt*] in Wiesbaden ("It was the broadest process of opinion formation one could imagine"), *Die Welt* painted opponents of the census as fantasists whose opposition itself was *prima facie* evidence that they believe "this cooperation never happened." The article urged readers to accept the declaration featured in official information spots: "every misuse [of data] is ruled out."[16]

There certainly were more weighty arguments to be made in favor of the census, arguments that, had they been developed to a depth matching that of many critiques, might have impacted public opinion substantially. One such argument was introduced by Günter Appel, head of the West Berlin statistical bureau, and paraphrased in taz: "More dangerous than the census would be the scenario in which interested offices, instead of [searching out] the securely stored data of the [official] statisticians, would cobble together the required information from other sources, [a procedure] which would no longer be covered by the strict provisions of the statistical law."[17] Was it really better, in other words, to force statistical agencies to find data wherever else they could, rather than having to get it directly from the population itself, which could thus at least ensure that it was correct? Such issues were not explored in much depth in the major national press. It is probably fair to interpret this in part as a matter of anti-government bias at *Der Spiegel*, *Die Zeit* and other major papers. But this "bias" in turn was partly the government's own doing, in the sense that it failed to elaborate defenses of the census that could have provided material for longer analyses. Perhaps the most potentially effective line of reasoning in support of the census expanded on basic argument number (2) above. Raised by Munich statisticians in the context of a discussion of the impact of the VoBo movement on the commitment of enumerators, their essentially biopolitical suggestion was that human rights could be negatively

15 Behr, Die Angst, ein gläserner Mensch zu werden; see also Anon., "Überfällig und unerlässlich"; Eickeler, Orwells Vision.

16 Nitschke, E. 1983a. Warum die Volkszählung nötig ist und stattfinden wird. *Die Welt*, March 31, n.p.n.

17 Anon. 1983. "Wem nutzt ein Boykott". *die tageszeitung*, March 25, p. 19. Ironically, cobbling together a census from various sources (notably, the *Melderegister*) instead of asking the entire population directly is now the basic strategy of the German government as it prepares for the 2011 census, the first comprehensive census of population since 1987 (see Conclusions).

affected "if because of inadequate morale among enumerators an undercount of residents would result." An undercount would lead to inadequate funds being allocated to local governments for social programs, and thus injure those residents who would otherwise have benefited.[18] This line of argument had the advantage of confronting the critiques of counting as a fundamental attack on human rights with a direct counter-position, and perhaps forcing census critics to argue, rather than merely assume, that the erosion of human rights they were warning against was more serious than that resulting from the under-funding of social programs. Götz Aly's acid critique of the disastrous results of the West Berlin government's use of statistics in urban planning suggested how such a counter-biopolitical argument might look. But boycott supporters were never forced to develop it further.

Instead, a dominant theme in the discourse of census proponents was that of the reliability and integrity of the public officials who might come into contact with personal information. Interviewed by West German Radio on March 10th, Interior Minister Zimmermann encouraged the interpretation of the boycott as an attack on the integrity of officialdom, giving his personal guarantee that no misuse of data would take place.[19] In the *Spiegel* interview Zimmermann expanded on his position: "Technically all manner of abuses are of course possible. But what does 'technically' mean? That would mean that the residency register of municipality XY be transferred whole to federal state Z. Something like that is unthinkable. Everyone involved would make himself punishable under the law." The *Spiegel* interviewers countered that it would be naive to assume the mere existence of a legal penalty would deter all transgressions, but Zimmermann stuck to his guns: "That is not naive … Fraudulent and corrupt people are to be found in every area of life … But one should begin by trusting those who are obliged to the state by their official positions to act according to the law."[20] Refusing to credit his interviewers' claim that there were now close to 500 VoBo Inis, Zimmermann insisted that census opponents remained a tiny minority, and confirmed his more sinister interpretation of the movement: it represented "less an attack against the census and more an attack against the whole system. The legal-constitutional state of the *Bundesrepublik Deutschland* is being challenged on the matter of whether or not it carries out a unanimously passed law."[21] Asked later in the interview what he thought about the suggestion of some information scientists that the census be reduced in scope but supplemented with more detailed representative samples, Zimmermann leveled a similar charge: "Information scientists who register reservations, I have to suspect, have [as their target] less the census than the system of the *Bundesrepublik Deutschland* if they become strident [on such points]."[22]

18 Anon., Heiße Ohren, p. 29.

19 Spoo, E. 1983. "Bei dem Zeitdruck kann keiner die Daten mißbrauchen". *Frankfurter Rundschau*, March 12, n.p.n.

20 Pötzl, and Mettke, "Wo ist denn die Intimität?", p. 45.

21 Pötzl, and Mettke, "Wo ist denn die Intimität?", p. 37.

22 Pötzl, and Mettke, "Wo ist denn die Intimität?", p. 45.

The important challenge, in other words, was not a substantive argument but a challenge to *authority*, and there was no significant difference in Zimmermann's mind between the individuals invested with that authority and the larger state apparatus they represented. As Michel Foucault had noted four years earlier in a lecture at the Collège de France, such thinking was a tenacious survival of the German *Polizeistaat* tradition originating in the 18th century.[23] Zimmermann would belatedly be forced to take the boycotts more seriously when by early April it had become abundantly apparent that the basic statist argument wasn't changing minds on a large scale. In a press conference on the 1st of April, he would even offer to send all residents who fully and truthfully filled out their census returns a copy of any information held on them in the NADIS database, one of the notorious databases maintained by the West German security services.[24] This "trust for trust" gesture was supposed to defuse overblown fears about the state's use of personal information. However, by early April, the publicity battle had effectively already been lost. This was partly also due to the late start made by a Kohl government only just elected in early March. Beyond that, however, the defections of some local and state governments and the interventions of some Data Protection Commissioners prevented any united front on the part of state officials themselves.

Dissenting officials and Data Protection Commissioners

Though highly visible and omnipresent in the press, Zimmermann and other champions of the census were not at the helm of a tight ship of state steering a clear course. The local party defections noted in Chapter 1 necessarily led to some officials distancing themselves from the census. The pro-boycott stance of the SPD and Greens in Hamburg meant that the state government (Hamburg and sister port city Bremen are federal states unto themselves) opposed the census. Accordingly, by March 10th, the Hamburg Senate had already halted preparations for the count.[25] The following week, the head of the Köln [Cologne] statistical bureau, Manfred Güllner, granted taz a lengthy interview, in which he declared the intention to forego the use of census data to correct his city's *Melderegister*. Güllner also expressed his full understanding for many of the fears raised by the anti-census publicity:

> [O]ne does not use personally-referenced aspects of the data one has acquired in order to make social structures and processes more transparent for citizens. But with a little bit of imagination there is the possibility, I don't wish to deny it, of creating the "glass person" out of this surfeit of data. This is why the entanglement

23 Foucault, M. 2008. *The Birth of Biopolitics: Lectures at the Collège de France 1978-1979* (trans. G. Burchell). Basingstoke: Palgrave Macmillan, 168-169.

24 Bergmann, *Volkszählung und Datenschutz,* p. 62.

25 Anon., Integration des VZ-Boykotts?

> of the census with administrative actions is so deadly. It produces justified anxiety, for the data are not statistically evaluated, compiled or aggregated in an anonymous way, but passed on in personal form, e.g. to the *Meldeämter*.[26]

In early April, the city of Kassel, too, announced that it would not carry out the corrections of the residency registers, and the mayor of Saarbrücken, Oskar Lafontaine (who would go on to lead the national SPD in the 1990s and *Die Linke* in the 2000s), gave notice that anyone in the city refusing to take part in or help with the census on grounds of conscience would be spared any fines.[27] The movement of government units into opposition expressed itself at the federal level when Hamburg and Bremen both voted in the *Bundesrat*, the house of the West German parliament representing the federal states, to postpone the *Volkszählung*.[28] Theirs was the minority position, and the *Bundesrat* voted to go ahead with the census, but not before hosting yet another public debate exposing rifts within and across political camps.

While such local defections were already important, and always reported with relish in boycott propaganda, a more crucial source of disunity among state officials in both 1983 and 1987 was the relatively new institution of the Data Protection Commissioner [DSB]. Paragraph 17 of the *Bundesdatenschutzgesetz* [BDSG] passed in 1977 established the official position of Federal Data Protection Commissioner [*Bundesbeauftragter für den Datenschutz* (or *Bundesdatenschutzbeauftragter*, henceforth BDSB], charged with ensuring that the stipulations of the data protection law were followed in government activities. Like other officials, holders of the office take an oath swearing to "dedicate [their] energy to the well-being of the German people, increase the benefits [it enjoys], prevent injury to it, defend the constitution and the laws of the Federation …". The BDSB is "independent in the exercise of his office and only subordinate to the law", but in administrative terms subordinate to the Interior Minister.[29] Paragraph 19 of the 1977 BDSG explicitly obligated government agencies to support the BDSB and to allow him or her access both to all files and documents related to the processing of personal data, and to all office spaces under their control.[30] State Data Protection Commissioners [*Landesdatenschutzbeauftragten* or LDSBs] were installed in all federal states and West Berlin on the heels of this legislation, and charged with the same mission. Quite apart from the specific activities and positions taken by Data Protection Commissioners in the course of the census

26 Dillmann, H.-U. 1983. "Die Tendenz, den Bogen nicht auszufühlen, ist bei mir ziemlich groß" Interview mit Manfred Güllner. *die tageszeitung*, March 17, p. 8.

27 Anon., Lehrer klagen gegen Zwangsverpflichtung.

28 Anon. 1983. Bundesrat besteht auf Volkszählung. *die tageszeitung*, March 21, p. 2.

29 *Gesetz zum Schutz vor Mißbrauch personenbezogener Daten bei der Datenverarbeitung, Bundesgesetzblatt* 1977, Teil I, Nr. 7, February 1, 1977, 206. Bonn: Bundestag.

30 *Gesetz zum Schutz vor Mißbrauch personenbezogener Daten*, p. 207.

controversies, their very existence already represented a rationality of government at odds with the statism and *Polizeistaat* mentality so stridently expressed by Zimmermann. Just as there could be no real difference in the statist view between properly passed laws and the Basic Law, or between the policy of two different branches of government, it was difficult for statists to take seriously the need for an internal government "watchdog" whose job might involve an adversarial relationship to other government agencies. In their view, the state was not only essentially legitimate but essentially unified and non-contradictory in its mission. The DSB, at whichever level, was a government office that from a purely statist perspective should not have been necessary at all: an office embodying what amounted to systematic distrust of other government offices. As David Flaherty would put it in a 1989 study of different national data protection systems, the law enshrining Data Protection Commissioners would prove a "strange object" within the West German state edifice, one that it was "hard to learn how to handle".[31] If state actions were seen to be legitimate by definition, and if a simple proclamation that no data misuse would take place were seen to be sufficient to calm all fears, there would be no conceptual space for something like a DSB. If they grudgingly had to live with DSBs, Zimmermann and other census supporters at least hoped that Hans-Peter Bull, the BDSB retained from the foregoing Schmidt government, and his colleagues at the state level would reassure West Germans about the census in unmistakable tones. The slogan summarizing the statist position was "*Datenschutz kein Tatenschutz*" ["data protection cannot be protection of crime"], a conception Zimmermann and his allies understood broadly to include such "crimes" as boycotting the census. Data protection was to be clearly subordinated to "security".[32]

Some critical analysts on the left were more cynical about the function of the DSBs, suggesting that perhaps the Data Protection Commissioners were in effect merely "trust-building measures" or indeed an "alibi agency" whose job it was to de-politicize data protection.[33] Busch, *et al.* tended toward this view in their influential *The Police in the Federal Republic*:

> Census and the personal identification card show once again that internally expressed reservations from the Data Protection Commissioners do not prevent the executive from continuing to pursue its intended course, even where this collides with data protection. If resistance strengthens among the public, the data protectors then really enter into an irresolvable conflict with the executive: on the one hand, on the basis of their express reservations, they are made at

31 Flaherty, *Protecting Privacy,* 76.

32 Hannes Schwenger notes the incongruity of the position of the police officials who coined this slogan: they found themselves criticizing an established state organ from within a culture that saw the state as an independent good, an end in itself (Schwenger, *Im Jahr des großen Bruders*, 83. See also Busch, *et al.*, pp. 209, 212).

33 Busch, *et al.*, *Die Polizei*, pp. 395, 399.

> least partly responsible for public resistance, on the other hand, they are pressed to give their blessings to the plans now caught in the crossfire, for they had, after all, already attested to the legitimacy in principle of the plans for residency registration, census or personal ID through their participation in preparatory discussions.[34]

In my view the role of the DSBs in the 1983 (and 1987) census controversies is not done justice with the dismissive term "alibi agency". The BDSB, Hans-Peter Bull, did seem to fit this profile. The *Frankfurter Rundschau* reprinted an information sheet prepared by Bull in which he argued for the necessity of the census, but also acknowledged that he had raised some reservations about the correction of the residency registers while the law was being drafted by the previous administration: "I had recommended to the legislators that they dispense with the transfer [of information] to the residency offices, so that the separation of statistics and administrative measures would be maintained. But it seemed more important to the legislator[s] that the *Melderegister* be brought up to date and corrected."[35] Bull here seemed ultimately to accept the notion of a circumscribed *Datenschutz*, and to be satisfied that he had done what he could. Bull's writings indeed turned out to be the strongest endorsement for the census the government was to receive from the ranks of DSBs. In a critical assessment published two days after the Constitutional Court issued its restraining order in April, Bull fleshed out his picture of the role of DSBs. His article was one of only two lengthy pro-census statements on the political significance of the controversy, and thus represents one of the best opportunities to see how the issue of data protection crystalized some of the tensions in West German political culture. Bull, unlike many census supporters with a more preemptively dismissive attitude toward the VoBo movement, recognized that it had some wider significance:

> What has been written and discussed here over the past few weeks in the broadcast media and press but also among neighbors and friends, in family circles and between co-workers regarding the census planned for the end of April reveals more about our political situation than [would] the statistics that could in the best case be gained from the great survey. The discussion betrays much about the attitude toward state and administration, about fears and civil courage, about the appraisal of the efficacy of law and the protections of law – above all, though, about how much citizens trust their politicians and public service, and trust them to do. For the much-discussed legitimation crisis of the state there is scarcely a better example.[36]

34 Busch, *et al.*, *Die Polizei*, pp. 397-398.

35 Bull, "Der Öffentlichkeit wurde zu wenig erklärt", p. 10.

36 Bull, H.-P. 1983b. Der Staat – nur ein datengieriger Riese? *Die Zeit*, April 15, p. 56. All quotes from this article have the same page reference.

Like Zimmermann and others, Bull rejected the notion that hypothetical possibilities for data misuse, or the widespread fear of such misuse, are legitimate grounds for opposition to the census. For Bull, it was enough to claim, for example, that "[a] few remaining and no longer rectifiable deficits [of the census plans] will in all probability not work out to the disadvantage of respondents." His advocacy of trust, and his insistence that scrutiny of the census should revolve around what is actually done with data rather than what might, hypothetically, be done, rested in part on the traditional presumption in favor of the honor and upright character of government officials. But Bull also added a more modern psychological argument to the authoritarian-paternalistic case for trust:

> Certainly: striving for power and ambition are at work everywhere, and the important thing is to hold them within limits. But what is often overlooked even by sociologists and psychologists [is that] the behavior of governors and administrators is determined to a significant degree by other impulses, positive and negative. Politicians wish not only to exercise power but also to be popular (for example in order to be re-elected). Bureaucrats want in general to distribute services to, rather than withhold [them] from, citizens. Many of [our] fellow citizens are conflict-averse, and it is not those who show particular hardness but rather those who can arrange themselves well who are rewarded within the administration.

The tendency not to recognize this benign, humane side of bureaucrats was compensated, in Bull's view, by an opposite but equally one-sided set of expectations about Data Protection officials like himself:

> So long as [DSBs] point up improprieties of governments and administrations they are considered by some to be "security risks" and by others to be courageous and credible. However, as soon as they ascertain that a measure taken by the executive is legal, doubts are expressed about the thoroughness of the examination, the willingness [to engage in] conflict or the independence of the [Data Protection] Commissioners.

Such doubts were fed also by recurring attacks on DSBs from administration officials:

> It is not so quickly forgotten if the Chief Federal Prosecutor or the President of the Federal Criminal Bureau mount heavy attacks against the *Bundesdatenschutzbeauftragter*, and it is of course widely noticed when a Parliamentary State Secretary in the Interior Ministry explains that the Federal Commissioner has "misunderstood" his position.

In general, government officials were nicer and more citizen-friendly than was often assumed. But in the special case of Data Protection Commissioners, the important question was how accommodating or unyielding they were *toward other officials*. And here, despite what Bull had just written regarding the rewards within the state apparatus for "arranging oneself with others", the assumption should be that DSBs have *not* chosen the least confrontational road. Attacks against DSBs from other officials should be taken not as a sign that data protection is being actively hampered but that it is being effectively championed. Bull was arguing, in essence, that Data Protection Commissioners were effective and necessary, but also that the need for them was occasional, not endemic. The thicket of cross-cutting arguments Bull got into is indicative of what might be termed the *liminal* position of Data Protection Commissioners. If DSBs pursued their mandate with energy, they would tend to generate internal disharmony; if they acceded to state plans, they would appear to be neglecting their duties. For Bull, the best way to negotiate this dilemma was to argue that vigorous prosecution of his duties might lead to the approval of government actions, as it led him to approve the census.

Crucially for the census controversy, though, many of Bull's state- and local-level colleagues did not subscribe to his reassuring line of thought. The LDSB of Baden-Württtemberg, Dr Ruth Leuze, and her colleague in Hessen, Dr Spiros Simitis, were quite critical of some aspects of the census law (and would again play high-profile roles in the 1987 controversy). Simitis had helped pioneer data protection legislation in West Germany, and would go on to play a central role in data protection policy at the European level, in a career that led one scholar to describe him as "the major international influence on the conduct of data protection".[37] In an interim report issued in mid-March of 1983, Simitis raised fundamental reservations about the 1982 census law, suggesting, among other things, that perhaps the entire counting method should be altered to a combination of a much more bare-bones census with only a few demographic questions, supplemented by a comprehensive but voluntary sample survey to flesh out the data relevant to planning.[38] He dwelt at length in parts of his report on the dangers posed by the plan to correct the residency registers, raising a very basic but interesting point. If the census data were used to correct the residency registers, Simitis observed, the corrected residency data would not retain traces of that correction. In other words, it would not be possible, once the correction had been carried out, to say which particular bits of information in the register had been updated by the census data and which not … it would all look the same. If the corrected residency registers were then used for administrative purposes (which was, after all the chief reason for their existence), this would lead, again inevitably, to the disadvantaging of some individuals, for example, through discovery of inaccurate reporting of primary or secondary residences. But this would mean, in effect, that the strict distinction between statistical and administrative data had been violated, and thus that the so-

37 Flaherty, *Protecting Privacy*, p. 50.

38 Simitis, S. 1983. Zwischenbericht des hessischen Datenschutzbeauftragten Professor Dr Simitis zur Volkszählung 1983. March 14. Typescript in Archiv Grünes Gedächtnis, Bestand B.II.1, Archivsignatur 3374, p. 3.

called *Nachteilsverbot*, which barred statistical data by law from disadvantaging individuals, had been broken as well.[39] It is easy to forget this peculiar property of information held in files or databases, namely, that, once recorded in whatever form is standard for a given filing system, it has often lost all trace of the various sources from which it might have come. This "cleansing" effect is particularly strong in the case of statistical, and especially electronic, information, but, as I will argue in the Conclusion, it is not inevitable. In view of this and other problems with the 1983 census, but also recognizing that the Federal Government planned to go ahead with it anyway, Simitis suggested that local municipalities voluntarily decline to correct their residency registers, as Köln's statistics chief Manfred Güllner had done (see above).[40]

At the end of March, the federal and state *Datenschutzbeauftragten* came together for a national conference in Bremerhaven, and approved a statement on the census which echoed Simitis on some points and implicitly validated many of the criticisms coming out of the boycott movement. Reprinted in *Frankfurter Rundschau* on April 12th, the statement opens thus:

> I. The conference perceives the growing uneasiness in the population regarding the upcoming census. The *Datenschutzbeauftragten* can understand the worries of the citizenry. The pending constitutional challenges offer an opportunity to examine the constitutionality of the census. The *Volkszählungsgesetz* involves some vaguenesses and weak points.[41]

The statement is largely devoted to clarifying these weak points, explaining all the rights of respondents not made clear in the law or on the census form, and detailing how the census would have to be carried out if it were to meet the requirements of Data Protection. Among the many things some readers may have learned for the first time upon reading this statement were the following: (1) every respondent could and should receive his or her own census form, to avoid a situation in which one individual's information would be revealed to another (as in the collective WGs); (2) enumerators were not to be put to work in or near their own neighborhoods; (3) any potential conflict of duties or interests should disqualify an individual from serving as an enumerator; (4) every citizen should be informed by enumerators of their right to return the census form by mail; (5) any information shared with *Einwohnermeldeämter* to correct the residency registers had to be culled from the actual census forms before being transferred – the census forms themselves were not to be shared; and (6) all respondents should be informed that the prohibition on disadvantage (*Nachteilsverbot*) would not protect them from every possible future

39 Simitis, Zwischenbericht, pp. 7, 12.

40 Simitis, Zwischenbericht, p. 8.

41 Konferenz der Datenschutzbeauftragten des Bundes und der Länder. 1983. "Der Bürger muß auf seine Rechte hingewiesen werden" [reprinted resolution]. *Frankfurter Rundschau*, April 12, n.p.n.

penalty as a result of the correction of the *Melderegister*. All of this was a far cry from a ringing endorsement for the census, and after the Constitutional Court's momentous decision the next day to stop the census with a temporary restraining order, Zimmermann's office was quick to single out the DSBs for criticism.[42] As Jochen Siemens put it in an editorial in the *Frankfurter Rundschau* on March 17th, Zimmermann and other champions of the census had displayed the "sensitivity of a steamroller".[43]

The Federal Constitutional Court's restraining order

The inability of hard-liners to make finer political distinctions ultimately rendered them incapable of perceiving that the VoBo movement was quickly gaining at least one ear of broad swathes of the West German public, and thus of putting anything imaginative or persuasive into the other ear. It also prevented them from taking seriously the misgivings of Data Protection Commissioners, dissident colleagues in local government, and other public authorities, in short, from recognizing that "the state" as a whole could not be marshaled together into a clear and unified position of support for the census. The lack of state unity, though, would become most shockingly obvious even to the most blinkered observer as a result of decisions taken by the Federal Constitutional Court [*Bundesverfassungsgericht* or BVerfG].

Toward the end of one of its updates on the VoBo in early March, the taz mentioned that two Hamburg attorneys had filed a constitutional appeal against the census with the Court.[44] Gisela Wild and Maja Stadler-Euler asked the court to issue a temporary restraining order before the enumeration date of April 27th, so that the court would have ample time to consider the deeper constitutional issues without allowing irreversible damage to individual rights in the meantime. *Die Zeit* would later summarize their reasoning concisely: "Once the data had been collected, a retrospective judgment forbidding the enumeration would have little more than platonic value. The government agencies would have to destroy the census forms, but the knowledge gained from them in the meantime could no longer be taken away."[45] For Wild and Stadler-Euler, as for the census critics cited in Chapter 1, the chief danger of the census lay in what might be done with the data once it was collected, not so much in the scope of the collection itself. But until the primary fears about data handling were addressed, they felt bound to oppose the gathering of the information in the first place. On March 7th, *Der Spiegel* reported that the BVerfG had formally agreed to consider the appeal.[46] Throughout

42 Süskind, M. 1983. Warten auf Orwells Jahr. *Süddeutsche Zeitung*, April 14, p. 3.
43 Siemens, Fast alles falsch gemacht.
44 Anon., Anweisung an Volkszähler.
45 Schueler, H. 1983. Angst vor dem gläsernen Menschen. *Die Zeit*, April 15, p. 2.
46 Anon. 1983. Höchst unredlich. *Der Spiegel*, March 7, p. 120.

March and into April, while the public debate raged, 1,221 other appeals against the census were filed with the Court,[47] and the justices had to decide which out of all of these complaints to have addressed in oral argument. Two appeals were selected, and the main arguments were conducted before the Court on April 12th by Wild, Stadler-Euler, and lawyers representing another plaintiff, the law student Gunther von Mirbach.[48] Testimony was taken from Federal Data Protection Commissioner Hans-Peter Bull, five state-level Data Protection Commissioners (including Simitis and Leuze), two state Senators from Hamburg, the federal Ministerial Director Schiffer, and the head of the *Statistisches Bundesamt* Kroppenstedt. Correspondents for taz, *Der Spiegel* and *Die Zeit* who attended the oral arguments agreed that the plaintiffs appeared to have done their homework and taken the matter more seriously than the relatively low-ranking government officials delegated to appear before the Court.[49]

The core claims put forward by the plaintiffs were that the possibilities of comprehensive statistical registration and automated data processing explored above represented a threat to the constitutionally protected rights to the "free unfolding of the personality", to the preservation of human worth, and to the free expression of opinion, as well as the guarantee of access to legal redress for injuries.[50] In her arguments on the last of these rights, Gisela Wild offered an image that would guide the thinking of the justices as they wrestled with the deeper issues over the coming months. She noted that violation of the principle of statistical secrecy was an *Antragsdelikt*, in other words, it required the injured party to bring a legal complaint against a clearly identified perpetrator. But "it is precisely the treacherousness of these data that they disappear into unfathomable channels and cannot be monitored or controlled. The injured party will almost never have the knowledge of the violation that would place one in the position to file a complaint."[51] The representatives of the government of course disagreed with the whole skeptical approach to the census, citing the arguments summarized earlier. The Data Protection Commissioners, invited as experts, differed on whether the census as a whole, or only the now infamous Paragraph 9, should be suspended. Federal Commissioner Bull and the LDSB from Hessen, Simitis, felt that the *Volkszählung* could go forward, but without the correction of the residency

47 Anon., "Ohne Drohgebärde, ohne Angst", p. 21.

48 Bundesverfassungsgericht 1983a. 1 BvR 209, 269/83, April 13, 1983. *Entscheidungen des Bundesverfassungsgerichts*, v.64. Tübingen: J.C.B. Mohr (Paul Siebeck).

49 Kurz, F. 1983a. Volkszählung erst später? *tageszeitung*, April 13, p. 2; Anon., "Ohne Drohgebärde, ohne Angst", 21-22; Schueler, Angst vor dem gläsernen Menschen; Süskind, Warten auf Orwells Jahr.

50 Kurz, F. 1983b. Verhandlung vor dem Bundesverfassungsgericht. *die tageszeitung*, October 18, p. 4.

51 Quoted in Anon., "Ohne Drohgebärde, ohne Angst", p. 22.

registers,[52] while Leuze, LDSB for Baden-Württemberg, based her objection to the whole census on a detailed critique of the broader flimsiness of the prohibition on disadvantage [*Nachteilsverbot*].[53]

On April 12th, the day of the oral arguments, taz printed the predictions it had solicited from seven prominent jurists, Data Protection Commissioners, information scientists and parliamentarians from across the entire political spectrum as to the likely outcome of the appeals.[54] There was no consensus, and only two of the experts (Prof. Steinmüller and Prof. Eggart Schwan, a scholar of governmental and administrative law at the Free University of Berlin) correctly foresaw the outcome. The very next day, the Federal Constitutional Court made history by issuing the temporary restraining order, halting the census in its tracks.[55] The justices had unanimously agreed to block the execution of the controversial Paragraph 9, which allowed for the use of census data to correct the *Melderegister*, and had voted 5 to 3 in favor of stopping the entire census. The crux of their reasoning was fairly straightforward:

> The constitutional appeals are neither inadmissible nor obviously unfounded. In the proceedings on the main issue fundamental questions will be raised regarding the protection of the rights of the individual, as a personality embedded in and related to community, under the special conditions of the [new] possibilities of statistics and automatic data processing [that have arisen] since the Micro-census decision of 1969, [questions] which require a thorough examination.[56]

Stopping only the correction of the residency registers foreseen in Paragraph 9 would not be adequate because personal information would already have been collected and stored. A majority on the Court followed the reasoning of Wild and Stadler-Euler:

> The question of whether these measures [gathering and storing the data] lead to an injury to constitutional rights under conditions of automatic data processing cannot be answered without thorough examination. So long as an injury to basic rights cannot be ruled out, even an injury committed only once and in sincere belief in the constitutionality of the measures must be seen as a serious detriment to the general good.[57]

---

52 Kurz, Volkszählung erst später?

53 Anon., "Ohne Drohgebärde, ohne Angst", p. 22; Leuze, R. 1983. "Auch das Nachteilsverbot schützt den Burger nicht" [reprinted testimony before the *Bundesverfassungsgericht*]. *Frankfurter Rundschau* April 26, n.p.n.

54 Fezer, G. 1983. Verfassungstoto. *die tageszeitung*, April 12, p. 2.

55 Bundesverfassungsgericht 1983a. The judgment was reprinted *verbatim* in *Die Welt*, April 14, 1983, and in *Dokument und Analyse*, May 1983.

56 Bundesverfassungsgericht 1983a, p. 70.

57 Bundesverfassungsgericht 1983a, pp. 70-71.

The Constitutional Court's restraining order was front-page news (*Der Spiegel's* cover story: "Bonn counted out"; *taz's* large-type caption to a photo of the justices: "Spoil-sports"; *Die Zeit*: "Red Light from Karlsruhe").[58] *Der Spiegel* noted that the Court's action represented the first time in West German history that "the third power stopped a law unanimously passed by the parliament – an un-dreamt-of procedure."[59] The distinctive focus of the analysis in *Der Spiegel* was Ernst Benda, the Chief Justice of the First Senate (the Constitutional Court in West Germany was – and in united Germany still is – made up of two groups of justices or "Senates", which share the case-load). The Hamburg weekly speculated that Benda had been the moving force behind the restraining order, noting that the high-profile CDU man had recently taken public positions stressing the responsibility of the Constitutional Court to protect human rights in an active way. Anticipating the political fallout, *Der Spiegel* suggested that Benda's future chances at the prestigious position of Federal President, or at least Mayor of West Berlin, were reduced to near zero by the First Senate's independent stance on the census.[60] Benda, in other words, appeared to have abandoned the statist commitments which for the conservative parties still served as a basic qualification for political leadership.

Without the same focus on individual justices, *Die Zeit* also framed the restraining order in terms of implicit expectations that the Court would defer to the government:

> The Federal Constitutional Court, criticized often and sometimes rightly in recent years for being all too pious toward the state [*staatsfromm*], has recalled its basic principles in the matter of the census: "It would not be possible to reconcile with the worth of the human being [a situation in which] the state could claim the right to force the individual [to submit to] the registration and cataloguing of his or her entire personality, even in the anonymity of a statistical survey, and thus to deal with the person like a thing available for any sort of inventory."[61]

The quotation was taken from the 1969 "Micro-census decision", and was directly followed in that earlier Constitutional Court judgment by another passage that would serve as a reference point for the plaintiffs again in oral arguments on the main census case in October of 1983:

> Such an intrusion into the realm of the personality through a comprehensive look into the personal relations of its citizens is prohibited to the state also because, for the free and responsible unfolding of the personality, an "interior

58 See title pages of *Der Spiegel*, April 18, 1983; *die tageszeitung*, April 14, 1983; *Die Zeit*, April 15, 1983. Karlsruhe is the southern German city in which the BVerfG was located, following a general policy of geographical de-centralization of government agencies.

59 Anon., "Ohne Drohgebärde, ohne Angst", p. 17.

60 Anon., "Ohne Drohgebärde, ohne Angst", pp. 18-19.

61 Anon. 1983. Rotes Licht aus Karlsruhe. *Die Zeit*, April 15, p. 1.

> space" must remain for the individual, in which one "possesses oneself" and "into which one can withdraw, to which the environment has no access, in which one is left in peace and enjoys a right to solitude".[62]

The exact extent of this "intimate sphere" or "space", the circumstances in which the state might enter it, and the question of whether its boundaries belong to it or to the environment would all remain at the center of the constitutional and political controversies over the census in 1987. Because the state's right to gather personal information was often understood legally in terms of the right to enter private space, the census controversies were inextricably bound up with different interpretations of how territorial sovereignty could be squared with "private space". One of the plaintiffs' arguments in testimony on the main census case in October of 1983 was that demanding personal information was equivalent to state agents forcibly entering private space, an intrusion against which West Germans were explicitly protected in the Basic Law.

In response to the restraining order, Interior Minister Zimmermann suddenly found himself able to take the political distance from the census law with which his *Spiegel* interviewers had tried in vain to tempt him three weeks earlier: "once more the old Schmidt administration has failed with a law before the Federal Constitutional Court."[63] But this rather transparent *volte face* on the failure could not mask the chastened surprise in Bonn. Diether Stolze, speaker for the Kohl government, admitted that "absolutely nobody in the Chancellor's Office took [the appeal] seriously", and Zimmermann's press officer Wighard Härdtl found it "not entirely understandable" that the justices would suddenly adopt "fringe reservations" regarding the census.[64] The *Frankfurter Allgemeine Zeitung* could only protest that "the Court let itself be misused."[65] The mood among census opponents was a mix of elation, relief, disorientation and disappointment. The reasons for disappointment were not difficult to grasp. Although the VoBo movement had indeed come to incorporate at least a sizable minority of the West German population, the organizational and motivational force behind many of the local Inis had remained the more experienced activists. Although there were of course many exceptions, these tended to be the people for whom blocking the census was no more than one step toward addressing the much larger threat posed by the security state. The activists were worried that mainstream citizens would quickly lose interest in this larger picture and break off their brief embrace of a common cause with their more radical fellow citizens. Reactions from VoBo Inis give a flavor of the concerns at work here:

---

62 Bundesverfassungsgericht 1969. 1 BvL 19/63. July 16. *Entscheidungen des Bundesverfassungsgerichts*, v.27. Tübingen: J.C.B. Mohr (Paul Siebeck), p. 7.

63 Quoted in Nitschke, E. 1983b. Der politische Streit ging immer nur ums Geld. *Die Welt*, April 14, p. 86.

64 Quoted in Anon., "Ohne Drohgebärde, ohne Angst", p. 18.

65 Quoted in, Anon., "Ohne Drohgebärde, ohne Angst", p. 17.

Berlin Info-Bureau:

Here dampened satisfaction holds sway, a bit of cluelessness. The thing has not disappeared. It is postponed, and after a little cosmetic work it will come forward again. And if that takes months, it will be difficult to maintain resistance at this level.

Hamburg Info-Bureau:

The mood is that it was a clever move on the part of the state, that they extended their antennae and realized that it would be a belly-landing. We want to work now more strongly against the machine-readable personal ID that is supposed to come in 1984. We will also suggest that the Hamburg VoBo Inis give themselves another name, in order outwardly to demonstrate [the shift in focus]. [We] found committees that address themselves more to data-fication [*Verdatung*] in general … The whole feeling of being directly affected [*die ganze Betroffenheit*] is now gone, and that will be the problem. And this feeling of direct affect has always been hard to produce on the other themes. That is the task now.[66]

As taz reported the next day, despite the unexpected news, roughly 100 people showed up for the regular Wednesday evening VoBo Ini meeting in West Berlin's Kreuzberg neighborhood. According to one activist, significant numbers seemed prepared to continue their engagement with the wider issue of the surveillance state. But the prospects for maintaining broad interest had lost their main flesh-and-blood focus: the anxiously anticipated enumerator appearing at the door.[67] The key question for many West Germans had been "What do I do when the enumerator comes?" Now that no bodily representative of the state would be appearing at the contested boundary between public and private space, the anticipated *Betroffenheit*, the feeling of being directly impacted, was free to fade back into abstraction and perhaps dissolve altogether. Another source of concern in many of the VoBo Inis was that the restraining order appeared to remove the main locus of struggle around the census from the broad, democratic arena of extra-parliamentary politics: "The initiatives take it as undemocratic that after broad discussions at public events, in union circles, in the media and in parliament, the decision on the census is now supposed to be made by a handful of judges". "We would rather have struggled on", is the word [among the Inis], and "Put off is not put to rest!" [*aufgeschoben ist nicht aufgehoben!*]"[68]

66 Anon. 1983. "Die ganz direkte Betroffenheit ist erst mal weg". *die tageszeitung*, April 14, p. 2.

67 Gaserow, V. 1983. Was tun wenn der Zähler kommt. *die tageszeitung*, April 15, p. 5.

68 Anon. 1983. Schwerpunkt: Informationsverarbeitung. *die tageszeitung*, April 19, p. 4.

These concerns raise the question of the degree to which the appeals to the Constitutional Court should be seen as part of or separate from the broad extra-parliamentary movement. While the attorneys Gisela Wild and Maja Stadler-Euler became heroines overnight for some in the movement, they did not themselves identify with it in any straightforward way. In fact, Wild characterized the temporary restraining order as an alternative to the collision course the movement was on with the government:

> It is not only chaotists and opponents of the [whole] system who reject this law, as some politicians feel free to say dismissively, it is citizens who fear that the push toward state omniscience will rob people of their private sphere; it is citizens who fear one day [ending up] as numbers ruled by automatic machines and administered by anonymous powers, because their data are networked in mysterious channels. This movement has assumed a scale that has it heading for confrontation. The Federal Government makes a show of state power and [invokes] reason-of-state. The citizens search out all possible ways to refuse, be it legally through [exploiting] weak points in the census form, or illegally through false responses or mass boycott. The temporary restraining order – and given the stage things have reached, only [this order] – can finally create the calm in which the *Volkszählungsgesetz* can be discussed and considered without hysteria and without threatening gestures.[69]

Wild was walking a precarious line here, rhetorically painting the VoBo movement as a tendentially dangerous force and thereby distancing the constitutional appeals from it, in order to make the appeals seem like the "sane" path. But in doing so, she played into the political worldview of many conservatives, who equated civil disobedience with subversion. The question of whether the VoBo movement had influenced the Constitutional Court's decision was a loaded one, and highlighted once again the fact that the whole census boycott phenomenon of the 1980s was never far from the root issues of postwar West German political culture. Again, a core zone of contention since the 1960s had been the legitimacy of extra-parliamentary (or more generally, extra-establishment) political activity, especially when directed against state policy. To those with statist leanings, a refusal to grant extra-parliamentary activism full legitimacy went hand-in-hand with a refusal to acknowledge that such activism could have any influence upon the workings of "official" democratic institutions. The Court did not put the connection in direct and explicit terms in justifying the restraining order, but its final decision on the census in December of 1983 would in fact confirm a link that was undeniable to many observers. *Der Spiegel* put it concisely: "And if the decision from Karlsruhe was not a concession to the protest on the street, but rather the legally appropriate reaction to two proper constitutional appeals of engaged attorneys, it is nevertheless

69 Quoted in Anon., "Ohne Drohgebärde, ohne Angst", pp. 18-19.

inexplicable without the climate of anxieties and worries that has come over the *Bundesrepublik* with the electronic age."[70]

The census judgment of December 1983

Discussion of the census in the media died off fairly quickly after the mid-April restraining order was issued. A front-page story in taz in mid-May noted with alarm that barely a month after the order, the *Bundestag* passed a law authorizing a new, sample survey or "micro-census", which would ask far more detailed questions than the census, and to which response would be mandatory for that sample of the population randomly selected to receive it.[71] But other papers did not feature the story, and no broad upsurge of protest comparable to the VoBo movement was ignited. The issuance of the restraining order was of course not the end of the story in 1983. The main case was still to be argued and decided later in the year, with the fate of the census hanging in the balance. The December 1983 decision would also bring a form of order to all the strands of argumentation that had been tangled up in the public discussions of the Spring, and resolve the federal state's position in important ways. But the restraining order certainly marked the ambivalent climax of the VoBo movement. After April 13th, the whole issue was transferred from the politically "wild" arena of extraparliamentary activity to the more regulated and respectable channels of judicial consideration. To that extent at least, defenders of the cherished values of "calm and order" [*Ruhe und Ordnung*] could breathe a sigh of relief. Yet the restraining order itself was a remarkable, and for many, profoundly unsettling occurrence. As *Der Spiegel* had pointed out, never before had the Constitutional Court put the brakes on a law that passed with the consent of all sitting parties. What did all of this mean?

Testimony took place over three days in late October, and press coverage as well as public statements of the protagonists ran as might have been expected. The 70-page December decision distilled by the justices out of the mass of testimony and documentation encompassed a wealth of insight into the whole census controversy, and finally laid out the various tacks taken by the plaintiffs and the state in their written and oral arguments.[72] Particularly the arguments of the government found a much more thorough presentation than in the national press. After a review of the relevant legislation and a parliamentary history of the 1982 law, the justices

70 Anon., "Ohne Drohgebärde, ohne Angst", p. 18.

71 Anon. 1983. Neuer Personalausweis. Run auf die Datenschützer? *die tageszeitung*, May 13, p. 1.

72 Bundesverfassungsgericht 1983b. 1 BvR 209, 269, 362, 420, 440, 484/83. December 15, 1983, *Entscheidungen des Bundesverfassungsgerichts*, v. 65. Tübingen: J.C.B. Mohr (Paul Siebeck). The passages cited in the analysis to follow are taken, in order, from pages 23, 31-32, 1, 1-2, 3-4, 39-40, 40, 41, 42-43, 44, 44-46, 47, 48, 49, 50, 57-61, and 61-69.

turned to a careful, extended paraphrase of the catalogue of arguments presented both by the plaintiffs and by the government. The former codify and systematize many of the lines of analysis presented in Chapter 1 above, adding a few additional legal and constitutional principles to the mix. The arguments of the government, especially since they had never been presented to the public in anything like this level of detail, bear summarizing here:

1. As modern societies grow ever more complicated, the need for comprehensive statistics was only growing more acute. And it was impossible to specify beforehand the range of exact uses to which statistics may be put once they have been gathered.
2. The 1970 census involved more questions than were to be asked in 1983, and also included a provision for using the results to correct the residency registers.
3. The guarantee of confidentiality in the census law was adequately protected by the oversight of Data Protection Commissioners and the Interior Minister.
4. Because the "personality" protected by constitutional rights was recognized in the Basic Law as always "embedded in and related to community" [*gemeinschaftsgebundene und gemeinschaftsbezogene*], it necessarily has an immanent social element, and it would thus be unrealistic to speak of a "fundamentally comprehensive self-determination of the individual".
5. The articles of the Basic Law defining the state as a "social state" responsible for the well being of the people imply a right to gather statistics.
6. Previous decisions of the Constitutional Court on statistical and privacy matters had not employed a standard of absolute anonymity of statistical data.
7. The legislature has decision-making prerogatives that cannot be too narrowly circumscribed by the courts. Within this room for maneuver, the 1982 census law met the proportionality principle as a reasonable way to address the lack of up-to-date information on the population.
8. The 1983 census would reach into the private sphere but not into the constitutionally inviolate "intimate sphere". No comprehensive "personality profiles" would be constructed with the data, especially since the reduced catalogue of questions asked (in comparison with the 1970 census) was generated precisely by eliminating questions touching the intimate sphere.
9. The offices responsible for planning, organizing and carrying out the census should be trusted to do their job properly, not suspected from the beginning of nefarious intent.
10. The democratic process that led to the passage of the 1982 census law involved sufficient opportunity for criticism and popular input. The fact that some citizens now opposed the census should not be a reason to halt it.
11. The census was preferable to gathering data from various other sources, because in order to do the latter, it would be necessary to establish the unique personal identification number for each citizen that had so alarmed census critics.

12. Sample surveys were not an adequate substitute for a census. For one thing, it would not matter to respondents whether they were being asked to answer a census vs. a sample survey. Sample surveys also do not provide the needed exactness and comprehensiveness of results. A voluntary survey would be methodologically unacceptable, and a combination of full enumeration and sample survey would be impracticable because the government lacked a unified underlying address file.
13. The Basic Law does not insist on a strict link between the stated purpose and the actual use of statistical data. Statistical data must be available for somewhat flexible patterns of use if they are to be an effective support for government policy and planning.
14. The sharing of data between agencies has a well-established precedent in the principle of "bureaucratic assistance" and "legal assistance" [*Amts- und Rechtshilfe*] recognized in earlier Constitutional Court decisions.
15. Opinion surveys had shown that most recipients of state assistance would rather see bureaucracies share information about them than be faced with more frequent requests for data from different agencies. Since it could even be argued that too-frequent requests for information are an injury to individuals, legislators had decided, when they formulated the Data Protection Law of 1977, against an absolute prohibition on using data only for their original purpose.
16. The federal statute governing statistics [BStatG] already incorporated strong and explicit safeguards against excessive data sharing.
17. There was ample legal justification in existing case law for the use of census data to correct the residency registers, and for the sharing of data with the other categories of agencies mentioned in Paragraph 9 of the 1982 law.
18. The mandatory character of response to the census did not injure basic rights. "Duties to respond that are ordered by the legislator, after weighing the relevance to the affected population, for the fulfillment of a justified state requirement for information, are an unobjectionable part of the constitutional order in the sense of Article 2, section 1 of the Basic Law." Only a duty to respond to a survey with information that would itself be the basis for punishment would be inadmissible. The protection against self-incrimination was in any case not absolute.
19. The 1982 census law fulfilled the essentiality requirement [*Wesentlichkeitsgebot*] because it was specific enough about how the law was to be carried out without attempting to preempt all administrative determinations about the details.
20. The checking of census responses for plausibility was crucially necessary to avoid expensive and time-consuming re-checking. Partly because this could be done most efficiently at the time of response, an enumerator-based census would be more accurate than one relying primarily on mail-in response. Thus also there was no adequate "milder" way of achieving the goals of the census.

The First Senate handed down its decision on December 15th, 1983. In the very first paragraph of the introductory overview, the justices, implicitly following testimony from Sebastian Cobler, posited a constitutional "right of informational self-determination" [*Recht auf informationelle Selbstbestimmung* or RISB], a right of individuals "themselves to make determinations about the surrender and use of [their] personal data". Their judgment on the census as a whole was anything but a wholesale condemnation, yet the need to respect this newly-formulated right of informational self-determination raised serious difficulties for the government:

> The program of data gathering of the 1983 *Volkszählungsgesetz* … does not lead to a registration and cataloguing of the personality that is irreconcilable with the worth of the human being; it also meets the conditions of clarity of norms and of proportionality. Nevertheless, [in order to] ensure the right of informational self-determination, it requires supplementary procedural [*verfahrensrechtliche*] precautions for the carrying out and the organization of the data collection … The … transfer rules foreseen in ¶ 9, sections 1 to 3 (among others, the correction of the residency registers) violate the general rights of personality.

The Court agreed that in these two ways, a general lack of procedural specificity and the specific section allowing the correction of the *Melderegister*, the constitutional rights of the plaintiffs were in fact injured by the census law. But it rejected all other claims of injury. Lest any doubt might have remained that the public controversy and the VoBo movement had entered the deliberations of the justices, a paragraph introducing the First Senate's reasoning would have dispelled them:

> The data gathering exercise ordered by this law has provoked uneasiness also in those parts of the population who as loyal state citizens respect the right and the duty of the state to generate the information necessary for rational and planned state action. This might be explained in part by the fact that there was widespread ignorance of the scope and purpose of the survey, and that the necessity of reliable enlightenment of those obliged to respond was not recognized in a timely manner, although the general [level of] consciousness has changed considerably in connection with the development of automated data processing since the micro-census surveys in the years 1956-1962. The possibilities of modern data processing are largely only transparent any longer to specialists, and can provoke fear of an uncontrollable registration of the personality even if the legislator only requests such responses as are necessary and not unreasonable. It may also have contributed to uneasiness, lastly, that experts, too, expressed the conviction that the census law of 1983, despite unanimous passage in the legislative bodies, did not sufficiently fulfill constitutional requirements, already in the instructions on the gathering of data, and above all in the provisions regarding its evaluation.

Whatever else can be drawn from this passage, the justices openly admitted that without the uneasiness crystallized in the VoBo movement, there would have been no pressing need to address the census legislation. But again, the overall message was ambiguous. The mild scolding of the government for its tardy attempts at justifying the census law to the public implies that the controversy was a matter of inadequate education of the public. But the First Senate also acknowledged that the dangers of automated data processing were complicated enough to challenge the understanding even of experts. Thus, in effect, the public could be excused for the fears arising from its ignorance, and these fears had to be taken seriously whether or not they ultimately prove to be grounded. In implicitly granting both that expert opinion could legitimately challenge state policies, and that even public opinion based on ignorance rather than knowledge could remain a valid touchstone and impetus for state action, the justices were suggesting a definition of democracy distinctly more expansive than that of statist conservatives. On the other hand, by ascribing opposition to the census to ignorance rather than to fully rational alternative understandings of state power, the justices refused to abandon fully the presumption that state institutions are the privileged seat of legitimate democratic processes.

It is not necessary to give an exhaustive account of how the justices decided on all the separate arguments for and against the census presented above. But a selection of the most interesting elements of their decision will give a flavor for how they attempted to negotiate a compromise position. First, they confirmed federal competency to gather all the data specified in the 1982 census law. They also noted that there was established precedent for allowing one level of government to gather information useful to another level: especially as the amount of information needed to govern had increased, there would inevitably be extensive overlap between the information resources needed at different levels. On the question of whether the request for census information was an invasion of private space, the justices answered no: "Living space in the sense of Article 13 of the Basic Law is only the spatial private sphere ... The basic right [specified in Art. 13] stipulates for the public authority a fundamental prohibition on entry into the living space or on lingering there against the will of the residents. This includes something like the installation of listening devices and their use in the living space, but not the gathering and collection of responses that can be undertaken without entry or lingering in the living space." If there was a state right to information about life in private space (what I have termed "epistemic sovereignty") but no state right to enter that space, the logical consequence is a right to require residents to report the needed information. To the plaintiffs' argument that they were protected against mandatory response to the census by the "negative freedom of opinion", the right not to express oneself that is part of the freedom of expression enshrined in Article 5 of the Basic Law, the justices counterposed a strict distinction between "opinion" [*Meinung*] and "fact" [*Tatsache*]: "Constitutive for the determination of what is included as expression of an 'opinion' in the protection of the basic right is the element of taking a position, of opining [*des Dafürhaltens*], of believing [*des Meinens*], in the framework of an intellectual encounter; it is not a matter of the value, the correctness, the reasonableness of the expression. The reporting of a fact is in the strictest sense not the expression of an opinion because it is lacking this element."

Having established the state's basic epistemic sovereignty, however, the justices proceeded to spell out the grounds for their notion of "informational self-determination". Existing statutes and case law support the inference of a right of informational self-determination out of the general constitutional protection of the personality. The need to concretize this new right was made more pressing by the new conditions of electronic technology that allowed unlimited storage and replication of information, its instantaneous transmission over great distances, and extremely rapid automated processing. All of this made possible the construction of a general "image of the personality" [*Persönlichkeitsbild*] beyond the knowledge and control of the affected individual. This in turn held the potential to lead to "psychological pressure" to conform. The mechanisms of this situation were spelled out in detail by the justices:

> Individual self-determination assumes – also under conditions of modern information processing technology – that the individual retains freedom of decision over actions to be taken or not to be taken, including the possibility also in fact to act according to such decision[s]. Whoever cannot with sufficient certainty oversee which information regarding them is known in specific areas of their social environment, and whoever is not able to some extent to estimate the knowledge of possible communication partners, can be essentially limited in their freedom to plan or decide on the basis of their own self-determination. A social and legal order in which citizens could no longer be certain who knows what about them when and on which occasions would not be compatible with the right of informational self-determination. Whoever is unsure whether anomalous or deviant behavior is at all times noted and stored over the long term, used or given to others, will attempt not to [make themselves] conspicuous by such behavior. Whoever can assume, for example, that participation in a meeting or a citizens' initiative will be officially registered and that as a result they could face risks will, possibly, forego the exercise of their basic rights [to assembly and expression]. This would restrict not only the chances for unfolding of the individual personality but also the general welfare, because self-determination is an elementary functional condition [of possibility] for a free democratic order based on citizens' ability to act and to cooperate. Out of all of this follows: the free unfolding of the personality requires under modern conditions of data processing the protection of the individual against unlimited collection, storage, use and sharing of his or her personal data.

Having so clearly laid out the grounds for the RISB, the justices then tacked back again, immediately qualifying it. Accepting the government's argument about the inherently social character of the constitutionally protected personality, they noted that "[i]nformation, even as far as it is personal, represents an image of social reality that cannot be ascribed exclusively to the affected [individual]." They thus affirmed that the individual "must reckon with limitations on the right of informational self-determination in the over-ruling general interest." Nevertheless, the new right required that every systematic limitation on self-determination be specified as explicitly as possible in law compatible with constitutional principles. Further, the challenges to the 1983 census were not the occasion for an exhaustive specification of the RISB. Indeed, such a specification would not be possible, according to the justices, because potential violations of this right were not associated only with certain kinds of data. There was, as the plaintiffs argued, no longer any such thing as inherently "meaningless" or "insignificant" personal data. Rather, any kind of information could potentially be dangerous depending on the specific context of its use. In the case of data the state might be interested in for its personal content, this made the need for careful prescription more urgent than previously recognized, and argued in favor of a general prohibition on storage for indeterminate periods of personal data not linked to specific state purposes. Also, the vigilance of independent Data Protection Commissioners was absolutely necessary.

By contrast, the justices argued, personal data gathered for *statistical* goals, that is, data which is personally referenced only for organizational purposes, and in which the government is interested chiefly for its *non-personal* or aggregate content, could not be subject to the same strict limitations. In particular, the ban on goal-independent storage of personal information could not apply in an absolute way to the census results, because these constituted a "secure data basis for further statistical researches and for the political planning process". The West German state was bound by the Basic Law to act for the general good. "If economic and social development is not to be accepted as unalterable fate but rather is supposed to be understood as a permanent task, it requires comprehensive, continuous and progressively updated information about economic, ecological and social relations." This biopolitical duty had to be acknowledged, the Court said, but here, too, the RISB demanded careful consideration of any perceived need to personalize data, so that, as the Court put it, the individual did not become a "mere information-object". The presumption should always be in favor of anonymized data, whether the statistics concern inhabitants of public institutions or workforce totals. The justices ordered a reconsideration of the1983 census law in so far as it asked for some data in personalized form which could serve state purposes just as well were it anonymous. And for those data that had to be personal, they ordered the formulation of special provisions to ensure the earliest possible erasure of identifying references (such as in address lists for enumerators) once these had fulfilled their organizational function. Finally, the justices insisted also on special rules to ensure the effective compartmentalization of databases holding personal information.

One of the most interesting passages in the decision openly acknowledged that trust on the part of citizens should be seen as a condition of possibility for the success of official statistics. Compartmentalization of data, anonymization, confidentiality and timely destruction of personally-referenced information all had to be both effectively carried out and made transparent to citizens if the data are to be reliable and accurate:

> Only under these preconditions can and may it be expected from citizens that they give the mandatory responses required of them … For the functionality of official statistics the highest possible degree of exactness and truth content of the collected data is needed. This goal can only be reached if the necessary trust can be generated, on the part of citizens obliged [to give information], in the compartmentalization of their personal statistical data, [a trust] without which it is not possible to produce a willingness to give truthful responses.

The First Senate came very close here to acknowledging a stronger form of "informational citizenship", an essentially participatory, active dimension to the seemingly a-political and passive experience of being counted. At the very least, the notion of "mandatory response" was complicated by the idea that mandatory responses to state surveys could only legitimately be expected if the state could successfully win the trust of citizens. Among other things, this suggested that epistemic sovereignty is qualified not only by the epistemic inviolability of the "intimate sphere" but also by the physical inviolability of private space. The state had a right to know some of what was happening in private spaces, but was forced to rely upon citizens to communicate this knowledge rather than gain it directly by entering private space. In other words, the knowledge-transaction at the doorway had come to be recognized implicitly as a reciprocal, *political* matter.

A subsequent section of the 71-page Constitutional Court decision was devoted to concrete guidelines for the government on how to render the census law compatible with the RISB. While not attempting to specify every detail, the First Senate suggested having enumerators personally deliver census forms in order to ensure they had been received, but then have the return of the forms occur entirely by mail. Further, the justices ordered the government in revising the census to stipulate (1) clear explanations to residents that each individual is entitled to be given his or her own form, and need not be registered as part of a household; (2) the holding of identifying information (name, address, form identification number and enumerator list number) separate from the substantive responses and the destruction of this information at the earliest possible moment; (3) a requirement that Data Protection Commissioners or their representatives exercise careful supervision of the processing of census data in the statistical agencies; (4) the formulation of rules preventing anyone from being obliged to act as an enumerator for whom a conflict of interest or duties might arise, and prohibiting enumerators from working in or near the areas where they live; and (5) careful inspection of the content of the census form to ensure its conformity to the census law. The final major section explained why the justices agreed that the correction of the residency registers was unconstitutional, and why other inter-agency data sharing as foreseen in the 1982 law also injured the RISB.

The decision of December 1983 would cast a long shadow, resurfacing repeatedly in West German (and then German) debates over surveillance and social control right up to the present day. The reactions at the time are pregnant with insights into West German political culture, and into the issues of epistemic sovereignty and informational citizenship through which I have been interpreting the spatial politics of the census. It is to these contemporary reactions that we now turn.

Public reactions to the census decision

On December 16th, 1983, the lead article in taz opened satirically under the headline "Put-down for the data collectors":

> It will no longer be possible to plan streets, in the area of residential building there will be "catastrophic effects", no politicians will any longer be able to rule according to the needs of their subjects, it will no longer be possible to "make state" [*Staat zu machen*] – the *Bundesrepublik* will be ungovernable for the unforeseeable future [*für unabsehbare Zeit*].[73]

The article quoted delighted reactions to the First Senate's decision from LDSB Ruth Leuze, attorney Sebastian Cobler and information theorist Wilhelm Steinmüller, and couched the decision as a clear victory for census opponents. In addition to aspects of the decision reviewed above, the justices' affirmation of the need for a stronger "informational division of powers" between local and higher-level government data jurisdictions, and between the databases of different agencies at every level, was noted approvingly.[74] *Der Spiegel* styled the decision a "heavy setback" for the administration, and mocked the attempt to claim the decision as a victory for the state: "Zimmermann's state secretary Horst Waffenschmidt and speakers for the CDU/CSU fraction tried to present what was an obvious matter of course in the decision, namely that the state may count its citizens, as a success."[75] Obvious it may have seemed before the controversy, but, as we have seen, the plaintiffs mounted a challenge to this basic dimension of sovereignty, and the justices spun out an interesting interpretation of the matter in confronting the challenge head-on. The *Spiegel* article noted, among other things, that the decision effectively expanded the purview of data protection law, which had hitherto governed only the sharing of information, to cover also the collection and the use of data.[76] Other major newspapers that had been more neutral or pro-census in their earlier coverage acknowledged more or less grudgingly that the

73 Anon. 1983. Abfuhr für die Datensammler. *die tageszeitung*, December 16, p. 1.
74 Anon., Abfuhr für die Datensammler, p. 3.
75 Anon. 1983. Schwere Schlappe. *Der Spiegel*, December 19, p. 19.
76 Anon., Schwere Schlappe, p. 21.

state had indeed suffered a setback. Erhard Becker, writing in the *Handelsblatt*, distinguished between a decision against the state as such and the First Senate's decision against overweening bureaucracy, and conceded that the Court had proven a more helpful constitutional organ than the other two powers: "The enthroned Constitutional Justices isolated in Karlruhe, it appears, have had their ear closer to the heart of the people and of the uneasy loyal citizens than have their elected representatives and the executive from which the law stemmed."[77] The *Frankfurter Allgemeine Zeitung*, self-appointed champion of the census throughout 1983, spun the decision as a confirmation of the right to take a census, but confined its report largely to a fairly balanced detailed summary of the decision. The editors could not resist a parting backhanded shot at the VoBo movement, noting that the judicial process in Karlsruhe had gone on "without any attempts at disruption".[78]

All major political parties other than the CDU/CSU reacted positively to the decision, though of course with different emphases. The SPD greeted the decision as a confirmation of its dual belief in the necessity of censuses and in the inviolability of human rights. The FDP, though the junior partner in coalition with the Christian Democrats, saw the judgment as a chance to remind voters of its distinctive profile as champion of personal liberty, and thus welcomed it as one of the most important constitutional decisions in recent years. The Greens, not unexpectedly, greeted it as an affirmation of their critique of the administration's "nearly boundless data collection fever [*Datensammelwut*]".[79] But the Greens were not unanimous in their celebration. On December 19th, the taz front page headline declared, "New Boycott Necessary", and the article quoted Green leaders criticizing the Constitutional Court for not going far enough in putting the brakes on the general expansion of surveillance technologies.[80] Expecting the government to be ready with a revamped census again in 1985, activists cautioned against calling for a boycott too early. But they insisted on the necessity of keeping alive the concerns that fuelled the 1983 VoBo movement, and of taking the lesson to heart that only a timely mobilization can avert the need to wage belated and defensive battles against dangerous laws.

LDSB Ruth Leuze's satisfaction with the decision was understandable in view of her apparent success in persuading the justices of the dangers of data sharing. But the larger community of data protection officials and activists did not unanimously share her enthusiasm. A detailed assessment of the decision published in January 1984 in the journal of the German Association for Data Protection criticized the abstractness of the "right of informational self-determination".[81] The (unidentified)

77 Becker, E. 1983. Gegen die Bürokratie. *Handelsblatt*, December 16, n.p.n.

78 Anon. 1983. Volkszählungen generell zulässig. Schutz gegen unbegrenzte Erhebungen. *Frankfurter Allgemeine Zeitung*, December 16, n.p.n.

79 Anon. 1983. Alle zufrieden? *die tageszeitung*, December 16, p. 3.

80 Anon. 1983. Neuer Boykott nötig. *die tageszeitung*, December 19, p. 2.

81 Anon. 1984. [No title]. *Datenschutz Nachrichten*, No. 1/2 (n.d.), pp. 9-11. afas 5.IV.1.3:1.

author noted that the RISB was formulated in the December decision as an absolute right but immediately qualified with reference to state needs that cannot be specified in advance. Thus, it is claimed, the only real content of this new right was comprised of qualifications to it. The lack of firmer guidance on what kind of data collection, sharing and processing might be off-limits in the future left the initiative in the hands of states and other large organizations that could be expected to continue finding new ways to exploit advancing electronic technology. The article suggested further that the BVerfG decision constituted a solution to a political problem faced by the newly installed CDU/CSU administration. The Kohl government could not back down from the census without losing credibility at the very beginning of its term, but if the enumeration had actually taken place, and had proven inaccurate due to widespread boycott, this, too, would have been a severe blow. By avoiding the latter scenario while affirming the government's right to count the population, and at the same time appearing to demonstrate that constitutionally mandated checks and balances actually worked, the Court had restored legitimacy to the state. But, according to the article, all of this did not touch on the fundamental political implications of electronic data processing, and thus did not promise any effective counter-trend to the rapid erosion of individual control over personal information.

Caught off-guard, conservative pundits and government officials had little to offer in the way of extended analysis of the whole affair. No comprehensive retrospective summaries appeared from this quarter after the December decision, but an article appearing in the *Frankfurter Allgemeine Zeitung* shortly before the October oral arguments bears a closer reading. Penned by Prof. Dr Max Wingen, at the time President of the *Statistische Landesamt* of Baden-Württemberg, the piece was intended to lay out "some social-psychological findings that extend far beyond the narrow problem-horizon of the census."[82] Wingen's basic premise was that

> the discussion in the Spring of this year and the modes of behavior that came to light in connection with it can be understood as a phenomenon which – if one [looks] beyond the hard core of refusers – carries clearly recognizable features of a collective psychosis, bearing in mind [also] the conjecture already put forward by Sigmund Freud that entire societies as well as individuals can be neurotically charged [*aufgeladen*].

Wingen saw a darker side to the fact that the VoBo movement was the product of a deliberate political campaign built on the uniquely favorable circumstance that every single West German could be made to feel personally affected [*betroffen*]: "The individual whose human worth and personal freedom were so passionately

82 Wingen, M. 1983. Wie es zu großer Unruhe über eine normale Sache gekommen ist. *Frankfurter Allgemeine Zeitung*, October 12, p. 11. All quotes from this article have the same page reference.

invoked was made into the object of a mobilization strategy." Being "made an object" clearly implies being manipulated; the campaign was, for Wingen, not a matter of rational persuasion. His argument was directed, then, at spelling out all the factors that rendered even "normal" citizens susceptible to manipulative propaganda. These factors were:

1. A diffuse sense of insecurity, stoked by rhetoric and based in an underlying cultural pessimism.
2. A closely connected and more specific mistrust of the state (as well as large non-state organizations), which made it easy for people to believe that unlikely possibilities for abuse of data were grave and present dangers.
3. A general feeling of dependency of the individual upon mysterious larger forces. "General anxieties regarding technological civilization were awakened by the example of a census supported by electronic data processing."
4. The irrational assumption that despite the extreme complexity of a modern society such as West Germany, everyone should be able to maintain a working understanding and overview of what is being done by the state.
5. The extension of the general mistrust of the state to official statistical offices and activities.
6. A growing sensitivity regarding the surrender of personal data to the state, explicable in terms of a widespread impression that the quantitative growth of data storage, transmission and processing capacities had advanced far enough to take on a qualitatively new character.
7. A narrow individualistic orientation, which led citizens to forget or ignore the social and collective aspects of modern life:

> It was alarming [*frappierend*] to see how a posture of refusal toward the census was paired with an especially strong feeling of entitlement toward state and society, whose social expenditures are a matter of course, whose efforts at residential building, for example, are supposed to satisfy a fundamental right to appropriate living quarters. That rights of the individual could be matched by duties (such as the provision of basic data for social planning in the broadest sense) appeared for many to be an idea without legs [*eine wenig geläufige Idee*].

8. The early seizure and subsequent retention of the initiative by the publicity machine of the VoBo movement. The media gave this oppositional publicity more play than that of the state because (according to the principles of information theory) there is more new information content in the unusual occurrence or interpretation than in the familiar.

What is most revealing about Wingen's analysis is the conviction running through it that such factors automatically discredited opposition to the census. Much of what he postulated may well have been at work, alongside explicit and rational arguments, in the shift in public opinion traced in Chapter 1. But Wingen (whose views can stand here for those of many other conservatives *and* liberals) clearly wanted to assume that political activity is only legitimate to the extent that it can be rationally justified, with reference to facts rather than feared possibilities. The justices of the First Senate had a more expansive view, implicitly acknowledging that the public opinion which must be taken into account by a responsive democratic government is often based on a mixture of the rational and the irrational. In the alternative view of democracy suggested by their December decision, public opinion is inherently important, regardless of whether it can ultimately be justified.

This chapter has surveyed three different types of positions on the census controversy taken by West German state officials in various parts of the state apparatus. This is of course only a limited sample of a much broader range of possible stances, but it is enough to convey a sense of differentiation among state officials on issues of the authority of state decisions, the meaning and legitimate scope of participatory democracy, and the degree to which political discourse must be "rational" in order to count as legitimate. All three positions, those of hard liners such as Interior Minister Zimmermann, of the state-level Data Protection Commissioners who expressed reservations about the 1982 census law, and of the Constitutional Court Justices who halted the census, raise interesting issues that can aid us in reconsidering the meaning of democratic citizenship in the information age. This is most obvious in the case of the December 1983 Court decision, which elaborated a "right of informational self-determination". But in another sense, the very existence as well as the critical opinions of the DSBs posed an interesting and more institutionally entrenched challenge to German statist and *Polizeistaat* traditions, broaching the possibility of conflicts of legitimate interest *within* the state apparatus, and hence, in principle at least, the idea that democratic processes are indispensable not just to parliamentary deliberations but to the very workings of executive agencies. Thus, in a sense, calls from the boycott movements to democratize the experience of being counted found some resonance in developments within the state, where, if from a different angle, administrative processes were also under pressure to incorporate a plurality of interests. The position of hard-liners is interesting because it insists on connections across the spectrum of intensity of government interventions and resistance to them. Zimmermann's claim that refusing to answer the census was essentially equivalent to violent resistance to the state, like the other issues raised in this chapter, would be explored far more searchingly in the heat of the 1987 struggle.

Interlude

> The [superintendent and inspector] sit watching the people walking along, none of them innocent, all of them guilty of something, and they wonder if that venerable-looking old gentleman, for example, is not perhaps the grand master of outer darkness, if that girl with her arms about her boyfriend is not the incarnation of the undying serpent of evil, if that man walking along, head down, is not going to some unknown cave where the potions that poisoned the spirit of the city are distilled.
>
> (José Saramago, *Seeing*, p. 194)

The 1983 census controversy was interesting in part because it showed how previously familiar political issues might look when transferred into the less-familiar context of officials statistics and electronic data processing. In fact the activities and arguments of the VoBo movement, in combination with the reasoning of the Constitutional Court in its December decision, begin to suggest the contours of a broader "informational citizenship". Informational citizenship can be defined at a general level as a participatory approach by individuals or groups to information-gathering exercises undertaken by states or other large organizations. Thus in practice it can challenge what was termed "epistemic sovereignty", the (usually implicit) claim by states to a right to know what goes on in the territories they govern. Epistemic sovereignty is always inherently spatial. This is because people, activities and resources are themselves always embodied and located. Thus any right of access to them is at the same time a (purpose-specific) right of access to the places, regions or bounded spaces in which they are to be found.[1]

The circumstance that lent the census boycott movements' form of direct democracy more teeth than most other extraparliamentary movements was the government's reliance on the willing and truthful response of every individual residing in the national territory. Members of the contemporaneous peace, women's or environmental movements could withhold their official participation and energetically pursue extraparliamentary activism, but at a basic level, the

1 John Agnew's argument that sovereignty is not always territorial is formulated against the traditional Westphalian account of the legitimate authority of states, which is keyed to *national* boundaries and implies a power that "fills" national *territory*. But there is nothing binding about this account, and Agnew's observations can be readily accepted without abandoning the notion that sovereignty involves forms of control over spaces and places. (Agnew, J. 2005. Sovereignty regimes: territoriality and state authority in contemporary world politics. *Annals of the Association of American Geographers* 95(2): 437-461, as well as Dean, M. 2007. *Governing Societies*. Maidenhead: Open University Press.)

government remained free to ignore all of this and continue pursuing its stated goals. The census boycott movement enjoyed the rare benefit of a clear and effective mechanism by which every individual could translate opposition to the census into effective resistance, whether or not they chose to involve themselves in public activism. In an electoral system of political representation, the withholding of one's vote might be seen to contribute incrementally to an undermining of the system's legitimacy, but only in rare circumstances is the electoral process successfully subverted *in the eyes of large swathes of the public* by lack of participation. A census, by contrast, can be essentially ruined by a much smaller rate of refusal; it can only serve its purpose effectively if almost everyone provides a truthful response. In this context, by treating the formerly passive condition of being counted as an active, political matter of self-representation, census opponents had found a way to challenge democratic centralism that the government could ill afford to ignore. If the population could have a voice not only in what is done with data but, even prior to that, in deciding what form and substance the information to be collected would have, and indeed, whether to surrender data in any given instance, it would be possible to speak of a more truly participatory process of policy formation.

Opportunities for actively challenging the extent and limits of epistemic sovereignty arise both in centralized institutions of the state (in West Germany, most clearly in the offices of Data Protection Commissioners) and in the millions of distributed, individual moments at which individuals are asked or simply expected to surrender personal information. The relations that link informational citizenship and epistemic sovereignty are thus both central and dispersed throughout the governed territory. One of the key points to emerge from the 1983 controversy is the crucial importance of the myriad, dispersed original moments of registration or counting. Especially given the ongoing technological advances over the intervening decades that render ever-easier all manner of sharing and manipulation after data have been collected, this initial moment of "being counted" has become, if anything, even more crucial to any possibility of truly effective informational citizenship. To a lesser extent, the 1983 controversy also began to shed light on issues of representation and politics within the burgeoning virtual world of state and private databases. The questions raised by critical analysts regarding the effects of imposed vs. elective groupings of individuals, and the relations between virtual data aggregation and lived, embodied political solidarities in what has more recently and inelegantly come to be known as "meatspace", would likewise remain salient in 1987 and since.

The 1987 census controversy was a more spectacular affair than its 1983 predecessor in part because the census was actually taken. Following the events of 1987 will allow us to fill in some of the thematic aspects of informational citizenship and deepen our understanding of how it can challenge epistemic sovereignty in practice. But in order to appreciate these new dimensions, it is necessary also to appreciate how the political context for the struggle had changed in the intervening four years. The single most important political development between late 1983 and the Spring of 1987 was the consolidation and expansion of the Greens as a party with a national electoral presence as well as continued strong links to local social movements. The Greens would not dominate the 1987 boycott, or impose complete uniformity upon it. But their ascendancy within the German Left and their institutional consolidation through their participation in "official" democratic processes would undeniably have major consequences for the controversy.

The Greens

The 1983 and 1987 census boycott movements were linked in activist calendars by a series of mobilizations, campaigns and controversies over various other pieces of the incipient *Kybernokratie* of the surveillance state. Hamburg, West Berlin and other "scene" hotspots had no shortage of occasions to decry the trends that had raised fears in 1983. To take just one example, the Hamburg left coalition GAL [*Grün-Alternative Liste*], the local umbrella party roughly equivalent to the AL in West Berlin, printed a newsletter supplement in early 1984 on "the machine-readable personal ID and the registration-state", describing the government's plans for the new ID card, the pending renewal (and weakening) of the data protection law, an interview with the Hamburg LDSB, informational pieces on the "cabling-over" [*Verkabelung*] of Hamburg, the building out of a local computer network, and related subjects.[2] The taz maintained a similar vigilance from West Berlin, with regular reporting on these and related issues. But more establishment figures were also kept busy providing commentary. In March of 1984, the *Frankfurter Rundschau* carried an article detailing Spiros Simitis's arguments for changing the next micro-census by allowing voluntary rather than mandatory response.[3] His colleague from Baden-Württemberg Ruth Leuze published an opinion piece in April of 1985 drawing up the balance sheet for the effects of the December 1983 Constitutional Court census decision. In her own federal state she noted a continued reluctance by higher government officials to regard data protection as anything other than an irritant and an obstacle: "Not a few politicians offer pithy words against data protection in the area of security, but on the other hand place a lot of stock in personal freedom and responsibility in the social sector."[4] These and many other commentaries did succeed in keeping public awareness and concern simmering along, to be re-ignited on a larger scale in the Spring of 1987.

2 Forschungsgruppe "Demokratie und Recht" der GAL Hamburg 1984. Rundbrief Extra zum machinenlesbaren Personalausweis und Erfassungsstaat. Supplement to GAL-Rundbrief Nr. 1/84. Hamburg Institut für Sozialforschung, Binder "EDV-Daten Anti 87".

3 Krumm, K.-H. 1984. Die Datensammler sind unter Zeitdruck geraten. *Frankfurter Rundschau*, March 21, 3.

4 Leuze, R. 1985. Freundliche Töne, doch keine Taten. *Süddeutsche Zeitung*, April 20/21, 10.

However, as suggested above, this discourse did not provide much in the way of dramatically new analysis or substantive argumentation. The 1987 boycotts would be so much bigger and more memorable than their predecessors not because of theoretical innovations but because the antagonists on both sides of the struggle were much better prepared, and because the census was actually taken, which meant the contest was prolonged over months and then years, and passed through many more phases than it had had a chance to in 1983. Some of the main, publicly visible personalities on both sides remained the same. But the most crucial change between the two boycotts was the consolidation of the Greens.

Much has been written on the Greens, and the intent here is not to provide an exhaustive or even adequate overview of scholarship on the party or the movements out of which it grew. However it is certainly worth sketching in broad outline some of the key aspects of the Green story, at least to the extent necessary to make sense of their involvement in the boycott in 1987. As noted in Chapter 1, the Green Party had just for the first time, in March of 1983, cleared the 5% hurdle (if a party receives 5% or more of eligible votes cast nationwide, it takes seats in the Federal *Bundestag*). The Greens passed the hurdle right in the middle of the burgeoning census boycott movement, and thus did not have the time necessary to translate this new electoral presence into new institutional forms of support for the boycott. A group of prospective Green delegates had issued a statement in support of the boycott in February, and it became part of the Green platform, but otherwise Green work on behalf of the VoBo was much like that of other oppositional groups and organizations. The Greens were important in 1983, but still chiefly at the level of local *Bürgerinitiativen* (citizens' initiatives), working with peace, anti-nuclear and other groups.[5]

The Green Party had emerged in the late 1970s out of long years of debate and discussion among *Bürgerinitiativen* focused on environmental politics, women's issues, peace, capitalism, participatory urban planning, nuclear power, fascism, racism, in short on practically every live issue across the landscape of oppositional politics. Horst Mewes estimates that by 1979, there were some 50,000 citizens' initiatives in West Germany, with an aggregate membership rivaling that of all the official political parties combined.[6] The local initiatives and networks out of which the Greens emerged were tremendously varied in their political emphases and their positions on the costs and benefits of trying to form a national party aimed at electoral representation. But local and state parties were already being floated in 1977, and some prominent figures in national peace and anti-nuclear organizations (such as Petra Kelly, Ossip Flechtheim, Rudolf Bahro and Rudi Dutschke, before his untimely death from long-term complications of the gunshot wounds he

5 See Bergmann, *Volkszählung und Datenschutz* for a more detailed discussion of Green activities in 1983.

6 Mewes, H. 1998. A brief history of the Green Party, in *The German Greens: Paradox Between Movement and Party* (trans. M. Schatzschneider), edited by M. Mayer and J. Ely. Philadelphia: Temple University Press, 29-48, p. 31.

sustained in 1968) were meeting to explore the idea of a national organization.[7] To make a long story short, the idea gained enough momentum to lead, via a series of meetings in 1979 and 1980, to the foundation of a national party in January of 1980. Unresolved in these meetings were an interlocking and cross-cutting set of tensions between different currents and political emphases, many based in different local oppositional traditions. Roland Roth and Detlef Murphy note that commentators have distinguished anywhere from two to seven major groupings in the early Green party. Roth and Murphy settle on four: (1) the "eco-socialists" with a stronghold in Hamburg but also well-represented in West Berlin, heavily influenced by radical members of communist cells, anarchists, and anti-nuclear activists; (2) "eco-libertarians" who opposed the ideological and organizational stringency of the eco-socialists, and were more likely to be found in smaller towns and rural areas of Baden-Württemberg and Schleswig-Holstein (though were also represented in West Berlin); (3) "fundamentalists" or "fundis" without a clear regional distribution but committed to ensuring that parliamentary politics always be subordinated to the more radical methods of the social movements; and (4) "realists" or "realos", urging professionalization of the Party and willingness to engage in conventional power politics. Members of this last group were more likely to hail from southern states such as Hessen, Bavaria and Baden-Württemberg, and some of their most famous figures, such as Joseph (Joschka) Fischer and Daniel Cohn-Bendit, rose to prominence in Frankfurt.[8]

Given this variety, it is not immediately clear why the party should have named itself in a way that suggested a clear primary commitment to environmental politics. At a mundane level, the major national West German parties had already claimed the colors red (SPD), black (CDU/CSU) and yellow (FDP), leaving the latecomers only blue and green among the classic colors. Andrei Markovitz and Philip Gorski suggest that the "Green" label is a product of the particular political conjuncture in which the party emerged, but that the real, underlying and unifying theme that cut across all currents was "defense of the reproductive sphere" in a broad sense:

> This included "ecological" policies aimed at maintaining what the Greens reverently refer to as the "natural bases of life" … But it also contained policies aimed at preserving the integrity of *sociocultural reproduction.* Under rubrics such as "autonomy" and "self-realization", many Green policies have aimed to defend the lifeworld, the realm of relationships, personality and expression, from distortion by the forces of the state and the imperatives of the market.[9]

---

7 Mewes, *Brief History*, pp. 32-35.

8 Roth, R. and Murphy, D. 1998. From competing factions to the rise of the Realos, in *The German Greens: Paradox Between Movement and Party* (trans. M. Schatzschneider), edited by M. Mayer and J. Ely, 53-59. See also Markovitz and Gorski, *The German Left*, pp. 41-51; 116-119.

9 Markovitz and Gorski, *The German Left*, p. 153.

While this characterization of the root commonalities of Green policy could be contested, it at least highlights a strand that helps clarify the interest and involvement of the Greens in the census boycotts. Another common and very relevant thread across all Green constituencies was a basic anti-authoritarianism inherited by many different pathways from the student movements of the 1960s. Yet despite these commonalities, the Greens remained a very diverse party with very different local situations and emphases.[10]

The percentage of votes gained in national elections by the Greens rose from 1.5% shortly after their founding in 1980 to 5.6% at the time of the first boycott in 1983 and then to 8.3% in 1987.[11] Thus within seven years they were in a position to challenge the Free Democrats (FDP) as the third party in West Germany. It would not be until 1998, however, after a period of recovery from miserable results attendant upon their missing the enthusiasm for re-unification in 1990, that the Greens would actually become part of their first ruling coalition. In the first decade of their existence as a national party, the chief overarching question facing the Greens would be the dilemma captured in the subtitle of Margit Mayer and John Ely's edited collection, namely, *Paradox Between Movement and Party*.[12] This short description hides a complex set of practical organizational, procedural and political problems, which would be dealt with more or less successfully over the 1980s, sometimes on the basis of pre-existing principle but also often through experimentation. Among the many innovations the Greens brought to the West German political establishment upon their entry into the halls of parliament in 1983 was a very different conception of the duties and privileges of delegates to the *Bundestag*, a conception based on the desire to translate aspects of grassroots democracy into the workings of official power. The four pillars of their approach were: (1) the "imperative mandate", dictating that delegates be bound strictly to party resolutions and aimed at preventing the development of opinion-formation insulated from the larger party membership; (2) the "principle of rotation", whereby Green delegates would all be allowed only limited terms in office, so as to prevent corruption and the formation of political elites; (3) the "separation of mandate and office", that is, a ban on delegates in parliament simultaneously holding party offices, intended to counteract any tendency for power to accumulate with specific individuals; and (4) equal representation of both genders on all committees and commissions.[13]

10 See Scharf, T. 1994. *The German Greens: Challenging the Consensus*, Oxford: Berg Publishers, for a detailed look at one of the many local party organizations.

11 Mez, L. 1998. Who votes Green? Sources and trends of Green support, in *The German Greens: Paradox Between Movement and Party* (trans. M. Schatzschneider), edited by M. Mayer and J. Ely. Philadelphia: Temple University Press, 72-93, p. 78.

12 Mayer and Ely, *The German Greens*.

13 Demirovic, A. 1998. Grassroots democracy: contradictions and implications, in *The German Greens: Paradox Between Movement and Party* (trans. M. Schatzschneider), edited by M. Mayer and J. Ely. Philadelphia: Temple University Press, 141-161, pp. 149-150.

These practices, coupled with a commitment to keep party conferences open to non-members, and a commitment to consensus-based decision-making, were supposed to construct as direct and undistorted a link as possible between social movement politics and parliamentary decisions. Of special importance for the census boycotts and other specific mobilizations was the practice of making resources available to social movements. Part of the calculation of Green founders had been precisely the anticipated access to, and creative political use of, these benefits of parliamentary representation: "the opportunity to intensify extraparliamentary protest by making use of the publicity effect accorded to parliaments; to obtain information available to parliament, as well as legal security and financial backing for the social movements' projects ..."[14] In the early years, delegates donated at least some of their parliamentary stipends to a fund for social movements.[15] In addition, as we shall see below, the local Green Party organizations often permitted oppositional groups and movement activists to use their offices and mail and telephone privileges.

The issue of Green commitment to these original grassroots measures, and to some of their signature policy positions, came to be polarized, by the mid-1980s, along lines of force laid out by the running confrontation between two of the four basic camps identified above, the "fundis" and the "realos". Perhaps inevitably, the longer the Greens survived in parliament, the greater the pressures became to gravitate toward established forms of politics based on the accumulation of experience and power in an emerging political elite, and a growing insulation of this elite from the impulses of the street, in short, toward professionalization. But this tendency called forth vehement opposition from the "fundis", who continued to insist that parliamentary goals remain subordinate to the movements. As Roth and Murphy put it, "The central paradox remains: a party deriving its energy and innovative impulses from the social movements' extraparliamentary and institutionally critical practices, but at the same time deriving the political power necessary for realizing its policies from elections and institutional representation."[16] By 1987, this basic rift had taken institutional form as a split between a *Bundestag* delegation in which "realos" such as Otto Schily and Joschka Fischer (respectively, future Interior Minister and Foreign Minister under SPD Chancellor Gerhard Schroeder) held sway and a "fundi" party leadership featuring Thomas Ebermann and Jutta Ditfurth, the latter a charismatic speaker who would eventually leave the Greens in disgust. Thus, while on the one hand, the 1987 boycott movement would

---

14 Klotzsch, L., Könemann, K., Wischermann, J., and Zeuner, B. 1998. What has happened to Green principles in electoral and parliamentary politics?, in *The German Greens: Paradox Between Movement and Party* (trans. M. Schatzschneider), edited by M. Mayer and J. Ely. Philadelphia: Temple University Press, 97-127, p. 100. See also Markovitz and Gorski, *The German Left*, p. 122.

15 Ditfurth, J. 2000. *Das waren die Grünen: Abschied von einer Hoffnung*. Munich: Econ Taschenbuch Verlag, p. 174.

16 Roth and Murphy, "From competing factions ...", p. 69.

undeniably benefit from Green Party organizational consolidation and the newly available resources this brought, it would at the same time be caught up in the high-profile struggle for national leadership, and control of the future direction, of the Greens. The boycott would receive massive and widespread support from Green party locals and some national leaders, while other prominent Greens would dissent. On this last point, it can be seen as something of an index of the changes brought on by institutional success that Otto Schily switched from staunch proponent of the 1983 census boycott to one of the critics of the boycott in 1987.[17] Details aside, the overall impact of Green success was undoubtedly to strengthen the 1987 boycott, but at the same time the more radical Green statements and actions made it easier for government officials to criminalize opposition to the census by demonizing the Greens as dangerous subversives.

From theory to practice: Informational citizenship in the 1987 boycott

At the discursive level, the 1987 controversy was much more two-sided than its 1983 predecessor. Government officials and other census supporters "showed up" this time. The general claim by opponents of the census that the government in West Germany was acquiring ever more of the trappings of a surveillance state was thus countered by a robust, more fully elaborated and equally polarizing suite of arguments to the effect that opposition to the census was criminal or worse. Much of the discursive controversy swirled around the conveniently concrete Green Party, which, as an officially recognized political party, could serve as the lightning rod for connecting the new issues of the information age to long-running debates regarding the constitutionality of civil disobedience or a "right of resistance", and the nature and conditions of legitimacy of state violence or alternatively, of bodily resistance to state measures. The state's implicit claim to epistemic sovereignty was now related in much more detail to general questions of the contested legitimacy of state enforcement of its policies. State officials were also much more aggressive and innovative than they had been in 1983 in their attempts to shut down the census boycott movement "on the ground", by means of institutional, legal and police measures. Here as well, the public figures and offices of the Green Party were a frequent target. As a number of commentators noted, the energy invested by state officials in suppressing the 1987 boycott movement seemed, even to many previously neutral observers, to confirm the specter of the surveillance state. At the same time, however, some few militant opponents of the census resorted to physical violence, thus appearing to confirm the statist demonization of resistance as tendentially subversive or even terrorist.

The concrete character of the 1987 struggle also brought to the fore the issue of the anonymity of citizens engaged in public politics. The parallels and overlaps noted in the Introduction between surveillance in the virtual world of electronic

17 Bergmann, *Volkszählung und Datenschutz*, p. 33.

information and surveillance of demonstrators in public space gained new urgency and immediacy as police forces and security services sought to register boycott activists and deter citizens more generally from joining the boycott. The fears expressed in 1983 about the geography of the boycott being turned into a "map of resistance potential" by the police and security services seemed in danger of coming true in 1987. The boycott movement, too, developed new strategies, particularly in the form of a more consistent implementation of the "hard boycott", aimed at safeguarding a notion of *anonymous* informational citizenship. Finally, another key aspect of informational citizenship lent additional detail by the 1987 controversy was, again, the crucial importance of the moment of data gathering. Since the census was actually taken in 1987, this issue was played out on the ground. The 1987 struggle made plain as the 1983 controversy could not that the moment of data gathering must be understood as part of an entire "product chain" of knowledge, that is, the concrete, geographically distributed media and pathways, complete with "break-in-bulk points" at which information is transferred from one format to another, through which knowledge is solicited, gathered and returned to centers of calculation to be evaluated, corrected, manipulated and made available to executive agencies or decision-makers. In truly surprising ways, the materiality of census data became a focus of attention in 1987, and the manner in which it did can add an important dimension to our understanding of the scope for informational citizenship more generally.

Chapter 3
A New "War of Religion": Ideological Battle Lines in 1987

> The time has come to inform this council of ministers ... that the espionage services under my orders, or rather, who answer to the ministry for which I am responsible, do not exclude the possibility that what happened may have its real roots abroad, and that what we are seeing may be only the tip of the iceberg of a gigantic, global destabilization plot, doubtless anarchist in inspiration, and which, for reasons we still do not comprehend, has chosen our country as its first guinea pig ... what we are facing today is terrorism, pure and unadulterated, it may wear different faces and expressions, but it is, essentially, the same thing, You should be careful about making such wild claims and such facile extrapolations, commented the justice minister, it seems risky to me, not to say, outrageous, to label as terrorism, especially pure and unadulterated terrorism, the appearance in the ballot box of a few blank votes ...
>
> (José Saramago, *Seeing*, pp. 32-33)

> The census and the authoritarian-technocratic concept of politics on which it is based are building blocks on the way to the "formed society" [*formierte Gesellschaft*], and democratic resistance is in order.
>
> (Roland Appel, specialist in the Law and Society Working Group, the Green Party in the *Bundestag*, 1986)[1]

The events of 1983 ensured that the West German public would take notice when the government was once again ready to try to count the population in 1987. The domestic political climate had changed considerably by 1987, with the conservative ideological "*Wende*" of two successive Kohl administrations tending to encourage federal, state and local officials in their determination to see the census through to completion this time. Perhaps the key difference was that in 1987, the census

1 Appel, R. 1986. Volkserfassung – zweiter Versuch. Das Volkszählungsprojekt 1987, in *Totalerfassung: "Sicherheitsgesetze", Volkszählung, Neuer Personalausweis, Möglichkeiten der Gegenwehr*, edited by M. Kutscha and N. Paech. Köln: Pahl-Rugenstein, 45-59, p. 56. The term *formierte Gesellschaft* originated with Ludwig Erhard, West German Chancellor from 1963 to 1966, as a counter-conception to the idea that West Germany was necessarily riven by class struggle. The *formierte Gesellschaft* would be characterized by cooperation among various socio-economic groups, under the benevolent protection of a strong state. The term was criticized at the time for its echoes of authoritarianism, and was taken up by the Left subsequently as a shorthand for authoritarian projects.

was actually taken. As we shall see, while this represented a victory for Interior Minister Zimmermann and the forces of "*Ordnung*", it was an ambiguous victory at best, and thus also something more complicated than a definitive defeat for the boycott movement. Even years after the count had been completed and the results had been announced, the census of 1987 remained, as Karl-Heinz Krumm foresaw in a November 1984 editorial, an "adventure with an uncertain outcome".[2]

A new law born into a tense environment

Following the momentous Constitutional Court decision of December 1983, Zimmermann's staff returned to the drawing board. Within a year, a new draft law was ready, but a tangle of political issues would need to be resolved.[3] According to *Der Spiegel*, a consensus text for the new census law awaited some sort of compromise between Zimmermann and FDP Justice Minister Hans Engelhard, who wanted to make sure the law was absolutely tight in data protection terms.[4] The original draft VZG foresaw April 23rd, 1986 as the day of enumeration.[5] But with a sizable minority of the population and the second largest political party still opposed, Interior Minister Zimmermann decided it was wise to secure SPD support before trying to push the law through the legislative process.[6] Time pressure was already sharp. Egon Hölder, the new head of the Federal Bureau of Statistics (*Statistisches Bundesamt* or StaBA), noted that the government had already agreed with the European Community on 1986 as the next West German census year, with the results serving as the basis for extrapolations in 1991, the year in which most other EC member countries would count their populations.[7] The planned 1983 census had already represented a delay with respect to the rhythm foreseen by the EC. Nevertheless, 1986, too, would fall by the wayside in the course of negotiations and debates in the early months of 1985. April 1986 had been selected chiefly to ensure that the census not get caught in the run-up to elections scheduled for Spring of 1987.[8] CDU officials doubtless remembered all too well how some politicians from their own ranks had flirted with public opposition to the 1983 census in their campaigns for the March elections, only to return to the party line once the votes

2 Krumm, K.-H. 1984b. Ein neues Abenteuer. *Frankfurter Rundschau*, November 14, n.p.n.

3 Krumm, Ein neues Abenteuer.

4 Anon. 1984. Porto zahlen. *Der Spiegel*, November 5, p. 29.

5 Reprinted in Anon. 1984. Grunddaten für die Politik und die Statistik. *Frankfurter Rundschau*, December 1, p. 10.

6 Strack, G. 1985. Ohne SPD keine Volkszählung. *Frankfurter Rundschau*, February 16, pp. 1-2.

7 Strack, Ohne SPD.

8 Bannas, G. 1985. Die Volkszählung erst nach der Wahl? *Frankfurter Allgemeine Zeitung*, January 21, p. 10.

were in. Writing in the *Frankfurter Allgemeine Zeitung*, Günter Bannas suggested it would be equally inadvisable to legislate a census with an enumeration date falling after the elections, since the outcome of the vote was uncertain.[9] Here, too, unpleasant memories of 1983 were doubtless at play: Zimmermann and company had not been able to dissociate themselves from the census by noting that the 1982 VZG had been the work of the foregoing SPD government. It is possible that his eventual willingness to agree to an enumeration date after the elections resulted from the belated recognition that the reversal of the positions of the two mass parties relative to 1983 changed the entire political calculation. If the CDU/CSU-led coalition passed the new census law and then lost the election, the SPD and its partners would be saddled with whatever controversy arose. If the CDU/CSU won again, the issue of straddling an election would be moot.

Some state-level SPD politicians, along with LDSBs Simitis and Leuze, suggested that the population could not be won over to solid support for the census before 1988. But misgivings emerged also with respect to financing and the quality of the results.[10] As in the years leading up to 1983, the division of financial burdens between different levels of government became an issue. Bonn had initially offered the federal states, which would carry out the bulk of the work, DM 2.50 per person counted. The *Bundesrat*, the second house of parliament structured to represent the interests of the states, requested a doubling of the federal contribution to DM 5 *per capita*, and Bonn countered with an offer of DM 4.[11] A compromise sum of DM 4.50 *per capita* was eventually written into the law.[12] In testimony before the Interior Committee of the *Bundestag*, representatives of local municipalities emphasized that although existing data was in a horrible state and new figures urgently needed, they would rather see a 1988 census done properly than a 1986 count rushed through.[13] What local statisticians and planners considered adequate was made clear at a conference of the German Institute for Urban Studies in West Berlin in March of 1985, where complaints were aimed primarily at the new data protection measures written into the draft law.[14] These protections, it was claimed, rendered census data almost unusable for communal purposes. While Leuze and others accused the government of minimal adherence to data protection guidelines, from the standpoint of local officials, Zimmermann's legislative experts had taken the 1983 Constitutional Court decision too seriously. By June 1985, the SPD and

9 Bannas, Die Volkszählung erst nach der Wahl?

10 Anon. 1985. Volkszählung 1986 oder 1988? Ansichten der Experten, politische Wünsche. *Frankfurter Allgemeine Zeitung*, April 18, p. 6.

11 Anon., Volkszählung 1986 oder 1988?, p. 6.

12 Bannas, G. 1986. Die Zählung ist noch nicht über den Berg. *Frankfurter Allgemeine Zeitung*, November 4, n.p.n.

13 Anon., Volkszählung 1986 oder 1988?, p. 6.

14 Duwe, P. 1985. "Zuviel Datenschutz schadet den Kommunen". *Volksblatt Berlin*, March 22, n.p.n.

the Kohl administration had agreed to aim for an as-yet unspecified later date.[15] In November of 1985 the law was finally passed with an enumeration date of May 25th, 1987.

The final version of the 1985 VZG would follow most of the language of the 1984 draft.[16] The first significant change from the 1982 VZG was a clear and explicit distinction between *Erhebungsmerkmale*, the substantive census information being requested, on the one hand, and organizational information such as file numbers and *Hilfsmerkmale*, or identification aids (names and addresses), on the other. The new draft allowed for the storage of organizational aids while the census data were being processed but also provided that personal identifiers be deleted after processing as soon as they were no longer needed (¶¶ 3-8, 15). The second key change appeared in ¶ 9: "For the carrying out of enumerations, census offices will be established. They are to be separated from other administrative offices both in terms of personnel and organizationally. It is to be ensured that the information in the forms not be used for other purposes."[17] The legislative staff at the Interior Ministry also expanded substantially on the somewhat cursory discussion of enumerators in the 1982 law. As before, every able-bodied West German between 18 and 65 was obliged to serve as an enumerator if requested to do so. This time, however, the law explicitly barred the deployment of enumerators in the neighborhoods where they lived, and excepted from enumerator duties those (such as police officers or social service workers) whose participation in the census might raise fears among respondents that the information given could eventually be used against them. Further, the law made it clear that enumerators were only allowed to enter living spaces with permission (¶ 10 (6)). The giving of a telephone number was now explicitly voluntary (¶ 12(6)), each respondent was free to choose whether to respond on an individual form or as part of a household, and could send the form by mail (¶ 13). This, however, had to be done within a week of receipt of the form, and the draft law specified that all the usual personal information contained in a return address in fact be written on the envelope (this probably in part to forestall the "must have gotten lost in the mail" tactic suggested by the 1983 boycott organizers). The provisions for sharing census data with other, non-statistical agencies were much more restrictive than in the 1982 VZG. As before, it was seen as unavoidable that some small local governments would need to request micro-level census information (including some individual-level data) from the state statistical agencies. But the nature and form of the data eligible for transfer was far more carefully specified, as were the conditions under which the transfer could occur (¶ 14).

---

15 Anon. 1985. Einvernehmen über die Verschiebung der Volkszählung. *Frankfurter Allgemeine Zeitung*, June 1, p. 1.

16 *Gesetz über eine Volks-, Berufs-, Gebäude, Wohnungs- und Arbeitsstättenzählung (Volkszählungsgesetz 1987)*. 1985. *Bundesgesetzblatt*, 1985, Teil I, November 8, pp. 2078-2083 [hereinafter VZG 1987]. Bonn: Bundestag.

17 VZG 1987, 2080.

The changes embodied in the new census law certainly represented a *plausible* response to the 1983 Constitutional Court decision; but of course the issue of whether they constituted an *adequate* response would be answered in dramatically different ways by supporters and opponents. There is no question that on paper, at least, the newly conceived "right of informational self-determination" was better safeguarded than in the 1982 VZG. But this new law was born into a troubled environment, and many ordinary West Germans, as well as the Data Protection Commissioners charged with defending their interests, turned an extremely sensitive and critical eye upon it. In the years between 1983 and 1987, Spiros Simitis, LDSB for the state of Hessen, and especially Ruth Leuze, LDSB for Baden-Württemberg, would make news with their concerns about data protection. Earlier in 1984, Simitis had already registered a critique of the planned "micro-census", a sample survey encompassing 0.1% of the population, which Bonn planned to take every year.[18] The key issues for Simitis were, first, that the sample survey was not based on specific legislation despite the Constitutional Court's insistence in its 1983 decision that all state information-gathering exercises have a legal basis; and second, that response to the micro-census was mandatory. Partly as a result of Simitis's misgivings on the first point, Bonn dropped the micro-census planned for May of 1984. The *Bundestag* debated a draft micro-census law along with the draft census law in November, and the micro-census draft included provisions for a comparative test of the accuracy of a sample based on voluntary response, Simitis's second point.[19] But no date for a micro-census was set. The question of whether response should be mandatory hung in the air unresolved throughout the 1987 controversy, and remains an important point of contention in the early 21st century.[20]

Simitis and his colleagues, who had seen multiple early drafts of the census law from Zimmermann's office, remained unsatisfied with the fact that the law did not dictate the exact content of the census form. More important, as it would turn out, was the problem of how to make sure census work remained truly separate from other administrative work in small, especially rural municipalities employing only a handful of officials.[21] As one of Simitis's staff put it, "How is a municipal bureaucrat in a small nest supposed to handle it? Is he supposed to forget everything that he learned statistically when he deals with the people on a daily basis?"[22] Ruth Leuze would insist on this point repeatedly throughout the 1987 controversy. In a talk in Gummersbach at the Theodor Heuss Academy in April of 1985, Leuze had offered an assessment of the state of data protection

18 Krumm, K.-H. 1984a. Die Datensammler sind unter Zeitdruck geraten. *Frankfurter Rundschau*, March 21, p. 3.

19 Anon. 1984. Die Stichproben-Erhebungen sollen wieder in Gang gebracht werden. *Frankfurter Allgemeine Zeitung*, November 14, n.p.n.

20 Feuck, J. 1985. Auskunftspflicht bleibt ein Zankapfel. *Frankfurter Rundschau*, August 19, n.p.n.

21 Anon., Porto zahlen.

22 Anon., Porto zahlen.

since the 1983 Constitutional Court decision.[23] According to Leuze, the decision involved three basic principles that should guide data protection: (1) the right of citizens to decide on the surrender and use of their data; (2) the importance of recognizing this right as a basis for a free democracy, and of keeping in view the threats posed to it by the diverse possibilities for using information technology; and (3) the duty of legislators to develop effective safeguards for this right. While the 1983 census decision had in effect halted what she perceived as the deterioration-by-neglect of the existing data protection infrastructure, and had prompted some rethinking, it had not resulted in the kind of new legislation envisioned by the justices. An overall concept of how the 1983 decision should transform data protection was still missing, according to Leuze, and this explained the fact that the Federal Data Protection Law [BDSG] had not yet been revised. In her own state of Baden-Württemberg, Leuze reported an attitude of, at best, indifference, if not outright hostility, toward data protection concerns among higher officials in state government. She acknowledged that occasions like a census, in which every citizen is made aware of personal data protection issues, are rare, and that in most cases, threats to individual data occur behind the scenes, without the affected individuals realizing that something might be amiss. For these reasons she remained pessimistic about the overall prospects for data protection in the future. On one point, though, Leuze was right to be optimistic. Her claim that "consciousness of data protection in the population has risen considerably" was borne out by public opinion polls.[24] The *Frankfurter Allgemeine Zeitung* reported in January of 1985 that 30% of West Germans had declared themselves unwilling to participate in a census even if it were conducted according to the principles recommended by the Constitutional Court in 1983.[25] The percentages differed strongly by party affiliation: 64% of Green Party adherents, 32% of SPD voters, 17% of FDP voters, and 18% of CDU/CSU voters claimed they would boycott. The high level of Green resistance to the census would anchor the 1987 boycott movement, and cause the Kohl administration endless headaches. But the biggest concern for Zimmermann and his colleagues was the SPD number, since 32% of the nation's other mass party meant a lot of people and a great deal of political influence. Indeed the SPD delegates in the *Bundestag* had been prepared to join the Greens in voting against the census law in its early 1985 form, and the Interior Ministers of the four SPD-controlled federal states, Hamburg, Bremen, Hessen, and the behemoth North-Rhine-Westphalia, the most populous West German state, had come out against the new law.[26]

In his early prediction that the new census would be an "adventure with an uncertain outcome", Karl-Heinz Krumm had correctly recognized that the key

---

23 Leuze, R. 1985. Freundliche Töne, doch keine Taten [Edited version of speech]. *Süddeutsche Zeitung*, April 20/21, p. 10.

24 Leuze, Freundliche Töne.

25 Bannas, Die Volkszählung erst nach der Wahl?

26 Strack, Ohne SPD keine Volkszählung, p. 1.

issue would be "*Akzeptanz*".[27] He stressed that in addition to addressing all the issues of data protection and informational self-determination, the government would have to do a much more thorough job of persuading the public that the numbers were really needed *and would be responsibly used.* What he had in mind here was not the possibility of invasions of privacy but a more fundamental problem with the role of statistics in policy-making:

> After all, although all the necessary data were available earlier, planning ruins are to be seen all over the country; relevant information lies in the offices of government experts, but policies have not always been based in any recognizable way on the correct conclusions to be drawn from [this information]. The reason for this traditional chasm between wish and reality lies in the fact that the political majorities in the administration and in Parliament shape their decisions above all on the basis of their own programs and values ... Up until now the prevalent impression has been that opinion polls, far more than the personal data requested from citizens, can influence political actions in Bonn. Not Egon Hölder, the President of the Federal Bureau of Statistics, but Elisabeth Noelle-Neumann, the public opinion researcher, is among the close advisers of Chancellor Helmut Kohl.[28]

As Horst Bieber would put it, "the saying that 'bad (statistical) data make for bad planning' may be correct, but it does not necessarily imply the converse, [namely] that from good data comes reasonable planning." Writing in February of 1987, Bieber shared Krumm's pessimism from late 1984: "it is already possible today to predict with some certainty that many incomplete census forms will come back to the processing centers."[29] Public opinion in the intervening period had shifted somewhat but still did not bode well for the census. According to a poll commissioned by the Interior Ministry in late October of 1986, while 77% of West Germans declared themselves wiling to respond to the census, 11% claimed they would refuse even if reminded of their legal duty to respond.[30] Egon Hölder, President of the StaBA, confirmed that a refusal rate of 10% would be damaging to the quality of the results. Perhaps more troubling, the poll found that despite a clear majority willing to answer census questions, 49.9% of the population (even 1/3 of those identifying with the CDU/CSU) believed the census was not necessary.[31] This meant that a sizable part of the population intended to comply out of a sense of duty (or perhaps resignation) rather than conviction. Strategically speaking, support for the census from this group thus had to be viewed as provisional and

27 Krumm, Ein neues Abenteuer.

28 Krumm, Ein neues Abenteuer.

29 Bieber, H. 1987. Viele Fragen – und welche Antworten? *Die Zeit*, February 20, p. 4. See also Anon. 1984. Bis ins letzte. *Der Spiegel*, November 19, pp. 138-139.

30 Bannas, Die Zählung ist noch nicht über den Berg.

31 Bannas, Die Zählung ist noch nicht über den Berg.

dependent upon the success of the government's publicity campaign in the face of a fairly well-organized boycott movement.

The first concrete signs of trouble for the census came in late 1986. In December, the boycott movement was already able to organize its first national coordination conference in Wiesbaden near Frankfurt.[32] As the call went out for enumerators around that time, Hamburg and West Berlin once again looked set to re-claim their status as hot-spots and headquarters for the boycott movement, Hamburg seeing only 2,500 of the required 11,000, West Berlin 4,000 of 20,000 enumerators voluntarily register.[33] Even at this stage, it seemed, thousands of West Germans were willing to translate their misgivings into action. In the face of such omens, Interior Minister Zimmermann and the other federal, state and local officials charged with carrying out the census might well have found Horst Bieber's metaphor apt when he compared the census to "an unloved child – necessary for success, but why does it cry so loudly?"[34] A second, unspoken question, whose answer was at least as central to the controversy, was "success at what, precisely?"

The struggle over "Akzeptanz"

The 1983 census fiasco had persuaded the Kohl administration that it had to take publicity seriously this time around. The publicity budget for the 1987 census dwarfed the paltry sums set aside in 1983, and plans for spending the money were forged much earlier. In October of 1985, under the header "Big public education campaign [*Aufklärungskampagne*] to secure the participation of all citizens", the business daily *Handelsblatt* reported the publicity budget at DM16 million, as compared with DM 50,000 four years earlier.[35] In February of 1987, an additional DM 30 million were approved, raising the total cost to DM 46 million.[36] Three weeks before the enumeration date, the taz judged the outlay "the most expensive advertising campaign in the history of the *Bundesrepublik*".[37] The campaign got into gear in the Spring of 1986, when the first ads began to appear in national newspapers. Inserts for targeted groups followed shortly thereafter, flanked by a

---

32 Paust, A. 1987. Diplomarbeit zum Thema Staatliche Legitimationsprobleme am Beispiel der Volkszählung 1987. Unpublished thesis, Universität Gesamthochschule Duisburg, Fachbereich 1 – Fach Politische Wissenschaft. Typescript provided by author, p. 80.

33 Plog, K. 1986. Hamburgs Volkszähler proben den Aufstand. *Frankfurter Rundschau*, December 19, p. 4; Anon. 1986. Terrier im Treppenhaus. *Der Spiegel*, December 15, p. 92.

34 Bieber, Viele Fragen – und welche Antworten?, p. 4.

35 Anon. 1985. Große Aufklärungskampagne soll die Teilnahme aller Bürger sicherstellen. *Handelsblatt*, October 1, n.p.n.

36 Roos, K. 1987. Grüne und Kommunisten. *Bayern Kurier*, March 21, p. 8; Pokatzky, K. and Sontheimer, M. 1987. Zähler und Gezählte. *Die Zeit*, June 12, p. 34.

37 Gaserow, V. 1987b. "Volgssählung? Nix gehört!". *die tageseitung*, May 6, n.p.n.

range of brochures, decals, plastic bags umbrellas, and even a special postage stamp. Television spots appeared in April.[38] The campaign message, developed by the Düsseldorf ad agency Publicis Intermarco-Farner in cooperation with the StaBA, was simple: "Ten minutes that help everyone".[39] One of the television spots was described dryly in the *Süddeutsche Zeitung* as follows:

> An advertising agency that recommended itself among other things on the strength of a highly successful campaign for a Scandinavian furniture concern invented as a symbol for the census a sort of gymnastics rack [*Sprossenwand*] on which nine black, red and gold figures resembling potato dumplings do gymnastics. The citizen by now knows that it is an "abacus", an antique calculating device, and every evening on the television a red and a gold dumpling, named Abakus and Abakine, talk shop [*fachsimpeln*] about the necessity and the use of the census.[40]

The StaBA struck a more serious note in the line of ads it sponsored in the taz, whose readers were of course much more likely than was the average West German both to oppose the census and to know why they opposed it. Each ad in the series featured a picture of a different local official or head of a voluntary social service organization standing next to the text of a reasoned plea for census information. For example, the ad appearing on May 4th featured a smiling Hartmut Engel, member of the board of directors of the German Society for the Promotion of Residential Construction [*Deutsche Gesellschaft zur Förderung des Wohnungsbaus*]. Engel's text made the point that housing supply cannot be built overnight, but must be planned on the basis of reliable extrapolations from current data. As with all these ads, the emphasis was on disadvantaged groups or issues likely to appeal to taz readers (Engel mentions future residential needs of youth and seniors). In the bottom left-hand corner was a framed head shot of the equally friendly-looking Ina Wiersgalla, an employee of the West Berlin Bureau of Statistics.[41] The ads were designed first and foremost to put a human, neighborly face on the community of statisticians and users of statistics and thereby to combat the image of a distant and authoritarian "Big Brother" bent on comprehensive social control. On the

38 Pokatzky and Sontheimer, Zähler und Gezählte; Dahl, S. 1987. Die Predigt wurde nicht verstanden. *Die Zeit*, November 27, p. 2.

39 Pokatzky and Sontheimer, Zähler und Gezählte; Anon., Große Aufklärungskampagne; Borchers, A. and Dahlheimer, A. 1987. Der programmierte Flop. *Vorwärts*, February 21, p. 7.

40 Holzhaider, H. 1987. Eine halbe Million Koffer voller Fragen. *Süddeutsche Zeitung*, May 20, p. 3.

41 Statistisches Landesamt Berlin. 1987. Wohnhäuser sind keine Kartenhäuser [Advertisement]. *die tageszeitung*, May 4, n.p.n. Interestingly, while the taz published pro-census ads without hesitation, the *Frankfurter Rundschau* rejected an anti-census ad, perhaps fearing legal consequences (Gaserow, V. 1987a. "FR" lehnt kritische Anzeige ab. *die tageszeitung*, April 1, n.p.n.).

national stage, the role of the reassuring familiar face eventually fell to statistics chief Egon Hölder, but not before other options failed to pan out. The government approached popular celebrities Wim Thoelke and Thomas Gottschalk, the latter still at the time of this writing in 2010 the host of the hugely popular game show *Wetten-Daß*, which he took over in 1987. Both (wisely) declined. Interior Minister Zimmermann was passed over as too tainted by the authoritarian image he had acquired in 1983. As Hölder would later recall, "suddenly it was said that we needed some sort of Weizsäcker", the former Federal President who had radiated calm authority and appeared to be above the dirt and tussle of politics.[42] The avuncular, white-haired Hölder fit the bill quite well, able as he was not only to project a benevolent paternalism but also to argue the issues from a solid technical understanding. Soon his face was familiar to all West Germans, often in a much-reproduced pose next to a giant mock-up of an abacus outside StaBA headquarters in Wiesbaden.[43] He gave interviews regularly, and never tired of pointing out how useful census statistics were for such things as environmental protection, reduction of unemployment, and furthering the interests of women.[44]

To make sure that all of these personable and service-oriented statisticians nevertheless presented a united front against attacks from census opponents, the StaBA distributed a "confidential" paper to all employees and to the various state and local statistical agencies, but a copy was obtained by the *Frankfurter Rundschau*. Entitled "Suggestions for responding to questions from Greens and Alternatives about *Volkszählung 1987* and the micro-census", the paper recommended an optimistically dismissive attitude toward the anti-census sentiment revealed by public opinion polls, and urged workers to reassure the skeptical that there were no computer programs dedicated to re-identifying individuals on the basis of anonymized data.[45] Excerpts from the confidential paper published in mid-February included more detailed answers to typical questions. For example, on the question of whether data would really be adequately protected, the internal paper offered the following:

> The *Volkszählungsgesetz 1987* has been most carefully examined, from the standpoint of statistical secrecy and data protection, in extremely thorough consultations as well as in public hearings. The Federal Data Protection Commissioner [BDSB] was active in all consultations. In addition, the law was checked with the Hessian LDSB [Simitis] as head of the Conference of Federal and State Data Protection Commissioners.[46]

---

42 Dahl, Die Predigt wurde nicht verstanden.

43 See for example Gaserow, V. 1987g. Vobo '87: Alles nur "Schall und Rauch'? Interview mit Egon Hölder. *die tageszeitung*, September 3, n.p.n.

44 Bannas, Die Zählung ist noch nicht über den Berg.

45 Voss, R. 1987. Geheime Argumente für Volkszählung. *Frankfurter Rundschau*, February 5, n.p.n.

46 Quoted in Anon. 1987. "Kleine Mogeleien können nicht aufgespürt werden". *Frankfurter Rundschau*, February 16, p. 14.

But later in this answer, as elsewhere in the paper, some of what the statisticians were to tell the public was not necessarily so reassuring. On the specific issue of names and addresses, the guidelines did little to dispel one of the arguments of census opponents, namely, that the personal information on enumerator lists could end up serving as a "refuser file". There was ultimately no getting around the temporary storage of such information as long as answering the census was mandatory, so the StaBA could not provide reassurance here. The subsequent assertion that the census law ruled out the sharing of such data with other state agencies, like the invocation of the approval of Data Protection Commissioners, signaled a continuing reliance on some of the failed argumentative strategies of 1983. In 1987, too, wide swathes of the West German public would not be content to hear that some distant authority had approved the law, nor that the law itself ruled out mischief in principle. On the other hand, it is hard to imagine what else the statisticians could have said. Once again, the difference between what census officials were expressly permitted, and what it was technically possible for them to do in a worst-case scenario, would be a terrain of contestation.

In addition to getting its own image and program of direct responses to inquiries in order, the government systematically and assiduously cultivated positive relations with the national press. As the first ads began to appear in March of 1986, the StaBA started inviting journalists to informational seminars.[47] The extent of the payoff in positive publicity is difficult to gauge in detail, but in any case it was not sufficient to produce any conspicuous larger shifts. As the controversy developed, the major newspapers fell out in a similar formation as in 1983. The *Frankfurter Allgemeine Zeitung* was once again a reliable defender of the census and bitter foe of all boycott-related activities. The conservative *Bayern Kurier* and CDU-affiliated *Rheinische Merkur* also proved tireless in their ideological support. In mid-April the *Rheinische Merkur* ran a long special section entirely devoted to the census, with articles on all aspects of preparations and expected benefits of the information, an interview with Egon Hölder, a piece on the cheerful participation of prominent politicians as enumerators, a litany of pleas for new data, and a long essay on the august history of censuses since ancient times.[48] One distinctive hallmark of pro-census coverage was the fact that the term "*Akzeptanz*" remained suspended in quotation marks. Although all census supporters recognized the need to take publicity more seriously, they remained fundamentally uncomfortable with the idea that the public had to be persuaded to obey the law. To abandon the quotation marks would have meant to accept *Akzeptanz* as a fully legitimate project.

As in 1983, the *Frankfurter Rundschau* generally remained neutral, documenting important arguments on both sides, though since there was now much more serious reasoning emanating from state officials and census supporters, the overall tenor

47 Pokatzky and Sontheimer, Zähler und Gezählte.

48 [Various] 1987. Volkszählung [Extra insert]. *Rheinischer Merkur*, April 16/17-1987.

of its coverage inevitably appeared to shift somewhat to the right. *Die Zeit* once again leaned slightly toward a pro-boycott stance. *Der Spiegel* remained, next to the taz, the most reliably anti-census of the major publications, though it also covered the less-flattering episodes connected to the boycott. One change from 1987 was the increased attention paid to the controversy by the Munich-based *Süddeutsche Zeitung*, where the coverage was neutral to slightly anti-census. In general, however, it is somewhat more difficult to be precise about the political positions of the major newspapers in 1987. As will become clear in what follows, the controversy was so much more intense than it had been in 1983 that a far larger percentage of the events and episodes connected with it would have been judged newsworthy even by fairly conservative papers. Thus, whatever their overall slant, most of the majors ran stories whose basic content at times tended to support, at other times to undermine, the boycott cause. In any event, it is impossible in retrospect to accuse the taz or the press more generally of having manufactured the controversy in 1987, and the extent to which supporters or opponents of the census came out looking virtuous or vile had less to do with which papers reported which stories than was the case in 1983. The dynamics of the controversy itself, in other words, drove press coverage, and resulted in a less decisive shaping role for the press in general and for any one newspaper. In any case, whether as a result of the government's publicity campaign or on the basis of independent conclusions drawn by West Germans following events as they unfolded, the initially ominous public opinion numbers would shift somewhat in favor of the census between early and mid-1987.

Boycott publicity and strategy

The 1987 anti-census publicity campaign mounted by the boycott movement closely followed the script from the 1983 in some ways, giving prominence to the links between the census, "security laws", machine-readable personal ID cards and the other trappings of what was portrayed as the emergent surveillance state. The Nazi use of statistics also made a renewed appearance in the critical discussion. But there were important differences as well, both in the scope and sophistication of the boycott enterprise and in the kinds of issues associated with it, especially once the census was actually taken in May. The taz once again acted as the central clearing-house for information, publishing lists of citizens' initiatives, establishing a census hotline, running a series on legal tips for those considering refusal, and in general, reporting everything that happened.[49] Boycott activists once again proved extremely imaginative in their publicity efforts, producing decals, buttons and

---

49 See *die tageszeitung*, April 1, 1987; April 3, 1987; April 6, 1987; April 8, 1987; April 9, 1987; May 5, 1987.

flyers, and, for example, plastering the Berlin Wall with empty census forms.[50] In mid-May, according to *Der Spiegel*, census opponents snuck into the Dortmund soccer stadium the night before a game and sprayed their message in huge letters on the turf: "Boycott and Sabotage the Census". When groundskeepers realized they would be unable to replace the affected turf before the game, they decided to supplement the call with additional text, so that the turf now read "The Federal President: Do Not Boycott and Sabotage the Census".[51] The fans were thus treated to a highly politicized game. By 1987, critical analyses of the security state had found and tapped into a lucrative niche market within the book publishing industry. Late 1986 and early 1987 saw titles such as *Careful, census! Registered, Networked, and Counted Out* and *Total Registration: "Security Laws", Census, New Personal ID – Possibilities for Self-Defense* go through multiple printings, the former selling 42,000 copies.[52] In mid-April, the *Süddeutsche Zeitung* reported that one such book published by 2001 press had gone through 18 printings and had sold 180,000 copies.[53] A small advice booklet offered by the same press ("What you can do against the micro-census and the census") had, according to *Der Spiegel*, sold 250,000 copies.[54]

In general, because the Constitutional Court had affirmed the constitutionality of censuses as such (while rejecting parts of the 1983 law), arguments against the census *per se* took a different tack in 1987. Whereas four years earlier, radical commentators such as Götz Aly had characterized censuses and other official statistics as dangerous in and of themselves, the focus now was more on the question of whether a census was necessary. Thus the sorts of criticisms of "planning ruins" noted above were more common, as was the observation that politicians often ignored whatever statistics were available and made their decisions on the basis of programs and values to which they were already committed. Implicitly or explicitly, these critiques referred to the admonishment of the justices in 1983 whereby the government was obliged to establish in each case that the proposed information-gathering exercise was indeed necessary, and was the least invasive means of gaining necessary data. Computer Science Professor Klaus Brunnstein once again played a prominent role in foregrounding the technical possibilities for re-identifying individuals on the basis of supposedly "anonymous" data. On

---

50 Anon. 1987. Klebriger Mauerspaziergang. *die tageszeitung*, June 1, p. 1; Fehrle, B. 1987a. Eine zartblaue Tapete für die Berliner Mauer, *die tageszeitung*, June 1, p. 5.

51 Anon. 1987. "Als sei es des Teufels eigenes Werk". *Der Spiegel*, May 18, p. 27.

52 Anon. 1987. Teufel an der Wand. *Der Spiegel*, April 13, 46, p. 49; Kutscha and Paech, *Totalerfassung*; Rottmann, V. and Strohm, H. 1986. *Was Sie gegen Mikrozensus und Volkszählung tun können: ein Ratgeber*. Frankfurt: Zweitausendeins; Appel, R. and Hummel, D. (eds.) 1987. *Vorsicht Volkszählung! Erfaßt, vernetzt und ausgezählt*. Köln: Kölner Volksblatt Verlag; Hohmann, H. (ed.) 1987. *Freiheitssicherung durch Datenschutz*. Frankfurt: Suhrkamp.

53 Anon. 1987. Das Unbehagen, als Schaf gezählt zu werden. *Süddeutsche Zeitung*, April 14, p. 15.

54 Anon., Teufel an der Wand, p. 46.

his advice, an explicit ban on re-identification was written into the 1985 VZG, but Brunnstein, like many West Germans, had little faith in the powers of legislative text alone.[55] With his student Simone Fischer-Hübner, he developed a simulation program showing how re-identification would work, and embarked on a tour of West German cities and towns, filling auditoria throughout the first half of 1987.[56] Ruth Leuze's arguments regarding the impossibility of keeping census work separate from other administrative tasks (and personnel) especially in small municipalities would have an ongoing impact. Although her voice would be heard more often through the summer of 1987, once the census was being taken and the processing of forms had begun, her early warnings already earned her the enmity of conservatives in her own state of Baden-Württemberg. There the CDU delegation in the state capital Stuttgart had demanded that the state government do what it could to ensure "that the impression not continue to persist that the Data Protection Commissioner is in solidarity with groups calling for a boycott of the census."[57]

Partly as a result of publicity efforts, and partly also simply because the boycott was not cut off before the census was taken, the scope of citizen participation in the 1987 boycott movement dramatically exceeded the 1983 mobilization. One rough yardstick is the number of citizens' initiatives. Whereas at the height of the 1983 controversy, the number of initiatives registered in the taz stood at 450 to 500, by May of 1987, there were some 1,500 VoBo Inis in existence.[58] A "coordination office" set up by the Green Party in Bonn claimed that "there is no longer a white spot on the map."[59] The existence of this coordination office points to another crucial qualitative difference between the 1983 and the 1987 movements. Although still fairly "grassroots" in character, the 1987 movement managed to settle on a unified boycott strategy long before the controversy reached its high-point in mid-year, and while there was still a good deal of local variation in tactics, most VoBo Inis did in fact follow the basic outlines of the strategy. Its keystone was a commitment to the so-called "hard boycott". The idea had first been mooted in 1983, and already in late 1986, Christian Ströbele, Green Party delegate in the *Bundestag*, was urging this form of boycott.[60] "Soft" boycott methods, which would include filling out the forms only partially or falsely but returning them, were in principle safer for individual boycott participants, but they had the great political disadvantage that the scale and effect of soft boycott would be impossible to gauge. If boycotters could be convinced to pursue the hard strategy, it would be easier to translate

55 Anon. 1987. Sicherster Ort. *Der Spiegel*, January 12, p. 89.

56 Anon., "Als sei es des Teufels eigenes Werk", p. 25.

57 Quoted in Willier, D. 1987a. CDU-Kampagne gegen Datenschützerin. *die tageszeitung*, May 5, n.p.n.

58 Pokatzky and Sontheimer, Zähler und Gezählte, p. 33; Dahlheimer, A. 1987. Den Planern geht die Puste aus. *Vorwärts*, July 11, p. 7.

59 Quoted in Anon., "Als sei es des Teufels eigenes Werk", p. 26.

60 Winter, M. 1987. Zähler sollen die Volkszählung zum Scheitern bringen. *Frankfurter Rundschau*, December 12, n.p.n.

the boycott into a compelling political message and to maintain commitment. In early 1987, though, two specific forms of hard boycott were still under discussion, the so-called "Bochum model" and the "Berlin model".[61] The former approach, advocated by the VoBo Ini *Bochum-Langendreer* and also by the Hamburg Inis, placed the accent on a refusal to accept the census forms in the first place, and on political work in residential apartment blocks to ensure the utmost solidarity among neighbors in presenting a united front of refusal. The political statement was to be direct and open, and the enumerators were to be told that refusals were part of the boycott. The Berlin model, by contrast, though not politicizing the immediate encounter with the enumerator at the doorway, generated an indirect and more global political statement. The Berlin model foresaw residents accepting the census forms without any overt indication of intent to boycott. The electronic bar codes identifying the addresses would then be clipped off, and the anonymized forms would be mailed or delivered by hand to local "alternative collection points". These alternative collection points would overlap to a significant extent with the institutions anchoring the oppositional geographies reviewed in the Introduction. In the May 1987 number of the local Köln city paper *Stadt-Revue*, for example, the list of collection points for anonymized census forms includes three community centers, two organic/health food shops, four bookstores, three university student offices and a cafeteria, two bars, a wine shop, a restaurant, a day-care center, the offices of the local FDP youth organization, and two local Green offices.[62] Volunteers at these alternative collection points could then photograph the stacks of empty forms and send the photos to the press. Eventually a more direct and exact method was decided upon: the collection points would keep running statistical totals of the empty returned forms, and report these numbers to a central office, which would in turn inform the press of the scope of the boycott. This system was in fact set up by May 1987, with the Bonn Green Party headquarters as the central tallying point charged with continually updating the so-called "boycott barometer".[63] As we shall see, the press did in fact keep tabs on the "barometer" numbers as the census went forward in May, June and July. This concept of an alternative running total was doubly elegant in that it served not only to give a clear indication of the strength of the boycott but also constituted an illustration of what a truly and purely *statistical* enumeration should be, in the sense that it was fully anonymous. An additional feature recommending the Berlin model was the fact that it would take much more effort on the part of the local census offices to

61 The description of the two models is paraphrased from an unpublished discussion paper: Tanneberger, S. and Gröger, A. 1987. Papier über die zwei, z.Z. am häufisten diskutierten Positionen zum Boykott der Volkszählung 1987, das sog. "Bochumer Modell" und das sog. "Berliner Modell". Archiv Grünes Gedächtnis, Bestand B.II.1, file no. 6017(1).

62 Anon. 1987. Volkszählungs-Boykott-Sammelstellen. *Stadt-Revue*, May 1987, p. 47, afas, 80.III.4.

63 Pokatzky and Sontheimer, Zähler und Gezählte, p. 33.

determine that individuals were in fact boycotting, and the prospect of being taken to court or being forced to pay fines was initially much more distant.

The risk involved in the hard boycott originated in the fact that the statistical offices still had their lists of names and addresses, their so-called *Hilfsmerkmale*. Thus by not turning their forms in to the statistical offices, individual boycott participants would make themselves vulnerable, in principle at least, to fines and other legal measures. Boycott organizers countered this fear by insisting that the state and federal governments would be completely incapable of pursuing individual boycotters if that meant initiating thousands of legal actions at once. The prospect of an utterly unmasterable "avalanche of legal actions" [*Prozesslawine*] would force governments to grant general amnesties.[64] As the drama unfolded over the spring and summer months of 1987, many West Germans were convinced enough of their own safety to participate in the hard boycott. Only later would the prediction of an "avalanche" prove to have been optimistic, and thousands of boycotters find themselves facing the legal powers of the state.

Census opponents as extremists

Roderich Reifenrath, writing in February of 1987, asserted that "[t]he republic stands before a new 'war of religion' [*Glaubenskrieg*]", a metaphor picked up and repeated in subsequent commentary.[65] The term *Glaubenskrieg* refers to what English speakers know as the "30-Years' War", the complicated 17th-century religious/political contest that ruined and exhausted large swathes of central and northern Europe before ending in the 1648 Peace of Westphalia commonly understood to have been a decisive step in the establishment of the modern system of nation-state sovereignty and international politics. The metaphor of a religious war is apt, in so far as the census controversy involved fundamental matters of political commitment, and revolved around tensions between the very different views of democracy, legitimate state power, freedom of conscience and action, and resistance surveyed in the Introduction. From the beginning of the 1987 controversy, the Kohl administration and census supporters focused their sharpest attacks on the Green Party, and not without reason. The Greens were the only party in the *Bundestag* to vote against the *Volkszählungsgesetz* in late 1985, and national and local Green Party organizations throughout West Germany played a prominent role in publicity and logistics for the boycott throughout 1987. *Der Spiegel* interpreted Green boycott support in part as a matter of electoral politics:

64 Pokatzky and Sontheimer, Zähler und Gezählte, p. 35.

65 Reifenrath, R. 1987. Legalität – Legitimität. *Frankfurter Rundschau*, February 25, n.p.n.

> For Green Party politicians the boycott campaign – shortly before the electoral battles in Hessen, Hamburg and Rheinland-Pfalz – fits especially well into the [overall] concept. They can try to portray the SPD, which voted for the *Volkszählungsgesetz* in its constitutionally-trimmed form, as a mute [*tumbe*] state-protection and surveillance party, and so expand the political market niche of the Alternatives at the expense of the SPD.[66]

Twenty-two Green delegates to the *Bundestag* made news when they unfurled a banner reading "Volkszählungsboykott" in Bonn, an act for which they were each later fined DM 8,400.[67] This was not uncontroversial within the Green leadership, with "fundi" support for the boycott strenuously opposed by the "realos", to whom the boycott appeared a convenient political excuse for the main parties to continue to paint the Greens as a fringe party not to be taken seriously or entrusted with any real power. Jutta Ditfurth, national Co-Chair, was a fiery champion of the boycott, urging her audience at the May 1987 state Green Party conference in Baden-Württemberg to join the boycott: "This boycott will help us to dismantle a piece of the surveillance state and thus to create space for something like democratic fresh air, which we in this state urgently need to counter this stale atmosphere [*stickigen Mief*] from the right."[68] Perhaps the most important action of the Bonn-based leadership in the longer-term was to have set up the central information clearinghouse from which the "boycott barometer" totals of empty returned forms were broadcast. At least as important as the national leadership was the work of local Greens in cities, towns and villages across West Germany. A look at the partial list of VoBo Inis published in early May of 1987 in taz gives a more fine-grained sense of the scope of Green influence. The contact addresses for the local Inis reveal the same mix of local book stores, cafes, social service bureaus, student organizations, anti-nuke organizations, etc. as in 1983, but the presence of the Greens is much more prominent. Roughly one quarter of all the contact addresses are local Green Party offices, and there was doubtless a good deal of Green involvement also in some of those institutions not explicitly identified as Green.[69] One important contribution some of these local Green organizations were able to make, especially if they were in office as part of local coalitions, was to provide space, phone lines, photocopying and other infrastructure for meetings and events. But two qualifications need to be registered with respect to Green involvement. First, it is not the case that the Greens dominated the boycott movement in any

---

66 Anon. 1987. Datenschrott für eine Milliarde. *Der Spiegel*, March 16, p. 45.

67 Anon. 1987. Nur Schafe. *Der Spiegel*, April 27, p. 132; see also Anon. 1987. "Boykott beeinflußt Ergebnis nicht". *Süddeutsche Zeitung*, April 30, n.p.n.

68 Ditfurth, J. 1987. Rede auf der Landesversammlung der Grünen Baden-Württemberg in Stuttgart am 23. Mai 1987. Archiv Grünes Gedächtnis Bestand A – Krieger, Verena, Archivsignatur 17, p. 4.

69 Anon. 1987. Volkszählung '87: mit Initiative(n) gegen den Erfassungsstaat. *die tageszeitung*, May 5, n.p.n.

sort of univocal and comprehensive way. They were, as the proportion of Green offices in the list of contact addresses suggests, the single most prominent group involved in the boycott, and they had at their disposal more resources than did the other organizations. But the movement drew its energy from a wider range of sources, and remained a grass-roots movement in many respects.[70] Second, again, any appearance of a unified anti-census stance even within the Green Party would be deceptive. The national party leadership at the time of the 1987 boycott was dominated by "Fundis" who tended to take a more uncompromising stance toward the census, and many of the active local party organizations were run by Greens aligned with them. But many other locals, and a number of *Bundestag* delegates, were not.[71] The 1987 census controversy was a clear illustration of the basic political dilemma faced by the Greens in the 1980s. Roderich Reifenrath neatly summarized the realo position on this dilemma: "The Party decided in favor of the parliamentary path, and it cannot claim legitimacy [now] for arbitrarily bending the instruments [of power] in its engagement with opponents, [for] being in the vanguard of illegal protest actions, when it seems politically opportune [to exercise] extra-parliamentary pressure."[72]

In short, the Greens offered an irresistible target to pro-census government officials and conservative commentators. Heinz Rosenbauer, State Secretary of the Bavarian Interior Ministry, asserted in an opinion piece for the *Bayern Kurier* that "for the Greens, the *Volkszählung* is only a means toward the end of challenging the state and moving further along the path of making our *Bundesrepublik* ungovernable."[73] For the editors of the *Frankfurter Allgemeine Zeitung*, the Greens were "not a constitutional party [*keine Verfassungspartei*]" at all.[74] This accusation suggested two damning resonances, one recent and connected with the "social movement" side of the Green dilemma, the other longer-term and linked to the idea of the Greens as a party. The recent resonance yoked the Greens to the domestic extremist groups of the 1970s and 1980s, and carried the implication that their open advocacy of civil disobedience was tantamount to subversion of the FDGO. The Greens were not alone in finding themselves on such a slippery slope. In late January of 1987, the left-leaning Republican Attorneys' Association [RAV] published an open letter (reprinted in the *Frankfurter Rundschau*) appealing to the Kohl administration and the *Bundestag* either to halt the census entirely or at least to recognize a "right to refuse enumerator duties". Citing a high degree of public mistrust, continued foot-dragging by state legislatures in complying with

70 Bannas, Die Zählung ist noch nicht über den Berg.

71 Anon. 1987. Bonn: Volkszählung verläuft positiv. *Süddeutsche Zeitung*, May 26, n.p.n.

72 Reifenrath, Legalität – Legitimität; see also Leicht, R. 1987. Staat im Visier, *Die Zeit*, May 1, p. 1.

73 Rosenbauer, H. 1987. Grüne rufen zum Rechtbruch auf. *Bayern Kurier*, February 28, p. 4.

74 Anon. 1987. Eine kleine Pflicht. *Frankfurter Allgemeine Zeitung*, May 21, n.p.n.

the 1983 Constitutional Court decision's requirement that they legislate explicit safeguards for local data processing, and the lack of evidence that planning failures can be attributed to bad statistics, the attorneys judged the 1987 census a threat to West German political culture. Failing any response by the government, they urged civil disobedience in the form of a boycott.[75] In late March, the civil rights organization the Humanistic Union [HU] launched a petition drive asking that the government either halt the census or, once it was carried out, destroy the collected data. As the head of the HU, legal scholar Jürgen Seifert, explained it, the organization deliberately refrained from calling for a boycott in an effort to counter the tendency in some official and media discourse "to transform citizen protest against the registration state [*Erfassungsstaat*] into revolt against the legal state [*Gesetzesstaat*]". The right of petition, Seifert noted, was guaranteed by Article 17 of the Basic Law.[76] Such caution availed little. As a result of their seemingly moderate actions, the RAV and the HU were soon to find themselves the objects of disturbing scrutiny. A taz report out of Hannover begins thus: "The Constitutional Protection Agency [*Verfassungsschutz*], which according to the law is permitted to track 'efforts against the free democratic basic order or the integrity [*Bestand*] and security of the federation and the states', busies itself now in Lower Saxony with misdemeanors [*Ordnungswidrigkeiten*]."[77] A confidential six-page *Verfassungsschutz* file had been obtained by Werner Holtfort, an SPD delegate to the Lower Saxony state parliament, wherein the RAV, the HU, the Greens and the *Jungdemokraten*, a left-liberal youth organization, were named in connection with the assertion that resistance to the census was "essentially initiated by political extremists".[78] If it had to be admitted that there was some substantive difference between refusing to answer the census and setting off a bomb, the Kohl government insisted it was only a difference of degree, and perhaps even just a passing difference. As reported in taz in early 1988, the Interior Ministry of Baden-Württemberg had asserted in the course of a position paper on the VoBo that "terrorists, too, start small."[79] The spectrum of forms of opposition, in this view, was best understood as a progression of stages along which resistance to state authority would inexorably intensify if disgruntled citizens were not deterred at an early point. This view of the matter seemed to be confirmed for the pro-census camp when violence did erupt in May, despite the fact that violent

75 Quoted in Anon. 1987. Weg zum Überwachunsstaat. *Frankfurter Rundschau*, January 28, p. 23.

76 Seifert, J. 1987. Gegen die Gretchenfrage. *Frankfurter Rundschau*, April 2, n.p.n.

77 Voges, J. 1987a. Vobo: Verfassungsschutz wird aktiv. *die tageszeitung*, April 16, n.p.n.

78 Voges, Vobo.; Spoo, E. 1987. Vom Volkszählungsgegener zum "Extremisten". *Frankfurter Rundschau*, April 24, n.p.n.

79 von Appen, K. 1988. Vobo's im Staatsschutz-Computer. *die tageszeitung*, January 12, n.p.n.; see also Plog, K. 1988. Boykotteure landeten in Polizeidatei. *Frankfurter Rundschau*, January 12, p. 1.

incidents were extremely small in number and were publicly condemned by the Greens and other boycott organizers (see Chapter 4). Interior Minister Friedrich Zimmermann strengthened the association between boycotters and terrorists when he expressed his conviction that the violence was the work of the Red Army Faction [RAF].[80] Chancellor Helmut Kohl, who in general refrained from commenting in great detail on the census issue, nevertheless made it known that he considered opponents of the census to have a "deeply fascist mindset".[81]

One of the most interesting attempts to place census boycotts on a continuum with violent resistance to the state took the form of a long article by Dr Elisabeth Noelle-Neumann for the *Frankfurter Allgemeine Zeitung* in mid-May, entitled "The census as a test of governability". Noelle-Neumann marshaled survey numbers from the *Institut für Demoskopie Allensbach*, the conservative-leaning public opinion research institute she had founded in 1947 with her first husband, to lend credence to the damning associations with which census opponents were being yoked.[82] The article opened with a clear recognition of the unique diagnostic value of a census: "A census is a test of a nation's governability. A legislatively approved measure of abstract, not easily explicable utility, which nevertheless does not pass by the majority of citizens but requires participation from each individual, is an ideal yardstick." But Noelle-Neumann did not linger on the specific of the census, instead immediately turning to a debate on the theme of "majority decisions in a democratic state" carried out by young West Germans on "Youth Day" 1986 in the *Bundestag*. Noelle-Neumann recalled that the debate seemed to cover many of the same basic questions around the "social contract" taken up by John Locke and associates in the 17th century. But the conclusions reached by the participants in 1986 suggested that the idea of a social contract meant little to contemporary West German youth: "That one must give up a part of one's individuality in the interest of peaceful co-habitation – and in the interest of external defense capabilities, one could also add – ... is no longer clear to a large part of our population and above all to the younger part." Noelle-Neumann explored this problem by means of polling numbers on the issue of the state's monopoly on violence. In an Autumn 1986 Allensbach poll, 60% of respondents had not heard of the term "monopoly on violence", and only 1.7% were able to explain it clearly. Forty-one percent associated the term with the limitation of citizens' rights and excessive state force; 13% explicitly mentioned the terms "police state" and/or "dictatorship". On the evaluative question of whether they were "for" or "against" the state's monopoly on violence, the answers fell out evenly: 45% in favor, 44% against. Among people

80 Anon., Bonn: Volkszählung verläuft positiv; see also Stumfall, F. 1987. Motive der Gegner. *Bayern Kurier*, May 30, n.p.n.

81 Quoted in Hartung, K. 1987. Selbstanzeige. Kohl bezichtigt Vobos der "faschistischen Gesinnung". *die tageszeitung*, May 14, n.p.n.

82 Noelle-Neumann, E. 1987. Die Volkszählung als Probe auf die Regierbarkeit, *Frankfurter Allgemeine Zeitung*, May 13, n.p.n. All of the following quotes from this article refer to the same page.

under 30 years old, 38% supported the monopoly on violence, 48% opposed it. Among Green voters, only 19% approved, while 74% disapproved. The non-binding view of state authority suggested by these numbers was also expressed in the way the young people in parliament on Youth Day 1986 summarized their debates on violence. A central theme for them was the "spiral of mutual violence [*gegenseitigen Gewalt*]", and participants reported agreeing that there must be a mutual effort on the part of both state and citizens to prevent the spiral from occurring. Noelle-Neumann commented: "Here we have an image of two equally justified opponents in strife, between whom peace must somehow be established." Labeling this idea a "confusion" [*Verwirrung*], Noelle-Neumann turned to another Allensbach survey question for further insights:

> If at a demonstration matters reach the point of a confrontation between demonstrators and the police, sometimes the police beat demonstrators, and demonstrators attack police officers. What do you think: is it acceptable that police officers use force against demonstrators who refuse to follow police orders, or may the police not use any force?

Slightly over 1/3 (36%) of all respondents thought use of force by the police acceptable, 40% thought it unacceptable (24% were undecided). For respondents under 30, only 25% approved of police coercion, and 49% thought the police should not be allowed to use force. Among Green voters, only 8% admitted a police right to use force, while 69% rejected such a right. Three times between 1980 and 1986 the Allensbach Institute also asked the following question:

> In a small town a factory is supposed to be built. The municipal council has approved the building of the factory, but the population is against it. A legal action resulted in a decision that the population can do nothing to stop it and that the factory must be built. In a public meeting, two speakers take the floor and say the following. With which speaker would you agree? [The first speaker says] The municipal council and the court have decided that the factory will be built. We elected the municipal council, so now we must accept this democratic decision, and may no longer try to defend ourselves against the construction. [The second speaker says] I see it differently. We, the citizens, are against the factory. If the municipal council cannot see that, the population can judge better. We must in any case hinder the construction of the factory, even if we might have to use force.

Overall, 23% of survey respondents agreed with the second speaker, with the number climbing to 34% for those under 30, and to 47% for Green voters. Noelle-Neumann interpreted these numbers, and the trend away from support of the state, as signs of a progressive dissolution of a pre-existing pro-state consensus. If the Greens were in some sense the political culprits, what had changed in the individual process of decision-making? Referring to another poll question on resistance to the building of a new runway at the Frankfurt airport (the "Startbahn West" controversy … see Introduction), Noelle-Neumann asserted that it was the individual *conscience* that had gained ground at the expense of state authority. If conscience could override obedience, this implied a "right of resistance." Here again, a polling question (this time about the right to resist the stationing of mid-range rockets on West German soil, another very current issue in the 1980s) served as confirmation: 45% of respondents under 30 believed there was a right of resistance, and the number climbed to 58% for Green voters. Noelle-Neumann drew all of this material together to conclude that there was a growing plebiscitary tendency in West German political culture, a move toward support for more direct democracy. Already in 1978, polls showed a majority of respondents believed, "in opposition to what the Basic Law says", that elected officials should not be able to vote against an opinion they know is held by a majority of the population they represented. Her editorial insertion here placed her squarely in the camp of those for whom the greatest danger to democracy emanated from the untutored masses, not from duly elected officials, who were implicitly to be trusted.[83] If too much democracy was the problem, the trends revealed in the statistics pointed not to a positive evolution of democratic thought but to an erosion of basic political understanding for the representative system, an erosion driven onward by the Green Party.

There were a number of contentious assumptions underlying Noelle-Neumann's argument, most obviously those allowing her to collapse civil disobedience and violent protest. At one level, this was a characteristic view among Germans of her generation (Noelle-Neumann was born in 1916), many of whom had emerged from the Nazi period convinced that the biggest danger to stable democracy lay with "the masses", who could so easily be misled by demagogues, and with popular politics unfiltered and un-channeled by "proper" institutional mechanisms of representation. But of course from the perspective of many younger West Germans, how people answer a question about police violence does not necessarily say anything about how they will answer a similarly structured question about whether citizens should pay parking tickets. Conversely, if large numbers of citizens are prepared to refuse participation in a census, this cannot immediately be ascribed to a fundamental unwillingness to recognize state authority in all spheres of life. More interesting are the mechanisms by which Noelle-Neumann's argument stigmatized the Greens. The strategy at work here had a number of elements. The structuring of the discussion of polling data according to a tripartite scheme involving the general population, people under 30 and Greens was important. No comparable distinctions between the survey responses of voters for other political parties were drawn, which allowed Noelle-Neumann to set Green voters off against "the population" as a solid mass of implicitly normal West Germans. It would have been interesting, for example, to know whether there were significant differences between CDU/CSU voters and SPD voters, many of whom were members of the industrial working class, on the police right to use violence at a demonstration.

83 See Sontheimer and Bleek, *Grundzüge*, pp. 184, 266.

Where there were undoubtedly degrees of opinion along a continuum, in short, Noelle-Neumann constructed a sharp break. Even leaving aside the category issue, the stigmatization of the Greens as "pro-violence" involved some creative interpretation of numbers that by themselves were not actually so clear. The survey results quoted by Noelle-Neumann established only that most Greens disapproved of the idea that the state had a right to exercise violence uncontested, on the simple presumption that any such exercise must be legitimate. This is not equivalent to a Green consensus that individuals have a right to use violence against the state.

If Noelle-Neumann constructed Green voters as always already tendentially violent, she also implicitly developed a specific corresponding model of the state as a political actor. The characteristic pattern of state behavior suggested by her argument was one in which the state could be expected to do whatever was necessary to force compliance, up to and including the exercise of violence. The state, in other words, would not take "no" for an answer. It could be counted on to escalate its side of any confrontation with disobedient citizens, and this escalation was naturalized in the way the survey questions were asked. Thus the suggestion of the young people in the *Bundestag* that the "spiral of violence" could be addressed by negotiation and mutual recognition had no purchase with Noelle-Neumann. Her rejection of this idea was of a piece with the insistence of conservative commentators upon placing the term "acceptance" in quotes. The idea that citizens need to "accept" a legal statute grated against a political worldview in which the executive organs of the state will and should always have their way regardless of circumstances. This underlying political philosophy was elegantly dissected by the television journalist Hoimar von Ditfurth (father of Green Party national Co-Chair Jutta Ditfurth) in an open letter to *Der Spiegel* explaining "Why I do not wish to be counted".

Von Ditfurth began by brushing aside the relevance of some of the more familiar arguments in favor of answering the census:

> The census law is "constitutional", or so I've been assured. I certainly hope so … But: in the end I don't warm up to a politician simply – we haven't yet reached that point – if he succeeds in persuading me that he's not corrupt. I wouldn't have anything to fear, so I've been further assured, because it is "most strictly forbidden" to use the data gathered in the count in other administrative areas … I am reminded of how long murder and theft have likewise been "most strictly forbidden" … But okay … I start from the optimistic position that what may not be [done] will (also under any future government) not be [done] (because it was strictly forbidden). I even go one step further and grant the officials delegated to the count in small municipalities the ability to adopt a state of schizophrenia at the behest of their superiors.[84]

84 von Ditfurth, H. 1987. Why I do not wish to be counted. *Der Spiegel*, May 18, pp. 34-39. Subsequent quotes taken from this article are to be found on pages 34, 37, 39 and again 39.

Even granted all of this, von Ditfurth argued, he was still not comfortable with the idea that he should surrender his personal information to the state. His imagined interlocutor countered by reminding him that the census law was passed according to the rules of democratic process. "Wouldn't there be a threat of total anarchy, the collapse of society, if every minority were allowed to decide which laws they felt like respecting?" Von Ditfurth answered in the negative, pointing out that some laws were more indispensable to the constitutional and social order than others. He would not dream, for example, of suggesting that the death penalty should be introduced or that the right of asylum should be stricken from the books. But laws regulating everyday life processes, traffic, etc. were simply not pillars of West German society. He went on to argue that especially such everyday regulations should serve the citizenry, not the other way around.

> For this reason the hunter is permitted to protest publicly against the inclusion of ravens in the list of protected species, and the homeowner likewise [to protest] undisturbed against what in his view are excessive protections for renters. Whether they are successful is a different question. But the public rightly considers their protest permissible, although it is directed against legal measures.

Why, then, von Ditfurth wondered, was the outcry from Zimmermann and other census supporters so shrill? At one level, he believed, it was indeed the old "authoritarian reflex" (here he quoted Heinrich Heine: "I know the style, I know the text/I know as well the honorable authors …" [*Ich kenne die Weise, ich kenne den Text/Ich kenne auch die Herren Verfasser*]). Was it a question of insisting on completely accurate census numbers? Von Ditfurth thought this would have been in keeping with the well-known German penchant for perfectionism, but again, it failed to explain the intensity of insistence. Ultimately, he believed, it had to do in part with an "authoritarian need for reparations for the 'Humiliation [*Schmach*] of 1983'":

> A right-wing ruling group [*rechte Obrigkeit*] does not recover from such a defeat overnight. It experiences the rebuff of the high court not as an orientation aid but as public humiliation. The excessive battering about the ears we have received regarding the guaranteed constitutional conformity of the present enumeration betrays just how deep the thorn sits. In plain text they are saying nothing other than, "This time we are in the right. This time there will be no escape for you. This time you will have to absorb the blows."

Volkszählung 1987 was, in other words, an obedience test. Both sides realized it, deep down. And in Hoimar von Ditfurth's view, this interpretation resolved the mystery of why the authorities insisted so relentlessly on compliance with what was actually an unimportant law. "[It is] precisely *because* the numbers are so 'harmless' [that] the act of their surrender which is demanded of us is so incomparably well suited as a symbol of our submission. And precisely because compelling grounds for the whole state action *cannot* be given …, the carrying out of this project offers an outstanding opportunity to demonstrate who is in charge." Having recognized what lay at the root of the government's insistence on the census, von Ditfurth also realized that he had reached a line he was not willing to cross.

> This administration, which demands in such a stiff-necked way the trust that we supposedly owe to it, has itself long since lost all the democratic courage [necessary] to show its citizens even the tiniest quantum [*Quentchen*] of trust. In its blindness it instead considers it high time to have us all, as objects of enumeration, jump through the hoops, so that we have the opportunity to prove ourselves reliable subordinates. I have to admit that my republican self-image simply revolts against this kind of test.

Especially in view of the unparalleled disasters that had resulted from the German mentality of subordination to authority, Hoimar von Ditfurth concluded by declaring himself fully prepared to pay the legitimate fine his personal revolt would bring upon him.

The communist taint?

The foregoing section shows that at one level, the demonization of the Greens and other census opponents as "extremists" was the flipside of a conception of state authority going back to the 18th century "police state" tradition and carried forward through the years of the *Bundesrepublik* as a peculiarly strong form of "state piety" [*Staatsgläubigkeit*].[85] As the review of Elisabeth Noelle-Neumann's discussion shows, this conception of state authority hardly needed to be advanced by opponents of the census seeking to construct their own "image of the enemy" [*Feindbild*]: the image was quite openly embraced by politicians and pro-census commentators themselves. A similarly uncompromising and authoritarian figure of state power was clearly at work in the second major defamatory association suggested by denying the Greens recognition as a "constitutional party". This smear tactic was of older and more hallowed provenance, but has regained currency since 1989, namely, an imputed connection with communism. Article 21, Paragraph 2 of the Basic Law prohibited parties that did not explicitly accept the West German constitutional framework from participating in the political system. Thus it was one of the ways in which West German democracy was to be "fortified". Originally formulated with a view to hindering the rise of any new Nazi-like party, this provision of the Basic Law was famously used to outlaw the Communist Party of Germany [KPD] in 1956. In 1968, for reasons to do in part with West Germany's international image as an open society, the foundation of a new party, the German Communist Party [DKP], was tolerated. This successor party retained very close ideological, personnel and financial ties with the SED,

85 Sontheimer and Bleek, *Grundzüge*, pp. 184-185.

the East German ruling party, and walked a fine line through the 1970s and 1980s in its efforts to further communist goals without falling too far afoul of the ever-watchful Constitutional Protection Agency [BVerfSch].[86] The political marginality of the DKP was in any case guaranteed by the carefully cultivated mainstream anti-communist consensus that stretched back in an unbroken line through all the political upheavals and sea-changes of the 20th century.

In associating Greens with communists, pro-census politicians were not conjuring their accusations entirely out of thin air. Unlike in 1983, the DKP and other communist groups did in fact play a visible, though subordinate, role in organizing the 1987 boycott. In March, the *Frankfurter Allgemeine Zeitung* paraphrased a report from (unnamed) West German security services claiming to have evidence of a campaign by the DKP to take over leading positions in the boycott movement.[87] Although communists could not realistically hope to supplant Greens as the most important single group, at least some local communist organizations were deeply involved in some of the earliest activity.[88] In March, Inge Kopp, a high official in the Socialist Unity Party of West Berlin [SEW], the local sister-party of East Germany's ruling SED, called for a boycott at a party meeting in Tempelhof.[89] In an article entitled "Greens and communists: hand in hand against the law", the *Bayern Kurier* noted that the DKP was inviting groups of public service workers to seminars on "counter-strategies" against the census.[90] Members of the Heidelberg DKP were fined along with local Green leaders for taking pro-boycott positions on behalf of their parties.[91]

For many mainstream West German voters, any *overt* involvement of communists in the census boycotts would already have been damning. Any evidence that the Stasi [*Ministerium für Staatssicherheit* (Ministry for State Security)], the feared East German secret police, were somehow *covertly* involved in infiltrating or steering the boycotts, would of course have robbed them of any last shred of credibility. There was no such evidence at the time of the boycotts, but the new availability of surviving Stasi files after the fall of the Berlin Wall and the unification of Germany offers an opportunity to query the boycotts from another angle. Research in the Stasi files has ignited a still-ongoing debate revolving around attempts to unearth and evaluate the extent of the Stasi presence in all facets of West German politics. Some researchers, most prominently Hubertus Knabe, tend toward the view that Stasi activities seriously compromised the

86 Sontheimer and Bleek, *Grundzüge*, pp. 224-225.

87 Anon. 1987. Die DKP übernimmt die Vorreiter-Rolle. *Frankfurter Allgemeine Zeitung*, March 11, n.p.n.

88 Hauptverwaltung Aufklärung. 1987. Informationen über Probleme der Volkszählung in der BRD. BStU, MfS Signatur HVA 47, p. 93.

89 Anon. 1987. VoBo – Boykott gerechtfertigt. *die tageszeitung*, August 21, n.p.n.

90 Roos, Grüne und Kommunisten, p. 8.

91 Anon. 1987. Anwalt muß für Boykotthilfe Bußgeld zahlen. *Süddeutsche Zeitung*, May 27, n.p.n.

integrity of wide swathes of West German public life.[92] A much discussed recent example of work in this vein is the exhaustive research by Bettina Röhl, daughter of Ulrike Meinhof (of RAF fame), demonstrating how thoroughly dependent the left magazine *konkret*, and indeed Meinhof herself and her husband Klaus-Rainer Röhl, were upon East German funding.[93] Other researchers would more likely agree with the judgment of Jens Gieseke in his history of the Stasi:

> The idea that the *Bundesrepublik* or at least essential parts of the political mainstream, or the (in the widest sense) left social movements of the 70s or 80s were subcutaneously steered from East Berlin, [and that] the "open society" *Bundesrepublik* was too lukewarm toward its "enemies" does not hold up under sober inspection.[94]

While I agree that newly unearthed connections to the Stasi should always be cause for careful ethical and political reassessment, I do not share Knabe's absolutist view of the automatic disqualifying effect of Stasi involvement in West German political issues. Certainly when it comes to the Green Party, the peace movement or the many other left political movements or issues in which the Stasi had some level of involvement, it makes little sense to claim that any such involvement retrospectively discredits these movements. Too many West Germans were independently concerned about these issues, and their concern cannot plausibly be portrayed simply as the product of cynical manipulation.[95] Thus, for example,

92 Knabe, H. 2001. *Die unterwanderte Republik: Stasi im Westen*. Munich: Ullstein.

93 Röhl, B. 2006. *So macht Kommunismus Spass! Ulrike Meinhof, Kaus Rainer Röhl und die Akte konkret*. Hamburg: Europäische Verlagsanstalt. Bettina Röhl, along with her twin sister Regine, was abandoned by Meinhof after she went underground to help found the RAF. Without informing her husband, Klaus Rainer Röhl, Meinhof left the two children in Sicily in the summer of 1970, with the intent to have them sent on to a Palestinian-run orphanage in Jordan. They were eventually located and returned to their father by Peter Homann and Stefan Aust (author of the standard history of the RAF and former acquaintance of Meinhof and Röhl). (Aust, *Baader Meinhof Komplex*, pp. 134-138).

94 Gieseke, J. 2006. *Der Mielke-Konzern: Die Geschichte der Stasi, 1945-1990*. Munich: Deutsche Verlagsanstalt, p. 245.

95 The most common form of connection with the Stasi, where there was one, would have been as a source of funding, especially for chronically cash-starved, all-volunteer social movements and initiatives requiring funds to generate publicity (printing costs, rental of public buildings, etc.). The intermediaries who knowingly passed on Stasi funding can rightly be called to account because they took money, in full awareness, from an organization known for a blatant and sometimes deadly disregard for human rights. But these agents or informers would have had a strong personal interest in keeping most people in the receiving organizations in the dark about their links to the Stasi. Even those activists seeking to learn more precisely where funding originated would have had limited resources with which to do so. In these cases, to condemn the entire organization or cause is to construct a very abstract and unrealistic picture of culpability.

even if it turned out that the census boycott movements had been supported in some systematic way by the Stasi, this would not discredit them completely. The task would be to discover exactly how and to what extent they were supported. As I will demonstrate below, it happens that they were not supported by the Stasi in any appreciable way, but the Stasi were nevertheless very interested in the boycotts. The reasons for their interest shed a unique light upon the question of how realistic the respective *Feindbilder* or images of the enemy held by census supporters and opponents ultimately were.

Before turning to the Stasi files, however, more needs to be said about the Stasi's activities in the West and about the larger discourse they have provoked. The most explosive evidence emerging from the files over the past 15 years concerns previously unknown activities of individual West Germans as "unofficial associates" [*inoffizielle Mitarbeiter* or IMs] of the Stasi, that is, informers not employed as full-time spies but simply paid for regular or occasional reports on some aspects of West German politics or society with which they were personally involved. The Stasi maintained some thousands of IMs in the BRD throughout the 1980s. Knabe estimates 20,000-30,000 were active at one time or another from the establishment of the Stasi until 1989, though an exact total number, or an exact number for any specific date, is difficult to establish, chiefly because the files on Western IMs were destroyed in 1989 and 1990.[96] The Federal Commissioner for the Records of the State Security Service of the former German Democratic Republic [BStU], the agency that now maintains the Stasi archives, estimates that 3,000 to 3,500 West German citizens were registered as IMs in 1989, though this would not have comprised the entire IM network.[97] Since the early 1990s, thousands of former East Germans and hundreds of former West Germans have seen their careers and lives ruined by being outed as former IMs, and debates have raged over the publicizing of this information.[98] A second form

96 Knabe, *Die unterwanderte Republik*, p. 10; see also Gieseke, *Der Mielke-Konzern*, pp. 114-115, 202-231.

97 Bundesbauftragte für die Unterlagen der Staatssicherheitsdienstes der ehemaligen Deutschen Demokratischen Republik 2009. Kurzinformationen zum Ministerium für Staatssicherheit (MfS). [Online]. Available at: http://www.bstu.bund.de/cln_028/nn_1328350/DE/MfS-DDR-Geschichte/Hintergruende-zur-Staatssicherheit/Kurzinformation/kurzinformation__node.html__nnn=true#doc765536bodyText7 [accessed: January 12, 2010].

98 The guidelines that accompany materials sent to researchers by the Federal Commissioner for the Records of the State Security Service of the Former German Democratic Republic go into great detail about the various conditions and procedures attendant upon the use and publication of anything concerning the activities of individuals. (Der Bundesbeauftragte für die Unterlagen des Staatssicherheitsdienstes der ehemaligen Deutschen Demokratischen Republik [BStU] (n.d.), Informationsblatt: "Verwendung von Informationen aus Stasi-Unterlagen für die Forschung" Berlin: BStU). One case of at least indirect relevance to the census boycotts was that of Karl-Heinz Roth, physician, historian and former associate of the B2J [*Bewegung 2. Juni*], who had spent time in jail after being

of Stasi involvement was funding of organizations. This was an important pillar of its attempts to gain and retain some influence within the extra-parliamentary Left that emerged from the 1960s.[99]

In his overview of the influence of the Stasi in the *Bundesrepublik*, Knabe surveys, among other topics, Stasi policy with respect to the West German political scene in the 1980s. Supporting the DDR government line in this area, Stasi chief Erich Mielke laid out the broader goals of the organization's work in the West for 1983, giving priority "to the uncovering of steps taken by [the Kohl] government against the reduction of tensions and [against] peace, to the encouragement of the process of differentiation in the parties of the BRD, to the support of forces, organizations and movements standing in opposition to this government ...".[100] By "differentiation", Mielke meant to encourage an increase in political distance and thus tension between the parties, which would of course render united action against the interests of the DDR more difficult. Not surprisingly, the Stasi were very interested in the Green Party, as they embodied a highly significant instance of political differentiation. But the Greens were not only a potential tool: they "were, on the one hand, valued in the context of protests against further NATO armament, but on the other hand appeared especially dangerous to State Security because of their contacts to like-minded people in the DDR."[101] Through IMs, which included a couple of prominent Greens, the Stasi attempted to discourage the Greens from taking an open anti-DDR line on foreign policy issues. The Stasi also invested a good deal of energy and undercover work in the new peace movement that reached its peak in 1983.[102] To my knowledge no direct evidence has been reported in the *secondary* literature showing Stasi involvement in the census boycott movements, but this may in part be a matter of the relatively scant attention the boycotts have received in comparison with better-known political issues. Certainly the Stasi focus on the Greens and the peace movement meant that it was very much present in the immediate environment of the boycotts.[103]

---

captured at the scene of a shootout with police. Roth, with Götz Aly, had carried out the research on the Nazi use of statistics that served as a mainstay of anti-census arguments in 1983 and again in 1987. After the Wall came down and researchers gained access to the files of the Stasi, Roth was accused in a 1997 article in the newsmagazine *Focus* of having spied for the Stasi as "IM Zeus". He has not reacted to this accusation. (Mailander and Zander, *Westberlin-Lexikon*, p. 48; Kraushaar, W. 2000. *1968: Mythos, Chiffre und Zäsur*. Hamburg: Hamburger Edition, p. 161.)

99 Kraushaar, *1968*, pp. 139-162.

100 Quoted in Knabe, *Die unterwanderte Republik*, p. 42.

101 Knabe, *Die unterwanderte Republik*, p. 71. See more generally pp. 71-88.

102 Knabe, *Die unterwanderte Republik*, pp. 243-255.

103 Knabe does mention one other piece of circumstantial information, namely that the Köln publisher Pahl-Rugenstein, which brought out one of the edited books attacking the census, security laws and new personal ID cards, was in some way "operatively" connected to (perhaps funded by) the Stasi. (Knabe, *Die unterwanderte Republik*, p. 254). The book in question is Kutscha and Paech, *Totalerfassung*.

It would have been quite surprising, therefore, if the census boycotts had had no presence whatsoever in Stasi files.

The files on the census boycott movements located by the archivists of the BStU confirm some of the general points made by Knabe about the Stasi's goals and hesitations with respect to Western social movements. For example, they include a photocopy of an open letter of May 1987 from 100 former DDR citizens to the Federal government of the BRD, a letter which must have annoyed Stasi officers:

> We former citizens of the DDR, now living in the *Bundesrepublik Deutschland* and Berlin (West), declare our intent to refuse [participation in] the imminent census of 25th May 1987. We are reminded by this census of our experiences with the government agencies of the DDR. In the DDR we were constantly exposed to a surveillance system of the state apparatus. We were registered and inspected through personal identification numbers, house-books [*Hausbücher*], personnel files (cadre files), questionnaires and spying systems and much else besides. With a targeted state planning and surveillance policy we were kept in line [*wurde über uns verfügt*] and the unfolding of our personalities hindered. We are not prepared once again to accept similar forms of state abuse of power …[104]

The letter went on to label the census unconstitutional (the phrase "unfolding of our personalities" was a direct reference to one of the two first Articles of the Basic Law on which the Constitutional Court had based its 1983 census decision). The letter already indicates one source of the ambivalence of the Stasi toward the VoBo: social movement protests in the BRD were generally considered a good thing, but when the theme was the surveillance state, the discourse could easily become uncomfortable. Another sense in which Stasi files on the boycotts reflected larger patterns is in their confirmation of the sourcing of information from IMs within the Green Party and West Berlin's *Alternative Liste* [AL], the umbrella left-wing party in that city's local government. A good deal of the information the Stasi collected on the census consisted of insider accounts of the planning and execution of VoBo-related activities.[105] Finally, there is some evidence in Stasi files that RAF members were present at early meetings on the boycott in Hamburg in January of

104 Anon. 1987. Offener Brief hundert ehemaliger Bürgerinnen und Bürger der DDR an die Bundesregierung (n.d.). BStU, ZA, MfS Signatur Sekretariat Neiber 429, p. 143.

105 See Hauptabteilung Terrorabwehr. 1987. Operativ-Information 062/836/87 über Aktivitäten der Alternativen Liste Berlin-West zum Volkszählungsboykott. March 25. BStU ZA, MfS Signatur HA XXII 794, vol. 43, pp. 1-4; Anon. 1987. Information G/009318/03/03/87/02. BStU ZA, MfS Signatur Sekretariat Neiber 429, pp. 160-163.

1987, and that the RAF and Revolutionary Cells [RZ] had expressed the intention to attack census offices.[106]

In general, however, the Stasi files contain nothing to indicate sustained, active involvement with the VoBo. A one-page memo from the 13th of February is all the archivists could find regarding the census boycott of 1983. The archival material for early 1987 up to the time of the enumeration totals 65 pages. Brief though it is, the 1983 memo, penned by a Stasi Oberst [Colonel], already indicates the main areas of Stasi interest in the census and the boycott. These lines of discussion would be developed at more length in 1987. The February 1983 memo shows plainly that, far from wishing simply to push forward the boycotts as a generic opportunity to make trouble for the West German government, the Stasi took boycott propaganda about the surveillance state seriously:

> It must be taken as a starting point that the opponent [the BRD state] will acquire with this broad program a plethora of data from the individual sphere of the West German and West Berlin population, [data] which, once saved in the appropriate computer systems, will form the basis for further surveillance and control activities of the enemy ... In connection with the planned census ... the following points need to be taken into account *in view of the security of the network of IMs* ...[107]

The key issue, thus, was the safety of Stasi informants, and this would remain the key issue in 1987. The 1983 memo went on to call attention to some additional details of the census that could constitute threats to the alibis or false identities of Stasi agents or informants in the West. At the end, there was an interesting bit of speculation on possible uses of the census: "It should be considered to what extent the deployment of volunteer helpers for the census is useful for the legending [*Legendierung* ... the construction of false biographies for agents and informers] of future political-operative measures in the operative area [*Operationsgebiet* ... the Stasi shorthand for West Germany]."[108] In other words, perhaps the Stasi could gain access to census files as a source for identity theft. In general it is not too much of a simplification to say that the Stasi were nervous about the census, but at least as nervous about participating in the boycott. Much in the way that boycott propagandists worried about the boycott itself becoming a "resistance map" allowing the government to pinpoint oppositional geographies,

---

106 Hauptverwaltung Aufklärung. 1987. Information über Probleme der Volkszählung in der BRD. BStU, MfS Signatur HVA 47, p. 93; Anon. 1987. Lageentwicklung im Operationsgebiet im Zusammenhang mit der "Volkszählung 1987". BStU ZA, MfS Signatur Sekretariat Neiber 429, p. 130.

107 Hauptabteilung Beobachtung, Ermittlung. 1983. Regimeinformation zur geplanten Volkszählung 1983 in der BRD und in Westberlin. February 16, 1983. BStU ZA, MfS Signatur HA VIII, 2936, p. 110, emphasis added.

108 Hauptabteilung Beobachtung, Ermittlung, Regimeinformation.

the Stasi worried that active participation in the boycott would bring unwelcome attention to its minions. However, and this is part of what makes the 1987 files so fascinating, the Stasi were nervous about boycott participation because they *knew,* through internal moles in the "adversary's state protection services" [*gegnerische Staatsschutzdienststelle*, which chiefly meant the *Verfassungsschutz* but could also have included the *Bundesnachrichtendienst* or BND], that the boycott movements were being closely observed by West German security agents. Thus, to some extent at least, the Stasi files offer confirmation, "through the back door", as it were, of some key claims made in boycott propaganda regarding surveillance by West German security services.

The Stasi files concerning the 1987 census, as mentioned earlier, consist in part of detailed reports on planning and execution of the boycotts, but much of this information was also reported in the press. The focus here will chiefly be on the theme of ensuring the safety and continued secrecy of informants and agents. The first detailed analysis of the 1987 census, prepared for Department VI of the Investigative Administration [*Hauptverwaltung Aufklärung, Abteilung VI*] appeared in July of 1985, before the final passage of the 1987 census law by the *Bundestag*. After an account of the political maneuvering among West German parties around the enumeration date, the report moved on to "operative guidelines and conclusions" regarding the security of Stasi agents and informants. The basic assumption behind this section of the document was that "the census is significant above all in regard to combinations of changes of residence" by Stasi informants and agents.[109] Thus the chief concern was to ensure that all the personal data for undercover associates and agents be consistent across the different agencies that had data, and that the data given on the census match all pre-existing information, especially the data in the residency registers. Stasi handlers were to ensure that all informants under their supervision be prepared to meet census enumerators with "a sure mastery of legends, a convincing manner, unhesitating completion of the questionnaire", and to ensure as well that they had the documentary evidence they needed to back up their stories.[110]

As the census drew nearer, memos and reports circulating between Stasi offices built on each other, accreting more and more detailed information, new layers of analysis specific to the tasks of different departments, and developing ever-more refined guidelines for what to do, as more was learned from agents in the census apparatus and in West German security agencies. A set of guidelines circulated in the Counter-espionage Department [*Hauptabteilung Spionageabwehr*] from February of 1987 noted that in addition to the need to ensure basic consistency between census responses and other existing files containing personal data, undercover agents and informants would have to make sure their responses to the census could pass the

109 Hauptverwaltung Aufklärung, Abteilung VI 1985. Überblick zur gegenwärtigen Lage bei der Vorbereitung einer Volkszählung in der BRD. July 5, 1985. BStU ZA, MfS Signatur BV Gera, Abteilung XV 0260, vol. 3, p. 4.

110 Hauptverwaltung Aufklärung, Abteilung VI, Überblick, p. 5.

"plausibility controls" with which the local census offices sought to flag incomplete or potentially false responses. This implied, as later memos would make explicit, that IMs and Stasi agents should in any case not participate in the boycott using "soft" measures such as filling out census forms with partial, incomplete or misleading information. Another piece of advice in the February 1987 document concerned travel: "Attempts at evasion [of the census], such as trips abroad, stays in hotels or pensions and moving house during the enumeration period will, as cases of counter-espionage-related [*abwehrmässig*] interest, as a rule attract enemy interest and analytical activity [*Bearbeitungsmaßnahmem*]."[111] A somewhat different version of the same memo circulating in the Investigative Administration [*Hauptverwaltung Aufklärung*] differentiated more carefully between the different types of person under Stasi control in West Germany. "Original persons" [*Originalpersonen*], that is, individuals living under their real names, most likely West German citizens operating as IMs, were urged to answer the census; fully or partly "legalized" persons (probably immigrants from the DDR for the most part) whose personal information could withstand scrutiny, were also permitted to answer the census. Difficulties could arise, so the document went on to point out, regarding conflicting information on primary and secondary residences.[112] This issue had turned up in press coverage of the boycotts primarily as a concern for young West German men who mendaciously listed West Berlin as their primary residence in order to avoid mandatory military service. The specific danger pinpointed by the Stasi, though, concerned a third type of person, the "*Doppelgänger*", an agent using the data of an "unitiated Original person" [*uneingeweihter Originalperson*] living elsewhere in the *Bundesrepublik*. A third, more detailed version of these guidelines, probably circulated slightly later but still at least six weeks before the enumeration date of 25th May, explained the problem of *Doppelgänger* at greater length, and urged specific measures to counter the danger:

> Plausibility comparisons between the questionnaires turned in by the Original person and excerpts from the residency registers would lead to differences regarding the ownership of a second home. Before the printing out of the enumerator lists for the locale of the Original person, the residency register there must have the record of the operatively used second home deleted. The latest time for the initiation of this de-registration process should be about six weeks before the enumeration date.[113]

---

111 Hauptabteilung II – Spionageabwehr 1987. Leiterinformation – Volkszählung 1987 in der BRD und in Westberlin. February 19, 1987. BStU ZA, MfS Signatur HA II 4421, p. 4.

112 Hauptverwaltung Aufklärung, Abteilung VI 1987. Überblick zum geplanten Ablauf der Volkszählung 1987 und den operativen Konsequenzen für die Sicherheit des IM-Netzes. BStU ZA, MfS Signatur BV Gera, Abteilung XV, 0260, vol. 2, pp. 3-4.

113 Anon. 1987. [No title or date]. [Unknown Stasi department – cover sheet missing]. BStU, ZA, MfS Signatur BV Gera, Abteilung XV, 0261, vol. 2, p. 7.

I read the first part of this instruction to imply that Stasi agents registered the addresses of *Doppelgänger*, both in the local residency register and in the local residency register of unsuspecting Original persons living elsewhere, as the second homes of those Original persons, who in reality owned no second homes. Thus, unbeknownst to these innocent West Germans, Stasi agents using their identities were living perhaps only a few hundred kilometers away in homes officially but fictitiously listed as their second homes. The latter part is particularly interesting for its demonstration of the sort of manipulation of West German records the Stasi felt confident it could undertake without detection. Despite all the attention paid to the general consistency of census responses with other sources of data, however, the Stasi had come to the conclusion by late Spring of 1987 that this was not where the chief danger for the network of IMs lay. Further on in the same document, the narrative turned to the issue of movement, and revealed a cat-and-mouse logic worthy of Cold War spy novels:

> On the basis of their partial awareness of [Stasi] methods, and in the knowledge of the pressure to act to secure the IM-network brought on by the census, the enemy counter-espionage organs are also in a position to work out the dates [by which the Stasi would have to have sorted out which IMs could stay in place and which would have to move due to inconsistent data]; counter-espionage measures against parts of the IM network will thus concentrate not in the first instance upon obvious discrepancies recognized during the enumeration but upon evasive movements before this time-span. Especially in large urban areas and population centers, calibrating information for data searches [*Rasterfahndung*] could already be derived before the census. Among these would be, for example, the possible comparison of the residency register with information that points to moving out of a house. This [latter] sort of information could include the closing out of rental contracts especially in large apartment complexes, the scheduling of freight services, the use of furniture storage facilities, the closing out or switching of telephone, radio/TV, energy, water or bank accounts. Operative evasion movements should therefore be ordered in time and legended such that in the context of natural population movements no causal relation to the census can be suspected.[114]

In the last sections of this document, the anonymous analyst turned to the issues of how the West German security agencies were likely to use census data in their struggle against subversion, and how (or whether) the Stasi itself might eventually be able to use the census results. On both points the conclusions were rather bland. With regard to uses of census data by "the enemy", it was thought most likely that because of its limitations, the census data would serve not so much as a direct locator of subversive individuals and groups such as Stasi agents or members of the RAF but rather indirectly, to improve the accuracy and completeness of

114 Anon. [No title or date], pp. 7-8.

the informational basis for *Rasterfahndung*.[115] Similarly, with regard to its own projects, the Stasi analyst considered and rejected three possible uses of the census data: as a large-scale source of personal data on BRD citizens, as an occasion to carry out specific espionage through enumerators, and as an occasion for deepening knowledge about how the BRD state carried out its work. In all cases, the nature of the potential benefits for the Stasi was judged minimal in comparison with the costs and risks involved.[116]

None of the material obtained from the BStU dates from after the 25th of May, the date of enumeration, so the eventual effects of the census (or the boycott) on the network of IMs in West Germany will have to await further research. However, a number of conclusions can be drawn, and a few speculative questions raised, regarding the involvement of the Stasi with the census boycotts. First it is clear that Stasi officers, far from taking a leading role in steering the boycott, were chiefly observers. Whatever advantage they may have seen in causing trouble for the West German government was not the ruling consideration. The West German DKP did get involved early on, but its profile had lowered dramatically by the time of the enumeration date. In view of the Stasi's concern that its IM network remain inconspicuous, it is at least possible that a signal was sent from East Berlin ordering the DKP to back off. Second, the Stasi definitely considered the census a threat to the integrity of its spy network, chiefly because of its potential use against Stasi operations by Western security agencies. Thus the "surveillance state" propaganda of the boycott movement received some implicit confirmation. Thirdly, however, the Stasi came to the view that the most threatening thing about the census was not the information it would produce but the indirect effect of the enumeration as a "beating of the bushes" that could force Stasi agents and informants into movements potentially detectable by the *Verfassungsschutz*. Finally, the Stasi ultimately did not consider census data attractive enough to be worth expending effort to obtain in any systematic way.

The ideological battles reviewed in this chapter connected the census boycott both to the issue of domestic extremism that had played so prominent a role in West German political discourse since the 1960s and to the longer and deeper 20th century theme of communism and subversion. Most of these connections were made by a newly mobilized and determined pro-census publicity discourse. The boycott movements did not work as hard to open up new vistas of political analysis, chiefly recycling the quite sophisticated critiques already developed in 1983. However, the newly unified strategy of the hard boycott constituted an important innovation with implications both for the course of the struggle itself and for the publicity battle. And the Green Party, with its infrastructure and resources, would play a key role in making that strategy work for census opponents. As noted in the Preface, I will not take a position on the basic question contested in all this publicity, namely whether the census boycotts were ultimately legitimate or worthwhile. However,

115 Anon. [No title or date], pp. 9-10.

116 Anon. [No title or date], pp. 11-14.

the unique perspective offered by the chance to look into the Stasi files suggests that at least in 1987, many of the fears on the Left of a burgeoning surveillance state did in fact have some basis in reality. The fact that the Stasi took the census seriously as a threat to their spy network is already interesting, but even more interesting is what the files reveal indirectly about the degree of infiltration and surveillance of legal oppositional social movements in the BRD by *West German* security services. Whatever can be said twenty years later in judgment on the boycott movements, the Stasi perspective certainly makes it more difficult to argue that the boycotts *should have been recognized as a pointless or alarmist exercise at the time*. Be that as it may, the high-energy ideological battle surveyed in this chapter set up the 1987 census to be a bitter struggle, and indeed it was. The next chapter turns to the battles in and for material public and private spaces, and the ensuing courtroom battles that would drag on, in some cases, to the end of the decade. The seemingly innocuous act of refusing to answer the census was to become what might be termed "the misdemeanor that roared".

Chapter 4
The Battle in the Streets, Stairwells and Courtrooms

> Dear fellow citizens, he said, the result of the elections carried out today in our country's capital was as follows, the party on the right, eight per cent, the party in the middle, eight per cent, the party on the left, one per cent, abstentions, none, spoiled votes, none, blank votes, eighty-three per cent.

> [PRIME MINISTER:] The armed forces and the police, whether acting within the ambit of their specific areas of competence or in joint operations, always observing the most rigorous mutual respect and avoiding any arguments over precedence that would prove prejudicial to our aims, are charged with the patriotic task of leading the lost sheep back to the fold, if you will allow me to use an expression so beloved of our forefathers and so deeply rooted in our pastoral traditions.

(José Saramago, *Seeing*, pp. 27, 56-57)

With the conservative press, the *Verfassungsschutz*, the Interior Minister and many state-level officials perceiving the VoBo as an essentially criminal, unconstitutional enterprise, it was not surprising that state officials at all levels felt free to react to boycott activities as serious crimes. As they had at the ideological level, defenders of the "free democratic basic order" began their "ground attack" long before the census was mobilized, and used all the tools at their disposal in a sometimes startlingly repressive effort to silence and intimidate census opponents. Especially in West Berlin, and in the southern states of Bavaria and Baden-Württemberg, the goal seemed to be to snuff out the boycott movement by any means necessary. The fact that refusal to answer the census was technically a misdemeanor, on a par with a parking violation, seemed to lose all significance in the grim campaign to enforce obedience.

Spatial strategies of repression

One aspect of the 1987 movement that set it apart from the 1983 mobilization was that it involved more and larger public demonstrations. Thus, at the level of concrete repression and resistance, the politics of virtual statistical space became more thoroughly entangled than they had been four years earlier with contemporaneous struggles over physical public space discussed in the Introduction. Just as census opponents challenged the anonymity, and hence the neutrality, of census work, the state in turn challenged the anonymity of census opponents. The campaign to deny boycott organizers the use of state-controlled spaces and infrastructures was in effect a rejection of the presumption that these individuals and organizations were simply generic citizens, anonymous constituents of the "general public" and as such entitled to use public facilities. As in 1983, boycott organizers planned a "VoBo week" of public events, this time in mid-May, aimed at highlighting the problems with the census and the intent of many citizens to boycott it. On the Kurfurstendamm, the main shopping street in West Berlin, a small group of demonstrators (approximately 200) cheered as a man climbed onto a local sculpture and began to drop shredded census forms as confetti onto the street, proclaiming a "recycling action". But as some demonstrators began to burn pieces of "confetti", police troops appeared, blocked the street and arrested 26 individuals, who were charged with arson and destruction of property [*Sachbeschädigung*]. The 26 arrests were made on the basis of films taken by police video teams.[1] A week later, a few thousand demonstrators accompanied a giant papier-maché octopus and a banner reading "Boycott the Surveillance State" along West Berlin streets. As the demo broke up, a small group reappeared on the Kurfurstendamm to attempt a spontaneous action. They were immediately surrounded by police, however, and forcibly escorted, still trapped in this "moving kettle" [*wandernden Kessel*] to a subway station, where they were issued "city bans" [*City-Verbot*] and put on trains headed to Kreuzberg.[2] The *Süddeutsche Zeitung* estimated the size of the West Berlin demo at 7,000 and reported that some 12,000 to 15,000 people had taken to the streets the same day in Hamburg.[3]

Spaces controlled by the state included not just public space in the traditional sense of streets, parks and city squares, but also buildings. In mid-March in the Bavarian city of Augsburg, an event scheduled by the Green Party under the heading "Resistance against the census" prompted the Bavarian Interior Ministry to send a telex to all local municipalities declaring all government buildings off-limits to boycott-related meetings. In response, the city of Augsburg cancelled the Green Party's rental agreement for the venue.[4] The event was moved to an inn, and two of the speakers were later cited for misdemeanors for having urged listeners to boycott. Augsburg city officials weighed the possibility of forbidding all future boycott-related activities scheduled to take place on any city property.[5] In West Berlin in May, the Interior Administration forbade the *Alternative Liste* [AL] councillors in the ward council houses to use their offices as alternative

1 Moderow, M. 1987. Aktionsraum Ku'damm. *die tageszeitung*, May 11, n.p.n.

2 Anon. 1987. Licht, Klang und Knüppel. *die tageszeitung*, May 18, n.p.n.

3 Anon. 1987. Streit um Volkszählung spitzt sich zu. *Süddeutsche Zeitung*, May 18, n.p.n.

4 Baur, D. 1987a. Von Augsburg soll ein Signal ausgehen. *Süddeutsche Zeitung*, March 21/22, n.p.n.

5 Baur, D. 1987b. Referenten droht Anzeige. *Süddeutsche Zeitung* March 27, n.p.n.

collection points for empty census forms.[6] A "*Volkszählungsfest*" set for May 9th in Nürnberg was forbidden by a local administrative court on the grounds that the name given to the event, "Count nothing" [*Verzählnix*] sent an unmistakable message of intent to promote the boycott (*Verzählnix* was a deliberate reference to the alternative *Tunix* ["Do nothing"] meeting in West Berlin in 1978). In lieu of the cancelled event, the organizers quickly called for a "Fest for freedom of opinion and information", and this was allowed to go forward.[7] The denial of state-controlled spaces to boycott organizers was extended by some local governments to include public means of communication, as in Ludwigshafen, where mayor Werner Ludwig ordered the telephone lines to the Green Party offices in the council house cut off upon learning that a boycott flyer listed those offices as a contact number. The local administrative court rejected the Greens' petition for a restraining order against the mayor's decision in no uncertain terms: "the provision of a telephone connection involved the obvious pre-condition that this official connection would not be used for illegal actions."[8] In Stuttgart, the Greens likewise found their telephones blocked on orders from Erich Schneider, President of the Baden-Württemberg parliament. Schneider, though, took a more refined approach than the Ludwigshafen mayor, arranging to have only *incoming* calls to the Green offices blocked, not outgoing calls. The telephone number had been listed in a flyer as a "*Zählsorge*" line (literally "count-care", a play in German on the almost identically pronounced *Seelsorge*, the religious "care of souls" undertaken by the pastorate).[9] Schneider wanted to ensure that the Green pastoral mission did not involve advising the flock to withhold from Caesar what was Caesar's. As the confrontation over the census became violent in a few cases during the period just before the official enumeration day of May 25th, authorities sometimes exercised their veto rights over the use of space pre-emptively. In a number of cases they demanded loyalty oaths from organizations suspected of being anti-census as a prerequisite for use of facilities or services. The mayor of Calw, where the Baden-Württemberg Greens were scheduled to hold their annual meetings in late May, threatened to deny them the use of the city auditorium unless they promised to declare, in legally binding terms, that they would not issue calls to boycott during the meeting, and further, that they would not stage any public boycott events anywhere in the town.[10] In the Hessian town of Idstein, the administrative council refused to answer questions from the local Green party unless it would distance itself from the boycott. Here, though, a local court struck down the move as an

6 Anon. 1987. Rathaus tabu. *die tageszeitung*, May 22, n.p.n.

7 Anon. 1987. VoBo ... *die tageszeitung*, May 9, n.p.n. On the *Tunix Treffen*, see von Dirke, *"All Power to the Imagination!"*, pp. 111-120.

8 Holz, M. 1987a. Vobo – Telefonsperre Rechtmäßig. *die tageszeitung*, April 13, n.p.n.

9 Zorn, H. 1987. Immer Ärger mit der Volkszählung. *die tageszeitung*, April 16, n.p.n.

10 Willier, D. 1987b. Bürgermeister zensiert Grüne. *die tageszeitung*, May 8, n.p.n.

insupportable instance of censorship.[11] Undeterred by the flimsy legal foundations of such a strategy, in July the Federal Youth Minister Rita Süssmuth threatened five national youth organizations with withdrawal of financial support unless they "provided legally binding statements that their organizations had not called for census boycott."[12]

Another method of combating the use of state-controlled infrastructure for boycott-related activities was to confiscate incoming mail. Despite the well-established legal sanctity of postal materials, this is precisely what a West Berlin judge did in late May with the mail destined for AL offices, reasoning that some empty, anonymized census forms would be among the items sent.[13] The next day, the taz reported that in fact the state's attorney's office in West Berlin had begun to confiscate mail headed for over 100 alternative collection points throughout the city.[14] Over the next few days it turned out that the scope of this strategy was much broader than initially supposed. The taz itself had had some of its mail held, as had the HU, and the taz learned that one local West Berlin court had held 850 pieces of mail. As news of these actions gained national attention, the SPD leader of the *Bundestag* Committee for Postal and Broadcast Systems initiated investigations.[15] *Der Spiegel* reported that some 300 empty census forms had been found in the postal action. In early June, the state's attorney's office, perhaps fearing more negative publicity and hoping to forestall more searching judicial review, claimed it was ceasing to confiscate mail, since nobody would send the forms now that the search activities had been made public.[16] In a few cases, shutting off access to public space even extended to repression of broadcasting and publication. The taz reported that two scheduled appearances in April by members of the HU to discuss the census on radio programs were cancelled.[17] In Darmstadt, bookstore owners learned that six books concerning the census and/or the surveillance state were blacklisted, with a fine of DM 1,000 for displaying the titles in stores.[18] In Bonn, a local administrative court ordered the alternative city paper *De Schnüss* to excise pages 6-9 of its May number, which reported favorably on the boycott movement.[19] On 8th May, 533 copies of the issue were confiscated from newsagents, but most had already been sold. The offending pages of *De Schnüss* were utterly typical of what was appearing in other city papers throughout the *Bundesrepublik*: critical

11 Anon. 1987. Ver-Zählt. *die tageszeitung*, May 20, n.p.n.

12 Gaserow, V. 1987e. Geld-Stopp wegen Vobo. *die tageszeitung*, July 4, n.p.n.

13 Anon. 1987. AL-Post beschlagnahmt. *die tageszeitung*, May 26, n.p.n.

14 Anon. 1987. Umleitung der VoBo-Post. *die tageszeitung*, May 27, n.p.n.

15 Bornhöft, P. 1987b. Proteste gegen Postbeschlagnahme. *die tageszeitung*, May 30, n.p.n.

16 Anon. 1987. Wird geschätzt. *Der Spiegel*, June 1, p. 28.

17 Voges, J. 1987b. Geheimpapier zur Volkszählung. *die tageszeitung*, April 23, n.p.n.

18 Sieber, U. and Gaserow, V. 1987. Staat mobil gegen Vobo-Gegner. *die tageszeitung*, April 23, n.p.n.

19 Anon. VoBo …

analysis of the VZ, a diagram of the legal process, lists of VoBo Ini contact information and addresses of alternative collection points for the hard boycott, an interview with Prof. Klaus Brunnstein (the traveling computer expert). What had perhaps drawn the attention of authorities was that the word "Boykott" appeared on the cover.[20]

In tandem with attempts to prevent boycott organizers from using state-controlled public spaces and infrastructures, the local police in many areas initiated a rash of searches aimed at gathering evidence of calls to boycott the census. The boycott movement, in other words, would have its right to *any* spaces contested, while the state would demonstrate its right to enter *all* spaces. The main Green Party offices in Bonn were forcibly entered and searched by police on a Saturday night in April, and 1,000 brochures (entitled "Only sheep let themselves be counted") confiscated.[21] The local VoBo Ini in Darmstadt, after having its offices searched on May 8th, distributed a flyer detailing the police action. Upon inquiring about the basis for the search, the Ini had been told that the action was justified by ¶ 86 of the Criminal Statutes [*Strafgesetzbuch* or StGB], the text of which the Darmstadt Ini reproduced on the flyer. The title of ¶ 86 is "Distribution of propaganda of anti-constitutional organizations", and the text specifies four types of organization by or on behalf of which public materials may not be distributed: (1) a party or association declared anti-constitutional by the Federal Constitutional Court; (2) an association that is legally forbidden because it is directed against the constitutional order or against internationally accepted principles; (3) an external government, association or institution working on behalf of the kinds of organizations specified in (1) and (2); and (4) organizations striving to continue the publicity work of former Nazi organizations.[22] Neither the Greens, the HU, the RAV nor any VoBo Ini fit into any of these categories, as none of them were illegal or forbidden organizations. But this seems neither to have clouded the conscience nor dimmed the enthusiasm of local police and states' attorneys, and ¶ 86 StGB continued to be invoked in searches. In Mainz, the offices of the student government at the university, as well as the local Green offices and those of the youth group the *Jungdemokraten*, were searched.[23] According to *Der Spiegel*, a police search of a local VoBo Ini office in the politically sensitive Kreuzberg neighborhood of West Berlin had dramatic results: "There was no judicial search order for the "night-and-fog" action; the state's attorneys office had decided there was a "clear and

20 I am grateful to Jürgen Bacia at the *archiv für alternatives schrifttum* [*afas*] for locating the excised pages from *De Schnüss* (afas archive signature 5.III.2), and for the details of the confiscation action.

21 Sieber und Gaserow, Staat mobil gegen Vobo-Gegener.

22 VoBo-Initiative Darmstadt 1987. Volkszählungs-Infobüro in Darmstadt von Staatsanwaltschaft und Polizei durchsucht!! [Flyer] May 8. *tageszeitung* archive, Berlin. [no archival signature].

23 Anon. VoBo ...

present danger" [*Gefahr im Verzuge*]; that evening Kreuzberg was in flames."[24] The *Süddeutsche Zeitung* reported searches of DKP offices in Bremen and three VoBo Ini offices in Hannover.[25] Book shops and other alternative collection points were repeatedly searched in Munich.[26] Already by May 13th, the Greens were able to compile a list of over 100 instances of events being forbidden or offices being searched throughout the Federal Republic, and the list continued to grow.[27]

Many local officials, judges and police forces were not satisfied merely to assert control over spaces and public infrastructure in order to smother the boycott movement as a public phenomenon. Materials confiscated in searches, and notes taken by observers at VoBo events, were often used to pursue legal actions against individual boycott organizers. Again, the tenacity of the authorities was sometimes quite impressive. In April, the Lower Saxony authorities took Klaus Eschen, head of the RAV [*Republikanische Anwaltsverein* or Republican Attorney's Association], to court for claiming in a taz interview that the census was anti-constitutional, despite knowing (so the official justification read) "that only the Federal Constitutional Court may establish incompatibility with the Basic Law."[28] Freedom of opinion in the *Bundesrepublik*, in other words, did not extend to opinions about constitutionality of laws. In May, Eschen was again in trouble with the Lower Saxony government, which fined him DM 7,355.80 for open encouragement of the boycott, on the grounds that he presided over a meeting at which the RAV voted to support the boycott.[29] Eschen was not alone: fines for almost any kind of association with the boycott movement had become standard practice throughout West Germany, and thinking up new activities for which boycott supporters could be fined proved fertile ground for the imaginations of local officials.[30] Eberhard Bueb, state speaker for the Bavarian Greens, was fined DM 500 in the small town of Mainleus on most unusual grounds. While attending a cabaret evening organized for the boycott, Bueb noticed two police investigators sitting with notebooks, ready to record any misdemeanors. When someone took the stage for to call for the boycott, Bueb went to the table where the investigators

24 Anon. "Als sei es des Teufels eigenes Werk", p. 26. The phrase "Night and fog action" [*Nacht- und Nebel-Aktion*] is a reference to the sort of technically illegal raids undertaken by the Nazis against perceived enemies of all kinds.

25 Anon. 1987. Stand der Volkszählung umstritten. *Süddeutsche Zeitung*, May 29, n.p.n.

26 Loerzer, S. 1987. Rund um die Volkszählung. *Süddeutsche Zeitung*, June 1, n.p.n.

27 Gaserow, V. 1987c. Volkszählung: Vernunft boykottiert. *die tageszeitung*, May 13, n.p.n.

28 Sieber and Gaserow, Staat mobil gegen Vobo-Gegner.

29 Anon., Anwalt muß für Boykotthilfe Bußgeld zahlen.

30 Anon. 1987. Ausgesuchte Sauerei. *Der Spiegel*, April 6, p. 37; Loerzer, S. and Meschede, E. 1987. Das Unbehagen, als Schaf gezählt zu werden. *Süddeutsche Zeitung*, April 14, p. 15; Anon. 1987. "Boykott beeinflußt Ergebnis nicht". *Süddeutsche Zeitung*, April 30, n.p.n.; Henkel, P. 1987. Boykottierer registriert. *Frankfurter Rundschau*, May 21, n.p.n.

sat and proceeded to talk to them loudly, intending to drown out the boycott call. As quoted in the *Süddeutsche Zeitung*, the official justification for fining him was that "despite repeated admonishment [Bueb] insistently talked at the investigators on the scene [*fortlaufend auf die anwesenden Kriminalbeamten eingeredet ... habe*] and thus supported Mr. H. in his call to boycott."[31]

Shortly before the enumeration day in late May, the *Süddeutsche Zeitung* learned that the Baden-Württemberg Criminal Bureau in Stuttgart had ordered registration of the license plate numbers of cars belonging to individuals believed to be census opponents. "Also completely uninvolved people who happened to park their cars in the vicinity of the inns [*Gaststätte*] under observation may well have ended up in the criminal files of the Bureau."[32] The state government quickly distanced itself from the action.[33] In Erlangen, however, automobiles continued to be a medium of incrimination long after the census had been taken. One Hans H. was fined DM 300 in January of 1988 for having lent his Opel to boycotters engaged in an unapproved public event in July of 1987. The event involved carrying for 50 meters through the downtown a banner pasted together out of empty census forms, after which the banner, attached to balloons, was released and flew away. The police were unable to gather personal information on the four individuals who had borrowed Hans H.'s car, but this posed no obstacle to the local administrative court, which imposed the penalty "for assistance in the staging of an unapproved march."[34]

Much in the way that groups were sometimes requested to give binding statements distancing themselves from boycott activities, individuals were sometimes subjected to the control strategy so infamously enshrined in the "employment ban" [*Berufsverbot*] used in the 1970s against left extremist groups. Here again, Baden-Württemberg led the way. In May, the state Finance Ministry circulated a paper advising local municipalities to strip any local officials active against the census (which in practical terms meant Greens) of their voting rights.[35] Two weeks later, the City Director of Aachen refused the normally *pro forma* confirmation of the newly appointed Green delegation manager [*Fraktionsgeschäftsführer*] Günter Schabram because his participation in calls to boycott the census demonstrated that he "could not be relied upon to uphold the law." Schabram challenged the move.[36] In these as in many other cases, the attempts at control were eventually rejected by the courts. As a rule of thumb, higher courts tended to be more skeptical of repressive measures than local courts. But the ultimate legal failure of attempts at repression often did little to counteract their success as strategies of intimidation.

---

31 Holzhaider, Eine halbe Million Koffer voller Fragen.

32 Anon. 1987. Polizei sammelt Daten von Volkszählungsgegener. *Süddeutsche Zeitung* May 21, n.p.n.

33 Henkel, Boykottierer registriert.

34 Anon. 1988. Auto verleihen verboten. *die tageszeitung*, January 14, n.p.n.

35 Henkel, Boykottierer registriert.

36 Harms, I. 1987. Volkszählung und kein Ende. *die tageszeitung*, June 6, p. 3.

The experience of Bettina K., an employee of the city administration in the town of Dinslaken, illustrates this point. Selected in March to be an enumerator, Bettina K. declared herself unwilling. Called to a hearing, she explained her misgivings about the constitutionality of the census, and the next day was granted a reprieve from the duty. But City Director Schmitz, when he was informed of the case, was not at all satisfied with this outcome. He immediately relieved her of her normal administrative duties, halved her pay, and initiated a formal investigation. In his notification to Bettina K., Schmitz (who was also head of the local census office) explained: "Any support of the census boycott is a violation of the duties of public service. Because this means there is no assurance that you will also be prepared in the future to observe laws in force, [your] remaining in office is insupportable." Schmitz, though, did not have the last word. He had to suffer the indignity of being taken to court for these harsh measures, according to the city employees interviewed for the taz story, by the same attorney who had bested him in an impromptu debate at a boycott event. The local administrative court expressed "serious reservations about the formal and substantive propriety [*Ordnungsmäßigkeit*]" of his actions, and the city was instructed to reinstate Bettina K. Shortly thereafter, Schmitz went into retirement, and Bettina K. resigned, shaken by the whole affair.[37]

This admittedly rather breathless litany of repressive measures should not be taken as an exhaustive inventory of everything that happened to census opponents, nor even as a representative sample. The instances described above were of course far outnumbered by instances in which no repressive measures were taken. But once such episodes came to the attention of the public through the media, they were bound to make a larger impression. Such spectacular acts of repression may indeed have intimidated many West Germans, and may help explain the gradual shrinkage of the pro-boycott numbers in public opinion polls throughout 1987. But they also did significant propaganda work for the boycott movement, as they seemed to confirm the connection between state information gathering and surveillance in the interest of social control. As Hans Holzhaider argued in the *Süddeutsche Zeitung*,

> The most effective backers of census opponents, at least in Bavaria, are to be found in the ranks of the police and the security agencies [*Ordnungsbehörden*]. The inventiveness with which actual and suspected boycotters have been pursued by the bureaucracy in recent weeks has provoked the feeling, even among citizens of good will, that the legal and constitutional state [*Rechtsstaat*] could be endangered not [so much] by the census itself as by the accompanying circumstances.[38]

37 Gaserow, V. 1987g. Wie das Volkszählen zum Urlaub wurde. *die tageszeitung*, September 18, n.p.n.

38 Holzhaider, Eine halbe Million Koffer voller Fragen.

Rezzo Schlauch, a state delegate for the Greens in Baden-Württemberg, told the *Frankfurter Rundschau* that although he had been skeptical at first of what seemed to him overly dramatic fears of the surveillance state, he now felt such fears were fully justified. He joked also that all the repressive measures highlighted a serious over-staffing of the police forces.[39]

Violence and safety for census infrastructure and enumerators

In the days before the official enumeration date of May 25th, 1987, some of the approximately 600,000 enumerators were already sent forth to begin their counts of businesses, residences, and the population itself. Opposition to the count heated up ahead of the date as well, sometimes to a temperature nobody had anticipated. The instances of violence in May of 1987, although disowned by all "above-ground" organizations, also represented a new dimension of resistance. Bombings targeted official centers of calculation and thus the centrally organized system of territorial control, and attacks on enumerators challenged the right of citizens to traverse public space as gatherers of knowledge for the state. Two weeks before the enumeration day, Helmut Trompeter, President of the Bavarian State Criminal Bureau [*Landeskriminalamt* or *LKA*] warned of expected bombings: "With the approach of the [census] date, attacks on State Statistical Bureaus, Residency Registration Offices or computation centers must be reckoned with, also in Bavaria."[40] Trometer anticipated a role in these attacks for the RAF and the *Revolutionäre Zellen* [RZ], but also expected autonomous regional militant groups to be involved. Two days later, the taz reported an arson attack on the census office in Heilbronn.[41] Citing this and other attacks, including a 1983 bombing of the Hamburg Cadastral and Geodesic Bureau [*Kataster- und Vermessungsamt*], and the bombing of the Leverkusen Residency Register Office in March of 1987, Chief Federal Prosecutor Kurt Rebmann applied in late May to the Federal Investigative Judge in Karlsruhe for permission to set up roadblocks and conduct searches throughout West Germany in pursuit of "militant census opponents."[42]

The public communiqué claiming credit for the Leverkusen bombing of March 10th, 1987 is interesting because it shows that at least some militant fringe groups did not accept the critical analyses of census propagated by the "Green-liberal spectrum".[43] Citing the sorts of social prophylactic planning measures discussed by "Sabine" in the Spring of 1983, the anonymous authors of the communiqué insisted

39 Henkel, Boykottierer registriert, n.p.n.

40 Anon. 1987. LKA-Präsident befürchtet Anschläge wegen Volkszählung. *Süddeutsche Zeitung*, May 14, p. 21.

41 Anon. 1987. "Volkszählung macht Spaß!" *die tageszeitung*, May 16, n.p.n.

42 Anon. 1987. Dünne Gründe. *Der Spiegel*, June 15, p. 116.

43 Anon. 1987. kommunikee – Die Bombe ist gezündet – der Widerstand auch. HISF Bestand SBe 444, Box 2: VoBo_Büro Hamburg – VoBo '87 Flugblätter, n.p.n.

that "for the statisticians and social planners it is not primarily about the individual 'glass person' (this is only a side-project, like more effective control of resistance) but rather [about] the population groups that in the course of economic restructuring can only be exploited [*verwertet*] and disciplined to a limited extent."[44] Foreigners and women were singled out as examples, as were "problem" neighborhoods in large cities. The communiqué closed with the call "BOYCOTT AND SABOTAGE THE CENSUS AND THE NEW PERSONAL IDENTIFICATION CARD! SOCIAL REVOLUTION AGAINST INHUMANE SOCIAL POLICY!"[45]

More disturbing than the bombings for many were the attacks on enumerators, which in some cases involved physical injury. These, too, started in mid-May. On the 20th, the taz reported muggings of enumerators in Hannover and Hamburg. In the latter case, four masked men made off with the enumerator materials.[46] Responsibility for the Hannover attacks was claimed by "Action-Group Enumerator-Intimidation [*Aktionsgruppe Zählerschreck*]".[47] In an editorial in the taz two days later ("The fun ends there"), Petra Bornhöft condemned such attacks, as well as anonymous letters urging "unmasked" [*enttarnte*] enumerators to commit suicide. Labeling this "psychoterror against individuals who certainly did not organize the total registration [*Totalerfassung*]", Bornhöft urged census opponents to reject all such tactics: "Here neither the direction nor the method is correct. The strength of resistance against the census lies not in fists."[48] Condemnations from the government and census supporters were also not long in coming. In a front page editorial, the *Frankfurter Allgemeine Zeitung* blamed the Greens ("not a constitutional party"), as did the FDP, the SPD and of course the CDU/CSU in the *Bundestag*.[49] CDU/CSU spokesperson Johannes Gerster accused the Green leadership of "outrageous instigation to sabotage", and of wanting to use the boycott "to revolutionize this republic".[50] Green Party delegate Gerald Häfner countered that the Greens "reject every act of violence against census enumerators", but his colleague Regula Schmidt-Bott insisted also that any discussion of violence against enumerators also mention the state violence that formed part of the context for it.[51] Asked on May 21st by the *Süddeutsche Zeitung* about the number of attacks on enumerators, the Interior Ministry reported fewer than 20 nationwide.[52] Small in number though they were, such incidents prompted Hamburg police to redirect some of their patrols in the interest of protecting

44 Anon., kommunikee.

45 Anon., kommunikee.

46 Anon., Ver-Zählt.

47 Anon. 1987. Voll in die Hose. *Der Spiegel*, May 25, p. 129.

48 Bornhöft, P. 1987a. Da hört der Spaß auf. *die tageszeitung*, May 22, n.p.n.

49 Anon., Eine kleine Pflicht.; Anon. 1987. Bundestag verurteilt Gewalt gegen Volkszähler. *Süddeutsche Zeitung*, May 22, p. 1.

50 Anon., Bundestag verurteilt Gewalt.

51 Anon., Bundestag verurteilt Gewalt.

52 Anon., Bundestag verurteilt Gewalt.

enumerators, and *Die Zeit* reported in mid-June that one enumerator in Nürnberg had decided to carry a revolver while doing his census rounds.[53] *Der Spiegel*'s May 25th issue reported on death threats received by enumerators, and on enumerators being forced to hand over their materials to census opponents at knife-point in Köln and at gunpoint in Wuppertal. Nevertheless, the influential weekly stuck by its anti-census position:

> The mood has been stoked [*geschürt*] not least by the snappy [*zackigen*] slogans with which Union politicians have inflated doubts about the census into traitorous agitation, and have demanded draconian penalties – skepticism about whether the data are really only to serve harmless statistics has befallen even cooperative [citizens]. The outrage regarding a few bloody noses and wrestling matches over enumerator boxes have distracted [the public] from official mis-steps and legal violations that have frequently accompanied the count.[54]

However one chose to interpret the attacks, the publicity surrounding them did intimidate enumerators in a few of the more politically charged areas of the *Bundesrepublik*, notably West Berlin and Hamburg. Urban neighborhoods known to be home to significant numbers of squatters [*Hausbesetzer*] or *Autonomen* were systematically avoided by enumerators.[55] *Der Spiegel* noted in early June that some of the political hot spots would probably never be fully counted, quoting the taz in reference to West Berlin's most flammable neighborhood, "Kreuzberg will be estimated [*Kreutzberg wird geschätzt*]".[56] The difficulty of the count in some areas contributed to a very uneven geographical pattern regarding the speed at which the census went forward. As will become clear below, this unevenness actually subverted one of the main strategies of the boycott movement.

To gain knowledge about the population, the state had to have access, through hundreds of thousands of delegated enumerators, to all the public spaces in the territory.[57] Few and far between as they were, violent incidents nevertheless succeeded in interfering with this access by instilling fear in many enumerators. Enumerators were denied the neutral, anonymous status of citizens fulfilling a legitimate obligation to the state. Instead, they were forced to think of themselves as vulnerable, embodied individuals traversing a public territory potentially fraught with danger. Working for the state by helping to take the census, in other words, was re-interpreted as a partisan activity which took place on contested

53 Anon. 1987. Polizeischutz für Volkszähler. *Süddeutsche Zeitung*, May 19, n.p.n.; Pokatzky and Sontheimer, Zähler und Gezählte, p. 33.

54 Anon., Voll in die Hose, p. 129.

55 Anon., "Als sei es des Teufels eigenes Werk", p. 32.

56 Anon., Wird geschätzt, p. 28; Anon. 1987. Kreuzberg wird geschätzt. *die tageszeitung*, May 25, n.p.n.

57 See Hannah, M. 2000. *Governmentality and the Mastery of Territory in Nineteenth Century America*. New York: Cambridge University Press, Chapter 5.

ground and which thus rendered individuals vulnerable to attack from the other side. A similar though differently articulated logic was at work in discussions of the safety of women enumerators. Here, too, West Germans participating in the census as enumerators were denied the twin comforts of a neutral anonymity and personal security in public spaces. A woman enumerator quoted in a long article on the census in the February 1987 *Vorwärts*, the monthly publication of the SPD, summarized the problem: "If we enter a residence and the door is closed behind us, what can happen then[?]…".[58] The article goes on to report that "bad experiences" in taking the building census that preceded the main *Volkszählung* led the Women's Commissioner of the city of Leverkusen, Susanne Hein, to request "protective accompaniment" for women enumerators. Friedrich Harfst, Hannover's chief statistician, expressed skepticism that this was really a problem, but the *Vorwärts* article claimed that multiple cases of unwanted advances by men occurred in connection with census tests in the Fall of 1986. Hein's counterpart in Mönchengladbach, Gabi Meyer-Ulrich, arranged for women enumerators to have access to free karate courses.[59] West Berlin's Interior Senator Wilhelm Kewenig joined Harfst in attempting to dismiss the whole issue, arguing that "womanly charm" would actually make the work of female enumerators easier.[60] The census law stated that all West Germans between the ages of 18 and 65 were in principle duty-bound to act as enumerators. This was fully consistent with Western democratic *ideals* of citizenship: just as every person receives certain privileges as a citizen, every person can be asked, in certain circumstances, to act as a representative of the state. The specifics of one's identity, in other words, should not matter. Citizenship, understood as a bundle of both privileges and obligations, is a baseline political identity attaching to every adult. But here, as in controversies over the role of women in the military, women's involvement in particular activities *in particular kinds of spaces* were perceived as problematic. In 1987, almost all of the challenges to women's work as enumerators came from census opponents, which means that they can be understood at least in part as opportunistic. In effect, some Greens and other census opponents appeared willing either to cede the census to men, thus reinforcing the patriarchal character of the state, or to make it more costly. Census supporters such as Kewenig and Harfst sensed that opportunism was at play, and were not prepared to let it get in the way of the recruitment of enumerators. Thus, although they were certainly no feminists, they found themselves insisting on women's full participation.

Again, at the core of a census is the activity of counting the population, and this activity, so long as it is carried out by embodied individuals, has two specifically spatial moments: moving through public spaces in order to locate and reach the households to be counted (and to return with the information gathered), and an

58 Borchers and Dahlheimer, Der programmierte Flop, p. 9.

59 Borchers and Dahlheimer, Der programmierte Flop, p. 9.; see also Anon., Datenschrott für eine Milliarde, p. 30.

60 Anon., Datenschrott für eine Milliarde, p. 46.

informational transaction at the boundary between public and private spaces. The gender-related concerns centered on both of these moments. In early March of 1987, the *Frankfurter Rundschau* reproduced a position paper by Theresia Riedmaier, Women's Commissioner for the city of Karlsruhe, in which the negotiation of public and private spaces by women in the context of a census is systematically analyzed.[61] On the basis of her analysis, Riedmaier made a series of clear-eyed recommendations. She began by rejecting two opposing suggestions, first, that women not serve as enumerators at all, and second, that (per Kewenig and Harfst) women should be deployed as enumerators without any special measures being taken, because there was no real danger. Riedmaier rejected the first suggestion on good feminist grounds:

> The demand that women not be deployed is equivalent to characterizing all women as incapable of dealing with everyday situations. Thought through to the end, this implies that women would have to avoid all possible endangerment, and thus avoid the public sphere altogether. [...] In the sense of a proactive [*offensiven*] demand to create more free space and independence in the life-context of women, I consider all limitations of the realm of their activities [*Wirkungsbereiches*] unacceptable.

The opposite suggestion, that there was no problem at all, Riedmaier considered opportunistic, since in other circumstances, it had become common policy for government officials to recommend that women follow particular danger avoidance strategies in specific times and places. "[B]ut because the deployment of women in the census cannot be dispensed with, these recommendation are relativized." The problem posed to women enumerators in the context of a census has to do precisely with these avoidance strategies:

> Every woman has her – conscious or unconscious – "avoidance strategies". She avoids dangers she knows or suspects, in that she takes detours, avoids dark paths, deserted [*unbelebte*] streets or abandoned open spaces [*ausgestorbene Plätze*]. She can do this in her everyday activities. As an enumerator deployed for the census, on the other hand, she must go to all residences in her area, must walk empty streets, and [make her way] over back lots and through passages. [...] She cannot use her avoidance strategies.

Given that, on the one hand, there were real issues regarding the safety of women enumerators, but on the other hand, it was unacceptable to remove women from service as enumerators, Riedmaier listed a number of recommended measures:

---

61 Riedmaier, T. 1987. Frauen und Volkszählung [reprinted position paper]. *Frankfurter Rundschau*, March 7, n.p.n. This is a one-page article, so all subsequent quotes are from the same page.

1. Officials responsible for recruiting enumerators should be told that they were only to engage women in numbers proportional to the percentage of the staff they represent within the various public agencies. "The disproportionate recruitment of women on the basis of the fact that they occupy lower positions, and [perhaps also on the basis of a] common opinion that they might therefore be more dispensable from office work, should be avoided."
2. Single parents (whether women or men) should not be asked to be enumerators.
3. While both men and women were given some scope to choose the areas in which they would like to be deployed, women should only be assigned to areas whose social and geographical structure appeared to minimize dangers (this suggestion implicitly brought gender and class issues into articulation).
4. Women enumerators who expressed anxiety about their safety in their assigned enumeration areas after the first time through (to hand out census forms) should be offered accompaniment thereafter.
5. In the enumerator preparation classes, the potential problems facing women should be explicitly thematized, and four points stressed, in particular: first, that they are not required to enter residences; second, that they are encouraged to bring pepper spray, whistles or other alarms with them (and to make sure they have practiced using them); third, that they should familiarize themselves with local police offices and emergency call boxes in their enumeration areas. Finally, women enumerators should be advised that if they are threatened or harassed, they should feel free to point out that the names and addresses of all households are known to the census office (this was an interesting suspension of the otherwise strict insistence on confidentiality).
6. Local police patrols should be reinforced during the enumeration.
7. The census publicity campaign should make it clear to the population that, on the one hand, enumerators are not obliged to enter residences, and on the other, residents are not obliged to allow enumerators into their living spaces (this last to address concerns about male enumerators entering the residences of women).

Some local governments adopted some or all of these recommendations; many did not. Riedmaier's argument is interesting not only because of the clarity with which she lays bare one aspect of the gender politics of territory, but also because these politics point to a further sense in which the politics of physical public space was crucial to the controversy surrounding the 1987 census. The bombings and muggings of enumerators challenged the "neutral" anonymity of the state by reminding office workers in local statistical bureaus and enumerators that doing the work of the state in public space was not necessarily safe. The focus on women pointed out that state-related use of public space was not entirely safe even in the absence of a deliberate violent campaign against the census. Both issues highlighted the specific, embodied identities of enumerators, and thus tended to distance census work from the political neutrality and public safety associated with legitimate exercises of the obligations of citizenship.

Stairwell terriers polishing doorbells: A census is taken

In the midst of all of the controversy, hundreds of thousands of enumerators swarmed out across West Germany in May and began taking the population census. By mid-July, the vast majority of forms had been returned, but the campaign to track down those residents who remained elusive dragged on into the autumn. The fact that the census was actually taken eventually proved to have been the beginning of the end of the boycott movement. Once the count had begun, Interior Minister Zimmermann, West Berlin's Kewenig and other prominent census advocates were quoted periodically to the effect that everything was going well, the mistakes were merely isolated incidents, and so on.[62] But especially in the first few weeks of most intense counting, most of the press coverage tended rather to convey the impression that the enterprise would be a complete flop. The taz and *Der Spiegel* were of course in the vanguard of such pessimistic reporting, but *Die Zeit* and the *Süddeutsche Zeitung*, which had been somewhat more balanced in their coverage up to that point, also emphasized the gap between what was supposed to happen and what actually happened.

Partly due to the boycott campaign itself, the level of state preparation for taking the 1987 census was uneven across the thousands of municipalities and urban districts that had to carry out the count. As in many other regards, the Kreuzberg neighborhood of West Berlin was notable for the unusual difficulty of the problems it posed. In addition to being a center of protest, for example, it was also home to the highest concentrations of foreign-born guest workers and their families. A few weeks before the enumeration date, the taz introduced the issue with delicious irony: "When the people are to be counted at the end of May in the *Bundesrepublik*, suddenly all those who are otherwise not wanted in this community belong to 'the people'."[63] But informal surveys of Kreuzberg residents from Turkey, Greece, Bulgaria and elsewhere suggested that the government's massive publicity campaign had not reached them. As in 1983, the boycott movement was generally advising non-German citizens not to take part in the boycott, so as not to jeopardize their residency status.[64] The government's promise to follow the provisions of the BStatG, whereby no personal disadvantage could result from a statistical survey like the census, would have to have been airtight

62 For example, Anon., Bonn: Volkszählung verläuft positiv.

63 Gaserow, "Volgssählung? Nix gehört!"

64 See for example Anon., Gefahren der Volkszählung für Ausländer; Nagler, A., Hinweise für Ausländer, p. 63.

and fully credible for guest workers, immigrants or asylum seekers to participate in the boycott without fear. But of course the lack of credibility for such claims was one of the reasons for the boycott in the first place. Yet even if these groups wished to answer the census, the taz reported, they might have had great difficulty doing so because of language barriers. Some cities were due to receive multilingual pamphlets translating the most important questions, and the census forms were to be accompanied, in heavily non-German neighborhoods, by a translation aid. But the forms themselves would be in German. Any sort of general translator service had been ruled out by the government on cost grounds, and the possibility of printing forms in languages other than German had been dismissed as posing too many problems for the automated form readers.[65] On May 25th, the official enumeration day, the taz followed up with a report that census offices in West Berlin were seeing much higher than usual error and incompletion rates on forms from Turkish families. The translation aids were clearly insufficient, and social workers were being flooded with requests from immigrants and guest workers for help filling out the forms. According to one Turkish resident, the social workers were refusing this help on data protection grounds, and instead handing out copies of a letter to be taken to the census offices requesting translators.[66]

But even in the many parts of West Germany where this kind of issue did not arise, the machinery was not necessarily humming along smoothly. The census law passed in September of 1985 had stipulated a number of specific conditions regarding the recruitment and deployment of enumerators. Among the most important were a prohibition on drawing enumerators from groups whose normal, daytime jobs might undermine residents' belief that their personal information would not be used to their disadvantage. Thus police officers or state prosecutors would typically not be assigned to count residents. A second important condition was that enumerators not be deployed in the very same neighborhoods in which they lived. The fact that these safeguards proved quite leaky can be seen in part as an indirect result of the early focus of the boycott movement on discouraging people from becoming enumerators. The scattered attacks on enumerators discussed in the foregoing chapter likely also had an effect. As noted above, shortages of enumerators persisted through the Spring of 1987, and many local census offices had to bend or break the rules to ensure that they had adequate numbers of bodies. Since they could not be too selective, reports also trickled in of sometimes quite startling breaches of confidentiality and enumerator incompetence or simple laziness.

A survey of incidents gives a flavor of the picture of chaos painted by press coverage. In the town of Viersen, the Social Bureau gave the Statistical Bureau a list of the names and addresses of welfare recipients, recommending them as enumerators.[67] On May 19th, the taz reported that members of the right

65 Gaserow, "Volgssählung? Nix gehört!"

66 Anon. 1987. Ausländer zählen nicht. *die tageszeitung*, May 25, n.p.n.

67 Anon., "Als sei es des Teufels eigenes Werk", p. 31.

extremist party NPD had signed up as enumerators in Münster "in order to locate non-EC foreigners living in Münster and thereby to counter the veiling efforts [*Verschleierungsbestrebungen*] of the red-green boycotters."[68] They were following the lead of members of the Hamburg group "Hamburg List for Banning Foreigners [*Ausländerstopp*]", who had likewise presented themselves at enumerator recruiting stations.[69] With the term "veiling efforts" the nationalists apparently wanted to suggest that the boycott was really intended to conceal the large number of "unwanted" foreigners in West Germany. The following day, the taz reported on problems in West Berlin: an enumerator simply handed over a bundle of empty forms to the house superintendent with instructions to the tenants that they should return their forms to the superintendent (a major breach of confidentiality); multiple calls to the census hotline complained of neighbors as enumerators, including a caller claiming to have been told to count residents in his own house; a police officer was assigned to count residents in Kreuzberg.[70] The West Berlin Data Protection Commissioner was alarmed enough at reports of neighbors as enumerators to begin looking into the matter of enumerator assignments.[71] In Stuttgart, an enumerator left his list of names and addresses sitting on a garden wall.[72] The temptation to hand over packs of forms to building superintendents instead of taking the trouble to count residents as prescribed in the census law proved irresistible to an enumerator in West Berlin as well.[73] Even in late July, there were reports of whole apartment blocks in Kreuzberg still waiting for census forms.[74] In Düsseldorf, residents of a student dormitory received forms that were already filled out, with a note from the enumerator asking them "to check and [where necessary] to complete the enclosed forms, which I have prepared for the sake of convenience." The enumerator, of course, should not have had access to personal information about the students, but it turned out that he was an official with the local Bureau of Statistics and Elections.[75] In North Rhine-Westphalia, likewise, numerous reports had come in regarding the "legally questionable deployment of officials from sensitive agencies – Residency Registration Offices, Social Bureaus, Youth Bureaus, Housing Assistance Offices [*Wohngeldstelle*], Tax Offices – as enumerators or even in the census offices."[76] The SPD monthly *Vorwärts* reported other incidents similar to these, concluding that "bureaucratic

68 Quoted in Anon. 1987. Zählerpannen. *die tageszeitung*, May 19, n.p.n.

69 Anon., "Als sei es des Teufels eigenes Werk", p. 31.

70 Gaserow, V. 1987d. Geburtsname von Adoptivkind in Liste. *die tageszeitung*, May 20, n.p.n.

71 Anon. 1987. Der Zähler von Nebenan. *die tageszeitung*, May 22, n.p.n.

72 Anon., "Als sei es des Teufels eigenes Werk", p. 31.

73 Anon., Voll in die Hose, p. 129.

74 Anon. 1987. "Ganze Hinterhöfe vergessen". *die tageszeitung*, July 23, n.p.n.

75 Anon., Voll in die Hose, p. 132.

76 Anon. 1987. Prügel und Kuchen als Wegzehrung. *Süddeutsche Zeitung*, May 23/24, p. 10.

mis-steps and violations of the law accompany the census throughout the entire republic."[77]

Those working in the census offices were, like the enumerators, not always adequately prepared or motivated to take their duties as seriously as the law required. In many cases, the mistakes and breaches of confidentiality were a result not of having too much information (as with the statistician who filled out student census forms himself) but of having too little. The taz reported a case on May 20th in which a Residency Registration Office in Köln supplying the names and addresses for the enumerator lists failed to transfer the special confidentiality mark [*Sperrvermerk*] forbidding the revelation of the names of the birth-parents of adopted children. One child's adoptive mother was unintentionally shown the child's birth surname by an enumerator puzzled at the fact that a person of that name apparently did not live in the building. Further investigation showed that the same thing had happened with other adopted children in Köln, and that women who had survived domestic violence and who wished to conceal their new addresses from abusers were also in danger of having their real locations revealed because the *Sperrvermerk* had been removed in the preparation of the census lists.[78] *Der Spiegel* turned up similar cases in West Berlin and Kassel.[79] In Wuppertal the census office filled in missing information on the building form not by contacting respondents again but by having the information sent from the local Building and Housing Office. In Ulm, the office staff compared the building forms it had received with the city address book and sent new inquiries to those respondents whose information did not appear to match up. This second survey, a violation of the Data Protection Law, was eventually sent to the shredder after Baden-Württemberg Data Protection Commissioner Ruth Leuze intervened.[80] In Hagen, census opponents searched the trash bins behind the local census office and discovered discarded lists of residents that should likewise have been sent to the shredder.[81]

Probably the strangest breach of confidentiality occurred in February of 1988, when a pile of some 1,700 filled-out census forms were discovered in the stairwell of an apartment house in München. The forms, it turned out, had been sitting in boxes in an automobile belonging to a woman contracted by the Bavarian State Statistical Bureau to bring them home and transfer the written responses into machine-readable code. But before she could remove the boxes, her car was stolen. Some of the respondents whose forms were found in the stairwell hired an attorney, Jürgen Arnold, who pointed out that the system of home-based piece-work for coding census forms was highly questionable in view of the census law's

77 Dettmer, M. 1987. Familie Licht wohnt hier nicht. *Vorwärts*, May 30, p. 10.

78 Gaserow, Geburtsname von Adoptivkind in Liste.

79 Anon., Voll in die Hose, 132.

80 Anon., "Als sei es des Teufels eignen Werk", p. 31.

81 Bornhöft, P. 1987c. Datenmüll-Fund in Hagen. *die tageszeitung*, July 14, n.p.n.

stipulations regarding confidentiality.[82] As the mistakes surveyed above make clear, this was only the most spectacular example of one of the basic problems Ruth Leuze, Spiros Simitis and other data protection experts had focused upon from the beginning: the practical impossibility of guaranteeing strict confidentiality and separation of census work from all other administrative work, especially at the local level. Leuze, in particular, was omnipresent as a critical commentator in much of the coverage cited above, and from late May onward came to be identified by both friends and foes of the census as the foremost critic of the practical execution of the count. Her annual report for 1987, made public in January of 1988, was much anticipated, for example in the taz: "For eight years now it has chased away the last friendly hopes for the new year, and for just as long it has been received as an unvarnished exposé of what has transpired: the report of the Data Protection Commissioner of Baden-Württemberg Ruth Leuze."[83] In her latest report, she lambasted authorities at all levels, not only for widespread indifference toward confidentiality and separation regarding the statistics themselves, but also for the aggressive stance taken by authorities, especially in Baden-Württemberg, toward census opponents. In the process of criminalizing the boycott, police and prosecutors had begun to set up precisely the sorts of "boycott databases" census opponents had feared from the beginning. Thus the breaches of data protection surrounding the 1987 census had, according to Leuze, taken on a second and even more troubling dimension.[84]

As noted earlier, the litany of transgressions reproduced in press accounts was not necessarily an accurate reflection of the degree of chaos on the ground. It can be assumed that the vast majority of individual acts of enumeration and data processing were carried out in a way that complied with the terms of the census law. Nevertheless, in legal and constitutional terms, even a small minority of instances in which the spirit and letter of the law was violated could have rendered the entire census null and void, had the courts been open to such challenges this time around. As it happened, they were not. But this was not a foregone conclusion, and in this sense it would have been beside the point to accuse the press of having conjured an inaccurate image of chaos. However inaccurate it was, even a few actual incidents of breaches of confidentiality did in fact potentially threaten the census. On the other hand, the press coverage probably did account to some degree for the personnel shortages that were behind some of the problems with the census. In any case, all of the difficulties noted above were at most indirectly traceable to the boycott movement. The direct effects of the boycott only made matters worse, and it is to these that we now turn.

---

82 Loerzer, S. 1988a. 1700 Volkszählungbogen waren verschwunden. *Süddeutsche Zeitung*, February 16, n.p.n.

83 Willier, D. 1988. Dateiterror gegen Volkszählungsgegener. *die tageszeitung*, January 19, p. 1.

84 Willier, Dateiterror gegen Volkszählungsgegner; Anon. 1988. Datenschützerin kritisiert Volkszählung. *Süddeutsche Zeitung*, January 9, n.p.n.

The scope of actual boycotting among West Germans in 1987 is somewhat difficult to pin down in retrospect. As noted earlier, public opinion polls revealed a steady shrinkage of the proportion of the population declaring an intent to boycott. Whereas the *Frankfurter Allgemeine Zeitung* had reported in January of 1985 that some 30% of the population would not want to take part in a census, the intervening two years had clearly reconciled many to what appeared increasingly inevitable.[85] By May 22nd, 1987, just three days before the count, an Emnid poll found the percentage of respondents intending to participate in the "hard" boycott (that is, send their empty, anonymized forms to alternative collection points) had recently dropped from 7% to 2%.[86] An Infas poll, however, still showed a hardcore boycott group at 9% of the population in mid-June.[87] The central "boycott barometer" put out by the Bonn Green Party office, meanwhile, showed a steadily increasing national total of empty forms returned: 220,000 by May 27th, 340,000 by May 29th, 420,000 by June 1st, 520,000 by June 12th, 817,000 by July 4th, and 840,000 by July 11th.[88] Reckoned against the total population of some 61 million that would eventually be reported, 840,000 represented between 1 and 2%.[89] What polling and barometer numbers did not capture was the extent of so-called "soft" boycotting (incomplete or false responses), nor could it provide a picture of the number or the impact of so-called "trojan enumerators", that is, enumerators who offered criticisms of the census as they passed out forms. *Der Spiegel* had hinted shortly before the count that some such subversives would definitely be active, though either they were very careful in deciding when to reveal their opposition or there were not very many of them, given that no subsequent reports of such activity turn up in the press coverage.[90] Soft boycotting, however, was probably quite common. One piece of circumstantial evidence to this effect can be seen in the fact that close to one half of all respondents, far more than the government had expected, insisted on taking the forms from enumerators with a promise to mail them back later.[91] This slowed the whole process and made it more expensive. Thus, checking back with residents to clear up questions was not a matter of face-to-face questions and answers but had to be done by mail or telephone.[92] If enumerators were unable to hand the forms directly to residents, they were often forced to fold them, and respondents, too, usually folded them to mail them back.

---

85 Bannas, Die Volkszählung erst nach der Wahl?

86 Gaserow, V. and Müllender, B. 1987. Sammelstellen warten auf Altpapier. *die tageszeitung*, May 22, n.p.n.

87 Pokatzky and Sontheimer, Zähler und Gezählte, p. 33.

88 Anon., Anwalt muß für Boykotthilfe Bußgeld bezahlen; Anon., Stand der Volkszählung unstritten; Anon., Wird geschätzt; Pokatzky and Sontheimer, Zähler und Gezählte, p. 33; Anon. 1987. Fehlerquote bis zu 60 Prozent bei "Volkszählung per Post". *Frankfurter Rundschau*, July 4, n.p.n.; Dahlheimer, Den Planern geht die Puste aus, p. 7.

89 Bieber, Neue Fakten übers Volk.

90 Anon., "Als sei es des Teufels eigenes Werk", p. 31.

91 Pokatzky and Sontheimer, Zähler und Gezählte, p. 33.

92 Anon. 1987. Zähler fertig, Zählung nicht. *die tageszeitung*, June 20, n.p.n.

But the folding rendered them unreadable by the equipment, so they had to be copied over onto new forms.[93]

More evidence that many had chosen the soft boycott route came to light as reports of error rates started to trickle in from census offices around the country in July of 1987. The *Frankfurter Rundschau* and *Vorwärts* cited officials in the federal states of Lower Saxony, Hessen and the Saarland who claimed that up to 70% of forms returned by mail were at least partly erroneous.[94] Under the banner "Stupid Germany!", the taz reported error rates ranging from 20% to 80% of returned forms, and bemoaned the "educational emergency" that seemed especially to plague large cities and university towns:

> Millions of federal citizens, so the first results of the census reveal, have such inadequate biological knowledge that they were not in a position to decide whether they were of the male or the female sex. Others, obviously not equal to the challenge of reading, were unable to decode the rent and size of living space from the lease and enter them into the appropriate boxes [on the forms].[95]

The reference to large cities and university towns indicates a phenomenon noticed by many commentators, namely that the census returns were in general far more reliable in rural areas and small towns than in areas of high population density. Some of this difference can be accounted for by a general pattern of "liberal urbanity", but some of it, is undoubtedly to be attributed to the lack of anonymity in smaller places. The lists of VoBo Inis published in the taz included many small-town addresses, especially in the early months before the census. But as the struggle wore on through the enumeration and into the late summer, rural Inis found it ever harder to hold out against sometimes quite invasive intimidation tactics.[96]

As we shall see below, such pressure eventually "trickled up" to take its toll even in the metropolitan centers of the boycott movement. But for months after the enumeration day, the outlook for the census appeared from press coverage to be rather grim. In late July, the taz published a detailed astrological prognosis for the West German state in its relation to the census. The author, "Astrodada", followed astrological good practice by relating the census's legislative birthdate (November 8th, 1985) to the birth date and time of the *Bundesrepublik* (5:00pm, May 23rd, 1949), reckoning the census to the third astrological "house" of the state (along with the traffic system, the postal system, the telecommunication system and the press, i.e., all institutions concerned with information and communication). The analysis that followed was uniformly dim:

---

93 Loerzer, Rund um die Volkszählung.

94 Anon., Fehlerquote bis zu 60 Prozent; Dahlheimer, Den Planern geht die Puste aus, p. 7.

95 Gaserow, V. 1987f. Dummes Deutschland! *die tageszeitung*, July 8, n.p.n.

96 Koch, L. 1987. "Es is so a netter Stammtisch wordn". *die tageszeitung*, August 6, n.p.n.

> Saturn, Uranus and Neptune are currently traversing the third house of the state's horoscope. Saturn as a symbol for obstacles and Uranus as a symbol of disquiet and surprise bring the realm of the third house strongly, and with tension, into the consciousness of state and citizen. Neptune gives an additional note of unclarity, of confusion, and of errors: communication fails, lies and dissimulation [*Vertuschung*], abuse can [all] play a role. These transits are from top to bottom somewhat problematic for the present counting project. [...]
>
> One misses strong relationships to the axes ("sensitive" points in the horoscope) that would be able to say something about the "momentary identity" or "goal orientation" of the state. A law whose execution is supposed to guarantee an inventory and thus a reflection of the identity of the state, out of which reliable projects could follow, would have had to be passed on a different, more advantageous day. [...] If nothing comes out at the end of a census costing a billion [DM] – to say nothing of the possible dangers of abuse of the data, which is also in the air due to the dominance of Neptune – that would be very damaging to the image of the republic.[97]

The battle in the courts, part 1: Form-clippers

Attempts to stop the 1987 census on constitutional grounds found little sympathy in West German courts. In 1983, the Federal Constitutional Court had struck down specific provisions of the 1982 census law, but had also affirmed the constitutionality of most of the statute, as well as the state's general right to take a census. Courts at all levels appeared to be deaf to any fundamental challenges in 1987, however willing some were to rein in the more egregious repressive innovations by local state officials. In October of 1987, the Constitutional Court definitively quashed any lingering hopes of census opponents by refusing to take on a series of complaints.[98] Thus although legal battles were of central and eventually decisive importance for the 1987 controversy, they concerned different issues than in 1983. The fact that refusing to answer the census was technically a misdemeanor provided census opponents with a very handy rhetorical tool. Commenting on the confiscation of mail addressed to the taz in West Berlin, Johannes Eisenberg's statement was typical: "If state's attorneys and judges place the pursuit of a misdemeanor [*Ordnungswidrigkeit*] – the smallest form of illegality – above

97 Astrodada 1987. Prima: Auch die Sterne boykottieren. *die tageszeitung*, July 22, n.p.n.

98 Anon., Wird geschätzt, p. 28; Anon. 1987. Bundesverfassungsgericht entscheidet zur Volkszählung. *Frankfurter Allgemeine Zeitung*, September 30, n.p.n.; Gaserow, V. 1987i. Volkszählung: Massenwiderstand endgültig abgehakt? [interview with P. Hauck-Scholz]. *die tageszeitung*, October 14, n.p.n.; Gaserow, V. 1987j. VGH segnet Volkszählung ab. *die tageszeitung*, October 16, n.p.n.

the freedom of the press guaranteed in the Basic Law, this is actually no longer comprehensible [*nachvollziehbar*]."[99] The absurdity appeared to be manifest, and many commentators saw in it a clear violation of the general constitutional principle of proportionality between punishment and crime. The anonymous author of a letter to the taz in March of 1988 put the matter clearly: "What is the state trying to accomplish with such a count, if from the start it deploys all of its power with such obvious disproportionality and [engages in] the criminalization of people who think otherwise [but] cherish and defend freedom?"[100] Reasonable as these questions might have seemed, the legal situation was not as clear-cut as census opponents pretended it was. Although police and state's attorneys did often try to impose serious fines upon citizens openly admitting their intent to boycott the census, the most extreme repressive measures were aimed at individuals *calling for* a boycott at *public* demonstrations and meetings. Clearly this was not the same thing as a private decision to boycott. But West German law simply did not foresee a specific infraction like "public instigation to commit a misdemeanor". Before the census boycott movements (and even after the 1983 movement), it did not occur to legislators to invent such a category. Thus one major stream of the legal activity that flowed from the 1987 boycott movement revolved around state attempts to find other ways to elevate the legal seriousness of boycott-related actions so that their grim response could be made to seem more proportional.

At public demonstrations against the census throughout West Germany, the call to participate in the boycott was often dramatized on stage by a ritual act of clipping the bar-code from an empty census form. Clipping was crucial to the whole "hard boycott" strategy. Boycotters who neglected to clip the bar code from their empty forms before sending them in would be immediately identifiable once the alternative collection points delivered the empty forms to census offices. They would find themselves much more quickly confronted with fines, and would not have recourse to any of the usual excuses (such as claiming that the form had been lost in the mail). In addition to its importance as a lynchpin of the hard boycott strategy, clipping had an intuitive appeal as a symbolic gesture. According to *Die Zeit*, state's attorneys in the city of Mainz were the first to hit upon the idea that clipping census forms was punishable according to ¶ 303 of the Criminal Statutes, as destruction of property, and thus as a crime rather than merely a misdemeanor. Calling for this form of boycott, then, would be instigation to destruction of property. Technically, the census forms were the property of the *Länder*, the individual federal states.[101] The first test of the destruction of property angle took place in early June of 1987 in the district court [*Landgericht*] of the North German city of Lübeck, which ruled that empty census forms were not substantial enough to be considered physical property in the sense of the Criminal

99 Quoted in Pokatzky and Sontheimer, Zähler und Gezählte, p. 35.

100 Anon. 1988. Ich bin nun siebzig Jahre alt [open letter to Berlin StaLa]. *die tageszeitung*, March 14, n.p.n.

101 Pokatzky and Sontheimer, Zähler und Gezählte, p. 35.

Statute invoked.[102] The district court in Karlsruhe echoed this judgment, arguing that although empty census forms were technically physical objects [*fremde bewegliche Sache*], their value was so vanishingly small as to be inconsequential. Further, the Karlsruhe court argued, empty census forms had no use value for the statistical offices that sent them out.[103] At the end of the month, an administrative court in Aachen elaborated on this argument, noting that when census offices did not receive forms from individuals, they simply sent new ones out. The individual physical form, in other words, was of no legal substance.[104] A year later (some of the court cases dragged on into late 1988), a Munich district court likewise ruled that the indefinite replaceability of a census form meant it could not legally be considered a "unique copy" [*Unikat*].[105]

Other local and regional courts, like the district court in Trier, were willing to uphold the treatment of clipping as a crime. The events following the clipping of a census form at a public demonstration in Trier in May became a sort of "Keystone Cops" legend. Investigators at the public event were somehow not able to establish the identity of the speaker who performed the ritual clipping (participants probably refused to name him). The following day, Ewald Adams, a local Green Party representative, received a phone call from a woman claiming to be a reporter from the local newspaper. After he refused to divulge the name of the speaker to the "reporter" (who later turned out to have been a criminal investigator), he was invited to a hearing with Horst Leisen, the local district attorney. Here, too, Adams refused to identify the clipper. Leisen then applied for a "coercive detention" [*Beugehaft*] order against Adams from the local Trier administrative court, but was rebuffed on grounds of the disproportionality of this method to the seriousness of the transgression. The district court, however, at the next level of the juridical hierarchy, was willing to comply with the request, whereby Adams would be required to serve jail time until he named names. Adams did not at first learn of the initial unsuccessful attempt to order his imprisonment; he merely received a summons to appear at the local jail, which he did. There, however, he was turned away, being told that the order had been rescinded. In the meantime, local activist Georg Wißmeier, the person who had actually clipped the form, held a public press conference to reveal his identity once he heard that Adams was being targeted. The fiasco was not yet, over, however. Judge Brühl, the Trier judge who had ordered Adams's detention, felt himself slandered by an outraged Green Party press release calling attention to the whole affair, whereupon he ordered searches of the studio of a local radio station, the local Green Party office, and

102 Bornhöft, P. 1987c. Keine Zeit für Statistik. *die tageszeitung*, June 6, p. 3.

103 Bornhöft, P. 1987d. Vobo-Schnibbelei nicht strafbar. *die tageszeitung*, June 18, n.p.n.

104 Müllender, B. 1987. Richter hebt eigenes Vobo-Urteil auf. *die tageszeitung*, June 29, n.p.n.

105 Anon. 1988. Schnippeln keine Sachbeschädigung. *die tageszeitung*, June 9, n.p.n.

Ewald Adams's home. Adams was eventually cleared of all wrongdoing.[106] But the case made a caricature out of the over-eager forces of order so maniacally bent on quelling the boycott movement.

Such bizarre stories, however, did not discredit the legal notion that clipping was a crime. In fact, as a range of cases dragged on further into 1988, the trend among higher courts appeared to be toward upholding such an interpretation. In an editorial for the *Süddeutsche Zeitung* in May of 1988, Heribert Prantl explained this trend by placing it in historical perspective. The tradition of precedent reaching back to the founding of the German nation-state in 1871 showed a very flexible and expansive view of the crime of "destruction of property". In the 19th century, it was interpreted to include such things as broadcasting weed seeds in rye fields, or dumping manure in a stream. In 1959, the definition of destruction of property was widened to include letting the air out of automobile or bicycle tires. As Prantl noted with pregnant symbolism, the great German authority on criminal law, Maurach, had even declared the freeing of a caged canary a form of destruction of property. The wave of higher-court decisions overturning acquittals for clipping census forms was thus, according to Prantl, entirely predictable, as was the accompanying argument that empty forms did in fact have value for the state, because they were in the aggregate expensive to replace. As Prantl summarized the matter, "the interests of owners have always been the [basic] factors of evaluation in German case law."[107] One eventual result of the 1987 census controversy was thus that most of the few dozen West Germans who had been charged with destruction of property for clipping census forms did eventually have to pay sometimes quite substantial fines.

It is worth pausing briefly to place this issue of the materiality of census forms side-by-side with the immateriality of electronic data, raised in the context of the 1983 census. The concern of boycotters and of Baden-Württemberg's LDSB Ruth Leuze had been that data in electronic form were, in a sense, imperishable: it was so easy to reproduce and store them that it was practically impossible to be certain that any electronic data had ever been fully deleted from *all* databases and thus had truly and definitively ceased to exist. In the context of data protection principles, this characteristic of electronic data lends support to Spiros Simitis's argument that, especially in the electronic age, the decision *whether to surrender personal information in the first place* should be considered an important element of the right of informational self-determination. If this right only covers what happens once personal information has been registered, it will always be extremely vulnerable to violation in practice, however strict the prohibitions in principle. But while a

106 Holz, M. 1987b. Beugehaft für Volkszählungsgegner. *die tageszeitung*, August 19, n.p.n.; Kurz, F. 1987. Vobo-Aktivist vom Knast abgewiesen. *die tageszeitung*, August 21, n.p.n.; Grabenströer, M. 1987. In der Römerstadt ist Justitia nur auf einem Auge blind. *Frankfurter Rundschau*, November 16, p. 7.

107 Prantl, H. 1988. Fahndung nach dem meßbaren Wert. *Süddeutsche Zeitung*, May 27, n.p.n.

good deal of critical analysis and boycott propaganda concerned the dangers of information once it had been transformed into intangible electronic data, most of the vulnerabilities and weaknesses of the census enterprise revolved around the specific physical properties of the paper forms on which the information first had to be entered. This "larval" paper stage of census information, before it "took wing" as electronic data, was the stage at which the information could actually go missing, could be taken by force from enumerators on the street, could be plastered to the Berlin Wall, could have coffee spilled on it or the bar codes clipped off of it. Indeed the entire hard boycott strategy was ultimately predicated upon two specific features of the materiality of paper forms: the fact that, on the one hand, they could be easily damaged by cutting, crumpling, soaking, etc., and on the other, that they were nevertheless relatively durable, and so could be collected and counted for the boycott barometer. This "intermediate" level of durability was what required the local census offices to shred rather than simply forget about the forms once the data had been entered.

Both the electronic and the paper stages of personal information could thus quite understandably have generated anxieties. For the enumerated, the moment at which an individual surrenders his or her data, either to the enumerator or by sending off a completed form, can be a moment of considerable anxiety. The personal information thus given up is not yet electronic, but there is no longer anything the respondent can do to prevent it becoming so. Yet for the managers of a system of information-gathering, too, anxieties might arise. In an equal and opposite sense to the way citizens might feel uneasy, census officials might well have felt anxious about the moment at which they were forced to send out paper forms and rely upon the cooperation of respondents to return them with the needed information. Leaving perishable and ephemeral census forms with households and relying upon residents to send them back undamaged and properly filled out thus represented the nadir of state control over the whole process. Just as the surrender of personal information may evoke feelings of being "delivered up" or "delivered over" to state power, the moment of leaving blank census forms in mail slots "delivered up" a durable but easily damaged physical instrument of state power to the sometimes not-so-tender mercies of millions of residents. The request for personal information had taken on embodied, mortal form, so to speak, and in its frail material vessel was surrendered into the private realm beyond the observational powers of the state. By clipping off the bar codes linking each census form to specific names and addresses, boycotters were zeroing in on the most intimate part of the material object that had been delivered up to them. Thus, though this can be nothing more than a conjecture, I think it is not too far-fetched to imagine that state officials' relentless focus on ritual clipping at boycott rallies was, at some level, motivated by a kind of governmental "castration anxiety". I suspect that some sort of subterranean awareness of this anxiety also helps explain the relish with which ritual clippings were carried out.

Whatever may be made of the hypothetical anxiety of government officials, there was certainly good reason for census opponents to be anxious about the consequences of clipping forms and calling for a boycott. As noted in Chapter 3, attacks on the boycott movement were based on a *Feindbild* ("image of the enemy") that portrayed all forms of left-wing opposition as tendentially revolutionary or terroristic (as the Bavarian Interior Ministry had put it, "terrorists, too, start small").[108] True to this story line, some local police and state's attorneys used the idea that clipping was a statutory crime as an excuse to enter personal information about boycott activists into the national criminal databases set up to register terrorists and other "enemies of the free democratic basic order" (specifically, the databases PIOS and APIS played host to information about boycott organizers … see Introduction). As the wide scope of this practice came to light in early 1988, it generated a second controversy connected to the legal status of clipping. Already in May of 1987, the *Süddeutsche Zeitung* reported that the State Criminal Bureau [*Landeskriminalamt* or LKA] of Baden-Württemberg had set up a special unit for boycott information, and had forwarded 134 reports of boycott activity for comparison with databases on terrorists. The information, which included names, was to be entered into corresponding databases at the BKA and the *Verfassungsschutz*.[109] This appeared to be an isolated incident, however, and nothing more on this front was reported until January of 1988. On January 12th, the taz ran a story in which Hamburg's LDSB Klaus Henning Schapper confirmed a similar practice in that city, with information on census form clippers landing in a file for "enemies of the state and terrorists."[110] The *Frankfurter Rundschau* also picked up the story, and quoted Schapper to the effect that someone calling for a census boycott could not be assumed thereby "to have begun his carrier as a criminal or even an enemy of the state."[111] Further inquiries over the next few days turned up similar practices in other federal states. The office of Spiros Simitis told the taz that already in July of 1987, some 40 individuals had been entered by the LKA of Hessen in APIS. Simitis had already urged the deletion of most of the information but had received no response from the Criminal Bureau.[112] The following day, the taz reported similar situations in Lower Saxony, Bavaria and West Berlin. The Lower

108 Quoted in von Appen, Vobo's im Staatsschutz-Computer.

109 Anon., Polizei sammelt Daten von Volkszählungsgegnern.

110 von Appen, Vobo's im Staatsschutz-Computer.

111 Quoted in Plog, Boykotteure landeten in Polizeidatei.

112 Mohr, R. 1988. Staatsschutz zählte mit. *die tageszeitung*, January 13, n.p.n. The actual name of the database represented by the acronym APIS is rendered differently in different reports. The report on Hessen gives the full name as *Arbeitsdatei für Personen, Informationen, Objekte, Sachen und Innere Sicherheit*, whereas a report from West Berlin the following day renders is as *Allgemeines Polizeiinformationssystem* (Anon. 1988. Alle Vobos im Computer? *die tageszeitung*, January 14, n.p.n.). A story in the *Frankfurter Rundschau* appears to clear up the confusion, calling it the Arbeitsdatei "PIOS" – Innere Sicherheit (Anon. 1988. Mehr Zählungsgegner in Datei. *Frankfurter Rundschau*, January 14, n.p.n.). PIOS is the acronym for *Personen, Informationen, Objekte, Sachen*. Thus APIS is an acronym within an acronym.

Saxony DSB Klaus Trebarth had likewise objected to criminal authorities entering 76 boycott participants into APIS.[113] The *Frankfurter Rundschau* put the number of census opponents entered into APIS by West Berlin authorities at 255.[114]

In May of 1988, the *Süddeutsche Zeitung* ran a story showing just how little one had to do to end up in anti-terrorist databases. One Rolf W., a patent attorney, had taken part in a census boycott event in an inn near Munich in early May of 1987, and had, according to eyewitness reports, snipped off the corner of a piece of paper with large scissors, in front of approximately 300 spectators. The exact sequence of events as recorded in court documents had Rolf W. taking the stage after a (lopsided) debate on the pros and cons of the census. He started by taking refuge in the subjunctive, saying he was not calling for a boycott but merely acting out what someone might do who wanted to boycott. The scene apparently involved a cabaret-like atmosphere, and Rolf W. got a laugh out of the crowd when he suggested that anyone wishing to do this at home should feel free also to wear facial covering so as to remain anonymous. The case against him rested on the assertion that all of this was a "call [to boycott] between the lines", a "silently expressed call". Although it undoubtedly was, the legal purchase of such a notion was highly questionable. Nevertheless, the judge accepted the prosecution's argument, Rolf W. was indeed fined DM 1,200, and the Bavarian authorities entered his personal information into APIS.[115] By late January of 1988, reservations about entering boycott participants into APIS had made it possible for Data Protection Commissioners to have many of the entries deleted (those remaining in APIS were there because they had been linked to attacks on enumerators or more substantial destruction of property).[116] But as late as July of 1988, West Berlin's Interior Senator Wilhelm Kewenig and other local authorities were still negotiating with their respective Data Protection Commissioner to enter more names into APIS when the individuals concerned had been "noticed" by police in more than one part of the country (for example at protests against nuclear plants or the "Startbahn West" runway controversy in Frankfurt).[117] The legal status of a call to boycott was not definitively resolved. But the fact that some census opponents who merely clipped empty forms at public rallies ended up in a database for enemies of the state and terrorists clearly illustrates both the worldview and the tenacity of many local and state-level authorities.

113 Anon., Alle Vobos im Computer?

114 Anon., Mehr Zählungsgegner in Datei.

115 Holzhaider, H. 1988. Das Zerschneiden eines Papiers und seine Folgen. *Süddeutsche Zeitung*, May 25, p. 11.

116 Anon. 1988. Kerkaus Datenputz. *die tageszeitung*, January 19, n.p.n.

117 Anon. 1988. Wer einmal "auffällt"… *die tageszeitung*, July 23, n.p.n.

The battle in the courts, part 2: Boycotters

> Each time the Berlin office worker Helmut M. leaves his apartment in the [West] Berlin district of Schöneberg, he has a weak feeling in his stomach. He can never be sure whether his domicile won't be broken into yet again. The burglars he fears don't climb over the roofs, they take the bureaucratic route: for almost a year and a half now, the father of three children, just turned 50, has refused to fill out a form – the one for the census. The angst inspired by the surveillance state sits deeply also among a dozen people who get together on a warm August evening for a summer exchange of experiences in the Berlin Alternative Center Mehringhof. "The VoBo Hardliner meetings", comments a man passing through the courtyard of the former factory building. A colorful mix of students, jobless people and office workers gathers there in the beer garden. The pitiful remnants of the once-powerful [West] Berlin boycott front.[118]

So begins an article in the taz in late August of 1988 chronicling the slow, fitful demise of the 1987 VoBo movement. By late summer of 1988, the enumeration had officially been declared complete everywhere but in Hamburg. What remained were legal proceedings in some of the federal states over the various types of fines that had been imposed upon boycotters. But final closure on these legal issues was still a long way off. The court cases still to be decided numbered in the tens of thousands nationwide, and in Hessen, for example, authorities reckoned it would take another two years to work through them.[119] Notwithstanding further months and years of legal struggle, however, the taz was right to suggest that the boycott itself was all but finished. On the terms in which the VoBo movement had decided to oppose the census, that is, by means of a "hard boycott", state authorities had won the war, sort of. The "hard boycott" strategy, once again, involved returning anonymized (clipped), empty census forms to alternative collection points, which would tally the total number received, report totals periodically to the "boycott barometer" central office in Bonn, and then send piles of empty forms to the local census offices for "recycling". The danger for hard boycotters lay in the fact that census offices would not receive properly filled out forms from them. On the basis of the lists of names and addresses supplied to the census offices by the local Residency Registration Offices [*Meldeämter*], which in turn were given to enumerators as "identification aids" [*Hilfsmerkmale*], it would be possible for the census offices to identify hold-outs and begin the process of warnings, followed by fines. To reassure citizens considering the hard boycott option, VoBo activists had initially claimed that there was safety in numbers. If thousands of people joined the hard boycott, were fined, and challenged the fines in court, local

118 Pilardeaux, B. 1988. Einbruch im Dienste des Rechtsstaates. *die tageszeitung*, August 30, n.p.n.

119 Pilardeaux, Einbruch im Dienste des Rechtsstaates.

and state courts would be buried in an "avalanche" of legal proceedings.[120] Being completely overwhelmed, so the argument went, authorities would be forced to grant amnesty or simply drop the fines.

In April of 1987, the taz had published advice columns covering, among other topics, the two basic kinds of fines hard boycotters could expect to face, the *Zwangsgeld* ("coercive fine") and the more general fine or *Bußgeld.* The first of these could be set as high as DM 2,000, and could be imposed repeatedly, but (like the *Bußgeld*) it did not establish a criminal record for the individual threatened with it. Its sole function was to force compliance, and it was thus always connected to a (one month) deadline for turning in the census form, after which it would come due. The taz advice column described the series of steps through which boycotters could, first, challenge the one-month deadline, then, if this challenge was rejected, appeal the decision to local administrative courts; or alternatively, if the deadline had passed and the fine was imposed, challenge the imposition of the fine. The coercive fine would evaporate either when the census form was received or "when the *Volkszählung* 1987 comes to an end." Noting that the processes connected with a coercive fine were "complicated and implied considerable expense for the authorities", the taz predicted that statistical offices, and especially the administrative courts, would not be able to deal with them by the thousands.[121] The steps recommended for challenging the normal *Bußgeld* were basically similar, and more of the burden of proof rested with the state authorities (namely, the need to prove that the census form had in fact been received by the person being fined). The upper limit for the *Bußgeld* was much higher than for the coercive fine (DM 10,000), and the fine did not automatically lapse once a response to the census was turned in. But the advice column reassured potential boycotters that fines higher than DM 350 were hardly likely. The outlook for safety in numbers was equally rosy, according to the article: "If thousands go before the courts to contest a fine, the administrative courts will be busy into the 1990s. The absolute statute of limitations is four years. If it is [a matter of] hundreds of thousands, nothing will happen any longer in the bureaucracy and the courts."[122]

Tens of thousands of challenges were in fact brought before the courts, and the prediction that court proceedings would last into the 1990s turned out to be accurate. But the image of a judicial system overwhelmed and utterly crippled by an avalanche of legal challenges failed to materialize. To a significant extent, the failure to clog the justice system can be attributed to local officials and administrative judges throughout West Germany, whose determination to master the census-related cases was expressed in a tirelessness and creativity at least as remarkable as the flowering of repressive innovations among police officers and state's attorneys noted earlier. One of the contentious innovations introduced

---

120 Pokatzky and Sontheimer, Zähler und Gezählte, p. 35.

121 Anon. 1987. Was tun? … gegen das Zwangsgeld? *die tageszeitung*, April 8, n.p.n.

122 Anon. 1987. Was tun? … gegen das Bußgeld? *die tageszeitung*, April 9, n.p.n.

by local and state courts involved mass, standardized decisions. Under the heading "Copy machine issues legal decisions" [*Kopierer spricht Recht*], the taz reported in October of 1987 on the case of an attorney attempting to sue for the reinstatement of the delaying effect of a legal challenge to answering the census. The census law for 1987 included a provision (as the 1983 law had) explicitly de-activating the delaying effect which an appeal against the execution of a law would normally have. The request to reinstate the delaying effect was rejected in writing, and when the attorney attempted to appeal that decision with a more elaborate explanation, he received an exact photocopy of the first rejection, despite the fact that the appeal should have been treated as a new case.[123] This strategy of appealing to the courts to have the delaying effect reinstated proved popular, and thousands of boycotters pursued it. In December, the *Frankfurter Rundschau* reported that an administrative court in Frankfurt was able to decide 30 such cases per day with the aid of a standard decision formula. A Kassel court confirmed the practice: "Without standardization it can't be done."[124] In all jurisdictions, only a tiny fraction of appeals were successful. The problem with standardized decisions, according to Frankfurt attorney Stephan Baier, was that they could be seen to violate individual appellants' rights to have the specific merits of their cases considered. However, according to Manfred Voucko, chief justice of the 7th chamber of the Hessian Administrative Court in Kassel, the Federal Administrative Court [*Bundesverwaltungsgericht*] had approved the standardized decisions. And in any case, Voucko added, the appeals themselves were often essentially identical in their wording.[125] The "cookie-cutter" procedures were allowed to stand, but even with this advantage, courts were still plowing through piles of cases through the latter half of 1988.[126]

Some boycotters were able to cover the court expenses generated by the whole appeals process with legal insurance, which had generated a minor controversy back when the enumeration was about to begin. On May 18th, 1987, the *Süddeutsche Zeitung*, following radio and television reports, quoted an (unidentified) speaker for the HUK, the umbrella organization of insurance companies, in what seemed to be very clear terms: "For the misdemeanor of *Volkszählungsboykott* the legal insurance companies will assume the legal expenses." Conservatives were outraged. The same article quoted CDU/CSU *Bundestag* Parliamentary Manager Friedrich Bohl: "Such a business decision is a punch in the face to law-abiding policy holders, who have to help finance these deliberate violations of the law by

123 Anon. 1987. Kopierer spricht Recht. *die tageszeitung*, October 5, n.p.n.

124 Riedel, A. 1987. Volkszählung: den Gerichten droht der Kollaps. *Frankfurter Rundschau*, December 14, n.p.n.

125 Reinhard, M. 1988. In den Gerichtsakten warten noch einige harte Nüsse. *Frankfurter Rundschau*, June 14, p. 10.

126 Loerzer, S. 1988b. Eine Volkszählung dieser Art wird es nicht mehr geben. *Süddeutsche Zeitung*, December 5, n.p.n.

census boycotters."[127] The next day, the *Süddeutsche Zeitung* reported a reversal: the HUK now stated its intent to refuse any financial assistance for boycotters, whether court costs or fines.[128] *Die Zeit* looked into the matter over the next few days and learned that the first reports over the weekend had unleashed a rush to the insurance company offices for new legal insurance policies. Klaus Sperling, head of the legal insurer DAS attempted to clarify the limits of insurable misdemeanors. While admitting that "we will have certain difficulties in borderline areas", Sperling explained that the key distinction was that between unintended and deliberate misdemeanors. But of course other misdemeanors such as parking violations are often intentional. The "helpless directive" agreed upon by most insurers was thus, according to Sperling, "Whoever looks like a boycotter will not be insured".[129] *Der Spiegel* picked up the story and delved further into the legal guidelines on insurance policies, finding that the "General Conditions for Legal Insurance" [ABR] explicitly included intentionally committed misdemeanors among the actions covered. Further, ¶ 17 of the ABR stipulated that misdemeanors would be insured regardless of the perceived chances of success in challenging fines in court (this was important because in practice, there appeared to be almost no chance of winning appeals). The only bright spot for authorities seemed to be that coercive fines [*Zwangsgeld*] would not be covered because challenges to them were handled in administrative courts [*Verwaltungsgerichte*] rather than municipal courts [*Amtsgerichte*]. A coercive fine could be imposed independently of whether an individual was charged with a misdemeanor, but once a misdemeanor was charged, it became an insurable matter for the *Amtsgericht*.[130] In March of 1988, a local *Amtsgericht* in Villingen-Schwenningen followed this reasoning, ruling that intentionality could not be a criterion for some misdemeanors and not others, and thus that legal insurance did in fact have to cover normal fines [*Bußgeld*].[131] In May of 1988, the *Frankfurter Rundschau* reported a similar decision by the Munich *Amtsgericht*.[132] The next month, the taz uncovered a new strategy pursued by judges unhappy with census-related appeals: a Berlin woman who had won an appeal on the basis of a bureaucratic error was nevertheless charged the court costs. In West Germany as elsewhere, of course, standard practice was to have the party winning an appeal reimbursed for court costs. The Federal Constitutional Court, whose consistent refusal to hear any challenges to the census did not stop

127 Quoted in Anon., Streit um die Volkszählung spitzt sich zu.

128 Anon. 1987. Doch kein Versicherungsschutz bei Boykott der Volkszählung. *Süddeutsche Zeitung*, May 19, n.p.n.

129 Quoted in Kahlen, R. 1987. Ungehorsam ist nicht versichert. *Die Zeit*, May 22, p. 28.

130 Anon. 1987. Tiefer Kotau. *Der Spiegel*, June 8, pp. 47, 50.

131 Gaserow, V. 1988a. Versicherung muß für Vobo zahlen. *die tageszeitung*, March 29, n.p.n.

132 Wittowski, B. 1988. Versicherung muß Prozeßkosten für Volkszählungsgegner zahlen. *Frankfurter Rundschau*, May 18, n.p.n.

ever more West Germans from sending in appeals anyway, likewise grew annoyed enough to start fining complainants DM 100 each for "misuse" of the court's time and energy.[133] If legally insured boycotters could expect financial help despite deliberate violation of the law, the reasoning seemed to be, then those boycotters not legally insured could expect to pay court costs even when they won.

While the courts were busy mastering the avalanche of cases and wrangling over the legal insurance issue, actually collecting those fines that had already been charged to boycotters posed another problem for local authorities. Here, too, the zeal, inventiveness and staying power of state authorities was impressive. As in so many other areas, West Berlin stood out. In September of 1987, the West Berlin Finance Senator issued a directive pulling all of the city's tax collection officers away from tax work to concentrate on bringing in the coercive fines that had been imposed upon suspected census boycotters. The boycott initiatives nevertheless counseled calm for those still holding out: even if the collection officials appeared at the door, they were not allowed to enter. They could thus be sent away, and would only be able to enter residences once they had obtained a warrant of entry. Residents who did not want to face confiscation of their property could in the meantime send in the census form (which then immediately eliminated the coercive fine).[134] Not content to rely upon such a time-consuming process, the West Berlin Financial Director's Office [*Oberfinanzdirektion*] began in early January of 1988 to impound the wages of boycotters. The Office had the right to obtain individuals' bank account numbers from banks, as well as names and addresses of employers from medical and automobile insurers. The employers were contacted and would then steer deductions from pay directly into the city's accounts. Although the procedure was technically legal, the taz reported that the West Berlin Data Protection Commissioner was unhappy with it, presumably because it represented a clear case of using data gathered for one purpose for a different purpose [*Zweckentfremdung*], one of the most basic violations of the Data Protection Law.[135] In July of 1988, the Finance Senator ordered tax secrecy protections lifted for some 6,000 remaining boycotters whose money was apparently not to be reached by these "ordinary" means. The rules stated that tax secrecy could be suspended only where "crime and intentional actions against life and limb [*Leib und Leben*] or against the state and its institutions are the object", or if "economic crimes are being pursued which are sufficient significantly to disrupt the economic order."[136] Tax law experts consulted by the taz were of the opinion

133 Gaserow, V. 1988b. Justitias Rache an den Vobos. *die tageszeitung*, June 15, n.p.n.

134 Fehrle, B. 1987b. Steuereintreibung stillgelegt. *die tageszeitung*, September 23, n.p.n.

135 Anon. 1988. Neuer VoBo-Dressurakt: Kontopfandung. *die tageszeitung*, January 16, n.p.n.

136 Quoted in Gaserow, V. 1988c. Illegale Schnüffelei per Erlaß. *die tageszeitung*, July 7, pp. 1-2.

that at the very least, a crime potentially punishable by imprisonment (as opposed to a misdemeanor) had to be involved.[137] The article also dryly noted the contrast between the ease with which tax secrecy had been lifted for census boycotters and the months-long battle over lifting the tax secrecy of political and economic elites in the so-called "Flick Affair", which had involved major political corruption. In any event, this was one step too many for West Berlin politicians from the AL and the SPD. Along with the West Berlin Data Protection Commissioner, they protested strongly against the suspension of tax secrecy, and the Finance Senator, Rexrodt, withdrew the order.[138]

In September of 1989, only two months before the Berlin Wall would come down, and more than two years after the enumeration day, there were still 4,000 fines outstanding in West Berlin alone, and the AL was urging a general amnesty.[139] There were certainly precedents to point to by that time: in May of 1988, the city-state of Bremen had declared the *Volkszählung* finished and had passed a measure granting amnesty on all outstanding regular and coercive fines.[140] But in the divided city, as in a number of other states throughout West Germany, the last, bitter scenes of the 1987 census controversy had yet to play out. As at the beginning of the whole census boycott drama in late 1982 and early 1983, the taz would be the main journalistic witness to these final doings. In February of 1989, one Dieter S. of the Karlsruhe area became the first West German to serve jail time for refusing to answer the census. When he declined to pay the DM 125 fine laid upon him and (his other option for avoiding jail) to swear an oath that he would turn in the census form, he was arrested and given six months.[141] Almost a year later, the same fate nearly befell a 77-year-old Pastor's widow living in a small town near Hannover. Eva Bormann, a long-time local peace and anti-nuclear activist, was fully prepared to serve her time. But the storm of protest raised by her activist comrades, and the anticipated embarrassment that would undoubtedly follow her incarceration, led the Hannover statistical office to grant her amnesty at the last minute. Mrs. Bormann admitted she was happy not to go to prison, but mainly because she didn't want to absorb the time and energy of activist groups who would doubtless carry on long-term actions on her behalf. She added that she was still waiting for an opportunity to carry on a substantive debate with statisticians or judges about the

137 Quoted in Gaserow, Illegale Schnüffelei, p. 1.

138 Gaserow, V. 1988d. Steuerschnüffelei bei Vobos gekippt. *die tageszeitung*, July 11, n.p.n.

139 Gaserow, V. 1989b. Keine Amnestie für VoBos. *die tageszeitung*, September 6, n.p.n.

140 Werner, A. 1988. Ende November sollen erste Ergebnisse vorliegen. *Frankfurter Rundschau*, June 14, p. 10.

141 Gaserow, V. 1989a. Knast für Volkszählungsgegner. *die tageszeitung*, February 23, n.p.n.

census.[142] In April, West Berlin resident Christian H. was sentenced to 8 days in jail for refusing either to answer the census or pay his fine.[143] In July of 1990, another local West Berlin *Amtsgericht* sentenced one Peter K. to five days.[144] But over the next few months, Peter K. refused to appear at the prison. In March of 1991, in a fitting endnote to the whole 1987 controversy, the taz reported that Peter K. was on the run from the law: "The tiny remnants [*Überbleibsel*] of a massive citizens' movement that once wanted to drive back the data-hungry surveillance state will not stand to have its will broken." According to Peter K.'s mother, the men who visited her house looking for him assured her that she would be left in peace once her son paid his fine.[145] The years after 1987 were marked by historic events that brought together the two Germanies and sent shock waves across the globe. But the determination of the (now formerly) West Berlin authorities would likewise "not stand to have its will broken." This was one of the most important lessons to be drawn from the painfully slow denouement of the 1987 controversy.

Sensing what the taz would later term the relentless "determination and effectiveness of the bureaucracy", some VoBo activists had anticipated the ultimate dissolution of the hard boycott as early as August of 1987.[146] Reinhard Bütikofer, then a Green city councilor in Heidelberg, told *Der Spiegel* at that time that the boycott was "without perspective in the long run", and Eberhard Bueb, speaker for the Bavarian Greens, announced "we don't want any martyrs."[147] Critical assessments of the boycott movement published in the taz drew some clear-eyed conclusions. West Berlin VoBo activists counted among the successes of the movement the willingness of wide swathes of the population to boycott a properly passed law, in other words, to participate in civil disobedience. Secondly, the repressive measures taken by state officials at all levels demonstrated as no activist public education campaign could have the interest taken by the apparatuses of the surveillance state in official statistics.[148] Longer analyses appearing in early June focused more intently on the failures of the boycott. A West Berlin activist writing under the name "Raimund" argued, first, that the initial position of the boycott movement in 1987 was less advantageous in some ways than in 1983. The obviously disturbing provision of the 1982 law allowing for use of personal census data to correct the Residency Registers [*Melderegister*] was no longer there, and in general the Interior Ministry and the Federal Statistical Bureau had gone to much

142 Lücke, O. 1990. Vobo-Aktivistin muß nicht ins Gefängnis. *die tageszeitung*, January 3, n.p.n.

143 Wildt, D. 1990. Vobo-Opfer wehrt sich. *die tageszeitung*, April 12, n.p.n.

144 Weber, A. 1990. Gnadenweg – aber warum? *die tageszeitung*, July 21, n.p.n.

145 Wildt, D. 1991. VoBo-Boykotteur ist auf der Flucht. *die tageszeitung*, March 4, n.p.n.

146 Anon. 1988. "Zum ersten Mal ein Gesetz boykottiert". *die tageszeitung*, May 25, n.p.n.

147 Quoted in Anon. 1987. Auf Dauer perspektivlos. *Der Spiegel*, August 31, p. 44.

148 Anon. "Zum ersten Mal ein Gesetz boykottiert".

greater lengths to broadcast the notion that the new census law was constitutional. Thus, despite the fact that the 1987 boycott movement was better organized, it lacked some of the emotional drive of the 1983 movement.[149]

The key point emphasized by Raimund had to do with the consequences of the census having actually been taken. Unlike in 1983, when such considerations never came into play because of the Constitutional Court's stoppage of the count, in 1987, the boycott organizers "did not want to see that the success of the coercive apparatus of the state was only a matter of time. The overwhelming majority of boycotters were not prepared to take on greater financial risks, and rightly so." Once the enumeration was underway, in other words, group actions (demonstrations, meetings, petitions) no longer had an impact beyond the maintenance of morale. As these actions became less frequent, thousands of individual boycotters were essentially left ever more completely alone to face the full power of a state apparatus far from unified but often bitterly determined. The structural conditions of the boycott led inexorably, *once the census was taken*, to an atomization of resistance. As Raimund perceptively put it, "[w]ith other acts of civil disobedience, for example, blockades, the collective illegal action is clearly defined and observable [*überschaubar*]. The potential experience of success is directly linked to the act of disobedience. With the *Volkszählungsboykott* participants face a long-lasting, steadily intensifying, motivation- and nerve-fraying [*-zermürbenden*] process." For this reason, it was probably a mistake for boycott organizers to focus so strongly on the "hard boycott" strategy: "the 'soft' boycott should be re-evaluated. In numerical terms it cannot be so precisely registered [which was of course one of the main reasons for choosing the 'hard' boycott], but the well-known complaints of the statistical offices regarding the low quality of the forms they received speaks volumes."[150]

149 Raimund [no surname given]. 1988. Dem Obrigkeitsstaat ein Schnippchen schlagen. *die tageszeitung*, June 4, n.p.n.

150 Raimund, Dem Obrigkeitsstaat ein Schnippchen schlagen.

Conclusions

> I must remind this council that a number of other states have expressed their concerns to me that what is happening here could cross the border and spread like a modern-day black death, You mean blank death, don't you, said the prime minister with a placatory smile, In that case, the minister of foreign affairs went on unperturbed, we can, quite correctly, speak of depth charges launched against the stability of the democratic system, not simply, not merely, of one country, this country, but of the entire planet.
>
> (José Saramago, *Seeing*, p. 51)

The chapters of this book have all borne as epigraphs passages from José Saramago's novel *Seeing*. Published in English in 2006, Saramago's fictional narrative parallels the events in West Germany in the 1980s in uncanny ways. In the novel, the bulk of the voting population of an unnamed European capital city decides to register its disapproval of the political system by turning in blank ballots on the occasion of a routine election. Eighty-three percent of the electorate in fact turn in blank ballots. The national government is completely taken by surprise and temporarily immobilized by this turn of events, but the cabinet, under the leadership of the prime minister, quickly concludes that the "blank ballot" phenomenon in fact represents the most extreme and subversive attack on the state, and that a sinister conspiracy must be behind it. The central government decides to withdraw from the capital city and seal it off militarily as a form of punishment, assuming that the lack of institutional organization will quickly result in the city's descent into chaos, followed by the citizenry seeing the error of its ways, promising to embrace the existing system again, and begging the government to return.

None of these expectations are fulfilled, which further disturbs the already deeply disconcerted ministers. Agents of the government then detonate a bomb near the railway station, hoping that the population will call it back in as the guarantor of security. But this response, too, fails to materialize. Meanwhile, acting on the assumption that a conspiracy must be at work, the Prime Minister secretly sends into the city a trio of police agents whose job it is to track down and kill an individual identified as the leader of the blank ballot "conspiracy". This purported puppet-master is a woman whose presumed connection with subversive activities is based not on any evidence possessed by the government but merely on conjecture following from the peculiar fact that four years previously, when the entire population went blind for weeks on end, she alone retained her sight (this story is the subject of Saramago's searing earlier novel *Blindness*, since made into a movie). The main plot of *Seeing* comes to revolve around the chief inspector in charge of the secret police trio smuggled into the city, who realizes that the woman has been selected arbitrarily as a scapegoat, that the government leadership really has no idea what it is doing and no justification for its deadly game other than a desperate desire to re-establish its authority. As the inspector's ministerial superior recognizes that his first assassin no longer intends to carry out the job, he decides to have him as well as the innocent woman killed, and the end of the novel moves hauntingly toward a denouement.

Saramago, a prominent leftist and long-time member of the Portuguese communist party, clearly wants to provoke questions with this novel about, among other things, the role and legitimacy of the state in modern societies, and particularly about the real purposes of "security" measures. The obvious parallel to the census boycott controversies is the way in which a peaceful and seemingly small-scale, innocuous form of resistance centered on counting comes to be seen as a grave threat to the legitimacy of the political order. Particularly in 1987, the actions and statements of some West German government officials suggest that some of the very same authoritative anxieties dissected so surgically by Saramago had been triggered by the census boycott. However, the anxieties of power are arguably Saramago's chief target; he is content to keep the focus on them, and not much interested, undoubtedly for very good narrative reasons, in exploring the origins and organization of the mass protest that provoked them. I would like to argue in this concluding chapter that the census boycotts, for all their mildness, likewise represent a profound challenge to state authority, specifically to what I have termed epistemic sovereignty. The "dark territory" of this book's title points toward a realm reducible neither to "private" nor to "public" space, but a realm which in any case should not be laid bare in ever greater detail to the gaze of states or other large organizations. Because we know much more about the census boycotts than about the rather mysterious and apparently spontaneous blank ballot scenario Saramago spins out, the boycotts allow us to explore in much more detail precisely what it is about such a movement that makes it so subversive. My argument, again, is that the census boycotts showcased the emergence of new forms of citizenship responding to the changing forms and meanings of "political representation" in the information age. The point of informational citizenship, as we will see below, is not so much to preserve dark territory as simply "dark", but rather to ensure that whatever images emerge from it are in part "polarized" (in the optical sense) or perhaps "filtered" in accordance with the interests and democratic input of members of the population. The main burden of the present chapter is to spell out these new forms of citizenship more explicitly, and to suggest new ways of thinking about political representation. But not all dimensions of this emergent form of citizenship were already clear and fully formed at the time of the census boycott movements. Some have only taken shape in the intervening decades, for example in connection with the accelerated globalization of capitalism, with the growth and new centrality of the internet, and with shifts in domestic and international political landscapes. This chapter will thus begin with a look at the immediate and longer-term aftermath of the boycott movements in West (and then unified) Germany, with an eye to distilling key features of the new citizenship. These will be systematized into a broad framework for citizenship in the second section, linking strategies and experiments from the 1980s to the wider landscape of informational struggles in the early 21st century. The intention is to reveal a form of coherence in these struggles that can point toward new possibilities for deepening and extending democracy. The core proposals for future political change are spelled out toward the end.

Fallout in (West) Germany

The first results of the 1987 *Volkszählung* were announced in late 1988. The conservative *Bayern Kurier* crowed that numbers confronted "Greens and communists" with the ultimate "bankruptcy" of their subversive efforts. The grand total of residents was 61,082,800, which represented an increase of only 432,000 over the total in 1970. The number of German residents dropped from 58.2 million in 1970 to 56.9 million in 1987, with the difference being made up by a 70% growth in the number of foreigners living in West Germany over this period. Other general trends included clear evidence of an aging population (the proportion of the population under 15 dropped from 23% to 15% in 17 years), confirmation of the impression that there were still too few residences, but also evidence that the average size of living spaces was increasing steadily.[1] Interior Minister Friedrich Zimmermann insisted that the effort had paid off, and that the census had produced a "good" result as a general inventory. He estimated the eventual scope of the boycott to have been less than 1%.[2] *Die Zeit*, however, noted what Zimmermann preferred not to emphasize, namely that the local quality of results varied considerably: his judgment "is *generally* valid; *locally* things look much worse, all things considered".[3]

Egon Hölder, head of the Federal Statistical Bureau, granted an interview to the taz in January of 1990. The obvious question posed by Vera Gaserow, the taz correspondent primarily responsible for the census coverage throughout, concerned the value of the 1987 results in view of the re-unification of Germany. The sudden flood of former East Germans into the "old states" of the *Bundesrepublik* surely rendered the population numbers just compiled totally obsolete, she suggested. Hölder strove to assure her that the reunification could be handled through standard statistical practice: "Already since the official enumeration date, additions to and subtractions from the [provisional] census results have been factored in. And we'll do exactly the same thing with those who come to us to re-settle." Hölder was willing to admit, however, that the sudden demographic shifts resulting from

1 Roos, K. 1988. Die Pleite der Boykotteure. *Bayern Kurier*, December 10, n.p.n.

2 Anon. 1988. Zimmermann: Volkszählung vollauf gerechtfertigt. *Süddeutsche Zeitung*, November 30, n.p.n.

3 Bieber, H. 1988. Neue Fakten übers Volk. *Die Zeit*, December 16, p. 4.

the re-unification would cause some problems for traffic and facilities planning (medical institutions, public swimming pools, etc.). Gaserow asked whether a new *Volkszählung* could be expected anytime soon. Hölder (referring to the EC guidelines, according to which all EC countries should synchronize their censuses decennially) answered that Germany would simply extrapolate from the 1987 totals in 1990/91, the next planned Europe-wide census year.[4] But many officials probably shared the opinion of Munich attorneys and census opponents Jürgen Arnold and Jutta Schneider that "a census in this form will not happen again".[5] A census was not taken in 1991, and the first census since 1987, due to be taken in 2011, will not be a traditional enumeration. This could be seen in retrospect as a vindication of the boycott movement, and of the unflagging insistence upon data protection principles by Data Protection Commissioners such as Spiros Simitis and Ruth Leuze. But, as census proponents had argued all along, alternative methods of obtaining data might not necessarily better protect the rights and interests of the enumerated. The 1990s would prove to be a decade of explosive growth in data gathering, exchange and processing, in Germany as elsewhere. Much of this growth would take place in the private sector, and the flow of data within the private sector, as well as between state and private institutions, and across international boundaries, would become much more difficult to control. Thus, while the census boycott movements may have posed real challenges to the West German state's information-gathering practices for a time, they certainly did not succeed in halting the general trend toward ever-more comprehensive registration of the population. Their main political significance, I will argue in more detail below, was in modeling a novel form of political action, and in the process exploring new terrain for democracy.

The fall of the Berlin Wall in 1989, the process of unification of the former East and West Germany under the latter's existing constitutional system over the subsequent two years, and then the social, political, economic and cultural fallout of this major watershed would understandably dominate German domestic politics through the first half of the 1990s. The relatively low profile of concerns about data protection and surveillance in connection with advances in information technology would be further reinforced by two specific features of the German political discourse during this period. First, the Greens, who had assumed the mantle of champions of data protection in the mid-1980s, were temporarily sidelined by their opposition to immediate re-unification via absorption of the East into the BRD system. As a result of their stance, they lost dramatically in the 1992 elections, and prejudiced their own chances in the former East for years to come.[6] Second, in so far as surveillance remained in the news, the most spectacular and absorbing stories concerned the operations of the spy and informant networks of

4 Gaserow, V. 1990. Volkszählung endgültig reif furs Altpapier? Interview mit Egon Hölder. *die tageszeitung* January 12, n.p.n.

5 Loerzer, S., Eine Volkszählung dieser Art.

6 Markovitz and Gorski, *From Red to Green.*

the East German State Security Service (Stasi) in the BRD during the 40 years of division. As noted in Chapter 3, debates around what to do with newly available information identifying West Germans who had passed information on to the Stasi were extremely fraught. For these reasons, the sorts of issues underlying the census boycott movements, resistance to machine-readable identity cards, etc. tended for a while to motivate only a relatively circumscribed group of activists and other concerned citizens. But by the latter half of the 1990s, the Greens were again ascendant, entering into their first ruling coalition at the national level with the SPD in 1998, and the relentless march of surveillance technology was again making headlines with some regularity, most notably in the 1998 controversy surrounding the passage of alterations to the Basic Law necessary to allow acoustic bugging of residential spaces by security services.[7]

Yet the nature of surveillance concerns was shifting throughout this period, as technological processes driving the information age meshed ever more thoroughly with the processes of capitalist globalization.[8] This shift is evident in the recipients of the German Big Brother Awards, first given out in the year 2000 and sponsored by a range of human rights and data-protection organizations. The British organization Privacy International had inaugurated Big Brother Awards in the UK in 1998, and over the next few years the practice developed of synchronized announcements of national prizes in a fast-growing number of participating nations (18 countries as of late 2009). Touted as the "Oscars for data leeches", the purpose of the German Big Brother Awards is explained on the website in terms of informational self-determination, and an extended quote from the Constitutional Court's 1983 census decision features prominently.[9] By the turn of the new millennium, the central importance of private corporations in generating, storing and sharing (or selling) electronic data was obvious. State officials associated with intrusive initiatives still earned ironic "recognition" for their "contributions" to the dismantling of citizens' rights, but often the most innovative and disturbing impacts upon the notional right of informational self determination were by-products of or tools mobilized in the search for profits. The critique of the "legitimate" use of data is just as relevant to private as to public data gathering exercises: periodic and eagerly reported cases of misplaced data or data theft involving organized crime, while serious matters when they occur, should not distract attention too much from troubling aspects of the far larger and ongoing aggregation of personal data by legal means.

In 2000, Big Brother Awards were given out in seven categories: business and finance, politics, bureaucracy and administration, communication, life-work, regional special prizes, and special prizes relating to the "scene", that is the

7 Schaar, *Das Ende der Privatsphäre*, pp. 106-110.

8 Castells, *Network Society*.

9 BigBrotherAwards.de 2009c. Why Oscars for data leeches? [Online]. Available at http://www.bigbrotherawards.de/why-en [accessed: September 3, 2009].

insider world of technicians, hackers and other computer surveillance experts.[10] The exact breakdown of categories would shift somewhat over the years, notably with the addition of a separate category for consumer concerns. Prizewinners the first time around included, in the politics category, Berlin Interior Senator Eckart Werthebach, for his advocacy of expanded police telephone surveillance, while Hartmut Mehdorn, head of the national railway agency Deutsche Bahn, came away with the prize for bureaucracy and administration, on the strength of his planned system of video surveillance in and around rail stations. The business and finance prizewinner was the Munich firm “Loyalty Partner” for its “PAYBACK” card system, a rebate card usable at thousands of participating businesses, which allows the consumer to accumulate bonus points toward rebates but also allows the firm to gather (and eventually sell) extensive personal data. The internet mail firm GMX won the communications prize for its inadequate protection of user data. The echo in the media was considerable. A list of articles in print, online, and of programs on radio and television calling attention to the 2000 awards, compiled by FoeBud e.V., the Bielefeld-based association of computer activists organizing them, included 14 articles in major national daily or weekly print media, two articles in foreign media, and two radio broadcast segments, as well as numerous pieces in computer, internet, and specialized journals, and in local city papers.[11]

Media coverage would grow steadily over the intervening years. While an exhaustive reporting of prizewinners through the first decade of the 21st century is beyond the scope of this chapter, some important moments deserve mention. The second year of the German awards was also the year of the September 11th attacks on the World Trade Center and the Pentagon in the United States. Like interior ministers in many other countries, Otto Schily, who had come a long way from his notorious stint as radical defense attorney for the RAF in the 1970s, wasted little time in attempting to strengthen security measures. For his “engagement against citizens’ rights, data protection and informational self-determination” he was nominated in numbers that far outweighed those of his competition, and he garnered the political award hands down. The text accompanying the award includes some choice quotes from the minister:

> Of all German politicians who have called into question data protection since the terrorist attacks in the USA, Otto Schily has most clearly stood out. Schily argued that data protection had to be “newly defined”, that “security interests should not be permitted to be hindered by data protection provisions”. Schily posed the question whether data protection is not often “overdone”. He had

10 BigBrotherAwards.de 2009a. Archive. [Online]. Available at: http://www.bigbrotherawards.de/archiv [accessed: September 3, 2009].

11 FoeBuD e.V. 2009a. Archive. [Online]. Available at: http://archiv.foebud.org/bba/#Unbekannt [accessed: September 3, 2009].

> his spokesperson warn that "data protection should not effectively end up as terrorist protection".[12]

This last admonishment of course updates the slogan "data protection is not perpetrator protection" [*Datenschutz ist nicht Täterschutz*], taken up by politicians and police officials in the early 1980s. Schily would receive the lifetime achievement award in 2005 for this and additional projects. The fallout from September 11th, 2001 has continued to resonate up to the present day through the Big Brother Awards in all countries that grant them. One of the 2008 German awards, for example, went to the EU Council of Ministers for its maintenance of a "terrorist" database cobbled together from input of member countries without any quality control, but coupled nevertheless with strictly enforced Europe-wide punishments for anyone unlucky enough to be included in it (the echoes of the APIS and PIOS databases into which personal information on some census boycott organizers was entered in 1987 are obvious). In July of 2009, Peter Schaar, the German Federal Data Protection Commissioner, issued a press release criticizing a new law passed by the *Bundestag* approving a wide-ranging exchange of personal data between the US and Germany, including DNA and digital fingerprint files.[13] Whereas governments tend to be nominated for proposals to gain access to, or to bring together, existing forms of data, many of the awards going to private firms such as software companies, telecommunications firms, and hotel chains have to do with the creation, extraction or packaging of new forms of personal information. The interface between state agencies and the capitalist economy is also a live site of new idioms of surveillance. The explosion of privatized government agencies and private contractors that have taken over ever more of the tasks formerly done by federal or state-level governments has bred major contenders, such as the agency GEZ entrusted with collecting radio and television fees for state-supported German broadcasters (2003), or the firm Toll Collect, for satellite-supported compilation into comprehensive movement profiles of data on vehicles passing through Germany's toll gates (2002).

Not only the Big Brother Awards but regular media coverage and a steady stream of books on surveillance seek to educate the German public.[14] It is perhaps not surprising that the taz, which played so central a role in the census

12 BigBrotherAwards.de 2009b. Prizewinner of the main prize (category "politics"). [Online]. Available at: http://www.bigbrotherawards.de/2001/.pol [accessed: September 3, 2009].

13 Federal Commissioner for Data Protection and Freedom of Information 2009. Press Releases. [Online]. Available at: http://www.bfdi.bund.de/cln_111/EN/PublicRelations/PressReleases/2009/20_09_SchaarCriticisesAgreementDataExchangesUSA.html?nn=410156 [accessed: September 7, 2009].

14 Gössner, R. 2000. *Big Brother & Co.: Der Moderne Überwachungsstaat in der Informationsgesellschaft*. Hamburg: Konkret Literatur Verlag; Prantl, H. 2002. *Verdächtig: Der starke Staat und die Politik der inneren Unsicherheit*. Hamburg: Europa Verlag.

boycott movements, maintains as a permanent feature of it website a "Dossier Surveillance", or that the Bündnis 90/Die Grünen, the post-unification successor to the Greens, announced a "data protection offensive" in May of 2009, aimed, among other things, at finally embedding the principle of informational self-determination explicitly in the Basic Law.[15] But concerns about data protection are in no way limited to the left side of the political spectrum or to an activist fringe, as a sample of recent survey results makes plain. A Europe-wide survey in January of 2008 found 86% of Germans concerned about the privacy of data held by state and non-state organizations.[16] A TNS-Emnid survey of 1003 households in July of 2008 found that 71% of respondents were concerned about the possibility that the government would search citizens' computers without justification.[17] A nationwide telephone survey by Infratest-dimap in August of 2009 found that 80% of respondents think better consumer privacy protection is needed in Germany. Ninety-three percent considered it important to know what was being done with their personal data, and 87% saw a pressing need for action in the area of data protection.[18] The "Pirate Party" [*Piratenpartei*] formed in 2006 around a core of internet activists, launched a bid to enter the *Bundestag* in the 2009 elections on a platform primarily focused upon data protection and defense of the internet against regulation.[19]

A brief glance at Big Brother Awards in other countries shows that while Germans are among the more sensitive populations in perceiving threats to data protection, these trends are not specifically German.[20] Underlying most of these disturbing developments are the same four basic technological trends identified in the Introduction: (1) ever faster, more miniaturized and less expensive information processing capacity; (2) ever-expanding, more miniaturized and less expensive

15 Bündnis 90/Die Grünen 2009. Grüne Datenschutzoffensiv. [Online]. Available at: http://www.gruene-bundestag.de/cms/datenschutz/dok/263/263067.gruene_datenschutz offensive.html [accessed: September 4, 2009].

16 European Commission 2008. Data Protection in the European Union: Citizens' Perceptions. [Online]. Available at: http://ec.europa.eu/public_opinion/flash/fl_225_en.pdf [accessed: October 14, 2009].

17 Statista.com 2009. Umfrage: Furcht vor online-Durchsuchung. [Online]. Available at: http://de.statista.com/statistik/daten/studie/1304/umfrage/furcht-vor-online-durchsuchung-privater-computer-durch-staat/#info [accessed: September 4, 2009].

18 Infratest-dimap 2009. 83 prozent sehen Handlungsbedarf bei Verbraucherschutz. [Online]. Available at: http://www.infratest-dimap.de/umfragen-analysen/bundesweit/umfragen/aktuell/83-prozent-sehen-handlungsbedarf-beim-verbraucherschutz/ [accessed: September 4, 2009].

19 Twickel, C. 2009. Piratenpartei will den Bundestag entern. *SpiegelOnline* July 5, 2009. [Online]. Available at: http://www.spiegel.de/netzwelt/netzpolitik/0,1518,634228,00.html [accessed: September 11, 2009]; Piratenpartei Deutschland 2009. [Online homepage]. Available at: http://www.piratenpartei.de/ [accessed: September 11, 2009].

20 Privacy International 2009. [Online homepage]. Available at: http://www.privacyinternational.org/ [accessed: September 4, 2009].

data storage and retrieval capacities; (3) ever-expanding, ever-faster transmission and switching capacities; (4) ever more efficient translation or conversion between various types and applications of electronic data based on their common digital base code. It is possible to identify two additional trends that have drawn upon and reinforced the interaction between these four basic developments to drive forward innovations in surveillance; (5) dramatic expansion of the range of human phenomena recorded in digital electronic form, a massive new "primitive accumulation" of data (here the digitization of optical images and sound are undoubtedly most important, but the embedding of tiny RFID chips transmitting location and other data in a rapidly growing number of products and documents has also generated alarm); and (6) increasingly sophisticated software engineered to recognize and extract potentially meaningful or abnormal patterns from the oceans of data generated by this expanding digitization (face recognition technology, software designed to flag suspicious bodily movements or postures, or data mining of telephone traffic in search of "terrorist" activity illustrate this trend). Coupled with the now quite advanced practice of tracking individual behavior for purposes of target marketing or calculations of insurance risk, all of this might well be taken to approach the real-world achievement of what 1980s activists in West Germany warned against: the construction of the "glass person". This is the basic point stressed again and again in the now-huge literature on the growth of surveillance and the evaporation of privacy.

But what significance can be attributed to the fact that much personal information is now gathered by innumerable private firms, innumerable "Little Brothers", and thus is not centrally stored by state agencies?[21] This dispersed geography of data does not seem to have prevented an across-the-board increase in the transparency of individual lives. It is ever more difficult, for example, for someone with a pre-existing medical condition to be accepted on a health insurance plan in the US, for someone with a checkered credit history to obtain a home loan, or for someone with a past criminal record to get a job in many countries. We are in general terms tied to our personal biographies in a more detailed way than was the case 30 years ago. But is it not at least reassuring that our personal data is scattered throughout hundreds or even thousands of unconnected databases? At least this dispersion makes our data less immediately accessible to state agencies. Developments in "security" techniques since September 11th, 2001 suggests that there is in fact little protection in dispersed private control over personal data. As long as information exists somewhere as digital data, governments can and increasingly do request or demand access to it in the name of "national security" or even just in the battle against "serious crime". This danger is illustrated by access to phone calling data granted to the US National Security Agency by US telephone companies in 2006, and by the EU's capitulation in the same year to US requests for access

21 Gössner, *Big Brother & Co.*

to data on international money transfers held by the Belgian company SWIFT.[22] These episodes highlight one of the key ways in which security caveats limit data protection legislation. If Italian philosopher Giorgio Agamben is correct that modern life is governed more and more frequently through "states of exception", in which governments claim the right to act against dire threats such as terrorism, it matters less and less that government agencies themselves may not collect or maintain comprehensive databases.[23] The normalcy of the exception will settle in over the coming years as the definition of domestic "security" expands, under the aegis of "risk prevention", to include large chunks of what used to be considered purely "social" (rather than "criminal" or "political") phenomena. In this way the threshold for state rights of access to privately held data will be lowered. An important implication of this trend is that the starvation or outsourcing of social programs by governments in the thrall of neoliberal ideology need not be paid for with decreased state access to knowledge about the population. Historically, fears about "Big Brother" were based implicitly upon the explosion of information states possessed on their respective citizenries by virtue of the range of social programs they administered. They gained this information by requiring citizens to sign up and register with state agencies, and while it was possible to object to state possession of personal data, its existence was connected to at least notional benefits for the population. This connection with benefits is no longer necessary. In short, the revolution in information technology is a major condition of possibility for states to detach the collection of personal data from provision of social welfare. They can now pursue robust "security" policies while abandoning any adequate *social* security. As Spiros Simitis already recognized in the mid-1980s, we should not make the mistake of assuming that state agencies are the only sources of danger to individual rights or interests.[24] But we should also recognize that even privately generated and privately held data can be accessed and used *by the state*, and that the neoliberal program of self-amputation through which states have been busy transforming themselves into miserly, dessicated and fearful "watchdogs" is no obstacle to this access.

---

22 Cauley, L. 2006. NSA has massive database of Americans' phone calls. USAToday, May 11, 2006 [Online]. Available at: http://www.usatoday.com/news/washington/2006-05-10-nsa_x.htm [accessed: September 6, 2009]; Bonse, E. 2006. Empörung über Pläne für US-Zugriff auf Bankdaten. *Handelsblatt* July 21, 2006 [Online]. Available at: http://www.handelsblatt.com/politik/international/empoerung-ueber-plaene-fuer-us-zugriff-auf-bankdaten;2434851 [accessed: September 7, 2009]; Reichstein, R. 2006. EU lässt das Thema Datenschutz schleifen. *Handelsblatt* November 29, 2006 [Online]. Available at: http://www.handelsblatt.com/politik/international/eu-laesst-das-thema-datenschutz-schlei fen;1175896 [accessed: September 7, 2009].

23 Agamben, *Homo Sacer*.

24 Simitis, S. 1987. Reviewing privacy in an Information Society. *University of Pennsylvania Law Review* 135(3), 707-746, p. 745.

Possibilities for active citizenship in the information age

The picture painted in this brief review is undeniably disturbing. In surveying all of these developments, however, it is crucially important not to lose sight of the continued reliance of data-gatherers on various forms of assent or participation by human beings. Here the census boycotts of the 1980s can help us pinpoint the key issues, and more importantly, to move beyond the usual defensive stance suggested by terms such as data *protection* and privacy. As the boycotts made clear, a crucial moment in the entire complex of issues surrounding personal information is the moment at which data is first gathered. Here a number of questions are clustered that can be seen as political questions of representation. I will discuss each of these questions at some length, in order to build up a systematic overview of *individual* dimensions of informational citizenship, before moving on to the more difficult but ultimately more promising possibilities for *collective* and institutional change.

(1) How much, and what kinds of, control do respondents have over whether being counted or registered is mandatory, voluntary, or "(dis)incentivized" (that is, voluntary but with a significant price to pay, for example in lost convenience, for not agreeing to be counted)?

Geographically speaking, the census boycotts dramatized the inherently spatially dispersed nature of the politics of being counted or registered, the fact that to gain knowledge about social reality, governments and other organizations must have access to extensive stretches of territory. Social life is territorially extensive and dispersed, so the harvesting of personal information obliges state agencies or private organizations to be present, physically or technologically, to gather information at myriad points on the social body. Individuals living their lives do traceable things at locatable points, whether Automatic Tellers, cash registers, internet connections, postboxes, traffic lights fitted out with automatic cameras, or, increasingly, sitting in one place and using iPhones™ or Blackberries™. It is at these millions of points that the question of choice in being registered plays out concretely. The continuing relevance of distributed geographies of knowledge gathering is one of the points so well dramatized by the Harald Juch caricature on the cover of the book.

In West Germany, census participation was mandatory in principle, but boycott organizers portrayed it as voluntary in practice, given what they anticipated would be insurmountable logistical difficulties as well as political risks for the government if it tried to prosecute thousands of boycotters. Yet it was not merely anti-authoritarian activists who favored a voluntary approach to the experience of being counted. Spiros Simitis, Data Protection Commissioner of the West German state of Hessen and the moving force behind much data protection legislation both in Germany and at the European level, had been arguing since the 1970s that a general move away from mandatory response was a necessary adjustment to the information age. Because of all the possible disadvantages to the individual of surrendering personal data, he argued that its collection should become the exception rather than the norm, and should only take place under strict rules and through dialogue with respondents. The burden of proof would then shift, so Simitis urged, onto those agencies (and ideally also private organizations) requesting the data, obliging them to make the case to the public that only personal data could achieve the required result.[25]

A statistical survey in which response is voluntary, such as an opinion poll, must of necessity rely on sampling to produce a picture of the entire population of interest. Being counted in a sample survey adds additional political considerations to the mix. If being counted is seen in part as a form of political representation, being counted in a sample is in fact a way of achieving disproportionate representation of one's views or personal situation. As sample results are extrapolated to entire populations, the relatively few individuals who respond see their own proportional role in the picture that emerges of the entire population grow far beyond the tiny contribution they would make in a classic enumeration. The decision about whether to respond to a survey thus becomes one of weighing the different advantages and disadvantages (either personal or socio-political and economic) to remaining invisible vs. registering one's response on particular matters of public concern. These issues came up with unusual clarity in debates leading up to the 2000 US Census over the permissibility of supplementing the enumeration with corrective sampling methods.[26] A number of issues were woven into this controversy, but all parties agreed that those members of the US population most likely to be undercounted by an old-fashioned enumeration, and thus standing to benefit most by the corrective effects of supplementary sampling, were the same groups that had traditionally been disenfranchised in the US. People of color, poorer people, children, immigrants, single mothers, all would have had their better interests served by census totals adjusted on the basis of sampling, because more accurate and complete counts of these sub-populations would have given them more numerically equal congressional representation. The primary purpose of the decennial US census since 1790 has been to re-adjust the number and boundaries of congressional districts in each of the states to reflect demographic changes, and thus to ensure equal proportional representation in the House of Representatives. Thus, predictably, conservatives opposed sampling, and the conservative members of the Supreme Court found ways to argue against its use to adjust census results for the purposes of divying up congressional districts.

One of the dangers of the proliferation of new forms of personal data since the 1980s, especially the tracking of communications and the digitization of optical images and sound, is that these data are generally gathered without consulting individuals, or without them even being aware of being observed. Similarly, much of the information composing the data trails left by the use of the internet or credit

25 Simitis, Reviewing privacy in an Information Society, p. 739.

26 Hannah, M. 2001. Sampling and the politics of representation in US Census 2000. *Environment and Planning D: Society and Space* 19, 515-534.

cards is stored without permission from the user. To some extent the latter trend can be countered by technological means. For example, FoeBuD e.V., the German organization that coordinates the Big Brother Awards in that country, now offers free downloadable internet browsing software on its website that allows users to browse without leaving traces of their activities.[27] In physical public space, maintaining anonymity is steadily becoming more difficult, especially in countries such as the UK, with comprehensive CCTV coverage of most public spaces. Video surveillance offers a much narrower range of options for remaining anonymous than did the receipt of paper census forms. As discussed in Chapter 4, the specific materiality of a piece of paper opened up a range of options for disrupting the flow of information back to centers of calculation. Video surveillance, by contrast, can only be interrupted by physical barriers to light reflectance. In the 1980s already, the West German government outlawed "masking" [*Vermummung*] at demonstrations, in order to ensure that the police had video access to the faces of demonstrators. It remains to be seen what impact recent European debates about the right of Muslim women to veil or wear *hijab* will have upon security legislation surrounding public space.[28] Rights to cultural self-expression might limit the right of police and security services to have unimpeded access to physical features of individual bodies for the purposes of identification. Federal Data Protection Commissioner Peter Schaar points to one potential technological measure that could generalize video-anonymity, namely the face-obscuring technology already routinely used to protect the privacy of individuals in public broadcasts of CCTV videos relevant to ongoing police investigations.[29] It is probably no great technological leap to link *all* video surveillance of public spaces to such software in such a way as to make anonymity the rule while still allowing the retrospective "de-scrambling" of the facial features of individual suspects in targeted investigations. This would restore, in the area of surveillance of public space, the presumption of innocence to which we are all supposedly still entitled. "Expense" is no more of an objection here than it was in the initial decisions taken to blanket public space with the cameras in the first place. The key factor is of course public pressure.

Such questions point to a further, ultimately quite profound issue. In the massive 1985 study of police in West Germany discussed in the Introduction, Heiner Busch and his co-authors noted that until very recently, information gathering by the police was not legally interpreted as an "intervention" in the lives of citizens.[30] They credited the 1983 census boycott movement in particular for having begun to change this, but pointed out that juridically, the constitutional requirement that

---

27 FoeBuD e.V. 2009b. PrivacyDongle: anonym im Internet surfen. [Online]. Available at: https://www.foebud.org/datenschutz-buergerrechte/vorratsdatenspeicherung/privacydongle/index [accessed: September 8, 2009].

28 See Kiliç, S., Saharso, S., and Sauer, B. 2008. Introduction: The veil: debating citizenship, gender and religious diversity. *Social Politics* 15(4), 397-410.

29 Schaar, *Das Ende der Privatsphäre*, p. 71.

30 Busch, *et al.*, *Die Polizei in der Bundesrepublik*, p. 116.

state interference in the private lives of citizens always be as minimal as possible, and "proportional" to the seriousness of the danger to be averted, would tend to make information gathering seem generally permissible.[31] If the alternative is more physically intrusive measures (searches, raids or what have you), the "lightness" or "ephemerality" of data gathering will tend to be perceived as the less intense, more modest form of intervention. As Simitis argued, however, this presumption leaves out of the picture the quite damaging potential *consequences* of the gathering of personal information. This is why he advocated reversing the burden of proof and making registration of personal information the exception rather than the rule. The experience of being counted or registered, at the moment at which it happens, may indeed be relatively painless. However, as I will discuss at greater length below, it must be seen in the context of its potential effects, some of which can make it quite a highly intrusive form of intervention. In addition, measuring its intensity in terms of its intrusiveness or obtrusiveness implies that the least intrusive, lightest form of information gathering would be of the sort that goes completely undetected. However, as should be plain by now, this militates directly against any sort of informational self-determination. Looking more critically at this issue of the proportionality of intervention suggests that some of the legal and juridical doctrines through which issues surrounding surveillance, privacy and personal data have been understood are in need of profound revision. It is not implausible, for example, to urge legal experts and judges to re-calibrate the "intensity" of a state intervention to include not just its "felt" impact but also, and perhaps in some instances more importantly, the multi-functionality and transportability of any knowledge resulting from the intervention.

It should be borne in mind in considering all of this that, given the choice whether or not to be counted, not all individuals in all situations would opt against enumeration. Large groups in wealthy societies and larger populations in the Global South suffer more from *invisibility* than from visibility.[32] Thus, for example, a coalition of the urban poor in Mumbai, the Alliance, has sought to call attention to the dire lack of housing and sanitation for slum dwellers in that city by training large numbers of people to *conduct reliable censuses on themselves and their neighbors*.[33] The information gathered in this way is communicated to local bureaucrats, international aid organizations and media to help make the case for infrastructural improvements and to demonstrate the initiative of the urban poor in doing what they can to alleviate their own condition. In a more general sense, it is clear that the existence of "official" statistical information pertaining to social

---

31 Busch, *et al.*, *Die Polizei in der Bundesrepublik*, pp. 225-226.

32 See for example Brown, M. and Knopp, L. 2006. Places or polygons? Governmentality, scale and the census in *The Gay and Lesbian Atlas. Population, Space and Place* 12(4), 223-242; Brown, M. 2000. *Closet Space: Geographies of Metaphor from the Body to the Globe*. London: Routledge, Chapter 4.

33 Appadurai, A. 2001. Deep democracy: Urban governmentality and the horizon of politics. *Environment and Urbanization* 13(2), 23-43, pp. 34-35.

issues is not only a matter of surveillance but also, and often more primordially, a condition of possibility for basic social problems to be addressed at all. In this sense the West German census boycott movements presupposed a generally adequate level of social provision for most of the population, which simply cannot be assumed in many cases. Nevertheless, whether in Frankfurt or in Mumbai, having the ability to treat being counted *politically*, as a matter of *representation*, constitutes a potentially profound enrichment of democracy.

(2) How much control, and what sort of control, do potential respondents have over the forms taken by the information to be surrendered (say, narrative vs. statistical), the categories into which responses are grouped, etc.?

This issue was most clearly raised by the *3 Tornados* in their tongue-in-cheek complaint about the West German government's *lack* of curiosity. Echoing Ernst von Salomon's controversial post-WWII response to the census taken by the US military administration occupying defeated Germany, the *3 Tornados* offered all sorts of gossip from everyday life in their residential collective, information that would have been of no use to the statisticians both because they did not ask for it and because of its narrative form. This kind of humorous suggestion has been resuscitated recently as well. US comedian Brian Unger's response, aired on National Public Radio in May of 2006, to news of the National Security Agency's request for data on millions of telephone calls, follows a similar logic.[34] Under the heading "Big Brother? Not Big Enough …", Unger suggests that the Bush administration's "gambling" with constitutionality and privacy does not go far enough: "The Unger Report sees your telephone calls and wants to raise you." There follows a litany of personal data that, he claims, should be thrown in for good measure:

> To really sweeten the pot, let's monitor what people eat. I'll bet there's some kind of dietary pattern that radical Islamists exhibit – an energy rich diet of oil, Middle Eastern grains, protein, to the occasional fast. If we collect data on people eating that diet, then compared it to those eating a non-terrorist diet – Big Mac's, Whoppers, Cheese Lovers' Pizza – then cross-reference those foods against a telephone database, especially calls made on the High Holy Days at suppertime, we might catch a terrorist at a supermarket or a Sizzler …
>
> Now, if we're gonna go all the way with this data collection business, let's monitor what TV shows people are watching. Now, there are 5,000 households in the National People Meter sample provided by Nielsen. This is what networks use to measure TV ratings. I'm betting if we add 280 million to the sample, we

34 Unger, B. 2006. Big Brother? Not Big Enough … The Unger Report, broadcast on National Public Radio (USA), May 15, 2006. [Online transcript]. Available at: http://www.npr.org/templates/story/story.php?storyId=5405422 [accessed: September 8, 2009].

> can really get inside people's heads. Presumably, terrorists love *24*, *Alias*, and *Malcolm in the Middle*. Cross-reference that with shows they probably hate: *Will and Grace*, *Desperate Housewives*, and *American Idol*. Compare it to the terrorist food intake index, then cross-reference it with phone calls made on High Holy Days, we'll catch terrorists flat-footed, bloated, in front of their TVs ...
>
> Now, if we really want to bet the farm on data collection, let's monitor who's dating who. [*sic*] It's done in Hollywood. Why not in real America? Any terrorist worth his weight wouldn't be wasting his time falling in love or going to a Sandals Resort with his honey. So, if we start surveilling people who drink alone, visit Internet dating Web sites, who stay home on Valentine's Day, then measure those people against the food they're consuming, cross-reference with the TV shows they're watching, then all of that analyzed against the phone calls they're making, I bet we'll catch a terrorist who's depressed, parked in front of his TV, getting fat, and waiting for the phone to ring.

Part of the reason this hypothetical updating of the technique of negative *Rasterfahndung* may strike us as only moderately funny is our awareness in the early 21st century that adding most of this additional personal data to that already gathered by the NSA would actually not be very difficult in technological terms.

Realistically, there is probably little scope for such improvised and creative responses to be adopted by large numbers of people, even where data requests still take the form of requests at all. As in 1946 and 1983, this kind of response can, however, contribute to strengthening awareness of surveillance issues in an artistic idiom. A complementary path to political influence over the form and categories of information gathered, for most citizens, is through collective action. An instructive example of this is the ongoing movement in the US to have a "multi-racial" category included in the official racial and ethnic categories used by governments and other organizations. ProjectRACE, founded in 1991, combines advocacy, lobbying at the state and federal levels, and the maintenance of an activist website to further its goals. The self-description of ProjectRACE links identity politics in its more familiar "cultural" sense with the reform of statistical categories:

> Biracial and multiracial people do not have a box to check on forms. Being forced to choose only one race forces us to deny one of our parents. It also requires us to do something illegal, since we are defining ourselves as something we are not. Multiracial people should have the option of recognizing *all* of their heritage. "Multiracial" is important so that children have an identity, a correct terminology for who they are. "Other" means different, a label that no person should bear. Also, without proper racial and ethnic classifications, multiracial people are "invisible" in the health care system.[35]

---

35 ProejctRACE 2009. About ProjectRACE. [Online]. Available at: http://www.projectrace.com/aboutprojectrace/ [accessed: September 8, 2009].

In 1997, the US Office of Management and Budget (OMB), which has responsibility for overseeing the statistical categories used by the US government, concluded a public consultation process in which it considered adopting the multi-racial category, among other suggestions. As a result it decided to allow individuals to tick as many boxes as applied from among the updated set of officially recognized racial categories.[36] Starting with the 2000 US Census, then, US population data could be analyzed for total numbers and various combinations of people self-identifying as belonging to more than one race. Whether or not one agrees with ProjectRACE's politics, it nevertheless indicates that significant numbers of non-specialist members of the public can be mobilized to get involved in decisions about categories of registration and identification.

(3) To what extent are respondents empowered to choose how they themselves will be identified or characterized within the range of possible forms of response (as opposed to being categorized "externally" by observers or procedures beyond their control)?

This question was highlighted by some of the "soft" boycott tactics suggested in 1983 and 1987, such as filling out census forms with partially erroneous or fictional information. When the census was taken in 1987, the West German government countered this tactic by applying "plausibility checks" to incoming census returns, though these would only have been able to detect some kinds of soft boycott. Another aspect of the controversy relating to self-identification was the emphasis placed by boycott initiatives upon the fact that census enumerators were not permitted to enter households. One fear was that entering the household would give enumerators independent, first-hand observations with which to correct or complete false or missing information entered on the census forms. More recently, a collective approach to the politics of self-identification was taken in New Zealand, the UK and Australia. In the UK, a circular e-mail persuaded enough individuals identified themselves as of the "Jedi" religion on the 2001 census to prompt the Statistical Office to assign "Jedi" its own unique code for the purposes of compiling the results.[37] The following year, a similar e-mail campaign resulted in over 70,000 Australian residents listing "Jedi" as their religion.[38]

36 United States Office of Management and Budget 1997. Revisions to the Standards for Classification of Federal Data on Race and Ethnicity. October 30 [Online]. Available at: http://www.whitehouse.gov/omb/rewrite/fedreg/ombdir15.html [accessed: September 8, 2009].

37 Anon. 2001. "Jedi" makes the census list. BBC News, October 9, 2001 [Online]. Available at: http://news.bbc.co.uk/1/hi/uk/1589133.stm [accessed: September 8, 2009].

38 Anon. 2002. "Jedi" religion grows in Australia. BBC News, August 27, 2002 [Online]. Available at: http://news.bbc.co.uk/1/hi/entertainment/2218456.stm [accessed: September 8, 2009].

These episodes raise a potentially much broader issue about the epistemological status of statistical categories representing human realities, an issue taken up by the US Office of Management and Budget in the 1997 decision about racial categories mentioned above. In its introductory comments to the revised racial categories adopted in that year, the OMB explicitly noted that "[t]he categories represent a social-political construct designed for collecting data on the race and ethnicity of broad population groups in this country, and are not anthropologically or scientifically based."[39] With this socially constructed character in mind, the OMB then claimed that the 1997 changes to racial categories "underscore that self-identification is the preferred means of obtaining information about an individual's race and ethnicity, except in instances where observer identification is more practical (e.g., completing a death certificate)". The OMB insisted as well that official categories "do *not* tell an individual who he or she is, or specify how an individual should classify himself or herself".[40] In other words, at least in the case of officially recognized race categories in the US, individuals have two levels of freedom: they are free to choose which race category to use in identifying themselves for official purposes, and they are free not to consider whatever choice they have made at this first level to be a determination of their "real" racial identities. This raises the question of how many categories of social statistics might in time come to be seen, not just by activists but by governments, as "socially constructed", and the closely related question of the limits (if any) to self-identification. An obvious candidate is gender. Trans-gender and queer activism in recent decades has highlighted the fluidity and performativity of gender identifications and sexualities. But many other social markers as well can certainly be seen as socially and politically constructed. If accepting that a category is socially constructed should lead in turn to allowing individuals to self-identify with respect to it, a very broad range of social statistics could become occasions for performative politics. In one sense, the logical conclusion of this development can be glimpsed already in the shape of the "avatar" in Second Life. As the Second Life website explains, "In a virtual world, an avatar is a digital persona that you can create and customize. It's you – only in 3D. You can create an avatar that resembles your real life or create an alternate identity. The only limit is your imagination. Who do you want to be?"[41] The user can customize many aspects of the avatar's identity (gender, age, profession, etc.) as well as its personal appearance in images. The second identity thus created becomes an actor in Second Life's virtual world, capable of doing things like dating, buying land, forming political parties, or committing crimes. It is possible to think of the avatar as a kind of "regulative ideal" for individuals' control over how they are identified in electronic databases. But the example of the Second Life avatar also raises the question of responsibility: in a fictional situation in which one had complete control over one's own data

39 United States Office of Management and Budget, Revisions.

40 United States Office of Management and Budget, Revisions.

41 Secondlife.com 2009. What is an avatar? [Online]. Available at: http://secondlife.com/whatis/avatar/?lang=en-US [accessed: September 11, 2009].

image, policing of real crime (such as harassment) would become more difficult. This raises the larger question of the relation between privacy or data protection and legitimate forms of transparency in public life; I will return to this below.

The first three large questions discussed up to this point, the mandatory or voluntary character of being counted or registered, the question of how and by whom forms of registration are determined, and the issue of whether individuals have scope to self-identify, all point to *the crucial importance of the moment at which personal information is first gathered.* The daunting litany of recent technological developments in the storage, sharing and processing of data should further reinforce the sense that, once data have been surrendered, the playing field is, so to speak, tilted ever more steeply in favor of state agencies, corporations and other large organizations that have impacts upon the daily life of residents. Especially the infinite reproducibility of electronic data, and the difficulty of achieving certainty that electronic data have ever been fully deleted once created, further emphasize the importance of this initial moment. However, the dimensions of informational citizenship extend as well into the realm of what is done with data once it has been gathered, and here, too, despite the tilted technological playing field, there are interesting possibilities for political action.

(4) What scope is there for controlling what happens to personal information after it is gathered?

This question was the focus of the 1983 census decision by the Federal Constitutional Court. Three of the main pillars of informational self-determination as laid out by the Court in 1983 were, first, that personal data should not be stored indefinitely, but should be deleted at the earliest time consistent with its purposes; second, that personal data should only be collected for specific purposes, should only be used for those purposes, and should not be held for unspecified future uses; and third, that the individuals whose personal data is held by some organization or agency should be consulted on, or at least informed of, any proposed transference of data to new uses or different organizations. Together these principles seek to establish a framework within which members of modern societies can attain at least a minimal level of confidence regarding who knows what about them. As the Court explicitly noted in its 1983 judgment, citizens who have no idea who knows what about them are much less able to live and exercise their rights freely in public life, to participate in public discussions, etc. In Germany and many other countries, these principles form the backbone of privacy law.

Yet, as Spiros Simitis explained, state agencies, particularly those concerned with "security" and policing, as well as private commercial firms, potentially have much to gain by storing personal data indefinitely, and by treating it as a *multifunctional resource*, as a "convertible" currency with "exchange value" rather than a dedicated, single-function "use-value".[42] This multifunctionality was what

42 Simitis, Reviewing privacy in an Information Society.

allowed Horst Herold to pioneer methods of computer searches [*Rasterfahndung*] as he hunted for RAF hideouts in the 1970s, and it is the condition of possibility for "dataveillance" today. Thus it is not entirely surprising that a boycott movement against the Canadian census of 2006 emerged, once it became known that the Canadian government had contracted out the processing of the census data to Lockheed Martin, the US defense contractor. One specific concern in this case was that Lockheed Martin would transfer the Canadian data files to US territory, where it would be legally accessible, under the USA PATRIOT Act, to US security agencies in their pursuit of information on terrorism.[43] Given the extreme physical liquidity of electronic data, and the obscurity of what is done with it from the perspective of the average individual, all three of the pillars of informational self-determination are extremely difficult to police. States and, to a lesser extent, private companies have made some moves to reassure the public, and to at least give the appearance of complying with privacy law. For example, it has become standard practice on commercial websites to offer customers the option of forbidding any sharing of their personal data, usually by checking a box on the electronic order form. However, a recent study by two German universities of the practices of 100 firms, including merchants, search engines, travel agencies and auction sites, revealed that only five were fully compliant with the data protection laws regarding storage, use and notification.[44] This is but one illustration of the fact that once personal data have made it into electronic databases, there is effectively little that can be done to control their subsequent careers.

In the 1983 Constitutional Court decision on the census, this issue was approached in terms of the crucial difference between statistical and administrative data gathering exercises by the state. However the basic distinction can be extended to cover private data-gathering as well. Statistical data gathering is aimed at registering larger patterns for the purposes of planning, infrastructural development, or in the private sector, market research. In so far as gathering such data requires the collection of personal information for logistical reasons (such as collecting names and matching them to specific addresses in the census, in order to ensure complete coverage), the Court urged that such information be deleted as soon as it had served its purpose, not stored indefinitely. The boycott movement of 1983 was motivated in part by provisions in the census law that foresaw the use of personal information from census forms to correct local residency registers. This, the justices concluded, crossed the line between statistical data, which should have no potential negative impacts for the individuals providing it, and administrative data (such as the residency registers), which must remain personally specific because it guides interactions between state agencies and individuals or households. Boycott activists

43 CountMeOut 2006. [Online homepage]. Available at: http://www.countmeout.ca/ [accessed: October 17, 2009].

44 Anon. 2009. Unternehmen ist Datenschutz egal. taz.de, September 3 [Online]. Available at: http://www.taz.de/1/politik/schwerpunkt-ueberwachung/artikel/1/unternehmen-ist-datenschutz-egal/ [accessed: September 10, 2009].

and many citizens feared in particular that personal data from the census would end up in the hands of security services, and that even "anonymized" data, that is, data stripped of names and addresses, could easily be re-personalized through simple computer-matching routines. These fears were not successfully allayed in the new census law for 1987. The strategic response by the boycott organizers, discussed in 1983 but put into practice in 1987, was the "hard" boycott. The hard boycott presaged the basic approach taken in the intervening years to more recent versions of this problem. Once again, participating in the hard boycott meant, first, clipping the identifying bar-code from the blank census form, and then sending or bringing the blank form to an "alternative collection point" (usually local Green Party offices, a community center, a cafe, a bookstore or a pub). The incoming anonymous forms would be tallied and the tallies reported to the central Green Party offices in Bonn, where national totals would periodically be announced as a "boycott barometer". The main point of this plan was of course to publicize the strength of the boycott while protecting the individual identities of participants. But what it also represented was a grass-roots form, indeed an instructive model, of purely *statistical* data gathering. A "hard boycott" involving return of anonymized but filled out forms would have modeled a fuller "shadow census".

The basic architecture of the hard boycott involved the insertion of an intermediate layer between the individual being counted and the larger database, a layer at which anonymity would be ensured before the data were passed on to their final destination (the census offices). This basic framework is, in my view, potentially crucial to emerging informational citizenship, but has thus far chiefly been addressed through individual-level market decisions that together can have only limited larger political impact. Many technical solutions are now becoming available to combat the uncontrolled proliferation and sharing of personal data on the Internet. The anonymous internet browsing software advertised by FoeBuD e.V., noted under point (1) above is merely one example of a wide range of similar products. Bugmenot.com, for example, provides information with which individuals can register in internet sites that require registration for access to services, but without providing their real names and other personal information to those sites.[45] This is accomplished through an intermediate database of usable login information. Similarly, so-called anonymous remailers are intermediate sites to which e-mails can be sent on their way to a final destination address. At the remailer site, the e-mail's identifying header information is stripped off and replaced with substitute information not traceable to the sender, before being sent on. There are various strategies for doing this and various additional measures that can strengthen the anonymity of a message. On the one hand, such strategies could protect the personal communication of workers, for example, from scrutiny by the firm. However, as an ethics report from the American Association for the Advancement of Science notes, there are dangers inherent in anonymous use

45 Bugmenot.com 2009. [Online homepage]. Available at: http://www.bugmenot.com/ [accessed: September 11, 2009].

of the internet, exemplified by the problems of untraceable harassment or child pornography.[46] Bugmenot.com addresses the harassment issue by not providing login information that grants access to online fora or message boards.[47] In other words, it makes less sense to guarantee anonymity of communication with other individual users.

The basic principle of an intermediate anonymizing relay for electronic information is presently a solution that individuals have to opt into. Given the value commercial firms place upon personal data provided by their customers, it is likely that any proposal to make such technologies universal, mandatory and subject to state oversight would meet with a storm of protest. However it is worth thinking along these lines. In general, it would be possible to take a differentiated approach to regulation, as Bugmenot has done, ensuring anonymity in different degrees depending the type of activity in question, preserving identificatory information in personal communications but not necessarily in communication with large organizations. It may be technically feasible, for example, to encode personal internet surfing activity in such a way that it is anonymous to firms unless they request and are explicitly granted access to it. In other words, the burden of proof, and of establishing what is done with personal data, could be shifted from the consumer to interested organizations. Firms could, for example, incentivize consumers to encourage the granting of access to data. But this would only be fair, arguably, as compensation for the use of personal data. The suggestion that anonymous internet traffic be supervised by a state agency highlights the dependence of the effectiveness and ethical character of anonymous communication upon the administrators of the "cloaking" services. I will return to this issue below.

The problem of notifying individuals whenever their information is shared is daunting, but can likewise be addressed in part through technical means. E-mail programs have long included the option of automatically notifying the sender that their message has been read. This basic approach could, in principle, be applied also to the sharing of personal data, so that any time personal data were sent to a different destination from an original database, an automatic notification would be generated and sent to the individual concerned. A designated "data sharing notification" folder (like those that can be set up to hold junk e-mails received) could be established and software developed to sort through the notifications and flag any that seem alarming. The problem here, as with anonymizing internet use, would be that of responsibility for administration and enforcement. The scenarios are not hard to spin out: a flurry of activity to develop software that could disable or block any such automatic notification system, cases of evasion and police investigations that uncover a massive underground data-sharing economy among

46 Fowler, A. 1996. Professional ethics report: anonymity on the internet. American Association for the Advancement of Science [Online]. Available at: http://www.aaas.org/spp/sfrl/per/per6.htm [accessed: September 11, 2009].

47 Merritt, T. 2005. Surf the web anonymously. CNET.com [Online]. Available at: http://reviews.cnet.com/4520-3000_7-6274488-1.html [accessed: September 11, 2009].

large firms … this brings us back again to the underlying fact that all of these issues will not be able to do much more than selectively slow down or temporarily obstruct the ongoing proliferation of data. The individual-level "citizenship" measures surveyed thus far would in practice still chiefly amount to the continuing challenge of defending privacy. But at the same time, a number of the tactics and solutions surveyed above have collective or institutional dimensions that could, if pushed in particular directions, begin to constitute real change with ramifications for democratic practices more generally.

(5) What possibilities are there for moving beyond a defensive, individual-level approach to personal information toward arrangements that would more seriously democratize information society?

This is the most important question and in a sense the culminating challenge posed by the West German census boycott movements of the 1980s. At one level, the political lesson of the boycott movements is that, whatever the shape of emerging informational citizenship, it will necessarily continue to rely on the entire, familiar repertoire of methods associated with radical extra-parliamentary social movements, from demonstrations, boycotts, petitions, perhaps to occupations of symbolic buildings or offices, internet campaigns and unforeseeable artistic interventions, to various forms of self-organization. As I will argue below, however, it will also at some point need to force through quite major institutional changes in the machinery of "official" democratic politics. In this final section I will move onto more speculative territory, spinning out possibilities still mostly immanent even in current, early 21st-century initiatives. The degree to which the strategies suggested here are "realistic" will have to await the course of future events. But my hope is that for interested strategists and commentators, the directions anticipated here can help clarify what is ultimately at stake in informational politics.

The "hard boycott" strategy implemented in the 1987 census boycott is worth returning to once again. It is in my view the most potentially radical aspect of the boycotts. If in an imperfect and limited way, it responded to an externally imposed information-gathering project not by seeking to block it defensively, but rather by creating a bottom-up detour around it, a way of creating an alternative form of information that on the one hand signaled a critical rejection of the official project but on the other actually modeled a more adequate practice of collecting truly anonymous (or "statistical" rather than "administrative") data. The "alternative collection points" set up by boycott organizers, the cafes, bookshops, pubs or local Green Party offices, mobilized the oppositional geographies outlined in the Introduction as a parallel local statistical structure. This implied a challenge not to the epistemic sovereignty of the state *in toto* but rather to the assumption that its right to know the territorially distributed population was to be understood as a right of *direct and unilateral* access to information. In Foucauldian terms, the distinction between the population as an essentially passive object of biopower and the citizenry as a collection of subjects enjoying some measure of political voice was blurred. The elegant scheme of reporting running totals of empty census forms turned in to these alternative collection points in a nationwide "boycott barometer" obscured this distinction further by blending the notion of "being counted" with that of "voting". These basic features of the hard boycott strategy are pregnant with possibilities still barely glimpsed.

What can be done with this approach in the early 21st century? A direct extrapolation of the hard boycott strategy's "alternative collection points" for blank census forms might be termed "data producer collectives". Since so much of the data gathering that goes on now, especially in the capitalist core, is digital/electronic in form, any sort of "alternative collection points" would essentially need to be databases. Whether "local" in the geographical sense or created by virtual communities scattered over wide areas, such alternative databases would have to be constituted and managed by individuals or organizations possessing both technical competence and the trust of the individuals registered. As informational parallels to "producer collectives", they would have as their main tasks the aggregation and anonymization of information from "members", and the management of its subsequent transmission to other parties. Data producer collectives would of course be limited in their control over information by legal requirements such as tax law, contract law or administrative regulations. But within these constraints, and *especially with regard to the transfer of information to private corporations*, they would still have considerable scope to strengthen anonymity and to develop policies for rules of sharing both individual-level and aggregate data. The key political aspect of such cooperatives would be the opportunities they afforded for direct democratic involvement in setting up the framework for the data portal through which members' information would pass, as well as in managing opt-in or opt-out possibilities. In principle, at least, such data producer cooperatives could also take on tasks such as receiving and evaluating automatically generated notifications of the use or transfer of personal data (see point 4 above). This, too, could be handled in ways affording much more direct democratic involvement in data policy. Since most adults are not particularly versed in the intricacies of data policy, the success of data producer collectives would likely depend on whether they provided or were linked with citizens' advice functions, that is, whether they could provide access to expertise and educational resources allowing busy individuals to learn enough to make minimally informed choices about the delegated management of their personal data. An intriguing forerunner of such an educational approach can be seen in the Bradford Community Statistics Project (BCSP), a non-profit organization set up to assist Bradford-area community groups in accessing and using statistics to strengthen the persuasiveness of their arguments for addressing specific problems.[48] Among other services, the BCSP offered training courses in the details of generating new statistical information to help illustrate the existence of a particular problem. This kind of advisory service

48 Bradford Community Statistics Project 2006. [Online homepage]. Available at: http://www.communitystats.org.uk/index.htm [accessed: October 16, 2009].

could as easily address personal data management issues. A modified form of this approach also underlies the Citizens' Advice Bureaux in the UK.

The emergence of data producer collectives would of course require political pressure, and would face huge political hurdles, foremost among these of course the resistance of private corporations. Were they ever to become common, data producer collectives would interfere quite seriously with the comprehensive territorial transparency that is the holy grail of target marketing firms and the countless other businesses that use their services. The map of shopping habits or medical risk could in principle become a patchwork of varying degrees of visibility or resolution. To push in this direction at all, in other words, would require some translation of grass-roots initiatives into pressure on legislators. At least as important, the whole idea presupposes some sort of official licensing or oversight system. Only if government agencies and other organizations could have some enforceable guarantee that the quality and accuracy of the data provided by collectives was of a high and uniform standard could such data ever become usable. It would be necessary, then, to evolve some legally recognized practice of licensing these organizations and the individuals managing personal data. Only thus, for example, would a scheme be imaginable in which ATM cards and credit cards would have coded in their strips the digital address of the particular collective to which an individual belonged, and thus to which alone his or her transaction data would be sent. Banks and tax authorities would of course have rights of access to this data, but any other organizations interested in it would have to contact the data producer collective to see whether or in what circumstances it would be available. If this general strategy were to begin to find real-world purchase, it would signal the end of what we might then look back upon as the early "Gold Rush" phase of corporate access to personal information, a window of a couple of decades in which firms enjoyed massive and unregulated access to personal data before the magnitude of destructive effects of such data-gluttony had been fully enough recognized to engender an overdue crackdown.

There are of course major difficulties with such a proposal. For example, the issue of what happens to any personal data that is legitimately passed on to external organizations would still exist. Once it is "out there", personal data can be shared. As noted above under point 4, there are some technological possibilities for at least keeping track of such outside data sharing. And keeping track of it is already one of the chief tasks of data protection officials. However, of course, the scope of data traffic far exceeds the capacity of a few watchdogs. These problems with the idea of data producer collectives point in two directions, one to do with organizational and institutional matters, the second and more radical, with the nature of the data produced. The impossibility of establishing anything like effective and recognized data producer collectives in an institutional vacuum points to the issue of the scope and centrality of data protection offices and resources within modern state institutions. The kind of re-balancing of control over what is done with personal information represented by data producer collectives would necessitate an ongoing, institutionally anchored and legally sanctioned investment of time and expertise beyond what can be expected of even the most vibrant social movement. As in every other major issue of social politics, here, too, the percentage of individuals willing and able to translate their concern into ongoing active political engagement will be limited. Spiros Simitis observed in 1985 that most adults in modern societies are simply incapable of keeping on top of what is happening with their own data, much less of wider developments in technology and data processing.[49] Thus he advocated the institution of Data Protection Commissioners in West Germany and equivalent positions in other countries. But ever since the appointment of the first data protection commissioner (in fact Dr Simitis's assumption of that post for the state of Hessen in 1971 made him the first such official in the world), it has been routine for data protection officials to bemoan the lack of resources at their disposal to do their jobs. This is emphatically *not* simply another in the endless litany of officials who would ideally have larger budgets and staffs. If, as I have been arguing, registration and "being counted" are coming to be seen and experienced as occasions for *active political participation*, if, that is, the "right of informational self-determination" initially sketched by the West German Constitutional Court is to acquire any proactive democratic content, any emerging grass-roots schemes such as data producer collectives will have to be supplemented by corresponding "docking points", that is, institutions and practices of *representational politics* within the state apparatus. Because the nature of personal data and its political impact is somewhat different from the simple aggregation of political will through voting, the representative infrastructure for shaping its policy impacts would have to span technical, juridical and legislative competence. As a starting point for imagining what this could mean, I would propose a dramatic increase in the number of data protection officials, and their installment as special legislative assistants and watchdogs within the office of *every* elected legislator. Each data protection specialist would be responsible, like traditional legislators, for defending the interests of constituents and for engaging in political discourse with them about matters relating to personal information and statistical data, both making and receiving suggestions or initiatives. In addition, as existing officials have long been urging, such "data representatives" should be given much more enforcement power in the event they discover illegal activities.

Here again, it is not difficult to think of huge obstacles or sticky questions. At what levels of government and in what numbers would such a new cohort of officials be most effectively installed? Leaving aside the predictable cost argument, which is always ultimately a question of political priorities, there is also the issue of how to reconcile the need for expertise with the notion of *elected* representation. There would be no difficulty in principle with the *ethics* of balancing expertise and political representation, since even now a data protection official is clearly an *advocate*, one whose technical expertise is mobilized *in the interest of one group* (the population of data subjects). But who should decide on filling the posts? One solution would be to set minimum standard qualifications for such officials, leave

49 Simitis, Reviewing privacy in an Information Society.

their appointment to elected legislators, but provide for popular recall; another would be to have them independently elected, as are, for example, local auditors of accounts in many parts of the US. However it is best approached, though, the chief point here is that a *dramatic expansion* of the number of data protection officials is urgently needed, as well as a fundamental transformation of their remit to include tasks that make them "data representatives". If I am right that various forms of informational citizenship are emerging along the dimensions sketched out above, the possibility of their gelling into a major political movement will depend in part on their ability to begin to force state apparatuses to develop much more serious and capable organs to address the politics of personal data.

The other direction in which the basic impulse of the hard boycott strategy can be developed is inspired by the idea of the "boycott barometer", and is potentially more radical. Again, the idea of a data producer collective mooted above still assumes a more or less pre-given range of existing or routinely refreshed data. A more profound threat to data-politics-as-usual would emerge if groups within civil society or local communities began to produce significant quantities of *their own* data, that is, information that was not only locally collected but also conceived according to forms and categories tailored to the problems and goals motivating local people. This is the more radical direction suggested by the Bradford Community Statistics Project mentioned above, and its political possibilities are more clearly illustrated by the activities of the Mumbai "Alliance", aptly described by Arjun Appadurai as "deep democracy".[50] Alliance activists in the Mumbai slums have been training fellow local residents to design and carry out censuses and other surveys on themselves and their neighbors in order to lend statistical weight to their claims about lack of services and other problems. As Appadurai explains, one of the key reasons that this activity is not simply ignored is that the Alliance has also carefully cultivated constructive relations with Mumbai city officials over many years, finding ways of balancing militant insistence on improved services with consultations on acceptable forms of data.

To extend this precedent more generally would be a matter, first, of widespread data-related capacity building among populations, as discussed above in connection with data producer collectives, and second, of putting in place requirements that states acknowledge and make use of grass-roots data. Dependence on local, ongoing negotiations with state officials does not constitute a sufficiently reliable basis for ensuring that community-generated information ends up playing the central role it should play in informational representation. Thus it makes sense to imagine a regulatory model which at first sight seems absurdly distant from data politics but which as a general mechanism for the regulation of "flows" can actually be seen as a close parallel. In 1978, during the administration of Jimmy Carter, the US Congress passed a law called the Public Utility Regulatory Policies Act (PURPA). This law was meant in part to respond to the newly perceived need for energy efficiency and the development of renewable energy sources prompted by the oil

50 Appadurai, Deep democracy: Urban governmentality and the horizon of politics.

shortages of the 1970s. In particular it was intended to encourage "the expeditious development of hydroelectric potential at existing small dams to provide needed hydroelectric power".[51] One of its key provisions legally obligated public utility companies to purchase at reasonable rates any electricity generated by independent hydroelectric projects. This basic model for governing a particular kind of energy flow suggests a potentially profound way of shifting the government of data flows. In this model, governments would be obligated to accept and to incorporate into policy-making any "grass-roots" data of the sort envisioned above, provided the data satisfied minimum standards in terms of how it was gathered, its provision in electronic form, and its compatibility with data processing software. If a local community, or perhaps a virtual community made up of individuals in a particular line of work, decided it was necessary to generate new data on, say, pollution from industry or overtime hours worked, they could, with the help of local expertise from data producer collectives, design and carry out their own surveys. The results of the surveys would then be provided to the relevant state agency, and the envisioned PURPA-like legislation would require that, at least in policy decisions relating to that specific district or group of individuals, the data they themselves had provided would be taken into account.

Such a model would have the potential to alter the entire relationship between populations and the institutions and practices of social governance. If some sort of PURPA-like legislation (for the sake of argument we might call it PIRPA, for Public Information Resources Policy Act) were to become commonplace, it is at least conceivable that a gradual increase in grass-roots information would bring major sea-changes in public policy at all levels, as the bedrock data on which policy decisions are made would increasingly come to reflect in a more direct way the concerns of living populations. It is possible to imagine, for example, that economic data *conceived and generated by citizens* would come to emphasize issues of inequality and basic economic security at the expense of the current focus on aggregate "growth" (GNP or stock prices) or competition. Organizationally, some sort of "PIRPA" legislation would need to be seen in the context of the other two major developments envisioned above, the emergence and proliferation of data producer collectives and the dramatic expansion of data representatives within the official institutions of democracy. Broadly, the data producer collectives would be a key source of initiative and expertise for the generation of new forms of grass-roots data. Both the collectives and the data representatives in government could play active roles in advising citizens on how to translate their concerns into new data. Additionally, the data representatives could monitor the extent to which the provisions of PIRPA laws were actually being followed by executive agencies. Whereas the data protection officials now scattered thinly throughout the state apparatuses of some nations have been concerned with the defensive

51 United States Congress 1978. US Code, Title 16, Chapter 46. Cornell University Law School, Legal Information Institute [Online]. Available at: http://www.law.cornell.edu/uscode/usc_sec_16_00002601----000-.html [accessed: October 16, 2009].

"protection" of personal data, their updated (and far more numerous) counterparts as conceived here would complement this role with the proactive role of ensuring the upward impact of a newly political "social body" on the state agencies tasked with governing it.

Learning from the West German census boycotts

The kinds of political issues discussed in this book do not exhaust the range of possibilities for more democratic engagement with information society. Although wading out into the deeper waters of theoretical debate is something I have deliberately resisted doing throughout, it is worth at least briefly noting that activists and scholars have been busy exploring different aspects of informational citizenship than those treated here. Notable among this larger array of strategies and projects are attempts to grapple with the meaning of more explicitly discursive (rather than merely statistical) forms of political expression and representation in the new technological media. Jeremy Crampton's subtle study of the possibilities of "fearless speech" and community formation in cyberspace, or David Bell's discussion of creative engagement with the possibilities of subverting surveillance mechanisms through practices of voyeurism and exhibitionism, indicate only two of the possible directions a more democratic approach to information gathering could take.[52] There is of course also the whole matter of making states and corporations more transparent to citizens and consumers, a huge field I have left aside.

What is clear in any case is that future forms of informational citizenship will have to involve multiple actors, institutional sites and forms of organization.[53] To summarize, the specific form of informational citizenship elaborated here would have four key components: (1) constitutional amendments and specific legislation establishing an updated version of the "right of informational self determination" for individuals, stressing especially the *right not be counted or registered* as a default presumption built into law as well as into public and private institutional practice; (2) procedures and standards for recognizing data producer collectives as the primary setting for the democratic management of personal data; (3) a vastly expanded infrastructure of data representatives, incorporating the older duties of data protection officials but adding to those more proactive advisory and advocacy duties as political representatives of segments of the population; and (4) ongoing dialogue between all of these components and social movements or mobilizations

52 Crampton, J. 2003. *The Political Mapping of Cyberspace*. Chicago: University of Chicago Press; Bell, D. 2009. Surveillance is sexy. *Surveillance and Society* 6(3): 203-212. Available at: http://www.surveillance-and-society.org [accessed: February 22, 2010].

53 Martin, A., van Brakel, R. and Bernhard, D. 2009. Understanding resistance to digital surveillance: towards a multi-disciplinary, multi-actor framework. *Surveillance and Society* 6(3): 213-232. Available at http://www.surveillance-and-society.org [accessed: February 22, 2010].

arising from new issues in informational politics. Together, these changes represent a rather dramatic, perhaps at first sight politically unrealistic extrapolation of the hard boycott strategy carried out in West Germany in 1987. Yet against the background of the larger sweep of developments in modern democratic political systems over the past two hundred years, it would actually involve changes that are fairly modest in scope. A few thousand additional public servants, some new regulatory legislation, and a new demand for expertise in information technology among activist groups would perhaps create a temporary burden on national educational systems, but such changes would not in and of themselves constitute major transformations of the institutions of politics. Crucially, they would not need to occur all at once, but could emerge unevenly and experimentally in different national and local contexts, with social movement pressure and state actions bringing piecemeal progress that would in turn contribute to general public understanding of the issues. However, the changes such relatively modest additions to democratic systems might eventually make possible in the nature and role of social knowledge in the governance of modern societies could be tectonic.

The scenario I have sketched here of the rudiments of a more democratic infrastructure of data politics may seem distant indeed from the original context of the West German census boycott movements in the early 1980s. However, 30 years later, modern Western societies are recognizing the high costs of not having seriously addressed the problems that first provoked social movements and made headlines in the 1970s and 1980s. Environmental destruction never ceased to be seen as a problem, though it has only returned to the front pages in the first decade of the 21st century. Fears of nuclear destruction through war receded for a time into the background after 1989, but then re-emerged again in the shape of concerns about rogue states and terrorist groups acquiring weapons of mass destruction or technologies to build them via the global arms trade. Nuclear power likewise temporarily lost its ability to provoke mass protest, chiefly through the success of earlier mass and local protests in bringing the building of new nuclear plants to a virtual halt in many parts of the wealthy core. But it is now on the table again as a proposed solution to anticipated decline in the global supply of oil, despite the continued inability of states possessing nuclear technology to find long-term solutions to the problem of disposal of nuclear waste. Thus the stage is set for a revival of conflict on this issue as well. The seemingly relentless trend toward an ever-more comprehensive "surveillance society" is also on the agenda again, as evidenced by the high levels of public concern over surveillance issues revealed by current polls.

A final broad trend that emerged around the same time as those noted above has made it extremely difficult to address any of these others. The development of a more unfettered and globalized capitalism, crucially accompanied by a very effective neoliberal ideological infrastructure, has severely limited the terms in which environmental responsibility may be pursued, lethal military technologies destroyed or effectively policed, alternative renewable energy sources developed, or the proliferation of personal data effectively brought under control. Neoliberal ideology has been crucial here, on the one hand, at the level of the stories it tells about what works and what doesn't. Thus, broadly speaking, a neoliberal position insists that no acceptable solution to climate change, energy shortages or infringements on privacy may involve significant limitations on the capitalist pursuit of profit. But neoliberal thought has also had major impacts at the less-often recognized level of the kinds of statistical knowledge it generates and promotes as important. On this latter count, neoliberalism is scandalously thin: it is not much of an exaggeration to say that the so-called "Washington Consensus" has been foisted upon the world on the basis of the outrageously reductive assertion that growth in profit rates, in national GDP and in stock market indicators tells us all we need to know about socio-economic well-being. The proliferation of personal data since the early 1990s is but one of the long list of questionable developments that can be justified, in the neoliberal view, by its aggregate contribution to these few simple numbers.

The larger potential significance of wresting personal and social data away from the control of states and large corporations, and turning it over to the direct "data producers", would be located here, at the level of ideology, or more broadly, of knowledge. In so far as the conception and generation of statistical knowledge through which social and individual life is governed could be returned to the hands of the governed themselves, a more authoritative and better grounded counter-knowledge could be built up and eventually become the basis for telling very different stories about what works and what doesn't. Parallel and complementary to the project of "indymedia" that came to prominence with the WTO protests in Seattle in 1999, an "indyinfo" or "indystats" project would further democratize social knowledge. Not only would specific fears of the surveillance state be addressed, but, more profoundly, a proactive, democratic form of informational citizenship could help break open the ideological cages that hamper attempts to deal effectively with a much wider range of social, economic and environmental issues and to set the larger direction of social change. To the extent that what Arjun Appadurai calls "deep democracy" becomes an accepted part of democratic systems, what we do about pollution, unemployment, racism or health care could come to depend much more on *what people directly confronted with these problems think should count*. This, then, a blueprint for making a different knowledge of government, is the more radical potential fallout from the West German census boycott movements of the 1980s. There are of course no guarantees of a "radical" or "progressive" substantive outcome from such a development, but this is the underlying risk of any enhancement of democracy.

References

Much of the story told here was constructed out of newspaper coverage of events at the time, supplemented by materials from social movement archives and government documents. The key archival sources were: *archiv für alternatives schrifttum* [afas] (Duisburg); the *Pressearchiv* of the *Otto-Suhr-Institut* at FU-Berlin; the *tageszeitung* archive in Berlin; *Archiv Grünes Gedächtnis* (Berlin); the *Hamburger Institut für Sozialforschung* (Hamburg) and the Stasi Archive [*Bundesbeauftragte für die Unterlagen des Staatssicherheitsdienstes der ehemaligen Deutschen Demokratischen Republik*] (Berlin). The material from these archives is uneven in terms of the completeness of bibliographical information. For example, some of the archival materials are without specific archival signatures, either because they had not been catalogued in the first place but were set aside as extra copies, or because my photocopies failed to capture the signatures. The key source for newspaper coverage (other than the taz archive) was the *Pressearchiv* at the *Otto-Suhr-Institut*, which has its material clipped and sorted according to theme. While this was an invaluable time-saver, many of the clipped articles did not have page numbers recorded. Thus some of the cited press coverage lacks page numbers. Secondly, a large number of newspaper articles, especially from the taz, were anonymously authored.

Newspaper articles (print)

Alternative Liste. 1983. Volkszählung? So nicht! [advertisement]. *die tageszeitung*, February 18, p. 18.

Anon. 1982. Politiker fragen – Bürger antworten nicht. *die tageszeitung*, December 16, p. 4.

Anon. 1983. Abfuhr für die Datensammler. *die tageszeitung*, December 16, p. 1.

Anon. 1983. Alle zufrieden? *die tageszeitung*, December 16, p. 3.

Anon. 1983. 11. Angestelltenkonferenz der IG-Metall – Metaller gegen Volkszählung. *die tageszeitung*, March 14, p. 4.

Anon. 1983. Anweisung an Volkszähler "… uns bei schwierigen Verweigerungen unterrichten". *die tageszeitung*, March 4, p. 4.

Anon. 1983. Auch Polizisten wollen keine Zähler sein. *die tageszeitung*, March 11, p. 20.

Anon. 1983. Bei diesem Thema nicht. *die tageszeitung*, April 8, p. 9.

Anon. 1983. Bereits über 50 Inititiativen zum Volkszählungsboykott. *die tageszeitung*, February 14, p. 3.

Anon. 1983. Bundesrat besteht auf Volkszählung. *die tageszeitung*, March 21, p. 2.
Anon. 1983. Das Bundesverfassungsgericht prüft Beschwerden gegen umstrittene Volkszählung. *Süddeutsche Zeitung*, March 12/13, p. 1.
Anon. 1983. "Die ganz direkte Betroffenheit ist erst mal weg". *die tageszeitung*, April 14, p. 2.
Anon. 1983. Die neue Welt von 1984. *Der Spiegel*, January 3, pp. 19-30.
Anon. 1983. Großer Bruder lässt zählen. *die tageszeitung*, January 26, p. 1.
Anon. 1983. Heiße Ohren. *Der Spiegel*, April 11, p. 29.
Anon. 1983. Höchst unredlich. *Der Spiegel*, March 7, p. 120.
Anon. 1983. Knast für Boykotteure angedroht. *die tageszeitung*, March 30, p. 16.
Anon. 1983. Lehrer klagen gegen Zwangsverpflichtung. *die tageszeitung*, April 11, p. 5.
Anon. 1983. Nach der Wahl. Albrecht dementiert. *die tageszeitung*, March 10, p. 3.
Anon. 1983. Neuer Personalausweis. Run auf die Datenschützer? *die tageszeitung*, May 13, p. 1.
Anon. 1983. Neuer Boykott nötig. *die tageszeitung*, December 19, p. 2.
Anon. 1983. [No title, passage reprinted from *Emsdettener Zeitung* of February 2, 1983]. *die tageszeitung*, March 4, p. 4.
Anon. 1983. "Ohne Drohgebärde, ohne Angst". *Der Spiegel*, April 18, p. 20.
Anon. 1983. Politiker fragen – Bürger antworten nicht! *die tageszeitung*, February 25, p.15.
Anon. 1983. Politiker fragen – Bürger antworten nicht! *die tageszeitung*, March 3, p.15.
Anon. 1983. Politiker fragen – Bürger antworten nicht! *die tageszeitung*, March 11, p.15.
Anon. 1983. Politiker fragen – Bürger antworten nicht! *die tageszeitung*, March 18, p.15.
Anon. 1983. Politiker fragen – Bürger antworten nicht! *die tageszeitung*, March 25, pp.14-15.
Anon. 1983. Rumpelstielz-Preis. *die tageszeitung*, April 11, p. 16.
Anon. 1983. Schutz von Meldeämtern wird verstärkt. *Frankfurter Allgemeine Zeitung*, April 12, n.p.n.
Anon. 1983. Schwere Schlappe. *Der Spiegel*, December 19, p. 19.
Anon. 1983. Schwerpunkt: Informationsverarbeitung. *die tageszeitung*, April 19, p. 4.
Anon. 1983. Staatsfeindlicher Akt? *die tageszeitung*, March 23, p. 16.
Anon. 1983. taz-Volkszählungs-Telefon. Wer schweigt hat viel zu erzählen! *die tageszeitung*, April 11, p. 5.
Anon. 1983. Trotz neuer Proteste und Verfassungsbeschwerden – Bundesrat besteht auf Volkszählung. *die tageszeitung*, March 21, p. 2.
Anon. 1983. "Überfällig und unerlässlich" neue Daten für Wirtschaft und Politik/ Kritik an der Volkszählung, *Frankfurter Allgemeine Zeitung*, February 25, n.p.n.

Anon. 1983. "… uns bei schwierigen Verweigerungen unterrichten". *die tageszeitung*, March 4, p. 4.
Anon. 1983. VoBo Termine. *die tageszeitung*, April 8, p. 11.
Anon. 1983. Volkszählung: "Lasst tausend Fragebogen glühen". *Der Spiegel*, March 28, p. 32.
Anon. 1983. Volkszählungen generell zulässig. Schutz gegen unbegrenzte Erhebungen. *Frankfurter Allgemeine Zeitung*, December 16, n.p.n.
Anon. 1983. Volkszählungsboykott: Aktionswoche ab 16. April. *die tageszeitung*, March 29, p. 4.
Anon. 1983. Volkszählungsnews. *die tageszeitung*, March 30, p. 15.
Anon. 1983. Volkszählungsnews. *die tageszeitung*, April 8, p. 20.
Anon. 1983. Von Aktivitäten überrollt, *die tageszeitung*, February 28, p. 3.
Anon. 1983. Vor 13 Jahren war alles noch so gut. *die tageszeitung*, February 17, p. 7.
Anon. 1983. "Wem nützt ein Boykott". *die tageszeitung*, March 25, p. 19.
Anon. 1983. Zählerei – Verweigerung aller Orten. *die tageszeitung*, April 11, p. 5.
Anon. 1984. Bis ins letzte. *Der Spiegel*, November 19, pp. 138-139.
Anon. 1984. Die Stichproben-Erhebungen sollen wieder in Gang gebracht werden. *Frankfurter Allgemeine Zeitung*, November 14, n.p.n.
Anon. 1984. Grunddaten für die Politik und die Statistik. *Frankfurter Rundschau*, December 1, p. 10.
Anon. 1984. Porto zahlen. *Der Spiegel*, November 5, p. 29.
Anon. 1985. Einvernehmen über die Verschiebung der Volkszählung. *Frankfurter Allgemeine Zeitung*, June 1, p. 1.
Anon. 1985. Große Aufklärungskampagne soll die Teilnahme aller Bürger sicherstellen. *Handelsblatt*, October 1, n.p.n.
Anon. 1985. Volkszählung 1986 oder 1988? Ansichten der Experten, politische Wünsche. *Frankfurter Allgemeine Zeitung*, April 18, p. 6.
Anon. 1986. Terrier im Treppenhaus. *Der Spiegel*, December 15, p. 92.
Anon. 1987. AL-Post beschlagnahmt. *die tageszeitung*, May 26, n.p.n.
Anon. 1987. "Als sei es des Teufels eigenes Werk". *Der Spiegel*, May 18, p. 27.
Anon. 1987. Anwalt muß für Boykotthilfe Bußgeld zahlen. *Süddeutsche Zeitung*, May 27, n.p.n.
Anon. 1987. Auf Dauer perspektivlos. *Der Spiegel*, August 31, p. 44.
Anon. 1987. Ausländer zählen nicht. *die tageszeitung*, May 25, n.p.n.
Anon. 1987. Ausgesuchte Sauerei. *Der Spiegel*, April 6, p. 37.
Anon. 1987. "Boykott beeinflußt Ergebnis nicht". *Süddeutsche Zeitung*, April 30, n.p.n.
Anon. 1987. Bonn: Volkszählung verläuft positiv. *Süddeutsche Zeitung*, May 26, n.p.n.
Anon. 1987. "Boykott beeinflußt Ergebnis nicht". *Süddeutsche Zeitung*, April 30, n.p.n.
Anon. 1987. Bundestag verurteilt Gewalt gegen Volkszähler. *Süddeutsche Zeitung*, May 22, p. 1.

Anon. 1987. Bundesverfassungsgericht entscheidet zur Volkszählung. *Frankfurter Allgemeine Zeitung*, September 30, n.p.n.
Anon. 1987. Das Unbehagen, als Schaf gezählt zu werden. *Süddeutsche Zeitung*, April 14, p. 15.
Anon. 1987. Datenschrott für eine Milliarde. *Der Spiegel*, March 16, p. 45.
Anon. 1987. Der Zähler von Nebenan. *die tageszeitung*, May 22, n.p.n.
Anon. 1987. Die DKP übernimmt die Vorreiter-Rolle. *Frankfurter Allgemeine Zeitung*, March 11, n.p.n.
Anon. 1987. Doch kein Versicherungsschutz bei Boykott der Volkszählung. *Süddeutsche Zeitung*, May 19, n.p.n.
Anon. 1987. Dünne Gründe. *Der Spiegel*, June 15, p. 116.
Anon. 1987. Eine kleine Pflicht. *Frankfurter Allgemeine Zeitung*, May 21, n.p.n.
Anon. 1987. Fehlerquote bis zu 60 Prozent bei "Volkszählung per Post". *Frankfurter Rundschau*, July 4, n.p.n.
Anon. 1987. Ganze Hinterhöfe vergessen. *die tageszeitung*, July 23, n.p.n.
Anon. 1987. Klebriger Mauerspaziergang. *die tageszeitung*, June 1, p. 1.
Anon. 1987. "Kleine Mogeleien können nicht aufgespürt werden". *Frankfurter Rundschau*, February 16, p. 14.
Anon. 1987. Kopierer spricht Recht. *die tageszeitung*, October 5, n.p.n.
Anon. 1987. Kreuzberg wird geschätzt. *die tageszeitung*, May 25, n.p.n.
Anon. 1987. Licht, Klang und Knüppel. *die tageszeitung*, May 18, n.p.n.
Anon. 1987. LKA-Präsident befürchtet Anschläge wegen Volkszählung. *Süddeutsche Zeitung*, May 14, p. 21.
Anon. 1987. Nur Schafe. *Der Spiegel*, April 27, p. 132.
Anon. 1987. Ordentlich schleppern. *Der Spiegel*, June 22, p. 23.
Anon. 1987. Polizei sammelt Daten von Volkszählungsgegnern. *Süddeutsche Zeitung*, May 21, n.p.n.
Anon. 1987. Polizeischutz für Volkszähler. *Süddeutsche Zeitung*, May 19, n.p.n.
Anon. 1987. Prügel und Kuchen als Wegzehrung. *Süddeutsche Zeitung*, May 23/24, p. 10.
Anon. 1987. Rathaus tabu. *die tageszeitung*, May 22, n.p.n.
Anon. 1987. Sicherster Ort. *Der Spiegel*, January 12, p. 89.
Anon. 1987. Stand der Volkszählung umstritten. *Süddeutsche Zeitung*, May 29, n.p.n.
Anon. 1987. Streit um Volkszählung spitzt sich zu. *Süddeutsche Zeitung*, May 18, n.p.n.
Anon. 1987. Teufel an der Wand. *Der Spiegel*, April 13, 46, p. 49.
Anon. 1987. Tiefer Kotau. *Der Spiegel*, June 8, pp. 47, 50.
Anon. 1987. Umleitung der VoBo-Post. *die tageszeitung*, May 27, n.p.n.
Anon. 1987. Ver-Zählt. *die tageszeitung*, May 20, n.p.n.
Anon. 1987. VoBo … *die tageszeitung*, May 9, n.p.n.
Anon. 1987. VoBo – Boykott gerechtfertigt. *die tageszeitung*, August 21, n.p.n.
Anon. 1987. "Volkszählung macht Spaß!" *die tageszeitung*, May 16, n.p.n.

Anon. 1987. Volkszählung ’87: mit Initiative(n) gegen den Erfassungsstaat. *die tageszeitung*, May 5, n.p.n.

Anon. 1987. Voll in die Hose. *Der Spiegel*, May 25, p. 129.

Anon. 1987. Was tun? … gegen das Bußgeld? *die tageszeitung*, April 9, n.p.n.

Anon. 1987. Was tun? … gegen das Zwangsgeld? *die tageszeitung*, April 8, n.p.n.

Anon. 1987. Weg zum Überwachungsstaat. *Frankfurter Rundschau*, January 28, p. 23.

Anon. 1987. Wird geschätzt. *Der Spiegel*, June 1, p. 28.

Anon. 1987. Zähler fertig, Zählung nicht. *die tageszeitung*, June 20, n.p.n.

Anon. 1987. Zählerpannen. *die tageszeitung*, May 19, n.p.n.

Anon. 1988. Alle Vobos im Computer? *die tageszeitung*, January 14, n.p.n.

Anon. 1988. Auto verleihen verboten. *die tageszeitung*, January 14, n.p.n.

Anon. 1988. Datenschutzerin kritisiert Volkszählung. *Süddeutsche Zeitung*, January 9, n.p.n.

Anon. 1988. Ich bin nun siebzig Jahre alt [open letter to Berlin StaLa]. *die tageszeitung*, March 14, n.p.n.

Anon. 1988. Kerkaus Datenputz. *die tageszeitung*, January 19, n.p.n.

Anon. 1988. Mehr Zählungsgegner in Datei. *Frankfurter Rundschau*, January 14, n.p.n.

Anon. 1988. Neuer VoBo-Dressurakt: Kontopfandung. *die tageszeitung*, January 16, n.p.n.

Anon. 1988. Schnippeln keine Sachbeschädigung. *die tageszeitung*, June 9, n.p.n.

Anon. 1988. Wer einmal “auffällt”… *die tageszeitung*, July 23, n.p.n.

Anon. 1988. Zimmermann: Volkszählung vollauf gerechtfertigt. *Süddeutsche Zeitung*, November 30, n.p.n.

Anon. 1988. “Zum ersten Mal ein Gesetz boykottiert”. *die tageszeitung*, May 25, n.p.n.

Astrodada. 1987. Prima: Auch die Sterne boykottieren. *die tageszeitung*, July 22, n.p.n.

Autonomie (Sabine). 1983. Volkszählung als Planungsinstrument: den Untergrund transparent machen. *die tageszeitung*, April 12, p. 3.

Bannas, G. 1985. Die Volkszählung erst nach der Wahl? *Frankfurter Allgemeine Zeitung*, January 21, p. 10.

Bannas, G. 1986. Die Zählung ist noch nicht über den Berg. *Frankfurter Allgemeine Zeitung*, November 4, n.p.n.

Baur, D. 1987a. Von Augsburg soll ein Signal ausgehen. *Süddeutsche Zeitung*, March 21/22, n.p.n.

Baur, D. 1987b. Referenten droht Anzeige. *Süddeutsche Zeitung*, March 27, n.p.n.

Becker, E. 1983. Gegen die Bürokratie. *Handelsblatt*, December 16, n.p.n.

Behr, A. 1983. Die Angst, ein “gläserner Mensch” zu werden. *Frankfurter Allgemeine Zeitung*, March 2, p. 10.

Bieber, H. 1987. Viele Fragen – und welche Antworten? *Die Zeit*, February 20, p. 4.

Bieber, H. 1988. Neue Fakten übers Volk. *Die Zeit*, December 16, p. 4.

Borchers, A. and Dahlheimer, A. 1987. Der programmierte Flop. *Vorwärts*, February 21, p. 7.
Bölsche, J. 1983. Der Geßlerhut des Orwell-Jahrzehnts. *Der Spiegel*, March 28, p. 47.
Bornhöft, P. 1987a. Da hört der Spaß auf. *die tageszeitung*, May 22, n.p.n.
Bornhöft, P. 1987b. Proteste gegen Postbeschlagnahme. *die tageszeitung*, May 30, n.p.n.
Bornhöft, P. 1987c. Keine Zeit für Statistik. *die tageszeitung*, June 6, p. 3.
Bornhöft, P. 1987d. Vobo-Schnibbelei nicht strafbar. *die tageszeitung*, June 18, n.p.n.
Brunner, E., Pokatzky, K. and Schwelien, M. 1983. Erfasst, registriert, entmündigt. *Die Zeit*, March 18, p. 11.
Bull, H.-P. 1983a. "Der Öffentlichkeit wurde zu wenig erklärt ..." [reprinted information sheet]. *Frankfurter Rundschau*, March 25, p. 12.
Bull, H.-P. 1983b. Der Staat – nur ein datengieriger Riese? *Die Zeit*, April 15, p. 56.
Dahl, S. 1987. Die Predigt wurde nicht verstanden. *Die Zeit*, November 27, p. 2.
Dahlheimer, A. 1987. Den Planern geht die Puste aus. *Vorwärts*, July 11, p. 7.
Dettmer, M. 1987. Familie Licht wohnt hier nicht. *Vorwärts*, May 30, p. 10.
Dickerlitz [no first name given] 1983. "Wunschpost TE" Interview mit dem Bundeskriminalamts-Aussteiger Berndt Schmidt. *die tageszeitung*, January 12, p. 3.
Die 3 Tornados. 1983. Wir sind unzählbar. *die tageszeitung*, March 21, p. 2.
Dillmann, H.-U. 1983. "Die Tendenz, den Bogen nicht auszufühlen, ist bei mir ziemlich groß" Interview mit Manfred Güllner. *die tageszeitung*, March 17, p. 8.
Duwe, P. 1985. "Zuviel Datenschutz schadet den Kommunen". *Volksblatt Berlin*, March 22, n.p.n.
Eickeler, R. 1983. Orwells Vision vom "gläsernen Menschen" ist noch eine Legende statt Realität. *Handelsblatt*, February 24, n.p.n.
Fehrle, B. 1987a. Eine zartblaue Tapete für die Berliner Mauer. *die tageszeitung*, June 1, p. 5.
Fehrle, B. 1987b. Steuereintreibung stillgelegt. *die tageszeitung*, September 23, n.p.n.
Feuck, J. 1985. Auskunftspflicht bleibt ein Zankapfel. *Frankfurter Rundschau*, August 19, n.p.n.
Fezer, G. 1983. Verfassungstoto. *die tageszeitung*, April 12, p. 2.
Fraktion Die GRÜNEN. 1983. Keine Totalerfassung des Bürgers. *Das Parlament*, No. 14, April 9, p. 3.
Gaserow, V. 1983. Was tun wenn der Zähler kommt. *die tageszeitung*, April 15, p. 5.
Gaserow, V. 1987a. "FR" lehnt kritische Anzeige ab. *die tageszeitung*, April 1, n.p.n.
Gaserow, V. 1987b. "Volgssählung? Nix gehört!". *die tageszeitung*, May 6, n.p.n.

Gaserow, V. 1987c. Volkszählung: Vernunft boykottiert. *die tageszeitung*, May 13, n.p.n.
Gaserow, V. 1987d. Geburtsname von Adoptivkind in Liste. *die tageszeitung*, May 20, n.p.n.
Gaserow, V. 1987e. Geld – Stopp wegen Vobo. *die tageszeitung*, July 4, n.p.n.
Gaserow, V. 1987f. Dummes Deutschland! *die tageszeitung*, July 8, n.p.n.
Gaserow, V. 1987g. Vobo '87: Alles nur "Schall und Rauch"? Interview mit Egon Hölder. *die tageszeitung*, September 3, n.p.n.
Gaserow, V. 1987h. Wie das Volkszählen zum Urlaub wurde. *die tageszeitung*, September 18, n.p.n.
Gaserow, V. 1987i. Volkszählung: Massenwiderstand endgültig abgehakt? [interview with P. Hauck-Scholz]. *die tageszeitung*, October 14, n.p.n.
Gaserow, V. 1987j. VGH segnet Volkszählung ab. *die tageszeitung*, October 16, n.p.n.
Gaserow, V. 1988a. Versicherung muß für Vobo zahlen. *die tageszeitung*, March 29, n.p.n.
Gaserow, V. 1988b. Justitias Rache an den Vobos. *die tageszeitung*, June 15, n.p.n.
Gaserow, V. 1988c. Illegale Schnüffelei per Erlaß. *die tageszeitung*, July 7, pp. 1-2.
Gaserow, V. 1988d. Steuerschnüffelei bei Vobos gekippt. *die tageszeitung*, July 11, n.p.n.
Gaserow, V. 1989a. Knast für Volkszählungsgegner. *die tageszeitung*, February 23, n.p.n.
Gaserow, V. 1989b. Keine Amnestie für VoBos. *die tageszeitung*, September 6, n.p.n.
Gaserow, V. 1990. Volkszählung endgültig reif furs Altpapier? Interview mit Egon Hölder. *die tageszeitung*, January 12, n.p.n.
Gaserow, V. and Müllender, B. 1987. Sammelstellen warten auf Altpapier. *die tageszeitung*, May 22, n.p.n.
Grabenströer, M. 1987. In der Römerstadt ist Justitia nur auf einem Auge blind. *Frankfurter Rundschau*, November 16, p. 7.
Harms, I. 1987. Volkszählung und kein Ende. *die tageszeitung*, June 6, p. 3.
Hartung, K. 1987. Selbstanzeige. Kohl bezichtig Vobos der "faschistischen Gesinnung". *die tageszeitung*, May 14, n.p.n.
Henkel, P. 1987. Boykottierer registriert. *Frankfurter Rundschau*, May 21, n.p.n.
Holz, M. 1987a. Vobo – Telefonsperre Rechtmäßig. *die tageszeitung*, April 13, n.p.n.
Holz, M. 1987b. Beugehaft für Volkszählungsgegener. *die tageszeitung*, August 19, n.p.n.
Holzhaider, H. 1987. Eine halbe Million Koffer voller Fragen. *Süddeutsche Zeitung*, May 20, p. 3.
Holzhaider, H. 1988. Das Zerschneiden eines Papiers und seine Folgen. *Süddeutsche Zeitung*, May 25, p. 11.

Imma [no surname]. 1983a. Volkszählung. Widerstand weitet sich aus. *die tageszeitung*, March 14, p. 7.

Imma [no surname]. 1983b. Man kann auf jeden zählen. *die tageszeitung*, April 12, p. 1.

Kahlen, R. 1987. Ungehorsam ist nicht versichert. *Die Zeit*, May 22, p. 28.

Karin and Rüdiger. 1983. Volkszählung – Leserbrief zum Artikel vom 2.2. *die tageszeitung*, February 9, p. 12.

Koch, L. 1987. "Es is so a netter Stammtisch wordn". *die tageszeitung*, August 6, n.p.n.

Konferenz der Datenschutzbeauftragten des Bundes und der Länder. 1983. "Der Bürger muß auf seine Rechte hingewiesen werden" [reprinted resolution]. *Frankfurter Rundschau*, April 12, n.p.n.

Krumm, K.-H. 1984a. Die Datensammler sind unter Zeitdruck geraten. *Frankfurter Rundschau*, March 21, p. 3.

Krumm, K.-H. 1984b. Ein neues Abenteuer. *Frankfurter Rundschau*, November 14, n.p.n.

Kurz, F. 1983a. Volkszählung erst später? *tageszeitung*, April 13, p. 2.

Kurz, F. 1983b. Verhandlung vor dem Bundesverfassungsgericht. *die tageszeitung*, October 18, p. 4.

Kurz, F. 1987. Vobo-Aktivist vom Knast abgewiesen. *die tageszeitung*, August 21, n.p.n.

Leicht, R. 1987. Staat im Visier, *Die Zeit*, May 1, p. 1.

Leuze, R. 1983. "Auch das Nachteilsverbot schützt den Burger nicht" [reprinted testimony before the *Bundesverfassungsgericht*]. *Frankfurter Rundschau*, April 26, n.p.n.

Leuze, R. 1985. Freundliche Töne, doch keine Taten [Edited version of speech]. *Süddeutsche Zeitung*, April 20/21, p. 10.

Loerzer, S. 1987. Rund um die Volkszählung. *Süddeutsche Zeitung*, June 1, n.p.n.

Loerzer, S. 1988a. 1700 Volkszählungbogen waren verschwunden. *Süddeutsche Zeitung*, February 16, n.p.n.

Loerzer, S. 1988b. Eine Volkszählung dieser Art wird es nicht mehr geben. *Süddeutsche Zeitung*, December 5, n.p.n.

Loerzer, S. and Meschede, E. 1987. Das Unbehagen, als Schaf gezählt zu werden. *Süddeutsche Zeitung*, April 14, p. 15.

Lücke, O. 1990. Vobo-Aktivistin muß nicht ins Gefängnis. *die tageszeitung*, January 3, n.p.n.

Ludger [no surname given] 1983. Verfassungsgericht soll entscheiden. *die tageszeitung*, April 8, p. 9.

Lummer, H. 1983. Boykott Bestrebungen aus "berufenem" Mund [reprinted letter from Berlin Interior Senator Lummer to SFB Intendant], *die tageszeitung*, February 23, p. 16.

Miehe, R. 1983. Eine Republik macht Inventur. *Frankfurter Rundschau*, February 19, n.p.n.

Moderow, M. 1987. Aktionsraum Ku'damm. *die tageszeitung*, May 11, n.p.n.

Mohr, R. 1988. Staatsschutz zählte mit. *die tageszeitung*, January 13, n.p.n.
Mückenberger, U. 1983. "Anonymität bedroht, Menschenwürde beeinträchtigt". *Frankfurter Rundschau*, March 24, pp. 14-15.
Müllender, B. 1987. Richter hebt eigenes Vobo-Urteil auf. *die tageszeitung*, June 29, n.p.n.
Nitschke, E. 1983a. Warum die Volkszählung nötig ist und stattfinden wird. *Die Welt*, March 31, n.p.n.
Nitschke, E. 1983b. Der politische Streit ging immer nur ums Geld. *Die Welt*, April 14, p. 86.
Noelle-Neumann, E. 1987. Die Volkszählung als Probe auf die Regierbarkeit, *Frankfurter Allgemeine Zeitung*, May 13, n.p.n.
Olaf [no surname]. 1983. [Letter to the editor]. *die tageszeitung*, February 22, p. 12.
Pilardeaux, B. 1988. Einbruch im Dienste des Rechtsstaates. *die tageszeitung*, August 30, n.p.n.
Plog, K. 1986. Hamburgs Volkszähler proben den Aufstand. *Frankfurter Rundschau*, December 19, p. 4.
Plog, K. 1988. Boykotteure landeten in Polizeidatei. *Frankfurter Rundschau*, January 12, p. 1.
Pokatzky, K. and Sontheimer, M. 1987. Zähler und Gezählte. *Die Zeit*, June 12, p. 34.
Pötzl, N. 1983. "Beten, dass die Sicherungen halten", Interview with W. Steinmüller. *Der Spiegel*, March 21, p. 109.
Pötzl, N. and Mettke, J. 1983. "Wo ist denn die Intimität?" Interview mit Innenminister Friedrich Zimmermann. *Der Spiegel*, March 28, p. 43.
Prantl, H. 1988. Fahndung nach dem meßbaren Wert. *Süddeutsche Zeitung*, May 27, n.p.n.
Projektgruppe Autonomie 1983. "Schon nach ihrem Wesen steht die Statistik der Nazionalsozialistischen Bewegung nahe" Statistiker als "wissenschaftliche Soldaten", *die tageszeitung*, March 18, pp. 12-13.
Raimund [no surname given]. 1988. Dem Obrigkeitsstaat ein Schnippchen schlagen. *die tageszeitung*, June 4, n.p.n.
Reifenrath, R. 1987. Legalität – Legitimität. *Frankfurter Rundschau*, February 25, n.p.n.
Reinhard, M. 1988. In den Gerichtsakten warten noch einige harte Nüsse. *Frankfurter Rundschau*, June 14, p. 10.
Riedel, A. 1987. Volkszählung: den Gerichten droht der Kollaps. *Frankfurter Rundschau*, December 14, n.p.n.
Riedmaier, T. 1987. Frauen und Volkszählung [reprinted position paper]. *Frankfurter Rundschau*, March 7, n.p.n.
Roos, K. 1987. Grüne und Kommunisten. *Bayern Kurier*, March 21, p. 8.
Roos, K. 1988. Die Pleite der Boykotteure. *Bayern Kurier*, December 10, n.p.n.
Rose, R. 1983. Aufruf zur Volkszählung [letter to the editor]. *die tageszeitung*, April 7, p. 12.

Rosenbauer, H. 1987. Grüne rufen zum Rechtbruch auf. *Bayern Kurier*, February 28, p. 4.
Schmidt, R., Baum, P., *et al*. 1983. Die Regierung fragt – Abgeordnete antworten nicht. *die tageszeitung*, March 10, p. 3.
Schroeren, M. 1983. Gemeinsam und offensiv [letter to editor]. *die tageszeitung*, February 21, p. 16.
Schueler, H. 1983. Angst vor dem gläsernen Menschen. *Die Zeit*, April 15, p. 2.
Seifert, J. 1987. Gegen die Gretchenfrage. *Frankfurter Rundschau*, April 2, n.p.n.
Sieber, U. and Gaserow, V. 1987. Staat mobil gegen Vobo-Gegner. *die tageszeitung*, April 23, n.p.n.
Siemens, J. 1983. Fast alles falsch gemacht. *Frankfurter Rundschau*, March 17, n.p.n.
Sommer, T. 1983. Freiheit, Freiraum und Fragebögen – Warum die Volkszählung verschoben werden sollte. *Die Zeit*, March 25, n.p.n.
Spoo, E. 1983. "Bei dem Zeitdruck kann keiner die Daten mißbrauchen". *Frankfurter Rundschau*, March 12, n.p.n.
Spoo, E. 1987. Vom Volkszählungsgegener zum "Extremisten". *Frankfurter Rundschau*, April 24, n.p.n.
Statistisches Landesamt Berlin. 1987. Wohnhäuser sind keine Kartenhäuser [Advertisement]. *die tageszeitung*, May 4, n.p.n.
Steinmüller, W. 1983. Der große Datenverbund. *die tageszeitung*, March 10, p. 3.
Sternsdorff, H.-W. 1983. Auf dem Weg zum Überwachungsstaat, *Der Spiegel*, January 10, pp. 46-64.
Strack, G. 1985. Ohne SPD keine Volkszählung. *Frankfurter Rundschau*, February 16, pp. 1-2.
Stumfall, F. 1987. Motive der Gegner. *Bayern Kurier*, May 30, n.p.n.
Süskind, M. 1983. Warten auf Orwells Jahr. *Süddeutsche Zeitung*, April 14, p. 3.
[Various] 1983. [Letters to the editor]. *die tageszeitung*, February 22, p. 12.
[Various] 1983. Betr. Artikel über Volkszählung v. 26.1.83 [Letters to the editor]. *die tageszeitung*, February 1, p. 12.
[Various] 1987. Volkszählung [Extra insert]. *Rheinischer Merkur*, April 16/17.
Voges, J. 1987a. Vobo: Verfassungsschutz wird aktiv. *die tageszeitung*, April 16, n.p.n.
Voges, J. 1987b. Geheimpapier zur Volkszählung. *die tageszeitung*, April 23, n.p.n.
von Appen, K. 1988. Vobo's im Staatsschutz-Computer. *die tageszeitung*, January 12, n.p.n.
von Ditfurth, H. 1987. Why I do not wish to be counted. *Der Spiegel*, May 18, pp. 34-39.
Voss, R. 1987. Geheime Argumente für Volkszählung. *Frankfurter Rundschau*, February 5, n.p.n.
Weber, A. 1990. Gnadenweg – aber warum? *die tageszeitung*, July 21, n.p.n.
Werner, A. 1988. Ende November sollen erste Ergebnisse vorliegen. *Frankfurter Rundschau*, June 14, p. 10.

Wildt, D. 1990. Vobo-Opfer wehrt sich. *die tageszeitung*, April 12, n.p.n.
Wildt, D. 1991. VoBo-Boykotteur ist auf der Flucht. *die tageszeitung*, March 4, n.p.n.
Willier, D. 1987a. CDU-Kampagne gegen Datenschützerin. *die tageszeitung*, May 5, n.p.n.
Willier, D. 1987b. Bürgermeister zensiert Grüne. *die tageszeitung*, May 8, n.p.n.
Willier, D. 1988. Dateiterror gegen Volkszählungsgegener. *die tageszeitung*, January 19, p. 1.
Wingen, M. 1983. Wie es zu großer Unruhe über eine normale Sache gekommen ist. *Frankfurter Allgemeine Zeitung*, October 12, p. 11.
Winter, M. 1987. Zähler sollen die Volkszählung zum Scheitern bringen. *Frankfurter Rundschau*, December 12, n.p.n.
Wittowski, B. 1988. Versicherung muß Prozeßkosten für Volkszählungsgegner zahlen. *Frankfurter Rundschau*, May 18, n.p.n.
Ziegler, G. 1983. Die Super-Befragung. *Frankfurter Rundschau*, March 10, n.p.n.
Zorn, H. 1987. Immer Ärger mit der Volkszählung. *die tageszeitung*, April 16, n.p.n.

Other archival materials

Anon. 1983. Alles was Du jetzt sagst, kann später gegen Dich verwendet werden! *der Tip* [Siegen], April, pp. 8-12. afas [no archival signature].
Anon. 1983. Ausgezählt! *Stadt Revue* [Köln] April, pp. 38-44. afas [no archival signature].
Anon. 1983. Ausländerrechtliche Hinweise für die Volkszählung. Hamburg Institut für Sozialforschung, Bestand SBe 444, Box 2: VoBo Büro Hamburg.
Anon. 1983. Gefahren der Volkszählung für Ausländer, in Dokumentation des bundesweiten Treffens der Initiativen zum Volkszählungsboykott, Bochum. afas 4.II.1983/3.
Anon. 1983. Meine Daten gehören mir! *Emma* (April 1983), p. 6. afas, 5.II [1983].
Anon. 1983. Volksquälung. *De Schnüss* [Bonn], no. 3 (March), pp. 4-6. afas [no archival signature].
Anon. 1983. Volks(v)erfassung. *De Schnüss* no. 4 (April), pp. 6-12. afas [no archival signature].
Anon. 1983. Volkszählungsboykott – Bilder, Plakate, Flugschriften, Tips zur Volkszählung. afas 83.I.2.
Anon. 1984. [No title]. *Datenschutz Nachrichten* No. 1/2 (n.d.), pp. 9-11. afas 5.IV.1.3:1.
Anon. 1987. Information G/009318/03/03/87/02. BStU ZA, MfS Signatur Sekretariat Neiber 429, pp. 160-163.

Anon. 1987. kommunikee – Die Bombe ist gezündet – der Widerstand auch. HISF Bestand SBe 444, Box 2: VoBo-Büro Hamburg – VoBo '87 Flugblätter, n.p.n.

Anon. 1987. Lageentwicklung im Operationsgebiet im Zusammenhang mit der "Volkszählung 1987". BStU ZA, MfS Signatur Sekretariat Neiber 429, p. 130.

Anon. 1987. [No title or date]. [Unknown Stasi department – cover sheet missing]. BStU, ZA, MfS Signatur BV Gera, Abteilung XV, 0261, vol. 2, p. 7.

Anon. 1987. Offener Brief hundert ehemaliger Bürgerinnen und Bürger der DDR an die Bundesregierung (n.d.). BStU, ZA, MfS Signatur Sekretariat Neiber 429, p. 143.

Anon. 1987. Volkszählungs-Boykott-Sammelstellen. *Stadt-Revue*, May 1987, p. 47, afas, 80.III.4.

Cobler, S. 1981. Herold gegen Alle: Gespräche mit dem Präsidenten des Bundeskriminalamtes. *Transatlantik* [n.v.n.], photocopy in Hamburg Institut für Sozialforschung, Bestand SBe 444, Box 2.

Ditfurth, J. 1987. Rede auf der Landesversammlung der Grünen Baden-Württemberg in Stuttgart am 23. Mai 1987. Archiv Grünes Gedächtnis Bestand A – Krieger, Verena, Archivsignatur 17, p. 4.

Dormagen, C. 1983. Die Häupter ihrer Lieben – Volks-ver-zählung. *Courage* (March 1983), p. 8. *archiv für alternatives schrifttum* [afas], 5.II [1983] n.s.

Forschungsgruppe "Demokratie und Recht" der GAL Hamburg. 1984. Rundbrief Extra zum machinenlesbaren Personalausweis und Erfassungsstaat. Supplement to GAL-Rundbrief Nr. 1/84. Hamburg Institut für Sozialforschung, Binder "EDV-Daten Anti 87".

Hauptabteilung II – Spionageabwehr 1987. Leiterinformation – Volkszählung. 1987 in der BRD und in Westberlin. February 19, 1987. BStU ZA, MfS Signatur HA II 4421, p. 4.

Hauptabteilung Beobachtung, Ermittlung 1983. Regimeinformation zur geplanten Volkszählung 1983 in der BRD und in Westberlin. February 16, 1983. BStU ZA, MfS Signatur HA VIII, 2936.

Hauptabteilung Terrorabwehr. 1987. Operativ-Information 062/836/87 über Aktivitäten der Alternativen Liste Berlin-West zum Volkszählungsboykott. March 25. BStU ZA, MfS Signatur HA XXII 794, vol. 43, pp. 1-4.

Hauptverwaltung Aufklärung, Abteilung VI. 1985. Überblick zur gegenwärtigen Lage bei der Vorbereitung einer Volkszählung in der BRD. July 5, 1985. BStU ZA, MfS Signatur BV Gera, Abteilung XV 0260, vol. 3, p. 4.

Hauptverwaltung Aufklärung, Abteilung VI. 1987. Überblick zum geplanten Ablauf der Volkszählung 1987 und den operativen Konsequenzen für die Sicherheit des IM-Netzes. BStU ZA, MfS Signatur BV Gera, Abteilung XV, 0260, vol. 2, pp. 3-4.

Hauptverwaltung Aufklärung. 1987. Informationen über Probleme der Volkszählung in der BRD. BStU, MfS Signatur HVA 47.

Initiative Volkszählungsboykott. 1982. Flyer in Archiv Grünes Gedächtnis, Bestand BII1, File 2896.

Küntzel, M., Kolodzeiej, G. and Ebermann, T. 1987. "Gewalt" – Debatte der Bundestagsfraktion Die Grünen am 2.6.87, unpublished typescript, Archiv Grünes Gedächtnis, Bestand B.II.1, File 3381.

Nagler, A. 1987. Hinweise für Ausländer, in Volkszählungsboykott: 10 Minuten, die Spass machen – Bilder, Plakate, Flugshriften, Tips für Volkszählung. Kassel: Kasseler Kunstverein, p. 63. afas [no archival signature].

Schroeren, M. 1982. Letter to activists, November 19. Archiv Grünes Gedächtnis, Bestand BII1, File 2896.

Simitis, S. 1983. Zwischenbericht des hessischen Datenschutzbeauftragten Professor Dr Simitis zur Volkszählung 1983. March 14. Typescript in Archiv Grünes Gedächtnis, Bestand B.II.1, Archivsignatur 3374, p. 3.

Strobl, I. 1987. Volkszählung. *Courage* (April 1987), p. 38. [afas], 5.II [1987] n.s.

Tanneberger, S. and Gröger, A. 1987. Papier über die zwei, z.Z. am häufisten diskutierten Positionen zum Boykott der Volkszählung 1987, das sog. "Bochumer Modell" und das sog. "Berliner Modell". Archiv Grünes Gedächtnis, Bestand B.II.1, file no. 6017(1).

VoBo – Initiative Darmstadt 1987. Volkszählungs-Infobüro in Darmstadt von Staatsanwaltschaft und Polizei durchsucht!! [Flyer] May 8. *tageszeitung* archive, Berlin. [no archival signature].

W./ Knast- u. Anti-Nato-Gruppe. 1983. Raster für Alle: Volkszählung und Widerstand. *Stadzeitung* [Freiburg im Breisgau] April, pp. 20-21. afas 80.III.4.

Government documents

Bundesverfassungsgericht 1969. 1 BvL 19/63. July 16. *Entscheidungen des Bundesverfassungsgerichts*, v.27. Tübingen: J.C.B. Mohr (Paul Siebeck).

Bundesverfassungsgericht 1983a. 1 BvR 209, 269/83, April 13, 1983. *Entscheidungen des Bundesverfassungsgerichts*, v.64. Tübingen: J.C.B. Mohr (Paul Siebeck).

Bundesverfassungsgericht 1983b. 1 BvR 209, 269, 362, 420, 440, 484/83. December 15, 1983, *Entscheidungen des Bundesverfassungsgerichts*, v. 65. Tübingen: J.C.B. Mohr (Paul Siebeck).

Bundesverfassungsgericht 1985. 1 BvR 233, 341/81, May 14. *Entscheidungen des Bundesverfassungsgerichts* v. 69. Tübingen: JCB Mohr (Paul Siebeck).

Gesetz über eine Volks-, Berufs-, Wohnungs- und Arbeitsstättenzählung (Volkszählungsgesetz) 1982. *Bundesgesetzblatt* 1982, Teil I, nr. 13, March 25, Z5702A, 369-372. Bonn: Bundestag.

Gesetz über eine Volks-, Berufs-, Gebäude, Wohnungs- und Arbeitsstättenzählung (Volkszählungsgesetz 1987). 1985. *Bundesgesetzblatt*, 1985, Teil I, November 8, pp. 2078-2083. Bonn: Bundestag.

Gesetz zum Schutz vor Mißbrauch personenbezogener Daten bei der Datenverarbeitung, *Bundesgesetzblatt* 1977, Teil I, nr. 7, February 1, 206. Bonn: Bundestag.

Online materials

Anon. 1955. It just happened, review of *Der Fragebogen*. *Time* January 10 [Online]. Available at: http://www.time.com/time/magazine/printout/0,8816,861117,00.html [Accessed: October 26, 2007].

Anon. 2001. Jedi makes the census list. BBC News October 9, 2001 [Online]. Available at: http://news.bbc.co.uk/1/hi/uk/1589133.stm [accessed: September 8, 2009].

Anon. 2002. "Jedi" religion grows in Australia. BBC News August 27, 2002 [Online]. Available at: http://news.bbc.co.uk/1/hi/entertainment/2218456.stm [accessed: September 8, 2009].

Anon. 2009. Unternehmen ist Datenschutz egal. taz.de September 3 [Online]. Available at: http://www.taz.de/1/politik/schwerpunkt-ueberwachung/artikel/1/unternehmen-ist-datenschutz-egal/ [accessed: September 10, 2009].

Bell, D. 2009. Surveillance is sexy. *Surveillance and Society* 6(3): 203-212. Available at: http://www.surveillance-and-society.org [accessed: February 22, 2010].

BigBrotherAwards.de 2009a. Archive. [Online]. Available at: http://www.bigbrotherawards.de/archiv [accessed: September 3, 2009].

BigBrotherAwards.de 2009b. Prizewinner of the main prize (category "politics"). [Online]. Available at: http://www.bigbrotherawards.de/2001/.pol [accessed: September 3, 2009].

BigBrotherAwards.de 2009c. Why Oscars for data leeches?. [Online]. Available at http://www.bigbrotherawards.de/why-en [accessed: September 3, 2009].

Bonse, E. 2006. Empörung über Pläne für US-Zugriff auf Bankdaten. *Handelsblatt* July 21, 2006 [Online]. Available at: http://www.handelsblatt.com/politik/international/empoerung-ueber-plaene-fuer-us-zugriff-auf-bankdaten;2434851 [accessed: September 7, 2009].

Bradford Community Statistics Project 2006. [Online homepage]. Available at: http://www.communitystats.org.uk/index.htm [accessed: October 16, 2009].

Bugmenot.com 2009. [Online homepage]. Available at: http://www.bugmenot.com/ [accessed: September 11, 2009].

Bundesbauftragte für die Unterlagen der Staatssicherheitsdienstes der ehemaligen Deutschen Demokratischen Republik 2009. Kurzinformationen zum Ministerium für Staatssicherheit (MfS). [Online]. Available at: http://www.bstu.bund.de/cln_028/nn_1328350/DE/MfS-DDR-Geschichte/Hintergruende-zur-Staatssicherheit/Kurzinformation/kurzinformation__node.html__nnn=true#doc765536bodyText7 [accessed: January 12, 2010].

Bündnis 90/Die Grünen 2009. Grüne Datenschutzoffensive. [Online]. Available at: http://www.gruene-bundestag.de/cms/datenschutz/dok/263/263067.gruene_datenschutzoffensive.html [accessed: September 4, 2009].
Cauley, L. 2006. NSA has massive database of Americans' phone calls. USAToday, May 11, 2006 [Online]. Available at: http://www.usatoday.com/news/washington/2006-05-10-nsa_x.htm [accessed: September 6, 2009].
CountMeOut 2006. [Online homepage]. Available at: http://www.countmeout.ca/ [accessed: October 17, 2009].
European Commission 2008. Data Protection in the European Union: Citizens' Perceptions. [Online]. Available at: http://ec.europa.eu/public_opinion/flash/fl_225_en.pdf [accessed: October 14, 2009].
Federal Commissioner for Data Protection and Freedom of Information 2009. Press Releases. [Online]. Available at: http://www.bfdi.bund.de/cln_111/EN/PublicRelations/PressReleases/2009/20_09_SchaarCriticisesAgreementDataExchangesUSA.html?nn=410156 [accessed: September 7, 2009].
FoeBuD e.V. 2009a. Archive. [Online]. Available at: http://archiv.foebud.org/bba/#Unbekannt [accessed: September 3, 2009].
FoeBuD e.V. 2009b. PrivacyDongle: anonym im Internet surfen. [Online]. Available at: https://www.foebud.org/datenschutz-buergerrechte/vorratsdatenspeicherung/privacydongle/index [accessed: September 8, 2009].
Fowler, A. 1996. Professional ethics report: anonymity on the internet. American Association for the Advancement of Science [Online]. Available at: http://www.aaas.org/spp/sfrl/per/per6.htm [accessed: September 11, 2009].
Infratest-dimap 2009. 83 prozent sehen Handlungsbedarf bei Verbraucherschutz. [Online]. Available at: http://www.infratest-dimap.de/umfragen-analysen/bundesweit/umfragen/aktuell/83-prozent-sehen-handlungsbedarf-beim-verbraucherschutz/ [accessed: September 4, 2009].
Kammerer, D. 2009. Police use of public video surveillance in Germany from 1956: management of traffic, repression of flows, persuasion of offenders. *Surveillance and Society* 6(1): 43-47 [Online]. Available at: http://www.surveillance-and-society.org [accessed: February 22, 2010].
Martin, A., van Brakel, R. and Bernhard, D. 2009. Understanding resistance to digital surveillance: towards a multi-disciplinary, multi-actor framework. *Surveillance and Society* 6(3): 213-232. Available at http://www.surveillance-and-society.org [accessed: February 22, 2010].
Merritt, T. 2005. Surf the web anonymously. CNET.com [Online]. Available at: http://reviews.cnet.com/4520-3000_7-6274488-1.html [accessed: September 11, 2009].
Piratenpartei Deutschland 2009. [Online homepage]. Available at: http://www.piratenpartei.de/ [accessed: September 11, 2009].
Privacy International 2009. [Online homepage]. Available at: http://www.privacyinternational.org/ [accessed: September 4, 2009].

ProjectRACE 2009. About ProjectRACE. [Online]. Available at: http://www.projectrace.com/aboutprojectrace/ [accessed: September 8, 2009].

Reichstein, R. 2006. EU lässt das Thema Datenschutz schleifen. *Handelsblatt* November 29, 2006 [Online]. http://www.handelsblatt.com/politik/international/eu-laesst-das-thema-datenschutz-schleifen;1175896 [accessed: September 7, 2009].

Secondlife.com 2009. What is an avatar? [Online]. Available at: http://secondlife.com/whatis/avatar/?lang=en-US [accessed: September 11, 2009].

Statista.com 2009. Umfrage: Furcht vor online-Durchsuchung. [Online]. Available at: http://de.statista.com/statistik/daten/studie/1304/umfrage/furcht-vor-online-durchsuchung-privater-computer-durch-staat/#info [accessed: September 4, 2009].

Twickel, C. 2009. Piratenpartei will den Bundestag entern. *SpiegelOnline* July 5, 2009 [Online]. Available at: http://www.spiegel.de/netzwelt/netzpolitik/0,1518,634228,00.html [accessed: September 11, 2009].

Unger, B. 2006. Big Brother? Not Big Enough … The Unger Report, broadcast on National Public Radio (USA), May 15, 2006. [Online transcript]. Available at: http://www.npr.org/templates/story/story.php?storyId=5405422 [accessed: September 8, 2009].

United States Congress 1978. US Code, Title 16, Chapter 46. Cornell University Law School, Legal Information Institute [Online]. Available at: http://www.law.cornell.edu/uscode/usc_sec_16_00002601----000-.html [accessed: October 16, 2009].

United States Office of Management and Budget 1997. Revisions to the Standards for Classification of Federal Data on Race and Ethnicity. October 30 [Online]. Available at: http://www.whitehouse.gov/omb/rewrite/fedreg/ombdir15.html [accessed: September 8, 2009].

Secondary print literature

Agamben, G. 1998. *Homo Sacer: Sovereign Power and Bare Life*. Palo Alto: Stanford University Press.

Agnew, J. 2005. Sovereignty regimes: territoriality and state authority in contemporary world politics. *Annals of the Association of American Geographers* 95(2): 437-461.

Aly, G. 1995. *"Endlösung": Völkerverschiebung und der Mord an den europäischen Juden*. Frankfurt: Fischer Verlag.

Aly, G. 1997. *Macht Geist Wahn: Kontinuitäten deutschen Denkens*. Frankfurt: Fischer Verlag.

Aly, G. 2005. *Hitlers Volksstaat: Raub, Rassenkrieg und nationaler Sozialismus*. Frankfurt: Fischer Verlag.

Aly, G. 2008. *Unser Kampf: 1968*, Frankfurt: Fischer Verlag.

Aly, G. and Heim, S. 2002. *Architects of Annihilation: Auschwitz and the Logic of Destruction* (trans. A. Blunden). Princeton: Princeton University Press.

Aly, G. and Roth, K.-H. 2000 [1984]. *Die restlose Erfassung: Volkszählen, Identifizieren, Aussondern im Nationalsozialismus*. Frankfurt: Fischer.

Aly, G. and Roth, K.-H. 2004. *The Nazi Census: Identification and Control in the Third Reich* (trans. E. Black). Philadelphia: Temple University Press.

Anon. (ed.) 1967. *Vorbereitung auf den Notstand? 10 Antworten auf eine aktuelle Frage*. Frankfurt: Fischer Bücherei.

Anon. 1981. Bullenparanoia und das Gefühl vom Paradies: Michael Wieczorek sprach mit Vertretern des "Kukuk", in *Hausbesetzer: Wofür sie kämpfen, wie sie leben und wie sie leben wollen*, edited by S. Aust and S. Rosenbladt. Hamburg: Hoffman und Campe, 97-126.

Anon. 1981. Rechtsfreie Räume, in *Hausbesetzer: Wofür sie kämpfen, wie sie leben und wie sie leben wollen*, edited by S. Aust and S. Rosenbladt. Hamburg: Hoffman und Campe, 127-169.

Appadurai, A. 2001. Deep democracy: Urban governmentality and the horizon of politics. *Environment and Urbanization* 13(2), 23-43.

Appel, R. 1986. Volkserfassung – zweiter Versuch. Das Volkszählungsprojekt 1987, in *Totalerfassung: "Sicherheitsgesetze", Volkszählung, Neuer Personalausweis, Möglichkeiten der Gegenwehr*, edited by M. Kutscha and N. Paech. Köln: Pahl-Rugenstein, 45-59.

Appel, R. and Hummel, D. (eds.) 1987. *Vorsicht Volkszählung! Erfaßt, vernetzt und ausgezählt*. Köln: Kölner Volksblatt Verlag.

Aust, S. 1998. *Der Baader Meinhof Komplex* (expanded and updated edition). Munich: Goldmann Verlag.

Balistier, T. 1996. *Straßenprotest: Formen oppositioneller Politik in der Bundesrepublik Deutschland*. Münster: Westfälisches Dampfboot.

Bergmann, N. 2009. *Volkszählung und Datenschutz: Proteste zur Volkszählung 1983 und 1987 in der Bundesrepublik Deutschland*. Hamburg: Diplomica Verlag.

Bethge, H., Bünemann, R., Enderlein, H., Kurz, I., Roßmann, E., Schiller, T., Stein, H. and Stuby, G. (eds.) 1976. *Die Zerstörung der Demokratie in der BRD durch Berufsverbot*, Köln: Pahl-Rugenstein Verlag.

Black, E. 2001. *IBM and the Holocaust: The Strategic Alliance between Nazi Germany and America's Most Powerful Corporation*. New York: Crown Publishers.

Braunthal, G. 1990. *Political Loyalty and Public Service in West Germany: The 1972 Decree against Radicals and its Consequences*. Amherst: University of Massachusetts Press.

Breyman, S. 1998. *Movement Genesis: Social Movement Theory and the 1980s West German Peace Movement*. Boulder: Westview Press.

Brown, M. 2000. *Closet Space: Geographies of Metaphor from the Body to the Globe*. London: Routledge.

Brown, M. and Knopp, L. 2006. Places or polygons? Governmentality, scale and the census in *The Gay and Lesbian Atlas*. *Population, Space and Place* 12(4), 223-242.

Brown, S. 1997. *Revolution at the Checkout Counter: The Explosion of the Bar Code*, Cambridge, MA: Harvard University Press.

Busch, H., Funk, A., Kauß, U., Narr, W.-D. and Werkentin, F. 1985. *Die Polizei in der Bundesrepublik*. Frankfurt: Campus Verlag.

Castells, M. 2000. *The Rise of the Network Society (2nd Ed.)*. Oxford: Blackwell.

Cobler, S. 1978. *Law, Order and Politics in West Germany* (trans. F. McDonagh). Harmondsworth: Penguin Books.

Crampton, J. 2003. *The Political Mapping of Cyberspace*. Chicago: University of Chicago Press.

Dean, M. 2007. *Governing societies*. Maidenhead: Open University Press.

Demirovic, A. 1998. Grassroots democracy: contradictions and implications, in *The German Greens: Paradox Between Movement and Party* (trans. M. Schatzschneider), edited by M. Mayer and J. Ely. Philadelphia: Temple University Press, 141-161.

Ditfurth, J. 2000. *Das waren die Grünen: Abschied von einer Hoffnung*. Munich: Econ Taschenbuch Verlag.

Enzensberger, H.-M. 1979. An address on German democracy to the citizens of New York. *New Left Review* 118 (Nov./Dec.), 3-14.

Enzensberger, U. 2006. *Die Jahre der Kommune I: Berlin 1967-1969*, Munich: Goldmann.

Flaherty, D. 1989. *Protecting Privacy in Surveillance Societies: the Federal Republic of Germany, Sweden, France, Canada and the United States*. Chapel Hill: University of North Carolina Press.

Foucault, M. 1982. The Subject and Power, in *Michel Foucault: Beyond Structuralism and Hermeneutics*, edited by H. Dreyfus and P. Rabinow. Chicago: University of Chicago Press, 208-228.

Foucault, M. 1994. Letter to certain leaders of the left, in *Power*, edited by J. Faubion. New York: New Press, 426-428.

Foucault, M. 2003. *Society Must Be Defended: Lectures at the Collège de France 1975-1976* (trans. D. Macey). New York: Picador.

Foucault, M. 2008. *The Birth of Biopolitics: Lectures at the Collège de France 1978-1979* (trans. G. Burchell). Basingstoke: Palgrave Macmillan.

Frei, N. 2001. *Karrieren im Zwielicht: Hitlers Eliten nach 1945*. Frankfurt: Campus Verlag.

Funk, A. 2000. Die Entstehung der Exekutivepolizei im Kaiserreich, in *Staat, Demokratie und innere Sicherheit in Deutschland*, edited by H.-J. Lange. Opladen: Leske und Budrich, 11-28.

Gieseke, J. 2006. *Der Mielke-Konzern: Die Geschichte der Stasi, 1945-1990*. Munich: Deutsche Verlagsanstalt.

Glotz, P. (ed.) 1983. *Ziviler Ungehorsam im Rechtsstaat*. Frankfurt: Suhrkamp.

Gössner, R. 2000. *Big Brother & Co.: Der Moderne Überwachungsstaat in der Informationsgesellschaft*. Hamburg: Konkret Literatur Verlag.

Habermas, J. 1975. *Legitimation Crisis* (trans. T. McCarthy). Boston: Beacon Press.

Habermas, J. 1992. *The Theory of Communicative Action* (2 Vol.) (trans. T. McCarthy). Boston: Beacon Press.

Hannah, M. 2000. *Governmentality and the Mastery of Territory in Nineteenth Century America*. New York: Cambridge University Press, Chapter 5.

Hannah, M. 2001. Sampling and the politics of representation in US Census 2000. *Environment and Planning D: Society and Space* 19, 515-534.

Hannah, M. 2008a. Die umstrittene Konstruktion von Vertrauen und Misstrauen in der westdeutschen Volkszählungsboykottbewegung 1983. *Social Geography* [Online journal], 3, 11-21. Available at http://www.soc-geogr.net/3/11/2008/sg-3-11-2008.pdf.

Hannah, M. 2008b. Mapping the under-scrutinized: the West German census boycott movement of 1987 and the dangers of information-based security, in *Geospatial Technologies and Homeland Security*, edited by D. Sui. New York: Springer, 301-314.

Hannah, M. 2009. Calculable territory and the West German census boycott movements of the 1980s. *Political Geography* 28, 66-75.

Hannover, H. and Wallraff, G. 1982. *Die Unheimliche Republik: Politische Verfolgung in der Bundesrepublik*. Hamburg: Rowohlt.

Hauser, D. 1997. *Baader und Herold: Beschreibung eines Kampfes*. Frankfurt: Fischer Verlag.

Hill, W. (ed.) 1984. *Widerstand und Staatsgewalt: Recht im Streit mit dem Gesetz*. Gütersloh: Gütersloher Verlagshaus Mohn.

Hirsch, J. 1983. *Der Sicherheitsstaat: Das "Modell Deutschland", seine Krise und die neuen sozialen Bewegungen*. Frankfurt: Europäische Verlagsantalt.

Hohmann, H. (ed.) 1987. *Freiheitssicherung durch Datenschutz*. Frankfurt: Suhrkamp.

Hoshino Altbach, E. 1984. The New German Women's Movement. *Signs* 9(3), 454-469.

Humanistische Union (Landesverband Berlin), Jungdemokraten Berlin, and Liberale Demokraten Berlin, 1983. *Volkszählung 1983 – Bürgerbefragung oder Zwangserfassung?* West Berlin: Elefanten Press.

Jaspers, K. 1966. *Wohin treibt die Bundesrepublik*, Munich: Piper.

Jesse, E. 1981. *Streitbare Demokratie*. Berlin: Colloquium Verlag.

Kiliç, S., Saharso, S. and Sauer, B. 2008). Introduction: The veil: debating citizenship, gender and religious diversity. *Social Politics* 15(4), 397-410.

Klein, M. 2002. *Ernst von Salomon: Revolutionär ohne Utopie*. Aschau i. Ch.: San Casciano Verlag.

Klotzsch, L., Könemann, K., Wischermann, J. and Zeuner, B. 1998. What has happened to Green principles in electoral and parliamentary politics?, in *The German Greens: Paradox Between Movement and Party* (trans. M. Schatzschneider), edited by M. Mayer and J. Ely. Philadelphia: Temple University Press, 97-127.

Knabe, H. 2001. *Die unterwanderte Republik: Stasi im Westen.* Munich: Ullstein.

Koenen, G. 2001. *Das rote Jahrzehnt: Unsere kleine deutsche Kulturrevolution.* Köln: Kiepenheuer und Witsch.

Koopmans, R. 1993. The dynamics of protest waves: West Germany, 1965 to 1989. *American Sociological Review* 58, 637-658.

Kraushaar, W. (ed.) 1978a. *Autonomie oder Getto? Kontroversen über die Alternativbewegung*, Frankfurt: Verlag Neue Kritik.

Kraushaar, W. 1978b. Thesen zum Verhältnis von Alternativ- und Fluchtbewegung, in *Autonomie oder Getto? Kontroversen über die Alternativbewegung*, edited by W. Kraushaar. Frankfurt: Verlag Neue Kritik, 8-67.

Kraushaar, W. 1998. *Frankfurter Schule und Studentenbewegung: von der Flaschenpost zum Molotowcocktail 1946 bis 1995* (3 Vols.). Hamburg: Rogner & Bernhard bei Zweitausendeins.

Kraushaar, W. 2000. *1968: Mythos, Chiffre und Zäsur*. Hamburg: Hamburger Edition.

Kutscha, M. (ed.) 1986. *Demonstrationsfreiheit: Kampf um ein Bürgerrecht*. Köln: Presseverlag Theurer.

Large, D. 1996. *West Germans to the Front: West German Rearmament in the Adenauer Era*, Chapel Hill: University of North Carolina Press.

Lemke, T. 1997. *Eine Kritik der Politischen Vernunft: Foucaults Analyse der modernen Gouvernmentalität*. Hamburg: Argument Verlag.

Mailänder, U. and Zander, U. 2003. *Das kleine Westberlin-Lexikon: von "Autonome" bis "Zapf" – die alternative Szene der siebziger und achtziger Jahre*. Berlin: Schwarzkopf und Schwarzkopf.

Markovitz, A. and Gorski, P. 1993. *The German Left: Red, Green and Beyond.* Oxford: Oxford University Press.

Mathes, R. and Pfetsch, B. 1991. The role of the alternative press in the agenda-building process: spillover effects and media opinion leadership. *European Journal of Communication* 6: 33-62.

Melucci, A. 1996. *Challenging Codes: Collective Action in the Information Age.* Cambridge: Cambridge University Press.

Melucci, A. and Avritzer, L. 2000. Complexity, cultural pluralism and democracy: collective action in the public space. *Social Science Information* 39, 507-527.

Mewes, H. 1998. A brief history of the Green Party, in *The German Greens: Paradox Between Movement and Party* (trans. M. Schatzschneider), edited by M. Mayer and J. Ely. Philadelphia: Temple University Press, 29-48.

Meyn, J.-H. 1988. *Die sogenannte Vermummung und passive Bewaffnung: Verfassungs- und verwaltungsrechtliche Probleme unter besonderer Berücksichtigung der Änderung des Versammlungsgesetzes von 1985.* Frankfurt: Verlag Peter Lang.

Mez, L. 1998. Who votes Green? Sources and trends of Green support, in *The German Greens: Paradox Between Movement and Party* (trans. M. Schatzschneider), edited by M. Mayer and J. Ely. Philadelphia: Temple University Press, 72-93.

Mommsen, H. 2003. *Aufstieg und Untergang der Republik von Weimar 1918-1933*. Munich: Ullstein.

Murakami Wood, D. 2009. The "surveillance society": questions of history, place and culture. *European Journal of Criminology* 6(2): 179-194.

Negt, O. 1977. The misery of bourgeois democracy in Germany. *Telos* 34 (Winter 1977-78), 123-136.

Negt, O. 2001. *Achtundsechzig: politische Intellektuelle und die Macht*. Göttingen: Steidl Verlag.

Neidhardt, F. and Rucht, D. 2001. Protestgeschichte der Bundesrepublik Deutschland 1950-1994: Ereignisse, Themen, Akteure, in *Protest in der Bundesrepublik Deutschland: Strukturen und Entwicklungen*, edited by D. Rucht. Frankfurt: Campus Verlag, 27-70.

Nicholls, W. 2009. Place, networks, space: theorizing the geographies of social movements. *Transactions of the Institute of British Geographers* NS 34, 78-93.

Niclauß, K. 1998. *Der Weg zum Grundgesetz: Demokratiegründung in Westdeutschland, 1945-1949*. Paderborn: Ferdinand Schöningh.

Offe, C. 1984. Ungovernability: On the Renaissance of Conservative Theories of Crisis (trans. A. Buchwalter), in *Observations on the Spiritual Situation of the Age*, edited by J. Habermas, Cambridge, MA: MIT Press, 67-88.

Orth, G. and Podlech, A. 1982. *Testfall Startbahn West: Erfahrungen und Perspektiven im Widerstand*. Wuppertal: Jugenddienst Verlag.

Palmer, R. 2001. *The Bar Code Book: A Comprehensive Guide to Reading, Printing, Specifying, and Applying Bar Code and Other Machine-Readable Symbols* (*4th Ed.*). Peterborough, NH: Helmers Publishing.

Paust, A. 1987. Diplomarbeit zum Thema Staatliche Legitimationsprobleme am Beispiel der Volkszählung 1987. Unpublished thesis, Universität Gesamthochschule Duisburg, Fachbereich 1 – Fach Politische Wissenschaft. Typescript provided by author.

Pickles, J. 2006. *A History of Spaces: Cartographic Reason, Mapping and the Geo-Coded World*. London: Routledge.

Prantl, H. 2002. *Verdächtig: Der starke Staat und die Politik der inneren Unsicherheit*. Hamburg: Europa Verlag.

Prozorov, S. 2007. *Foucault, Freedom and Sovereignty*. Aldershot: Ashgate.

Reichel, P. 2001. *Vergangenheitsbewältigung in Deutschland: Die Auseinandersetzung mit der NS-Diktatur von 1945 bis heute*. Munich: C.H. Beck.

Rosenbladt, S. 1981. Nürnberg: "Die großen Lumpen schwer aufs Hirn hauen", in *Hausbesetzer: Wofür sie kämpfen, wie sie leben und wie sie leben wollen*, edited by S. Aust and S. Rosenbladt. Hamburg: Hoffman und Campe, 60-96.

Roth, R. and Murphy, D. 1998. From competing factions to the rise of the Realos, in *The German Greens: Paradox Between Movement and Party* (trans. M. Schatzschneider), edited by M. Mayer and J. Ely, 53-59.

Rottmann, V. and Strohm, H. 1986. *Was Sie gegen Mikrozensus und Volkszählung tun können: ein Ratgeber*. Frankfurt: Zweitausendeins.
Röhl, B. 2006. *So macht Kommunismus Spass! Ulrike Meinhof, Kaus Rainer Röhl und die Akte konkret*. Hamburg: Europäische Verlagsanstalt.
Sanitäter-Gruppe 1981. Im Fadenkreuz: Drei Mitglieder der Sanitäter-Gruppe über sich selbst, in *Hausbesetzer: Wofür sie kämpfen, wie sie leben und wie sie leben wollen*, edited by S. Aust and S. Rosenbladt. Hamburg: Hoffman und Campe, 170-192.
Saramago, J. 2006. *Seeing*. London: Harvill Secker.
Sassoon, D. 1996. *One Hundred Years of Socialism: The West European Left in the Twentieth Century*, New York: New Press.
Schaar, P. 2007. *Das Ende der Privatsphäre: Der Weg in die Überwachungsgesellschaft*. Munich: Bertelsmann.
Scharf, T. 1994. *The German Greens: Challenging the Consensus*, Oxford: Berg Publishers.
Schenk, D. 1998. *Der Chef: Horst Herold und Das BKA*. Hamburg: Spiegel Buchverlag.
Schiller, M. 2001. *Es war ein harter Kampf um meine Erinnerung: ein Lebensbericht aus der RAF*. Munich: Piper.
Schönbohm, W. 1979. *Verfassungsfeinde als Beamte? Die Kontroverse über die Streitbare Demokratie*. Munich: Günter Olzog Verlag.
Schwenger, H. 1983. *Im Jahr des grossen Bruders: Orwells deutsche Wirklichkeit*. Munich: Piper.
Seifert, J. 1965. *Gefahr im Verzuge: Zur Problematik der Notstandsgesetzgebung*. Frankfurt: Europäische Verlagsanstalt.
Simitis, S. 1987. Reviewing privacy in an Information Society. *University of Pennsylvania Law Review* 135(3), 707-746.
Sontheimer, K. 1976. *Das Elend unserer Intellektuellen*. Hamburg: Hoffmann und Campe.
Sontheimer, K. 1979. *Die verunsicherte Republik: Die Bunderepublik nach 30 Jahren*. Munich: Piper.
Sontheimer, K. 1980. *Der unbehagliche Bürger: vom deutschen Umgang mit der Demokratie*. Zürich: Edition Interfrom.
Sontheimer, K. and Bleek, W. 1999. *Grundzüge des politischen Systems der Bundesrepublik Deutschland*. Munich: Piper.
Taeger, J. (ed.) 1983. *Die Volkszählung*. Reinbek bei Hamburg, Rowohlt.
Third Russell Tribunal 1978. *Berufsverbote Condemned*. Nottingham: the Bertrand Russell Peace Foundation Ltd.
Thomas, N. 2003. *Protest Movements in 1960s West Germany: A Social History of Dissent and Democracy*. Oxford: Berg.
Till, K. 2005. *The New Berlin: Memory, Politics, Place*, Minneapolis: University of Minnesota Press.

Tolmein, O. 1999. *"RAF – Das war für uns Befreiung": Ein Gespräch mit Irmgard Möller über bewaffneten Kampf, Knast und die Linke*. Hamburg: Konkret Literatur Verlag.

Vieten, G. 1983. Holland – ein Land lässt sich nicht zählen, in *Die Volkszählung*, edited by J. Taeger. Reinbek bei Hamburg: Rowohlt, 270-282.

von Dirke, S. 1997. *"All Power to the Imagination": The West German Counterculture from the Student Movement to the Greens*. Lincoln: University of Nebraska Press.

von Salomon, E. 2007 [1951]. *Der Fragebogen*. Hamburg: Rowohlt.

von Salomon, E. 1955. *The Questionnaire*. New York: Doubleday.

Wirsching, A. 2006. *Abschied vom Provisorium: Geschichte der Bundesrepublik Deutschland 1982-1990*. Munich: Deutsche Verlags-Anstalt.

Wise, M. 1998. *Capital Dilemma: Germany's Search for a New Architecture of Democracy* Princeton: Princeton Architectural Press.

Wisniewski, S. 1997. *Wir waren so unheimlich konsequent: ein Gespräch zur Geschichte der RAF mit Stefan Wisniewski*. Berlin: ID Verlag.

Zipes, J. 1977. From *Berufsverbot* to Terrorism. *Telos* 34 (Winter 1977-78), 136-147.

Index

For Product Safety Concerns and Information please contact our EU representative GPSR@taylorandfrancis.com
Taylor & Francis Verlag GmbH, Kaufingerstraße 24, 80331 München, Germany

www.ingramcontent.com/pod-product-compliance
Ingram Content Group UK Ltd.
Pitfield, Milton Keynes, MK11 3LW, UK
UKHW020013200926
475702UK00014B/1854

* 9 7 8 1 1 3 8 2 7 3 6 3 4 *